JN113884

ミゲールの世界の沖縄空手事情

ミゲール・ダルーズ著

Overview of Okinawa Karate in the World

Miguel Da Luz

沖縄タイムス社

序文　Foreword

宮城篤正
元沖縄県立芸術大学学長
Miyagi Tokumasa
Former President of
the Okinawa Prefectural University of Arts

今から約30年位前のことになるだろうか。
フランス国北西部のブルターニュ地方出身の青年が空手の本場沖縄にやって来た。彼の名前はミゲール・ダルーズという。15歳の時地元の剛柔流空手道場に入門して空手を習ったという。彼は来沖まもない頃、私に出会った際に次のような話をした。1993年4月、フランス・パリ市のベルシー体育館で開催された「第8回世界武芸祭」（メーン・テーマ〝沖縄の空手道〟）を空手の師匠に伴って見に行き、「沖縄空手・古武道国際交流団」（主催　沖縄県、沖縄タイムス社、沖縄空手・古武道国際交流団）が演武した沖縄伝統空手を観て感激したこと。更に続けてあの時の感動が沖縄行きを決意したと語った。

来沖すると翻訳・通訳の仕事に就くが、途中からNPO法人沖縄空手道・古武道支援センターが発行する「沖縄空手通信」の編集人となった。そのニュースレターは県内外・海外の情報を幅広く発信する内容で、ミゲール氏は精力的に取材活動を展開した。ところがNPO法人が受託した沖縄県の「沖縄空手交流事業」（平成16年度、17年度）の終了に伴い「沖縄空手通信」は発行中止となった。そこでミゲール氏は関係者から了解を取り付けて、個人的に発行を継続し、現在に至っている。

沖縄タイムス社は2017年4月に「週刊沖縄空手」を創刊するにあたり、彼に「ミゲールの世界の沖縄空手事情」の執筆を依頼した。彼は世界の国や地域に広く普及発展している沖縄空手をルーツに持つ空手・古武道家の道場や門下生達の修行の様子をレポートして端的に伝え、132回（2022年6月5日付）の連載を数える。今回この連載記事が1冊の単行本として出版される。このたびの発刊を心から喜び、祝意を述べる。そして世界中の多くの空手愛好家や一般県民に対して私は自信と誇りを持って推奨する次第である。

Wasn't it about 30 years ago?

A young man from Brittany region in the northwest of France came to Okinawa, the birthplace of karate. His name is Miguel Da Luz. At the age of 15, in his hometown, he joined a local Gōjū-ryū karate dōjō and learned karate. Shortly after arriving in Okinawa, he told me the following when we first met. "In April 1993, I accompanied my karate master to the 8th World Martial Arts Festival (main theme: Okinawan karatedō) held at the Bercy Gymnasium in Paris, France, and I was moved by watching traditional Okinawa karate performed by the Okinawa Karate Kobudō International Exchange Group" (sponsored by Okinawa Prefecture, Okinawa Times and the Okinawa Karate Kobudō International Exchange Group). He continued saying that the deep impression that the event left on him was what made him decide to go to Okinawa.

Having arrived in Okinawa, he worked as a translator and interpreter, meanwhile becoming the editor of the "Okinawa Karate News" published by the NPO Okinawa Karatedō Kobudō Support Center. The newsletter was designed to widely disseminate information from inside and outside the prefecture and overseas, and Miguel energetically expanded his coverage activities. However, with the end of the Okinawa Karate Exchange Project (FY2004, FY2005) entrusted to the NPO, the issuance of "Okinawa Karate News" was discontinued. After obtaining the consent of related parties, Miguel continued to publish it privately, and so does he to this day.

The Okinawa Times newspaper commissioned him to write "Miguel's Overview of Okinawa Karate in the World" when it launched the "Weekly Okinawa Karate" serial publication in April 2017. He has since reported 132 times (as of June 5, 2022) about dōjō and practitioners of karate and kobudō who have their roots in Okinawa karate, an art which is spreading and developing widely in various countries and regions around the world. This series of articles is being published as a single book. I am very pleased and offer my congratulations on this publication. And I have confidence and pride in recommending it to the many karate enthusiasts around the world and to the citizens of Okinawa.

序文　Foreword

仲本政博
沖縄県指定無形文化財「沖縄の空手・古武術」保持者

Nakamoto Masahiro
Holder of the Okinawa Prefecture designated intangible cultural asset "Okinawa karate and kobujutsu"

『ミゲールの世界の沖縄空手事情』の出版、おめでとうございます。「週刊沖縄空手」での連載は内容が豊富で充実しており、私自身興味を持ち、毎回楽しみにしていました。待ち遠しい読み物がついに書籍になるという事を聞き、「人生は短しされど芸術は永し」と昔からの言葉にあるように、末永く多くの武道愛好家たちに深い感動を与える本になると信じています。

私は著者のミゲール・ダルーズ氏とは長いおつきあいがあります。彼は空手の本場聖地沖縄だけではなく、世界各国の交流会派の事情に詳しく、私自身情報を得てとても助かっています。在沖米軍基地で実施されている米兵（特に新兵）の沖縄に対する理解を増進する目的で毎年行われているセミナーで空手と古武術を教える時には、通訳でお世話になりました。私が出版した本の翻訳もしてもらいました。

彼は、文筆家であると共に、本場沖縄に住んで、名師を訪ね本格的に沖縄の伝統空手古武術を修行している武道家でもあります。相当な鍛錬を重ねていますが、隠れ武士として、社会的な表層に自己を顕示することはしません。彼の慎み深さに敬意を表します。『ミゲールの世界の沖縄空手事情』がベストセラーになるよう願っています。

Congratulations on the publication of Miguel's "Overview of Okinawa Karate in the World." This serialization in the "Weekly Okinawa Karate" is rich and fulfilling, and being personally interested in it, I look forward to it every time. When I heard that the long-awaited book would finally be published, I believed that it would be a book that would deeply impress many martial arts enthusiasts for many years to come. As the old expression says, "Ars longa, vita brevis – Art is long and life is short".

I have a long relation with the author, Miguel Da Luz. He is very knowledgeable about karate circles not only in Okinawa, the birthplace of karate, but also in various countries around the world and he has been a very helpful source in order to gather information. When I taught karate and kobujutsu at annual seminars held on U.S. military bases in Okinawa to improve the understanding of Okinawa among U.S. soldiers (especially new recruits), he was a helpful interpreter. He also translated some of the books I published.

In addition to being a writer, he is also a martial artist who lives in Okinawa, where he visits famous masters and trains in traditional Okinawa karate and kobujutsu. Despite his considerable training, like a kakure bushi, a hidden master, he does not reveal himself to the social surface. I admire his modesty. I hope that Miguel's "Overview of Okinawa Karate in the World" will become a bestseller.

序文　Foreword

東恩納盛男
沖縄県指定無形文化財「沖縄の空手・古武術」保持者

Higaonna Morio
Holder of the Okinawa Prefecture designated intangible cultural asset “Okinawa karate and kobujutsu”

この度は『ミゲールの世界の沖縄空手事情』の発刊誠におめでとうございます。

2017年から長期にわたり沖縄タイムス紙の「週刊沖縄空手」で連載されている企画を毎回楽しく愛読させて頂いています。世界71カ国と地域の空手家・武術家を紹介していますが、ミゲール・ダルーズ氏の類まれな情報収集力にはただ敬服するばかりです。

ミゲール氏は、国際沖縄剛柔流空手道連盟の会員であり、空手発祥の地で沖縄剛柔流空手のさらなる研鑽を積むため、1993年に来沖いたしました。

当初、東恩納空手道場で寝泊まりし稽古に励んでおりましたが、2011年に任意団体の「沖縄伝統空手総合案内ビューロー」を設立し、爾来海外の空手愛好家と沖縄の空手道場を繋ぐ橋渡し役を長年にわたり担ってきました。今やミゲール氏は沖縄空手界になくてはならない存在であるといっても過言ではありません。

いつの頃からか執筆活動にも励み、これまでの活動の集大成ともいえる本書籍の出版となり誠にご同慶の至りであります。

ミゲール氏は、ウチナーグチを流暢に話し、泡盛をこよなく愛し、カラオケで翼に乗れば沖縄の民謡も上手に歌う、まさしく碧眼のウチナーンチュであります。

ミゲール氏の今後さらなる活動が、沖縄伝統空手の普及継承発展に多大なる影響を及ぼすであろうことを確信し、第二、第三のさらなる発刊を待ち望むものであります。

My sincere congratulations on the publication of Miguel’s “Overview of Okinawa Karate in the World.” Since 2017, I have been enjoying reading the articles that have been serialized in the Okinawa Times’ “Weekly Okinawa Karate” for a long period of time. As his articles introduce karate and martial arts practitioners from 71 countries and regions around the world, I have nothing but admiration for Miguel Da Luz’s extraordinary ability to gather information.

Miguel, a former member of the International Okinawa Gōjū-ryū Karatedō Federation, came to Okinawa in 1993 to further his study of Okinawa Gōjū-ryū karate in the birthplace of karate.

At first, he stayed and slept at the Higaonna Karate Dōjō and practiced hard. In 2011, he established the “Okinawa Traditional Karate Liaison Bureau”, and since then has been acting for many years as a bridge between overseas karate enthusiasts and Okinawan karate dōjō. Today, it is no exaggeration to say that Miguel is now an indispensable presence in the Okinawa karate world.

As he has been striving in his writing activities for some time now, I am truly grateful for the publication of this book, which can be said to be the culmination of his activities so far.

Miguel speaks fluently Uchināguchi, the Okinawan language, loves Awamori and sings Okinawan folk songs skillfully when on the wings of karaoke.

I am convinced that Miguel’s further activities will have a great impact on the spread, inheritance and development of traditional Okinawa karate, and I look forward to the further publication of the second and third editions.

目次 Contents

注記 Notes

●本書は『沖縄タイムス』内の「週刊沖縄空手」2017年4月9日~2022年4月3日に掲載された記事の中から122編を選んで収録しました。

●文字数に限りがあるため、英語の翻訳は新聞に掲載された日本語の記事の完全翻訳ではありません。

●同じ国に複数の道場が紹介された場合、道場主の年齢順で記載しています。

●記事に記載されている段位、所属、職業等は、掲載当時に提供された情報に基づいています。これらの情報は、本書発行時点と異なる場合があります。

- This book contains 122 articles selected from the articles published from April 9, 2017 to April 3, 2022 in the "Weekly Okinawa Karate" of the "Okinawa Times" newspaper.
- The Hepburn romanization system is used to stay as close as possible to the original pronunciation of Okinawan and Japanese words, e.g., Ryūkyū instead of Ryukyu.
- For Japanese people, names are written the Japanese way, meaning that the family name comes first and the given name comes second. For non-Japanese people, the given name precedes the family name.
- Due to space limitation, English translations are not the full translations of the actual published Japanese articles.
- In case of multiple dōjō introduced for one single country, they are listed according to the age of the main persons featured in the articles.
- Ranks, affiliation, professions and facts mentioned in the articles are based on the information provided at the time of the interview. These information might be different at the time of the publication of this book.

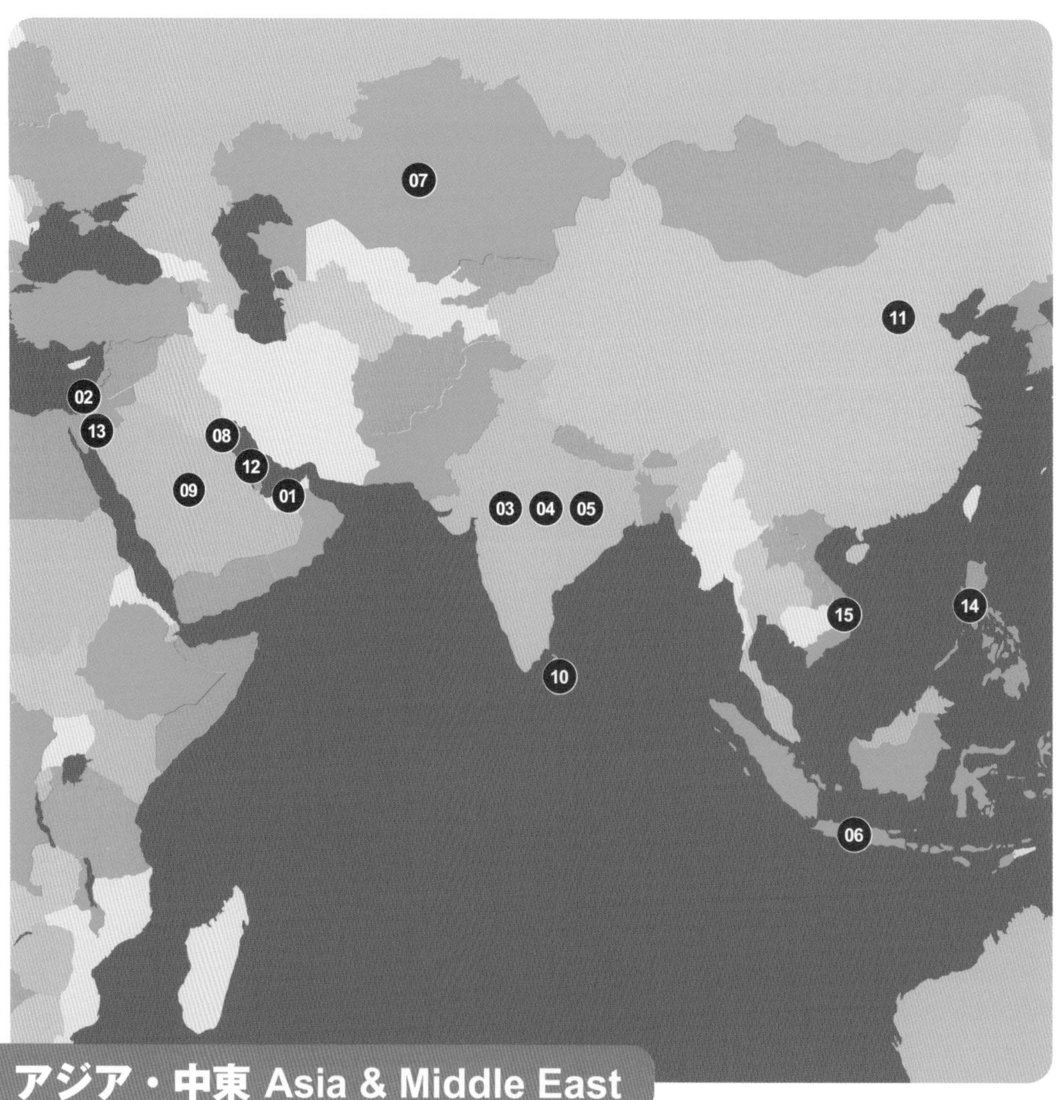

アジア・中東 Asia & Middle East

アジア・中東
Asia & Middle East

2018年03月11日

01 アラブ首長国連邦

兄弟で汗 諦めぬ精神

国際連合空手団

アラビア半島のペルシャ湾に面する連邦国家のアラブ首長国連邦（UAE）は、長年イギリスの支配下に置かれ、1971年に独立した。人口920万人余の内88％余は外国籍の住民で、インド人だけで140万人いるという。

1958年インドケララ州コーチ生まれのモハメド・イクバル氏が、76年に入門したのは当時、インドで2万5千人の弟子を数えていた沖縄少林流聖武館のクプスワミ氏の道場。後に、兄のナジームと弟のジャリール両氏も稽古を始め、現在も兄弟3人で空手の道を共に歩んでいる。彼らにとって最初から沖縄少林流に出合えたことは、幸いなことで誇りでもあるという。

79年、より良いキャリアを求めるイクバル氏は、人気移民先UAEのドバイに移住し、プロとして空手の普及に挑んだ。しかし75年のころまで武術は、軍人や警察官のみが習えるものであったため苦労の連続だった。

「当初の稽古場は屋上や裏庭を使う青空道場だった。少しずつ空手の稽古が大衆に認められ、ちゃんとした道場が開設できた」と振り返るイクバル氏。

兄弟と共に鍛錬を積むイクバル氏（右から3人目）＝提供　Mohamed Iqbal (3rd from the right) training with his brothers.

その後も稽古を重ね、聖武館ドイツのマレーシア出身のジャマル・ミヤサラ氏の下で研究を深めた。93年には初めて同館館長の島袋善保氏より直接指導を受けた。

現在ドバイ本部道場では約500人が稽古し、UAE全国8道場や学校、故郷のケララ2道場で門下生が空手を楽しむ。少林流のほかに沖縄市に本部を持つ神武会の古武道や合気道も指導している。

空手7段、古武道6段で聖武館支部長のイクバル氏は、中東に聖武館を広めクウェート、バーレーン、イランでも指南している。活発な活動の動機を聞くと、「より多くの人々に空手の恩恵を受けてほしいから」と語った。

イクバル兄弟は、幼いころ父を亡くしている。「父親の存在なくとも迷わず悪い習慣に陥らなかったのは空手のおかげ」とイクバル氏。「空手は正しき道へと導き、立ち上がる勇気、自信と諦めない精神を与えてくれる。常に生活の中で正しい行動と判断力への規律も養われる」

これまで5度、沖縄を訪れたイクバル氏は、多くの空手家のように、本場での本部道場の初訪問が最も大切な記憶となっている。「北谷町吉原の聖武館に足を踏み入れたとき、師から聞かされた歴史が目の前にあり、発祥の地の神髄を感じさせられた」という。

8月には第1回沖縄空手国際大会がある。今年も聖地・沖縄へ30人を率いて訪れ、神髄を探し求める。

Under British control for many years, the United Arab Emirates (UAE) became independent in 1971. Of a population of 9.2 million, it is said that 88% are foreign nationals, among which 1.4 million are Indians.

Born in 1958 in Cochin in the Indian state of Kerala, Mohamed Iqbal started karate in 1976 in the dōjō of Mr. Kuppusamy, Okinawa Shōrin-ryū Seibukan instructor who had at that time approximately 25,000 students. His brothers Najeem and Jaleel also started karate and even today, they follow together the way of karate. They feel fortunate and proud to have met Okinawa Shōrin-ryū from the beginning.

Published on 2018/3/11

01 United Arab Emirates

United Karate Group International

Brothers sweating in the spirit of never giving up

In 1979, seeking a better career, Mohamed Iqbal moved to Dubai and challenged himself to spread karate as a professional. However, until around 1975, teaching martial arts was restricted to the military and police and thus the first years were a series of hardships.

"Our dōjō was really nothing more than some space on a rooftop or a backyard. Over a period of time, martial arts teaching was legalized for the public and that is when we established a proper dōjō," Iqbal recalls.

Along the way, they deepened their research under Jamal Measara, a Malaysian Seibukan instructor living in Germany. In 1993, Iqbal received for the first time direct instruction from the head of the Seibukan, Shimabukuro Zenpō.

Today, the Dubai honbu dōjō has about 500 students, 8 branches in the country and 2 in Kerala. They also teach Okinawan Jinbukai kobudō and aikidō.

A 7th dan in karate and 6th dan in kobudō, Iqbal has helped Seibukan grow steadily over the years in the Middle East. Apart from the UAE, he also teaches in Kuwait, Bahrain and Iran. When asked about his motives, he says, "I want more people to benefit from karate across the world."

The Iqbal brothers lost their father very early in life. "Even without a father figure, thanks to karate we didn't go astray and fall into bad habits," says Mohamed Iqbal. "Karate showed us the light. It gave us the courage to stand up for ourselves, self-confidence and the spirit of never giving up. Karate develops discipline that leads to correct behavior and judgment in life at all time."

Having visited Okinawa five times so far, Iqbal's most cherished memory is his first visit to the honbu dōjō in Chatan. "When I stepped in the Seibukan, it brought to life all those stories I had heard from my teachers, and made me feel the true essence of the land of karate".

In August will be held the 1st Okinawa Karate International Tournament. This year too, Iqbal will lead 30 people to the sacred place of karate to continue his search.

2017年04月23日

02 イスラエル

沖縄固有の武術鍛錬

体心館

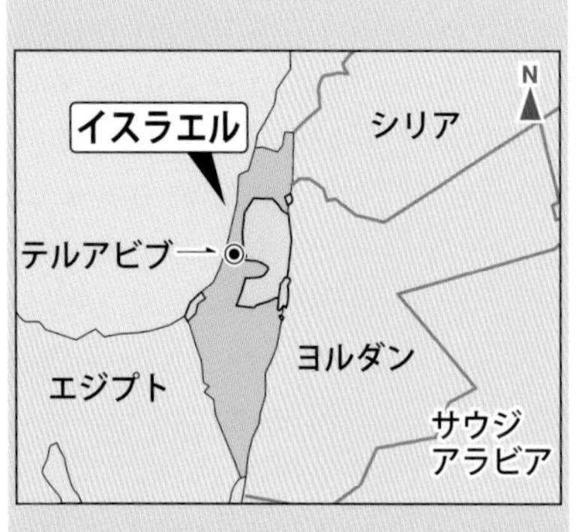

2005年7月、駐日イスラエル大使エリ・コーヘン氏が来沖し、沖縄で開催されたイベント「シャローム!イスラエル」で空手の演武を披露したことを知る人はかなりの空手通だろう。同大使は松濤館空手最高師範としても知られ、演武はイスラエルと空手の強いつながりを示すものだった。

1948年に建国されたイスラエル。この国には松濤館などの本土系の空手が多く存在しているが、一方で空手の本場・沖縄の小林流、剛柔流、上地流や古武道など10の流会派も定着し、活動している。

主要都市の一つテルアビブには、沖縄固有の武術を研究する「体心館」という道場がある。館長は同市出身のイツィック・コーヘン氏だ(上記大使と親類ではない)。現在54歳。コーヘン氏は75年ごろ、糸東流三身館の門をたたいた後、約35年間、県出身の故摩文仁賢和を流祖とする本土系四大流派の一つとされる糸東流の道を歩んだ。↗

イスラエルの3年間の兵役義務を終えた当時20歳のコーヘン氏は、エンジニアリングの学問に進みハイテク業界で成功した。その間も稽古を続け、89年故郷で道場を開設した。

そして99年には沖縄の古武術にも目を向けた。きっかけは、ハイファ市で指導していた同門のエフィー・シュラエン氏が、琉球古武道信武館の赤嶺浩館長とポール・バーミーグリオ氏を招き、主催した同年の古武道セミナーだった。セミナーは同国における、琉球の古武術普及の始まりともいえる。

イスラエルの道場でヌンチャク対棒の組手を行うイツィック・コーヘン氏(左)=提供　Itzik Cohen performing nunchaku vs. staff kumite in his dōjō (left).

2006年、ビジネスと空手道の両立に困難を感じたコーヘン氏は難しい判断を下し、空手と古武術を人生の道に選んだ。そして11年、沖縄の伝統の技に打ち込みたいと、糸東流から小林流への転向を望んだ氏は、赤嶺氏の紹介で比嘉稔氏の小林流究道館に入門した。

沖縄の武術の両輪のごとくである空手と古武術に人生をささげたコーヘン氏は、15年前から定期的に沖縄を訪れ、最近ではほぼ毎年来沖している。また10年間、個人メモや小論を重ね、今年4月に『Karate Uchina-Di　沖縄手』を題とした620ページの書籍を発行した。技術集ではなく、琉球の歴史、文化や地政学などにのっとった沖縄空手のルーツと進化の研究論としてまとめられている。

心技体の鍛錬は道場で行うものとして、現在コーヘン氏は、テルアビブで2カ所の道場で約60人に琉球古武道と小林流を精力的に指導している。弟子らは師と共に汗を流し、沖縄の伝統武術の技と精神を磨く。

Few are the ones who know that the then Israeli Ambassador to Japan Eli Cohen came to Okinawa in July 2005 and demonstrated karate during the event "Shalom! Israel". Known as one of the supreme masters of Shōtōkan karate, his demonstration exemplified the strong connection between Israel and karate.

In this country founded in 1948, there are many mainland karate schools but 10 Okinawan organizations are also well established and active.

In Tel Aviv, there is a dōjō called Teishinkan where martial arts unique to Okinawa are studied. Born in the same city, the kanchō is Itzik Cohen (54 years old, no relation with the above mentioned

Published on 2017/4/23

02 Israel

Teishinkan

Training unique Okinawan martial arts

ambassador). Around 1975, Cohen joined the Shitō-ryū Sanshinkan and for about 35 years, studied the Shitō-ryū way.

After completing the three years of mandatory military service in Israel, Cohen, then 20 years old, went on to study engineering and succeeded in the high-tech industry. Meanwhile, he continued to practice and opened a dōjō in his hometown in 1989. It is in 1999 that he became interested in Okinawan kobudō. The opportunity was a kobudō seminar held the same year and hosted by Effi Schleyen, a fellow Shitō-ryū instructor in Haifa City. Schleyen had invited the head of Ryūkyū Kobudō Shinbukan Akamine Hiroshi and Paul Vermiglio. The seminar can be said to be the beginning of the spread of Ryūkyū kobudō in the country.

In 2006, as he found it difficult to balance business and karate, Cohen chose karate and kobudō as his way of life. Then, in 2011, wishing to devote himself to the traditional techniques of Okinawan martial arts, he decided to switch from Shitō-ryū to Shōrin-ryū. Through an introduction by Akamine Hiroshi, he joined the Shōrin-ryū Kyūdōkan of Higa Minoru.

Cohen, who devotes his life to karate and kobudō, the two wheels of Okinawa's martial arts, has travelled to Okinawa for the last 15 years and recently, he has visited the island almost every year. After 10 years of personal memos and essays, he published this April a 620-page book entitled "Karate Uchina-Di". Not a collection of techniques, it is an exploration of the roots and evolution of Okinawa karate based on the history, culture and geopolitics of the Ryūkyū.

Believing that the training of the mind and body is done at the dōjō, Itzik Cohen is currently energetically instructing about 60 people in Ryūkyū kobudō and Shōrin-ryū at two dōjō in Tel Aviv. There, disciples work together with their teacher to polish their traditional Okinawan martial arts skills and spirit.

アジアの武術の発祥の地ともいわれているインドでは、空手はとても盛ん。道場だけではなく、教育機関の学生や警察、軍、刑務所等の職員指導でも行われている。関係者いわく、空手人口は50万人を上回る。

欧米の国々と違って、インドで初めて紹介されたのは、松濤館ではなく、剛柔流という。タミル・マニ氏は東京で宮城長順氏の弟子山口剛玄氏に師事し、帰国後1965年、南にある州のチェンナイで指導を始めたが、94年、50歳の若さで亡くなった。

もう一人のインドにおける空手の父は、45年ムンバイ生まれのパーベス・ミストリ氏だ。

13歳の時、柔道を始め、19歳で武術アカデミーを生まれ故郷で開設した。67年、京都に行き、剛柔流空手を学んだ。帰国の69年から指導に励み、競技空手にも挑んだ。75年、米ロングビーチで行われた第3回世界空手道選手権大会で、氏は唯一のインド代表選手として出場した。その際、沖縄剛柔流の東恩納盛男氏の空手を初めて見た。「型スーパーリンペイの演武を見て、これだ！　と思った」とミストリ氏は思い返す。

2016年沖縄で開催された武道祭で指導するミストリ氏（中央）＝ローマン・ボードリエフ氏提供　Mistry (center) instructing at the 2016 Budosai in Okinawa (photo from Roman Boldyrev).

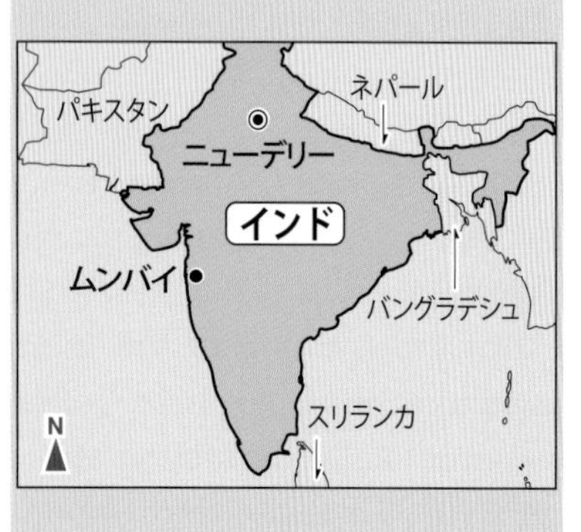

2017年07月09日

03 インド

伝統志向 熱心な研究

武術アカデミー

77年、インド空手連盟の技術顧問を務めつつ、伝統空手の追求は続けていた。同年東京に滞在し、3カ月間、東恩納氏に師事し、国際沖縄剛柔流空手道連盟（IOGKF）インド支部長に任命された。

しかし、空手の主要人物になるために生まれたわけではなかった。4歳の頃ぜんそくを発症した氏は、ヨガ教室に連れられ、呼吸法等を学んだ。ヨガと空手を両輪として磨き、剛柔流の基本型の三戦（サンチン）、転掌（テンショウ）とヨガとの共通点に気付き、研究を深めた。医師との共同研究、運動療法、指圧等の資格習得、専門書『三戦、三つの戦い』の編集も行った。結果論として「空手とヨガは異なる道ではあるが、同じ目標である『心、身体、精神の統一への理解』につながる」と氏は確信し唱える。

2012年、8段に昇段したミストリ氏は、これまで軍人や警察官などさまざまな業種の人に指導してきた。現在、伝統空手の指導の他、障がい者や身体まひの患者に集中して指南している。

「インドでは、ほとんどの（空手の）組織はスポーツ志向であり、伝統志向の空手は珍しい。IOGKFインドは、一番小さな組織かもしれません」と永遠の微笑で親しまれている氏は語る。小さな組織ではあるが、30年以上氏のそばで鍛える有段者が多く、同国で間違いなく、最も尊敬されている道場である。

Karate is very popular in India, which is said to be the birthplace of Asian martial arts. There, karate is not only taught in dōjō, but also in educational institutions, in the police, military, and to prison guards, etc. Karate experts believe that the karate population exceeds 500,000.

Unlike in western countries, the first style introduced in India was not Shōtōkan but Gōjū-ryū. Tamil Mani studied under Yamaguchi Gōgen in Tōkyō, and began teaching in Chennai in 1965 upon his return. He passed away in 1994 at the young age of 50.

Another Indian karate father is Pervez Mistry, born in Mumbai in 1945.

Mistry started jūdō at the age of 13 and

Published on 2017/7/9

03 India

Bujutsu Academy

Tradition-oriented enthusiastic research

opened a martial arts academy at the age of 19 in his hometown. In 1967, he went to Kyōtō to study Gōjū-ryū. After his return in 1969, he taught karate and got involved in competitions. In 1975, he participated as the only Indian athlete in the 3rd World Karate Championships in Long Beach, USA. This is when he first met Higaonna Morio of Okinawa Gōjū-ryū. “Seeing the demonstration of the kata Sūpārinpē, I thought that’s it!” he recalls.

While serving the Indian Karate Federation as a technical director, Mistry continued to pursue traditional karate. In 1977, he stayed in Tōkyō to study under Higaonna for three months and was later appointed as the head of the Indian branch of the International Okinawa Gōjū-ryū Karatedō Federation (IOGKF).

However, Mistry wasn’t born to become a major figure of karate. When 4 years old, he developed asthma and was taken to a yoga class to learn how to breathe. He honed yoga and karate as the two wheels of a bicycle, and deepened his research by noticing the similarities between Gōjū-ryū’s kata Sanchin, Tenshō and yoga. Collaborating with doctors, he acquired qualifications in acupressure massage, reflexology, etc., and edited the book “Sanchin, Three Battles”. He advocates that, “Karate and yoga are different paths, but they lead to the same goal of understanding the unity of mind, body, and spirit.”

Mistry, who was promoted to 8th dan in 2012, has been instructing people in the military and police. Currently, next to instructing traditional karate, he specializes in teaching people with disabilities and paraplegic patients.

“In India, most karate organizations are sports-oriented and traditional-oriented karate is rare. IOGKF India may be the smallest organization,” says he. A small organization, but that counts many black belts who have been training by his side for more than 30 years, making his dōjō one of the most respected in the country.

2021年09月12日

04 インド

指導普及に意気込み

小林流翔武館

アジアの武術の発祥の地とも言われるインドの古い武術としてカラリパヤットは有名だ。

1948年タミル・ナードゥ生まれのスワッキ・レティナム氏は、9歳のころに同武術や地元の棒術を学んだ。22歳でテコンドーに転向し、6年後の76年に空手に入門した。当時、スリランカ小林舘のガミニ・ソイサ支部長の下で故仲里周五郎氏の空手を習い、80年に小林流の道場を開設した。

「伝統空手、インドの武術、医学、精神生活との関係性」という主題で博士号を取得した氏は、カラリパヤットと空手の共通点を長年追求してきた。例えば、入門前の試し期間、尊敬と信頼に基づく師弟関係、立ち方、基本動作、関節技、急所術などだという。さらに、棒、ティンベー（楯）とローチン（小刀または矛）、鉄柱（てっちゅう）など、技法が異なっても沖縄の古武道とカラリパヤットには同じような武器がある。ヒンズー教の神シヴァが片手に持つ三叉槍（さんさそう）のトリシューラは、古武道の釵（さい）の原型という説もあると氏は語る。

97年、沖縄県立武道館落成記念として開催された世界大会に参加したレティナム氏は、那覇市安謝にある仲里氏の小林舘本部で稽古し、当時

3人の子息に囲まれたレティナム氏（中央）＝提供　Rethinam (center) with his three sons.

の高段者と交流を深めた。2016年仲里氏の死去後、高弟の一人で10年年上の儀保宜裕氏の沖縄小林流翔武館協会に加盟した。

「古武道のすべては、儀保先生に師事し習得した」と氏は言う。師弟関係に加え、両国でのライオンズクラブ活動においても共感する。

レティナム氏は13年前に60歳となり、勤めていたインド最大の国営生命保険会社を退職した。長年道場や警察で空手を指導した氏は11年に、故郷の州都チェンナイに「沖縄小林流翔武館空手古武道インド協会」の本部道場を設置し、現在は高段者30人や子ども40人が汗を流している。首都のデリーや国内8つの州にある支部で2千人余りが空手と古武道を学ぶ。19年に9段を授与された氏の子息3人も道場主として普及に努めている。

指導の他、ヨガ医療所も経営するレティナム氏は「私が習ったカラリパヤットは主に呼吸法と人間の急所を刺激する武術であり医療法である。いろんな意味で空手とカラリパヤットは似ていて、優れた健康法でもある」と両武術への意気込みを伝える。

戦わないための武術である空手の普及と偉大な師の奮闘を顕彰し、拳聖の足跡をたどることによって、空手のより深い概念を実現することが氏の使命感であり、指導への原動力である。

Published on 2021/9/12

04 India

Shōrin-ryū Shōbukan

Enthusiasm for teaching martial arts

Born in Tamil Nadu in 1948, Swakky Rethinam learned kalaripayattu, the ancient Indian martial art and the local stick art from the age of nine and started karate in 1976. At that time, he learned the karate of Nakazato Shūgorō with Gamini Soysa, head of the Sri Lanka branch of Shōrin-ryū Shōrinkan. Rethinam later opened a Shōrin-ryū dōjō in 1980.

With a PhD in the subject of "Traditional Karate - how it is connected to Indian Martial Arts, Medicine and Spiritual Life," Rethinam has long researched the similarities between the two arts. For example, he mentions the patience test before a master accepts a student, the teacher-student relationship based on respect and trust, the stances, basic movements, joint techniques and vital points among others. In addition, although the techniques are different, there are similar weapons in kobudō and kalaripayattu, like bō - silambam and tinbe-rochin - valum parijaim among others. He adds that the Hindu god Shiva's trident Trishula is believed to be the prototype of the Okinawan trident called sai.

In 1997, as Rethinam visited the Nakazatō's Shōrinkan headquarters in Aja, Naha City, he trained with high-ranked disciples of the master. After the passing of Nakazato in 2016, he joined the Okinawa Shōrin-ryū Shōbukan Association of Gibo Giyū, one of Nakazato's top students who is 10 years older than him. He stresses, "I learned all my kobudō from Gibo sensei." Both men also share in common their Lions club activities in their respective countries.

Rethinam turned 60 years old 13 years ago and retired from his position at a state-owned life insurance company. In 2011, after having taught karate in many dōjō and to police forces for decades, he set up the headquarters dōjō of the "Okinawa Shōrin-ryū Shōbukan Karate Kobudō India Association" in his hometown of Chennai. He now instructs 30 of his senior instructors and 40 children. More than 2,000 people also train within his organization that has branches in Delhi and in eight states. Promoted to 9th dan in 2019, he keeps teaching with his three sons who support him in his activities.

In addition to teaching martial arts, Rethinam also runs a yoga medical clinic. "The kalaripayattu that I learned is a martial art and medical method that mainly stimulates breathing and human vital points. In many ways, karate and kalaripayattu are similar and both are also excellent health methods."

Rethinam follows the footsteps of the grand karate masters of the past, praising their achievements and promoting an art that aims at preventing fighting. Teaching being his driving force, he firmly believes it is his mission to spread the deep meaning of karate.

2021年01月24日

05 インド

伝統の技 源流を追求

剛柔流・琉球古武道

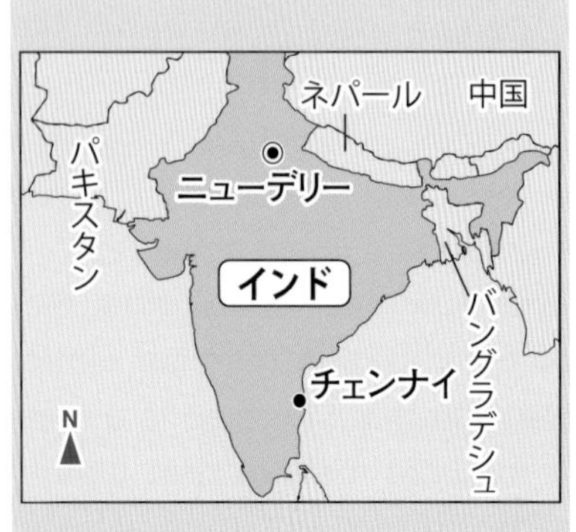

南インドの玄関口、タミル・ナードゥ州の州都チェンナイ。1961年、この街に生まれたスブラマニアム・ハリバブ氏は12歳の頃からテコンドーを習い始め、79年から指導も任されたという。

当時のその師匠は81年にマレーシアで沖縄剛柔流を学び、帰国後に空手の指導者になった。ハリバブ氏も師の意向を継いで空手に転向した。

だが、3年間で二段に昇段したハリバブ氏は疑問を感じていた。「マレーシアで学んだ指導者は沖縄と関係はなく、段位を売ることが主な目的だったから関係を断った」と振り返る。

真の師を求めハリバブ氏は、84年からニューヨークで尚礼館沖縄剛柔流を指導するスコット・レンジ氏を紹介され、ビデオ指導で剛柔流を改めて学んだ。

尚礼館は比嘉世幸氏や剛柔流々祖・宮城長順氏に師事した故渡口政吉氏が54年に創立した道場。上京した渡口氏は、代々木、目黒や中野で指南に当たった。

86年にはハリバブ氏はイタリアを拠点に普及活動に努めた渡口氏の高弟・玉野十四雄氏を訪ねて師事、初段にも合格した。

空手の源流を求め、ハリバブ氏は5年間かけて文書で渡口氏に受け入れを求めた。願いがかない91年に中野の尚礼館本部道場の門をくぐり、6カ月の間技術指導を受けた。後に93年から5年間、師の他界まで東京に住み鍛錬を重ねた。

門下生を前に型の分解を披露するハリバブ氏（手前左）＝提供　Haribabu (front to the left) showing an application of a kata.

古武術にも興味を持ったハリバブ氏は2001年に与儀清氏と出会い、武器術の手ほどきを受けた。後に中野の道場の先輩だった池原英樹氏の紹介で琉球古武道保存会会長・金城政和氏に弟子入り。剛柔流と同様に古武道に打ち込むことを決心し、03年から07年まで沖縄に住み研究を重ねた。

1986年に開設した尚礼館インド総本部は2004年から琉球古武道保存会のインド本部としても活動している。道場では約60人、国内9支部や約20の学校や大学で約2千人がハリバブ氏、渡口氏にも師事した妻、娘2人や育った指導者の下で空手と古武道を習う。

日本と沖縄通のハリバブ氏は日本語も堪能。これまでインドを訪れた多くの県出身空手師範の通訳も務めた。その功績が認められ、18年に在チェンナイ日本国総領事から表彰を受けた。

「武道は海に例えられる謎。深く行けば行くほど、貴重な恵を発見できる」。ハリバブ氏は、伝統空手と古武道を通じて日本とインドの友好親善と相互理解を目指し、沖縄生まれの武術の魅力を伝え続けている。

Published on 2021/1/24

05 India

Gōjū-ryū & Ryūkyū kobudō

Pursuing the origin of traditional techniques

Born in 1961 in Chennai, the capital of Tamil Nadu, Subramaniam Haribabu began learning taekwondo at the age of 12 and started teaching in 1979.

As his instructor went to study Okinawa Gōjū-ryū in Malaysia in 1981, Haribabu followed his master and switched to karate. However, as he was promoted to the rank of 2nd dan in three years, Haribabu became skeptical. “I came to understand that the Malaysian master did not have any connection with Okinawa as he was claiming, and that he was more interested in selling ranks than teaching karate,” he recalls.

In search of a true master, Haribabu was introduced in 1984 to Scott Lenzi, who teaches Shōreikan Okinawa Gōjū-ryū in New York, and studied with him through video instruction.

The Shōreikan is a dōjō founded in 1954 by the late Toguchi Seikichi, who later moved to Tōkyō to spread karate.

In 1986, Haribabu visited Tamano Toshio, a high-ranked student of Toguchi based in Italy, and trained with him to finally be awarded the 1st dan.

Seeking the roots of karate, Haribabu wrote for five years to Toguchi asking to be accepted as a student. In 1991, he finally entered the Shōreikan in Nakano Tōkyō and studied there for six months. He later lived and trained in Tōkyō for five years, from 1993 until Toguchi’s passing.

Interested in kobudō, Haribabu later became a student of Kinjō Masakazu, the chairman of the Ryūkyū Kobudō Preservation Society. The introduction was made by a senior of the Nakano dōjō, Ikehara Hideki. Willing to devote himself to kobudō as much as he did for Gōjū-ryū, Haribabu lived in Okinawa from 2003 to 2007 and deepened his research in Okinawan weaponry.

The Shōreikan Indian headquarters, which was established in 1986, have also been active as the Indian headquarters for the preservation society since 2004. Approximately 60 people at the dōjō, and some 2,000 people in 9 branches and 20 schools and universities across India, study karate and kobudō under Haribabu and his wife, who also trained directly with Toguchi. They are supported by their two daughters and the many instructors they have raised along the way.

A Japan and Okinawa enthusiast, Haribabu is fluent in Japanese and has served as an interpreter for the many masters who have visited India. In recognition of his dedicated services, he received a commendation award from the Consulate General of Japan in Chennai in 2018.

“Budō is a mystery. It is like an ocean. The deeper you go, the more precious things you find.” In this spirit, Haribabu continues to convey the charms of Okinawa-born martial arts, aiming for friendship and mutual understanding between Japan and India through traditional karate and kobudō.

2019年09月08日

❻ インドネシア

武術の奥義求め精進

文武館ソロ道場

1万3千島を有する島国のインドネシアは、東南アジアに伝わる拳法と武器術で混合される伝統的な武術プンチャック・シラットが盛んだ。その一方で空手も普及している。

1971年生まれのワヒュー・アミーン・シャフェイ氏は、小学校で剛柔流空手、中学生の時にシラットを学んだ。高校に入学すると空手に戻り、その後カンフーも体験した。

24歳から、自身も卒業した母校ディポヌゴロ大学の講師を務めた。2006年から10年まで、九州工業大学で学んだ際に、文武館の空手と古武道を指導する同大学教授の尾知博氏に出会い師事した。

尾知氏(60)は、高専や大学時代に競技空手を中心に練習し、27歳で琉球大学の助手として沖縄に移ったころ、沖縄伝統古武道保存会文武館に入門した。後に師範免状を取得し九州やベトナムなどで指導を行っている。↗

那覇市首里鳥堀町にある沖縄伝統古武道保存会文武館は、県指定無形文化財保持者の仲本政博氏が1971年に開設した道場で、現館長は息子の守氏が務めている。

大会でサイの型を披露するシャフェイ氏(手前)=提供 Syafei (front) demonstrating sai at a tournament.

インドネシアに帰国後シャフェイ氏は、ディポヌゴロ大学工学部無線研究の准教授を務めながら、自身が住むジャワ島のスラカルタ(愛称ソロ)に本部道場を開設。約10年間で国内に6カ所の空手、古武道の道場を持つまでになった。

首都ジャカルタに空手が導入されたのは1963年のことだという。翌年インドネシア空手競技連盟が設立された。現在、本土系の各流会派が広く普及しているが、2010年に設立された文武館インドネシア支部は、同国初の沖縄空手古武道の組織だという。

仲本氏から空手・古武道の3段と指導員の証を授与されたシャフェイ氏は、2007年以降10回沖縄を訪れている。思い出について問うと「空手と古武道の奥義に導かれることはもちろんのことだが、沖縄の人々はいつもフレンドリーで温かく、魅力的で親切です。環境と天気がよくて、ハラルフーズもおいしい!」と答えが返ってきた。イスラム教徒であるシャフェイ氏は、肉なし豆腐チャンプルーやゴーヤーチャンプルーも好む。

「真の空手は、ただのスポーツだけではなく、生涯活動の一つだと思う。稽古を通して健康、自己と感情のコントロール、しつけ、強さ、他人への尊重、すべてのものや生物への感謝が学べる」と空手の魅力を分析するシャフェイ氏。将来は、無料で沖縄空手と古武道を教えることを目標にさらなる精進の道を歩む。

Published on 2019/9/8

06 Indonesia

Bunbukan Solo Dōjō

A dedication to seeking the secret of martial arts

Indonesia, an island nation with 13,000 islands, is home to the traditional martial arts Pencak Silat, a full body and weapons method that has been handed down in Southeast Asia. On the other hand, karate is also widespread.

Born in 1971, Wahyul Amien Syafei studied Gōjū-ryū karate in elementary school and Silat in junior high school. When he entered senior high school, he returned to karate and then experienced kungfu.

After serving, from the age of 24, as a lecturer at Diponegoro University from which he graduated, Syafei went on studying at the Kyūshū Institute of Technology from 2006 to 2010. There, he met and studied the karate and kobudō of the Bunbukan with Ochi Hiroshi, a professor at this same institute.

Ochi (60) practiced mainly competitive karate when he was a technical college and university student. When he moved to Okinawa to work at the University of the Ryūkyūs at the age of 27, he entered the Okinawa Traditional Kobudō Preservation Society Bunbukan. Later obtaining a master's license, he has been teaching martial arts in Kyūshū and Vietnam since then.

The Bunbukan, located in Shuri Torihori-chō, Naha City, is a dōjō that was opened by Nakamoto Masahiro in 1971 and today his son, Mamoru, stands as the kanchō.

After returning to Indonesia, Syafei opened his headquarters dōjō in Surakarta (colloquially Solo) on Java Island, where he lives, while serving as an associate professor at the Faculty of Engineering, Diponegoro University. In about 10 years, he has opened 6 karate and kobudō clubs in the country.

It is said that karate was introduced in the capital Jakarta in 1963. The following year, the Indonesian Karate Sports Association was established. Currently, while mainland Japanese karate schools are widespread, Bunbukan Indonesia, established in 2010, stands as the first Okinawa karate and kobudō organization in the country.

Syafei, who was promoted to 3rd dan in karate and kobudō and handed a certificate of instructor by Nakamoto, has visited Okinawa 10 times since 2007. When asked about his memories of his trips, he answers, "Of course, next to being guided to karate and kobudō's hidden techniques, Okinawans are always friendly, warm-hearted and charming people. The environment and weather are great, and the halal cuisine is delicious!" As a Muslim, Syafei likes tōfu and gōyā chanpuru without meat.

About the charms of karate, he says, "True karate is not only a sport but a lifelong activity. Through practice, one learns about health, self-control, discipline, strength, respect for others and the appreciation of all things."

In the future, he will continue to devote himself to teaching for free Okinawa karate and kobudō.

2019年05月12日

07 カザフスタン

不屈の魂 研究に情熱

第二本部道場

元大相撲力士風冨山泰雅の出身国カザフスタン。カスピ海とアラル海に面しているこの内陸国に定着した民族は、元々遊牧民だった。そのため男たちは、乗馬と刀や棒を含む五つの武器術を習得しなければならなかったという。現在は、カザフのレスリングしか残っていないが、格闘技は極めて盛んだ。

1980年代、松濤館系と極真系の空手がこの国に紹介された。91年ソビエト連邦からの独立を受けて、世界空手連盟に加盟する国家連盟が発足し、現在も競技空手は活発に行われ普及している。

南の都市アルマトイを故郷とする57年生まれのスヴゥトラナ・キム氏は、89年、32歳の時偶然に空手と出合い、同国空手パイオニアの一人バレリ・カルポフ氏の下で松濤館系の空手を習った。

91年に、カルポフ氏は同市に剛柔流の東恩納盛男氏を招きセミナーを開催した。そこから、師と共にキム氏は剛柔流に転向した。現在剛柔流6段のキム氏は、支部長のカルメノフ・アーマン氏の下で研究と指導に挑んでいる。

「好戦的な人々の歴史ゆえ、カザフスタンではさまざまな格闘技が普及している。空手の流派も多く、競技空手、フルコンタクト空手やテコンドーの大会も盛んに行われている。そんな中、強い指導者の育成、伝統の保存、健康増進をコアとする沖縄空手は人気」と現況を語る。

古武術の武器を持って構えるキム氏（中央）と門下生たち＝提供　Kim (center) and her students holding the various weapons of kobudō.

96年に道場を開設。古武道にも興味をもったキム氏は、2010年に沖縄伝統古武道文武館の仲本政博氏を紹介され古武術も習い始めた。

「今のところ、カザフスタンでの古武道は、始まったばかり。だが、多くの空手指導者が古武道に興味を持ち始めている。新たな修業法、空手技法の発展、記憶の訓練につながるなどがその理由」と文武館支部長のキム氏は解説する。

今年初めてキム氏は、国内2カ所、ロシアとデンマークで古武道のセミナーを実施した。また技術向上に向けて今年4月に、文武館の仲本守と喜屋武盛和両氏を招き、首都のヌルスルタンでセミナーを開催した。その際キム氏は、古武道の4段に昇段した。

「無比である古武道は話題を呼んでいる。このような講習会を通して国内の古武道の発展と技術向上が促進される」とキム氏。これまで16回沖縄を訪れ、研さんを積んでいる。

これからも「決してあきらめないこと」をモットーに、剛柔流をしっかり受け継ぎながら、独自の力学と特徴を有する古武道の研究を深めていく。

Published on 2019/5/12

07 Kazakhstan

Honbu Dōjō No.2

An indomitable soul and a passion for research

In the landlocked country Kazakhstan, the original settlers were nomads and it is said that men had to learn five weapons techniques, including horse riding, swords and sticks. Currently, only Kazakh wrestling remains, but martial arts are extremely popular.

In the 1980s, Shōtōkan and Kyokushin karate were introduced to this country. Following the independence from the Soviet Union in 1991, a national federation which became member of the World Karate Federation was established, and competitive karate is still widely practiced to this day.

Born in 1957 in the southern city of Almaty, Svetlana Kim discovered karate in 1989, studying Shōtōkan karate under one of the country's karate pioneers, Valery Karpov.

In 1991, Karpov invited Higaonna Morio for a Gōjū-ryū seminar. From there, along with her teacher, Kim switched to Gōjū-ryū. Currently a 6th dan in this style, she continues to train and study under Aman Karmenov, the national chief instructor.

"There is an intense interest to martial arts in Kazakhstan, perhaps because of the war-oriented past of Kazakh people. There are a lot of styles of karate, so there are many competitions in sport karate and Kyokushin among others. Our success comes from the core elements of our Okinawa karate school that are nurturing strong instructors, preserving the traditional systems of karate and kobudō and popularizing healthy lifestyles."

Kim opened her dōjō in 1996. As she was also interested in kobudō, she was introduced to Nakamoto Masahiro of the Okinawa Traditional Kobudō Bunbukan in 2010 and began learning weaponry.

As the official representative of Bunbukan, she says, "At the moment, kobudō is in the beginning of its development in Kazakhstan. However, a lot of karate instructors are interested in kobudō for many reasons: development of karate skills, training of memory, concentration, coordination and other aspects."

This year, for the first time, Kim held seminars on kobudō in Russia and Denmark. Furthermore, in order to improve the local skill level, she invited in April Nakamoto Mamoru and Kyan Morikazu of the Bunbukan for a seminar in the capital city of Nur-Sultan. On this occasion, she was promoted to kobudō 4th dan.

"Kobudō attracts interest because of its uniqueness. I'm sure that such seminars promote the development of kobudō in Kazakhstan and will also boost mastery level," says she. In order to deepen her knowledge, she has also visited Okinawa sixteen times.

With the maxim "Never give up," she will continue to firmly inheriting Gōjū-ryū while deepening her studies on Okinawa weaponry's mechanics and characteristics.

2021年11月28日

08 クウェート

千人以上に空手指導

少林流聖武館

2020年東京オリンピックの空手競技には36の国から81選手が出場し、形競技に出場した1人がクウェート人であった。予選敗退となったが、空手が盛んなこの国の空手家に大きな刺激と希望を与えたことだろう。

クウェート空手連盟のウェブサイトを見ると、松濤館系の道場を主として15の空手組織が紹介されている。そのほか、極真系など非加盟の道場も存在し、沖縄空手もこの国で普及している。

クウェートの総人口の約70%は移民が占めており、その内、インド人とエジプト人が最大の外国人コミュニティーだという。

マニ・パップ氏(63)は、インド西南部のケララ州にあるコーリコードで生まれた。1977年に、ブルース・リー主演映画『燃えよドラゴン』を見て、故郷にあった空手道場に入門した。氏がくぐった門は、マレーシア出身空手指導者のクプスワミ氏が開いた少林流聖武館の道場だった。

より良い仕事を求め、パップ氏は85年にクウェートへの移民を決めた。数年間の困難な時期を乗り越え、輸入品を取り扱う企業のストアマネジャーとなった。懸命に働き、大学へと進学させた娘は医者となり、現在は夫と一緒にスウェーデンに住んでいる。

クウェートの門下生一部とパップ氏(後列左端)=提供　Pappu (far left in the back row) with some of his Kuwaiti students.

生計を立てながら、空手の稽古を重ねたパップ氏は87年に初段を取得。翌年、首都クウェート市内にあるレクリエーションセンターで空手の指導を始めた。12年間同施設で指導し、他数カ所でもクラスを開校した。92年に、島袋善保氏が会長を務める国際沖縄少林流聖武館空手道協会への加盟が認められた。

その後、首都の南の地域マンガフにあるインド人向けの学校法人に拠点を移し、普及活動を続けた。他の二つの支部では、クウェート人や多くの外国人に空手を指南したという。

教育施設で指導してきたパップ氏は、5歳から18歳の児童生徒に空手を教えた。彼らの多くは、より高度な学問を続けるためにさまざまな国に移民した。千人以上に指導した傍ら、学校現場の状況に制限があり、島袋氏を招くことができなかったことがパップ氏の後悔の一つだと言う。

今年7月、パップ夫妻は、故郷のケララ州に帰郷したが、クウェート支部長として現地の道場主と日々連絡を取り合っている。世界が新型コロナウイルス感染症を乗り越えられたら、再び36年に住んだペルシャ湾の先端に位置するクウェートに渡り、大好きな沖縄空手の指導に励みたいと4段のパップ氏は思っている。

Published on 2021/11/28

08 Kuwait

Shōrin-ryū Seibukan

Teaching karate to more than a thousand people

Among the 81 athletes from the 36 countries who participated in the karate competition of the 2020 Tōkyō Olympics, there was one kata competitor from Kuwait who must have been a source of great inspiration for the karateka in this country.

On the website of the Kuwait Karate Federation, 15 karate organizations, mainly Shōtōkan dōjō, are introduced. Next to other groups like Kyokushin schools, Okinawa karate is also practiced.

Immigrants make up about 70% of Kuwait's total population, of which Indians and Egyptians are said to be the largest foreign communities.

Mani Pappu (63) was born in Calicut, Kerala, India. In 1977, after watching the movie "Enter the Dragon" starring Bruce Lee, he entered a karate dōjō in his hometown, a club run by a Malaysian Shōrin-ryū Seibukan instructor by the name of Kuppusamy.

In search of better work opportunities, Pappu decided to move to Kuwait in 1985. Overcoming several years of difficult times, he succeeded in becoming a store manager for an import business company. Working hard, he sent his daughter to college and she became a doctor who now lives in Sweden with her husband.

While earning a living, Pappu kept practicing karate and was awarded the 1st dan in 1987. The following year, he began teaching karate at a recreation center in the capital Kuwait City. Teaching at this facility for 12 years, he also opened classes in several other locations. In 1992, he was officially recognized as a member of the International Okinawa Shōrin-ryū Seibukan Karatedō Association, chaired by Shimabukuro Zenpō.

Later on, Pappu moved his karate classes to an Indian public school in Mangaf, in the south of the capital, and continued to teach and promote Okinawa karate. With two other branches, he says that he has taught karate not only to Kuwaitis but also to many foreigners.

As he has been teaching at educational facilities, Pappu taught karate to students aged 5 to 18 years old. Many of them immigrated to different countries to continue their higher education. Although he has instructed more than a thousand people, one of Pappu's regrets is that he was unable to invite Shimabukuro Zenpō due to the facilities he was teaching at.

This July, Mrs. and Mr. Pappu returned to their hometown of Kerala but as the head of the Kuwait branch, Pappu keeps in touch with the local dōjō owners on a daily basis. Once the world has overcome the Covid-19 pandemic, he plans to travel again to the tip of the Persian Gulf country where he lived for 36 years and teach his beloved Okinawa karate.

2018年06月10日

09 サウジアラビア 

不屈の精神 続く挑戦

小林流と古武道

間近に迫ったサッカーのワールドカップ（W杯）の開幕試合で、開催国ロシアはサウジアラビア（KSA）と対戦する。イスラム教最大の聖地「メッカ」があるこの王国は、これまで世界で唯一女性の自動車運転が禁じられていたが、今月で解禁されるという。

1960年代から松濤館系の指導者がKSAを訪れ空手を指導してきた。現在でも、全日本空手道連盟とサウジアラビア空手連盟の交流が続けられ、派遣事業が続いている。

53年フィリピン、マニラ生まれのジュン・カバリエロ氏は、13歳のときド・パレノ氏の下で空手を始めた。フィリピンでは、60年代以降、県出身指導者の伊波清吉氏や城間盛義氏により小林流志道館の空手が普及した。カバリエロ氏もその空手を継いだ。

70年から大手の一般消費財メーカーに勤めながら、小林流の普及に挑んだ。97年、沖縄を訪れた際に、志道館館長故宮平勝哉氏に初めて会い、師事した。琉球古武道の赤嶺栄亮氏と息子浩氏にも紹介され古武道を始めた。

99年に、KSAのあるスポーツセンターの空手指導者募集広告を見つけたカバリエロ氏は、移住を決め

「前里の鉄甲」を演武するカバリエロ氏＝提供　Caballero performing "Maezato no Tekkō".

た。応募して採用され、ペルシャ湾に面するダンマームで指導を始めた。2012年より同市の「ボディフィットネス&護身術センター」を拠点とし、子ども135人、大人65人に小林流と古武道を指南するほか、国内数支部やクウェートにも出掛けて指導する。

アラビア語を知らない状況で、身ぶり手ぶりで指導した。国内の松濤館の権威に動じず、沖縄空手・古武道を披露し、普及のために競技大会にも参加し名を成した。

しかし一番のハードルは習慣の違いだったという。「KSAは厳格な国。女性の人権は固く規制されている。公共の場での男女共同稽古は禁止。女性は、自宅または女性専用施設で習うしかない。長く滞在するには、その国のルールに従わなければなりません」

その一方で免税と雇用補償の良さ、友人や弟子の支援が大きな支えという。「空手を通して、あらゆる人生の挑戦に対し不屈な精神を養う。どんな状況でも柔軟性をもって応じられるようになる。個人的に、異文化の地で暮らすのも大きなチャレンジです」

空手8段、古武道3段のカバリエロ氏は、イラストレーターでもある。沖縄の武術の道を歩むことが最も大切と考え、その新たな一歩として8月の第1回沖縄空手国際大会に参加する。8度目の"空手のメッカ"訪問となる。

Published on 2018/6/10

09 Saudi Arabia

Shōrin-ryū and kobudō

An indomitable spirit for a never-ending challenge

The kingdom of Saudi Arabia (KSA), home to the Mecca, the holiest city of Islam, was the only country in the world where women were banned from driving, but this month the ban will be lifted.

Since the 1960s, Shōtōkan instructors have visited KSA to teach karate. Even now, karate exchanges between the two countries and instructors' dispatching continue.

Born in Manila, the Philippines in 1953, Jun Caballero started karate under Do Pareno at the age of 13. In the Philippines, Shōrin-ryū Shidōkan karate became popular in the 1960s due to the teaching of Okinawan instructors Iha Seikichi and Shiroma Seigi. From the start, Caballero studied this system of karate.

From the 1970s, while working in a multinational company, Caballero started teaching karate. In 1997, when he visited Okinawa, he trained for the first time under Miyahira Katsuya, the head of the Shidōkan. He was also introduced to Akamine Eisuke and his son Hiroshi and started practicing Ryūkyū kobudō.

In 1999, having found an advertisement for a karate instructor at a sports center in KSA, Caballero decided to move to the Arabian Peninsula country. Hired, he began teaching in Dammam, which faces the Persian Gulf. Since 2012, based in the Body Fitness & Self-Defense Center in Dammam, he teaches Shōrin-ryū and kobudō to 135 children and 65 adults while travelling to several branch dōjō in the country and in Kuwait.

Not knowing Arabic, he taught by sign languages. Unshaken by the established presence of Shōtōkan, he strived to popularize his karate and kobudō, and participating in tournaments, made a name for himself.

However, the biggest hurdle was the difference in customs. "KSA is a strict country. Women's human rights are strictly regulated. Men and women's joint training is prohibited in public places. For women, the only choice is to train at home or in women-only facilities. If you want to stay long, you must follow the local rules."

On the other hand, good tax exemption, employment compensation and support from friends and students are a huge help, he says. "Karate develops an indomitable spirit for all the challenges in life. People will be able to respond with mental calmness and flexibility in any situation."

An 8th dan in karate and 3rd dan in kobudō, Caballero is also an illustrator. As he follows the path of Okinawan martial arts, his next new step will be to participate in the 1st Okinawa Karate International Tournament in August. This will be is eighth visit to the "Mecca of karate".

1976年9月25日、沖縄タイムスの紙面に「軍隊で空手を指導~垣花さんスリランカへ」と題された記事が掲載された。

当時、小林流小林館協会の故仲里周五郎氏の弟子垣花恵春氏（70歳、現小林流尚倫會会長）は、この島国を訪れ2カ月間指南した。記事には、スリランカ陸軍の訓練長・ガミニ・ソイサ氏が派遣を実現させたと記載されている。

51年生まれのソイサ氏は、18歳のころに中国の武術などを始め、2年後松濤館空手に移った。

「偶然、73年発行の米雑誌で仲里先生のことを知った」と氏は思い返す。すぐに小林流を習いたいと手紙を出したが3カ月がたっても返事はなかった。諦めず、1年以上7通の手紙を送り続けた結果、仲里氏から英字の手紙が届いた。文書には「習いたいなら、ビデオを見て学ぶか、沖縄に来るか」と選択肢を与えられたが、指導者の派遣を依頼し、76年に小林流の道を歩み始めた。

その後小林館の道場を開設し、国家公務員の職を勤めながら指導したが、82年にプロとなった。

87年には、初めて来沖を果たした氏は、那覇市安謝にある小林館本部道場で汗を流し、スリランカ支部長に任命された。

門下生を指導するガミニ・ソイサ氏（中央）＝提供 Gamini Soysa (center) teaching his students.

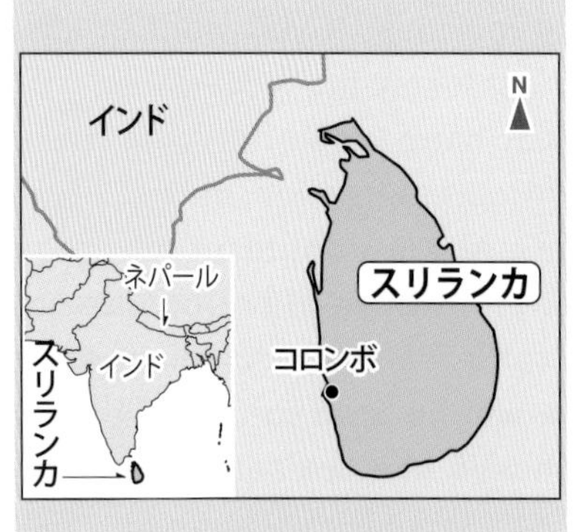

2017年08月13日

⑩スリランカ

不屈の精神 普及に力

南亜細亜小林舘協会本部

新生活を求めて91年に、家族と共にニューヨークに移住し、約17年間空手指導者として生活を送った。「ある日、ブロンクスで2人の泥棒に絡まれたが、沖縄空手の稽古と技のおかげで無事に逃れた」と氏は述べる。日本語も学び、訪米した仲里氏のセミナーに参加し、師匠との交流も深めた。

2005年の2回目訪沖後08年に、故郷の最大都市コロンボの郊外にあるボラレスガムワに定住し、道場を再開。そして南アジアにおいて小林館の空手と古武道の普及に挑んだ。

1975年に創立されたスリランカ空手道連盟には現在、350道場が登録されているが、さまざまな機関で空手が指導され、ソイサ氏によると空手人口は15万人余という。沖縄に本部を持つ支部は10以上あるようだ。

指圧療法士をしながら空手8段のソイサ氏は、本部道場で約150人を指導している。国内七つの支部道場に加えて、インド、モルディブ、ドバイ、アラブ首長国連邦の国々に千人以上の愛好者がいる。来年開催される第1回沖縄空手国際大会に弟子と共に参加する予定。

40年前に、自ら道を開き逸脱しなかったソイサ氏。物柔らかな心と不屈の精神を磨きながら、無限である沖縄の武術の研究と普及に努めている。

Published on 2017/8/13

10 Sri Lanka

South Asia Shōrin-ryū Shōrinkan Hdqrs.

Spreading karate with an indomitable spirit

On September 25th, 1976, an article titled "Instructing Karate in the Army - Mr. Kakinohana goes to Sri Lanka" was published in the Okinawa Times newspaper. At that time, Kakinohana Keishun (70 years old, current chairman of Shōrin-ryū Shōrin-kai), a disciple of the late Nakazato Shūgorō, visited this island country and taught for two months. The article stated that Sri Lanka Army's instructor Gamini Soysa made the visit possible.

Born in 1951, Soysa started Chinese martial arts at the age of 18 and switched to Shōtōkan karate two years later.

"I happened to know about Nakazato sensei in a US magazine published in 1973," he recalls. He immediately wrote that he wanted to learn Shōrin-ryū, but didn't get reply. Not giving up, he sent seven letters in one year and as a result, he received a letter in English from Nakazato that gave him two options: "If you want to learn, do it watching videos or come to Okinawa." Asking for an instructor's visit, Soysa started his career in Shōrin-ryū Shōrinkan in 1976.

Although he opened a dōjō while working as a civil servant, Soysa became a professional in 1982. In 1987, he was appointed as the Sri Lankan branch chief training at the Shōrinkan honbu dōjō in Aja, Naha City.

In 1991, Soysa moved to New York with his family in search of a new life and lived as a karate instructor for about 17 years. Having learned Japanese, he attended the seminars of Nakazato Shūgorō in the USA and deepened his relation with his master.

In 2008, following his second visit to Okinawa in 2005, he settled in his hometown Boralesgamuwa in the suburb of Colombo, reopened a dōjō and took on the challenge of spreading Shōrin-ryū Shōrinkan karate and kobudō in South Asia.

According to Soysa, the Sri Lankan national karate federation, which was founded in 1975, currently has 350 registered dōjō with more than 150,000 practitioners nationwide. It seems there are more than 10 organizations with a honbu dōjō in Okinawa.

While working as a shiatsu therapist, 8th dan karate instructor Soysa teaches about 150 people at his main dōjō. In addition to the seven branch dōjō in the country, he has more than a thousand members in India, the Maldives, Dubai and the United Arab Emirates.

Gamini Soysa has not deviated from the path he has chosen for himself 40 years ago. While refining a gentle heart and an indomitable spirit, he strives to research and popularize the infinite Okinawan martial arts.

2020年08月09日

⑪ 中国

武術大国で空手普及

剛柔流空手道弘孝館

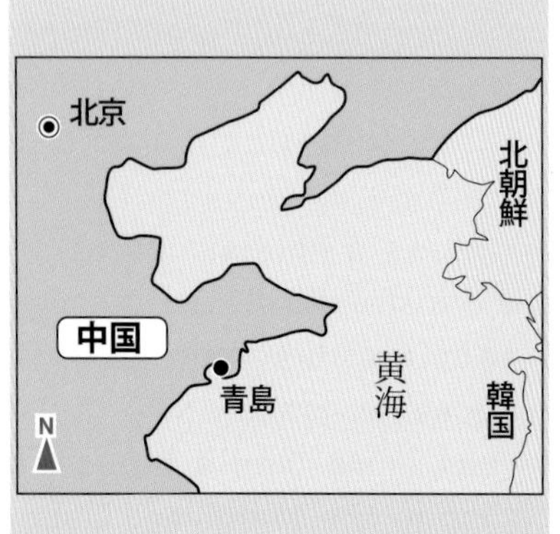

長き歴史を誇る武術大国、中国。今日では空手が盛んになっている。1990年代以前は中国大陸と日本の間で文化や武術交流は少なかった。香港においては60年代前半から空手が日本の商人によって紹介されている。

このころラム・キング・ファン氏は香港で剛柔流の手ほどきを受けた。74年に沖縄で剛柔流の上原恒氏、宮城安一氏、東京で指導していた東恩納盛男氏に師事した。香港に帰った後、2018年に亡くなるまで沖縄空手の普及に努めた。

1990年に沖縄出身で小林流系の空手を習っていた銘苅拳一氏は上海に移住し、教育機関等で広く空手を普及させた。以降、日本と中国本土の武術交流が増え、空手も広まった。

「しかし、沖縄空手はあまり知られていない。フルコンタクト系の空手や東京五輪で正式種目となった競技空手が一番人気」。こう指摘するのは沖縄剛柔流空手道協会の何泓孝氏（カ・オウコウ）氏だ。

1980年内モンゴル自治区生まれの何氏はドキュメンタリーやアニメで空手を知り、2003年から稽古を始めた。「故郷に道場がなかった。北京で大学に入学した際にフルコン系の道場に入門した」と振り返る。翌年、世界各地で沖縄剛柔流を指導していた村松真孝氏（73）に出会った。

北京で行われたセミナーで。何氏（後列左から2人目）と村松氏（同3人目）、参加者ら=2019年（提供）　He Hongxiao (second from the left in the back row) and Muramatsu (third from the left) in Beijing in 2019.

沖縄剛柔流空手道協会副会長、範士9段の村松氏は1966年から8年間、那覇市の順道館で故宮里栄一氏に師事した。1976年に帰郷し、静岡県富士宮市で「榮道館」を開設している。

村松氏のセミナーに参加した何氏は、沖縄剛柔流に魅了された。2008年には、それまで中国商業連合会で働いていた仕事を辞め、空手のプロ指導者になろうと決心した。

2007年に北京で道場を、09年には青島に移り住み、二つ目の道場を開設した。両道場では150人が空手を学び、何氏は北京大学でも指南している。中国国内では、6都市に協会加盟の支部があり、約400人が稽古しているという。

沖縄の海、風土が大好きだという空手5段の何氏は、沖縄を5回訪れている。「中国はさまざまな異文化を受け入れる用意がある国。良いものである限り、学びたい人はたくさんいる。中国伝来武術は多いが、空手を含む海外の武術に興味を持つ人も多い。中国人には、日本の文化を好む者も多い」と説明する。

剛柔流々祖・宮城長順の師・東恩納寛量が武術を習った中国。何氏は異文化交流を深めながら、その系統の空手普及に励んでいる。

China, a country with a long martial arts history. Before the 1990s, cultural and martial arts exchanges between mainland China and Japan were rare. Yet, karate was introduced in Hong Kong by Japanese merchants in the early 1960s.

Around this time, Lam King Fung started learning Gōjū-ryū in Hong Kong. In 1974, he studied under Gōjū-ryū Uehara Kō, Miyagi Anichi and Higaonna Morio. After returning to Hong Kong, he strived to popularize Okinawa karate until his death in 2018.

In 1990, Shōrin-ryū karate instructor Mekaru Kenichi from Okinawa moved to Shanghai and spread karate widely in educational institutions. Since then, martial arts exchanges between Japan and mainland China have increased, and karate has become widely popular.

Published on 2020/8/9

⑪ China

Gōjū-ryū Karatedō Kōkōkan

Spreading karate in the great land of martial arts

"However, Okinawa karate is not well known. Full contact karate and competitive karate are the most popular," says He Hongxiao, a member of the Okinawa Gōjū-ryū Karatedō Association.

Born in Inner Mongolia in 1980, He Hongxiao learned about karate through documentaries and anime, and began practicing in 2003. "There was no dōjō in my hometown. When I entered university in Beijing, I joined a full-contact karate club," he recalls. The following year, he met Muramatsu Masataka, who was teaching Okinawa Gōjū-ryū all over the world.

Muramatsu, a 9th dan and Vice Chairman of the Okinawa Gōjū-ryū Karatedō Association, studied under the late Miyazato Eiichi at the Jundōkan from 1966 to 1974 before opening the Eidōkan in Shizuoka.

He Hongxiao attended Muramatsu's seminar and was fascinated by Okinawa Gōjū-ryū. In 2008, he decided to quit his job at the China Commercial Federation and became a professional karate instructor.

After opening a dōjō in Beijing in 2007, he moved to Qingdao in 2009 and opened a second dōjō. At both dōjō, 150 people are studying karate, while He Hongxiao also teaches at the Peking University. Today, there are branches affiliated with the association in 6 Chinese cities, with about 400 members.

Fond of the sea and climate of Okinawa, He Hongxiao has visited the prefecture five times. He comments, "China is a country willing to accept the multiculturalism of various countries. As long as people think it is worth studying, many are willing to try and learn. There are many kinds of martial arts in China but many people are willing to learn other kinds of arts. Many Chinese also like Japanese culture."

In a country where Higaonna Kanryō, the teacher of Miyagi Chōjun, studied martial arts, He Hongxiao is working hard to popularize Okinawa karate in China while deepening cross-cultural exchanges.

2020年05月24日

⑫バーレーン

伝統の技と魂を追求

究道館バーレーン

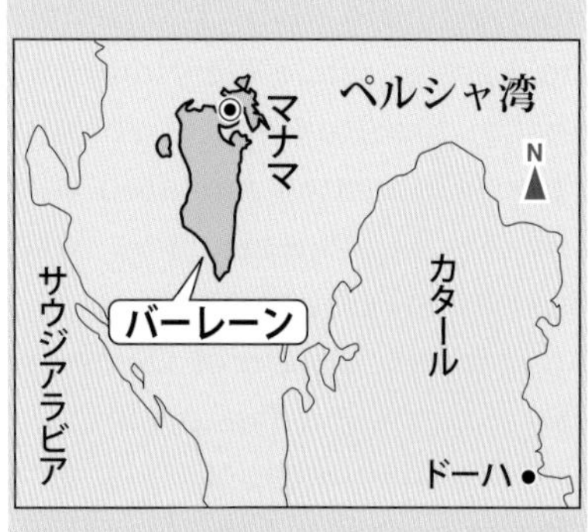

ペルシャ湾に浮かび、沖縄本島より小さい島国、バーレーン。人口150万人余の半数は外国人労働者が占める。こうした状況から空手は定住した外国人によって発展したという。

バーレーンで小林流究道館比嘉手連盟の代表を務めたロベルト・カリヨ氏(29)によると、最初に普及した流派は松濤館と小林流で、松濤館は英国出身の空手家、小林流はフィリピン出身のベルニ・サルモンテ氏によって広まった。

フィリピンで小林流を継承する鷲目会に所属するサルモンテ氏は1980年代にバーレーンに移り、ソラス(牡牛座)空手クラブを開設した。その後、同じくフィリピンから移り住んだヘスス・アブラニダ氏が引き継ぎ、90年代初期に首都マナマで新たな道場を立ち上げた。同道場は国際鷲目会とワールド小林流究道館空手道比嘉手連盟に所属している。↗

比嘉手連盟の代表を務めるのはアルゼンチン生まれでイタリアパレルモ在住のオスカー・まさと・比嘉氏(75)。究道館初代比嘉佑直氏の弟でアルゼンチンにおいて空手を普及した比嘉仁達氏の子息。現在、29カ国で支部を展開している。

サマコ氏(後列左端)、カリヨ氏(同中央)と門下生たち=提供 Samaco (far left in the back row) and Carrillo (center) with their students.

フィリピン・マニラ生まれのカリヨ氏は、中近東各国で多くの土木プロジェクトに従事していた父に連れられ、2002年にバーレーンに定住し、アブラニダ氏の道場に入門した。

18歳の時、師匠が帰国するとカリヨ氏は道場を任された。武道センターを立ち上げ、自身の空手道場を「究道館バーレーン」と改称した。「バーレーンを初訪問した沖縄空手の範士は2013年の島袋善保先生。翌年、オスカー・まさと・比嘉先生を招き、セミナーを開催した」とカリヨ氏は振り返る。

しかし、数年にわずか数回しか師に会えないことから、自身の技術向上が困難と感じたカリヨ氏は、比嘉氏の近くで学ぶためイタリアの大学への入学を目指し、2015年にイタリアに渡った。現在はトスカーナ州ピサを拠点に比嘉氏に師事しながら、欧州委員会の研究機関で働く。究道館バーレーンでは、サミ・サマコ氏(3段)が道場生20人以上を指導している。

「人格形成と道徳付与に導く空手は、暮らす社会をより良い環境にすることに役立つ」とカリヨ氏。バーレーンで30年余、継承されてきた小林流空手。比嘉祐直氏が掲げたモットー「究道無限」の魂は、沖縄から遠く離れた中近東の稽古場でも重んじられている。

Published on 2020/5/24

Kyūdōkan Bahrain

Pursuing traditional techniques and spirit

Bahrain is an island country that floats in the Persian Gulf and is smaller than the main island of Okinawa. Foreign workers make up half of the 1.5 million population. Under these circumstances, karate is said to have been developed in this country by foreigners who settled there.

According to Roberto Carrillo (29), the representative of the Shōrin-ryū Kyūdōkan Higa-te Federation in Bahrain, the first styles to spread were Shōtōkan and Shōrin-ryū. The first was introduced in Bahrain by a British karateka while Shōrin-ryū was brought by Bernie Samonte from the Philippines.

Samonte belongs to Washimekai, a Shōrin-ryū system in the Philippines. He moved to Bahrain in the 1980s and opened the Taurus Karate Club. After that, Jesus Ablanida, who also moved from the Philippines, took over and set up a new dōjō in the capital Manama in the early 90's. This dōjō belongs to the International Washimekai and the World Shōrin-ryū Kyūdōkan Higa-te Federation.

The head of the Higa-te Federation is Oscar Masato Higa (75), who was born in Argentina and lives in Palermo, Italy. He is the son of Higa Jintatsu, the younger brother of Higa Yūchoku, and a man who popularized karate in Argentina. Currently, the federation has branches in 29 countries.

Born in Manila, the Philippines, Carrillo was taken to Bahrain in 2002 by his father who was a civil engineer working on many projects across the Middle East. There he entered Ablanida's dōjō.

At the age of 18, when his teacher returned to the Philippines, Carrillo was assigned as the head of the dōjō. Setting up a martial arts center, he renamed his own karate dōjō Kyūdōkan Bahrain. "2013 was the first time an Okinawa karate master, Shimabukuro Zenpō sensei, visited Bahrain. The following year, we invited Oscar Higa sensei for a seminar," he recalls.

However, because he could meet his master only a few times in a few years, Carrillo found it difficult to improve his karate. He thus moved to Italy to be close to Higa and is currently based in Pisa, Tuscany, studying karate under Higa and working on multiple research and innovation projects for the European Commission. In Bahrain, 3rd dan Sami Samaco runs the Kyūdōkan Bahrain dōjō instructing more than 20 students.

"I believe that karate which leads to the development of one's character and impart values helps make the world we live in a better place," says Carrillo.

Shōrin-ryū karate has been passed down in Bahrain for over 30 years. Far from Okinawa, the soul of Higa Yūchoku's motto "Kyūdō Mugen" is still valued in the far away Middle East.

ユダヤ教、キリスト教、イスラム教の聖地であるエルサレム。1995年、世界最古の都市の一つでもあるエルサレム生まれのファド・ナシフ氏は8歳の時にパレスチナのラマッラー市で松濤館空手道を習い始めた。

その後、さまざまなセミナーに参加した際、フランスで空手と古武道を指導するモンセフ・アブデルワヘド氏に出会った。

フランスで松濤館の普及に努めた故加瀬泰治氏に師事したアブデルワヘド氏(65)は現在松濤館7段、無心国際協会の代表も務める。初めて訪沖した2002年以降、ほぼ毎年沖縄を訪れ、松林流、剛柔流など流派を超えた研究を重ねている。06年からは、沖縄伝統古武道保存会文武館の仲本政博氏に弟子入りが認められ、現在は古武道5段でもある。これまで数回、フランス空手連盟主催の古武道杯で優勝を果たしている。↗

アブデルワヘド氏と出会った後、ナシフ氏はイスラエル政府の制限がかかり、稽古をいったん中断したが、09年にアブデルワヘド氏と再会、15年まで毎年指導を受けられるようになった。翌年、アブデルワヘド氏の組織に加盟。「先生の受け入れは私を幸せにしてくれた。先生は師匠であり、精神的な父でもある」と感謝の思いを示す。

空手を学ぶ道場生と共に。アブデルワヘド氏(前列中央)とナシフ氏(後列左から3人目)=提供　Abdelwahed (center in the front row) and Nassif (third from the left in the back row) with some dōjō members.

2020年11月08日

⑬パレスチナ 

神の聖地 武道を追求

ファド武術アカデミー

裕福な家族の長男に生まれたナシフ氏は、大学卒業後、家族が住む東エルサレムで家業のガソリンスタンドの経営に携わる。同時に、16年に開設した道場で約100人の児童や大人を指導している。

道場では年に一度アブデルワヘド氏を招き、技術指導と昇段審査が行われる。道場開設以降、古武道の指導を受けるナシフ氏は、門弟にも古武術の手ほどきをするという。「アブデルワヘド先生の古武道の演武を見ると、君子の武術である古武術への情熱と献身を感じる」とナシフ氏。「国内に支部はないが、古武道への関心が増しており、新支部の開設の可能性はある」と未来を見据えた。

空手・古武道の細かい指導を受けるため、ナシフ氏はアブデルワヘド氏のヨーロッパ各地のセミナーに同行、18年と19年には沖縄に渡って文武館総本部などで指導を受けた。

東エルサレム最北端の区域で暮らすナシフ氏は現在25歳。空手2段、古武道3級でもある。アブデルワヘド氏の指導と沖縄で得た知識と経験を生かし、門下生と共に生涯武道を追求していく。

Jerusalem, the holy city for Judaism, Christianity and Islam. Born in Jerusalem in 1995, Fuad Nassif began learning Shōtōkan karatedō in Ramallah, Palestine at the age of eight.

After that, as he attended various seminars, he met Moncef Abdelwahed who teaches karate and kobudō in France.

Abdelwahed (65) studied under the late Kase Taiji, who worked to popularize Shōtōkan in France. Currently a 7th dan in Shōtōkan, he heads the Mushin International Association. Since his first visit to Okinawa in 2002, Abdelwahed has visited the birthplace of karate almost every year and has been training in systems such as Matsubayashi-ryū and Gōjū-ryū.

Published on 2020/11/8

13 Palestine

Fuad Academy of Martial Arts

Pursuing martial arts in the sacred land of God

Since 2006, he has been admitted as a student of Nakamoto Masahiro, chairman of the Okinawa Traditional Kobudō Preservation Society Bunbukan. Nowadays a 5th dan in kobudō, he has won several times the Kobudō Cup sponsored by the French Karate Federation.

After meeting Abdelwahed, Nassif was temporarily suspended from training due to restrictions from the Israeli government, but he reunited with his instructor in 2009 and studied with him every year until 2015. The following year, Nassif joined Abdelwahed's organization. "Sensei's acceptance made me a happy practitioner. He is more than my teacher, he is my spiritual father," comments Nassif.

Born as the eldest son of a wealthy family, Nassif graduated from college and is now involved in running the family gas station business in East Jerusalem, where his family lives. At the same time, he teaches about 100 children and adults at the dōjō he opened in 2016.

Once a year, Nassif invites Abdelwahed for technical guidance and promotion examinations. As he also studies kobudō since the opening of his dōjō, he teaches the basics of weaponry to his students. "When I see Abdelwahed sensei performing kobudō, I can feel his passion and total dedication to this noble art," says Nassif, who adds, "There is no branch in the country, but there is a growing interest in kobudō, and thus a possibility of starting a new chapter."

In order to receive detailed instruction on karate and kobudō, Nassif accompanies Abdelwahed on his seminars in various parts of Europe, and in 2018 and 2019 he travelled to Okinawa to train at the Bunbukan honbu dōjō.

Nassif, who lives in the northernmost area of East Jerusalem, is now 25 years old. A 2nd dan in karate and a 3rd kyū in kobudō, he vows to pursue martial arts with his students, making the best of the teachings of Abdelwahed and the knowledge and experience he gained in Okinawa.

2018年08月26日

⑭フィリピン

教え守り 小林流継承

デ・ラ・サール志道館

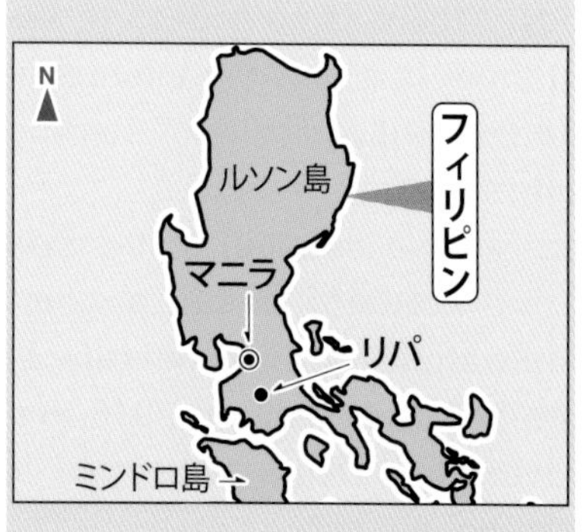

沖縄県内には、約1900人のフィリピン人が在留する。戦後の米軍駐留により多くの外国人労働者が沖縄に流入し、1950年代後半にはフィリピン人の労働者だけで6千人を超えていたという。

60年代、沖縄在住のフィリピン人、フェリックス・マナクサ氏が沖縄小林流空手道協会2代目会長・志道館館長の宮平勝哉氏に師事した。マナクサ氏は、志道館を母国に広めたいと指導者の派遣を求めた。念願がかなって、宮平氏の「左腕」であった伊波清吉氏が63年マニラを訪れ、11カ月間、沖縄小林流を指導した。後に同門の城間盛義氏も指南した。

54年生まれのマリオ・ダカナイ氏は、15歳のとき、セブ市にあった志道館の道場に入門した。館長はマナクサ氏の弟子ロランド・シラオ氏だった。

空手の稽古、指導と共にダカナイ氏は学問にも励み、92年に宗教学博士号、2001年に経営技術学博士号を取得した。その後、ルソン島のリパ市にあるローマンカトリック系私立大学デ・ラ・サールリパ大学に勤務した。現在、同大学学長オフィスのコンサルタントとして、大学所属のトップアスリートやコーチへのラサーリアン精神の普及、チームビルディングなどさまざまな面で人材育成を担っている。

デ・ラ・サール志道館で行ったセミナーで指導したサウジアラビア在住ジュン・カバリエロ氏(前列左から4人目)とダカナイ氏(同3人目)=提供
Jun Caballero (front row, fourth from the left) who lives in Saudi Arabia and Dacanay (front row, third from the left) teaching a seminar at the De La Salle Shidōkan.

95年ダカナイ氏は城間氏より4段の昇段を認められ、97年リパ市で道場を開設した。「空手は人格形成である。ラサーリアンのクリシェ(考え)を借りれば、『教養を与え、人の心に触れ、人生を変える』。いわゆる、親切で慈悲深い人になること」と修道士(ブラザー)でもあるダカナイ氏は説く。

現在、フィリピンの沖縄小林流空手道協会志道館の加盟道場は18ある。代表としてダカナイ氏は、8月1~7日に開催された第1回沖縄空手国際大会に出場し、首里・泊手系シニア男子の部で優勝を果たした。

伝統の型を演武し、高い評価を受けたダカナイ氏は「長い伝統の連続性の精神が各世代に継承されたと感じる。それは生き続けるべくアイデンティティーであり、受け継がれるべきものだ」と強調する。伝統を維持するため、宮平氏の技と心を受け継ぐ高段者に定期的に指導も受けている。

国際大会後ダカナイ氏は、範士10段の城間氏より9段の称号を充許され、フィリピンで最高位の師範となった。「東洋の真珠」ともいわれる国で最も古い伝統空手の「志道館」の教えを守り、小林流を継承し続けている。

Approximately 1,900 Filipinos reside in Okinawa Prefecture. Many foreign workers flowed into Okinawa due to the postwar US military presence, and it is said that in the latter half of the 1950s, the number of Filipino workers alone in Okinawa exceeded 6,000.

In the 1960s, Filipino Felix Manacsa studied karate under Miyahira Katsuya, the head of the Shidōkan, while living in Okinawa. In order to spread this system in his country, Manacsa requested Miyahira to send instructors to the Philippines. The request approved, Miyahira sent his trusted disciple Iha Seikichi to Manilla in 1963 and for eleven months, Iha taught there. Later, Shidōkan's member Shiroma Seigi also instructed in the Philippines.

Published on 2018/8/26

⑭ Philippines 

De La Salle Shidōkan

Preserving the inherited teachings of Shōrin-ryū

Born in 1954, Mario Dacanay entered a Shidōkan dōjō in Cebu City at the age of 15. The head of the dōjō was Rolando Silao, a student of Manacsa.

While practicing and teaching karate, Dacanay earned a Master in religious studies in 1992 and a Master in management technology in 2001. He then worked at the University of De La Salle Lipa in Lipa, Luzon. Currently, as a special assistant to the office of the president of the university, he is in charge of human resource development in various aspects such as spreading the La Sallian spirituality, forming and creating developmental programs for athletes and coaches and team building.

In 1995, Dacanay was promoted to 4th dan by Shiroma Seigi and in 1997, he opened a dōjō in Lipa City. As the kanchō, Lasallian Brother Dacanay explains that, "Karate is character formation of (to borrow the Lasallian cliche): 'Teaching mind, touching hearts and transforming lives' so as to become a kind and benevolent person".

Currently, there are 18 dōjō members of the Okinawa Shōrin-ryū Karatedō Association Shidōkan in the Philippines. As a representative, Dacanay participated in the 1st Okinawa Karate International Tournament held from August 1st to 7th and won the kata championship in the Shurite & Tomarite senior men's division.

Praised for his traditional kata performance, Dacanay commented, "I feel that the spirit of continuity of a long tradition has been passed down to each generation. It is an identity that must stay alive and should be perpetuated." In order to maintain the tradition, he regularly receives instruction by high-ranking instructors who inherited the technique and spirit of Miyahira Katsuya.

After the international tournament, Dacanay was granted the rank of 9th dan by Shiroma, and thus became the highest ranking instructor in his country. Preserving the teachings of the Shidōkan, the oldest traditional karate system in a country known as the "Pearl of the East", he strives on passing on Shōrin-ryū karate.

2018年12月23日

⑮ベトナム ★

貫く信念 普及に情熱

沖縄伝統空手・古武道

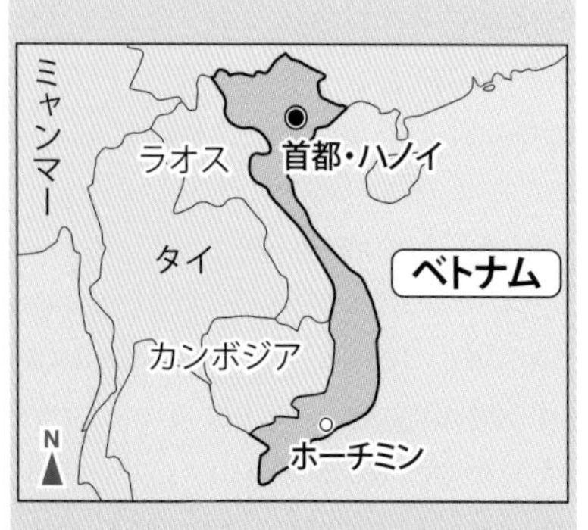

琉球とベトナムの交流は1509年にさかのぼる。安南と呼ばれたこの国に1度、琉球船が派遣されたと記述がある。現在沖縄とベトナムは、産業等の分野で交流を展開している。

ベトナムには、1936年にさまざまな武術を基に考案された「ヴォヴィナム」という独自の武術がある。空手の導入については、故ホ・カム・ナック氏が40年代に日本を訪れ空手を習った。現在では、松濤館系の山田会として継承されている。宮城県出身の故鈴木長治氏も重鎮である。44年、日本海軍の指揮官として中部の都市フエに立ち寄り、戦後、「鈴長空手」の伝播に努めた。

空手が盛んな国でありながら、本場沖縄と繋がりのある道場はまだ少ない。

69年ドイツ・ドレスデン生まれのマイケル・コロッスラー氏は、若いころ右耳の聴覚を失い、病院に通いながら青春時代を過ごした。学校でいじめを受け、強くなろうと柔道に入門し、86年に空手に転向した。

陶磁器技術を学んでいる時代に、松濤館空手を習い始めた。当時、ドイツでは空手の稽古は禁じられていた。「少数の空手道場のほとんどは、秘密警察のシュタージに管理されていた」とコロッスラー氏は振り返る。

88年に稽古が解禁され、東ドイツで初の競技大会が開催された。コロッスラー氏は、形競技で4位に入った。さらに修行に励み、91年にドイツで指導する沖縄少林流聖武館のジャマル・ミヤサラ氏に弟子入りを決めた。

道場で指導するコロッスラー氏(右端)=提供 Kloesser (far right) teaching at his dōjō.

コロッスラー氏は、99年からベトナムで休暇を過ごし、この国に心を奪われた。旅するたびに空手の普及活動という夢を描き、2011年、ミヤサラ氏のエールを受けて、ホーチミン市に移住を実現した。現在、国内4道場で50人余りの門下生を指導する。

定期的にベトナムを訪れる沖縄伝統古武道保存会の尾知博氏にも古武道を師事する。移住のきっかけを問うと、「2回目の訪問の際、帰国した気分でした。その後、国民の親切さと自然の美しさに魅了された」と答える。

「ベトナムは安全な国ですが、都会では高い犯罪率に直面する。護身術を求めて空手を始める人は少なくない。しかし、競技に興味をもって入門する者も多い」。だが、多くの道場では技術のみが伝授され、歴史と文化の側面が失われている状況も指摘する。

現在は、沖縄の伝統空手への関心が高まりつつあり、セミナーの指導依頼が増えているという。コロッスラー氏は、沖縄の武術への信念にこだわりを持つことで、ベトナムでの空手と古武道への考え方や理解に好影響を与えると信じている。

Published on 2018/12/23

Okinawa Dentō Karate Kobudō

An unstoppable faith and a passion for teaching

The exchange between Ryūkyū and Vietnam dates back to 1509 as there is a historical trace that a Ryūkyūan ship was dispatched once to this country called Annan. Nowadays, Okinawa and Vietnam are developing various relations among which the ones in the industrial field.

Vietnam has its own martial art called "Vovinam", which was devised in 1936 based on various martial arts. Regarding karate, the late Ho Cam Ngac visited Japan in the 1940s to learn karate. Today, his karate is inherited by the Yamadakai. The late Suzuki Chōji from Miyagi Prefecture is also a major figure. In 1944, he stopped by the central city of Hue as a commander of the Japanese Navy and worked on spreading his "Suzuchō karate" in the country after the war.

Although karate is popular, there are still few dōjō that teach Okinawa karate.

Born in Dresden, Germany in 1969, Michael Kloesser lost the hearing in his right ear when he was young and spent his youth frequently going to hospitals. Bullied at school, he started jūdō to become stronger and switched to karate in 1986.

While studying to become a porcelain modeler, he started learning Shōtōkan karate. At that time, karate training was prohibited in Germany. "Most of the few existing karate clubs were run and supervised by the secret police called stasi," Kloesser recalls.

The ban on karate lifted in 1988, the first competition was held in East Germany and Kloesser finished fourth in the kata competition. In 1991, he decided to become a student of Jamal Measara, an instructor of the Okinawa Shōrin-ryū Seibukan in Germany.

Kloesser, who enjoyed visiting Vietnam for vacation since 1999, became fascinated by this country. Dreaming of promoting karate in the country, he received the blessing of Measara in 2011 and moved to Ho Chi Minh City. Today, he currently teaches more than 50 students in four dōjō nationwide.

He also studies kobudō with Ochi Hiroshi, a member of the Okinawa Dentō Kobudō Preservation Society, who visits Vietnam on a regular basis.

About Vietnam, he says he is fascinated by the kindness of the people and the beauty of the nature. "Vietnam is quiet safe. But especially in big cities, we face a high crime rate. Many enter karate for self-defense. Many others start as they are interested in competition." However, he also points out that many dōjō only teach the technical aspect while the historical and cultural aspects are lost.

Recently, the interest in traditional Okinawan karate is growing and requests for seminar guidance are increasing. Kloesser believes that sticking to his faith in Okinawan martial arts will have a positive impact on the way karate and kobudō are apprehended and understood in Vietnam.

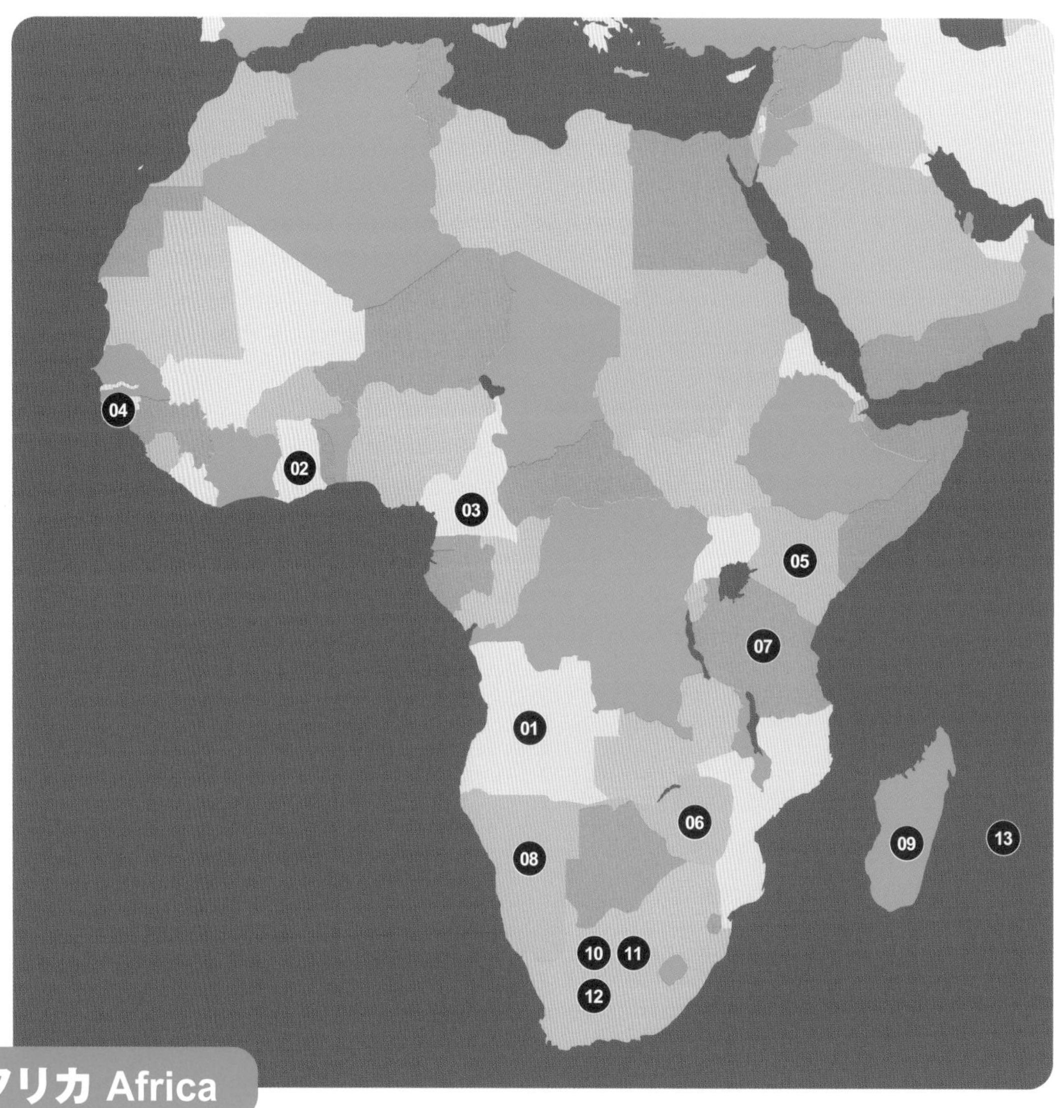

アフリカ Africa

アフリカ
Africa

アフリカ大陸南西にある国、アンゴラ。旧ポルトガル植民地であるこの国は1975年、独立戦争を経て共和国となったが、ポルトガルとの交流はさまざまな面で続き、公用語もポルトガル語となっている。

1960年同国生まれのフィヤリョ・フィロメノ氏は、19歳の時松濤館空手の門をくぐった。建築を学んでいた氏は83年、ポルトガルのポルト市に留学した際に、剛柔流と出合った。

その時指導したのは、剛柔流の故宮里栄一氏や東恩納盛男氏らに指導を受けたアンゴラ出身のジェイミ・ペレイラ氏だった。アンゴラの「空手の父」とも称されるペレイラ氏は、72年に稽古を始め、後に日本で修行し、76年ポルトガルに定住して沖縄剛柔流を普及させた。

84年に帰国したフィロメノ氏は、生まれ都市の首都ルアンダで剛柔流を教え始めた。当時から今日まで道場となっているのは、サッカーチームのクラブハウスであると同時に、さまざまなスポーツが学べる施設。ルアンダで現在、45人が沖縄の空手と古武道を稽古し、同国内では6道場200人ほどが同系統の練習に打ち込んでいる。

空手の道を歩みながらフィロメノ氏は、アンゴ

弟子と共に型を修練するフィロメノ氏=提供 Fialho training together with his students.

2017年12月24日

01 アンゴラ

剛柔流の普及使命に

ペトロ・アトレティコ

ラ国立銀行頭取の顧問を長年勤めた。「2003年のとき同銀行にスカウトされ、少しずつ昇進した。06年から、4人の頭取の下で顧問の仕事をし、16年で退職。全国で多くの従業員の管理で忙しい毎日が続いた中、空手を通して身体と精神を良い状態に保つことができ、冷静に多くの難題への対応ができた」と振り返る。現在は元の専門であった建築業に戻り、大学で建築術も教えている。

アンゴラ空手連盟の会長も8年間務めた。「アンゴラという国は18の州で構成され、それぞれの州には県連がある。すべての道場はその州の県連に加盟する責務がある。松濤館、剛柔流、常心門、糸東流が主な流派で、それぞれが日本本土または沖縄と良い交流を保っている。全国でおよそ5千人が空手を習っている」と解説する。

競技団体に属してもフィロメノ氏は、沖縄剛柔流からは離れない。これまで8回沖縄を訪れた氏は、那覇市安里にある宮里善博氏が館長を務める沖縄剛柔流空手道総本部順道館のポルトガル支部長ヌーノ・カーデイラ氏に相談し、昨年9月、ポーランドで開催された同会のヨーロッパ合宿に参加した。来年来沖を予定するフィロメノ氏は再び、宮里栄一氏が建てた順道館で稽古をすることを楽しみにしている。

Published on 2017/12/24

01 Angola

Petro Atlético

On a mission to popularize Gōjū-ryū

Angola, a country in the southwestern part of the African continent. The former Portuguese colony became a republic after the war of independence in 1975, but exchanges with Portugal continued in various ways and the official language is still Portuguese.

Born in Angola in 1960, Filomeno Fialho entered a Shōtōkan karate dōjō at the age of nineteen. Having studied architecture, it is in 1983 when he went to Porto in Portugal for a professional seminar that he met Gōjū-ryū.

The one who taught him was Angolan Jaime Pereira, who studied under late Miyazato Eiichi and Higaonna Morio of Gōjū-ryū. Known as the "father of Angolan karate", Pereira started karate in 1972, trained in Japan, established himself in Portugal in 1976 and strived on spreading Okinawa Gōjū-ryū.

Returning home in 84, Fialho started teaching Gōjū-ryū in his hometown and capital Luanda. Since then, the dōjō has been in a soccer team clubhouse where people can learn various sports. Currently, 45 people in Luanda and about 200 people in 6 dōjō in the nation are practicing Okinawa karate and kobudō.

While following the path of karate, Fialho has served many years as the consultant to the governor of the National Bank of Angola. "In 2003, I was invited to integrate the National Bank of Angola and was steadily promoted. From 2006, I ended up working as a consultant of 4 different governors. I left the Bank in October 2016. While I was busy managing many employees all over the country, I was able to keep a good physical and psychological condition through karate, which allowed me to calmly handle many issues." Today, he is back to architecture and teaches it at a local university.

For 8 years, Fialho has also served as the president of the Angola Karate Federation. "Angola is made of 18 provinces and each has a karate federation. All dōjō must be registered to the province's federation. Shōtōkan, Gōjū-ryū, Jōshinmon, Shitō-ryū are the major schools and all have good relation with Japanese or Okinawan organizations. There are about five thousand practitioners in the country."

Although his group belongs to a sport federation, Fialho is first an Okinawa Gōjū-ryū karateka who has visited Okinawa 8 times. Through Nuno Cardeira, the representative in Portugal for the Okinawa Gōjū-ryū Karatedō Sōhonbu Jundōkan under Miyazato Yoshihiro, he was allowed to join a Jundōkan seminar held in Poland last September.

Fialho, who is scheduled to visit Okinawa next year, is looking forward to practicing again at the Jundōkan built by Miyazato Eiichi in Asato Naha.

2019年10月27日

02 ガーナ

生涯武道 求めて研究

上地流

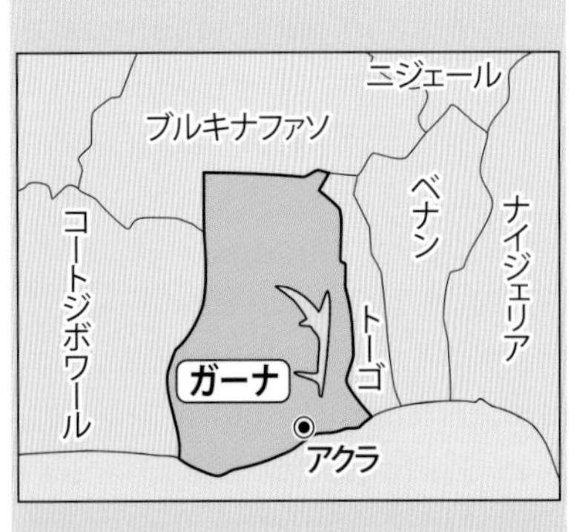

日本でガーナというと、板チョコレートが頭に浮かぶ。カカオの産地、陸上競技サニブラウン・アブデル・ハキーム選手の父親の出身国でもあるガーナで空手が紹介されたのは1980年後半の頃だという。

近隣国との交流によって空手は少しずつ普及したが、国からスポーツとして認められたのは97年。その年、ガーナ空手道連盟が開設され、競技空手主体で若者向けの空手を中心に広まった。

73年首都アクラ生まれのアイサック・アンポンサー氏は、9歳の時、連盟の創始者の一人サムエル・アクパル氏の道場に入門し、松濤館空手を習い始めた。15歳のころから指導にも関わったアンポンサー氏は現在4段で、船越義珍氏に師事した金澤弘和氏の国際松濤館空手道連盟に所属する。

だが、生涯続けられる伝統空手の普及が望まれているという事を知り、アンポンサー氏は、インターネットで伝統空手を調べ、上地流空手の魅力にひかれた。

2016年にアンポンサー氏は、ガーナ空手道協会と改名された連盟のナショナルチームの4人と共に来日し、松濤館、和道流、上地流の空手を体験。上地流の研さんは、アンポンサー氏が自ら連絡を取った関東で活躍する沖縄上地流唐手道協会(沖唐会)東京本部で実現した。

弟子と共に型を稽古するアンポンサー氏(前列左)　Amponsah (front row left) practicing kata with his students.

当時受け入れに携わった角田仁司氏は「来日の目的は、将来ガーナに上地流空手を普及させることでした。今後は、沖縄にある協会総本部と連携し、ガーナ空手協会への必要な支援と助言を行っていく」と展望を示す。

研究を深めるためアンポンサー氏は、再び17年10月に来日し、東京本部で2週間の研修を受けて帰国した。

現在、アンポンサー氏の道場「中山松濤館空手道」では、52人の会員が松濤館の空手に取り組みながら、上地完文氏を流祖とする上地流空手の技法を学ぶ。

指導と同時に、建設大工職人で生計を立てるアンポンサー氏は、ガーナ空手道協会の役職者であり、審判長、コーチ、技術委員も務める。全国にある50余りの道場、1000人の空手家に技術指導を行いながら技術向上に努めている。

ガーナでは沖縄伝統空手として上地流の普及を求める声が多く上がっていることから、アンポンサー氏はDVDやメールでのやりとりを通して、沖唐会と交流をさらに深めている。上地流の神髄を正確に理解するため、一歩一歩研究を進めていく。

In the country of origin of the father of Japanese athlete Abdul Hakim Sani Brown, it is said that karate was introduced in the latter half of the 1980's.

Karate gradually became popular due to exchanges with neighboring countries, and it's in 1997 that karate was recognized as a sport by the government. That year, the Ghana Karatedō Federation was established, and mainly youth-oriented competitive karate spread.

Born in Accra in 1973, Isaac Amponsah began learning Shōtōkan karate at the age of nine when he entered the dōjō of Samuel Kudjo Akpalu, one of the founders of the federation. Amponsah, who has been involved with teaching since the age

Published on 2019/10/27

Uechi-ryū

Researching and practicing a lifelong martial art

of 15, is currently a 4th dan who belongs to the International Shōtōkan Karatedō Federation founded by Kanazawa Hirokazu, a direct student of Funakoshi Gichin.

However, realizing that the diffusion of a traditional karate that could be practiced for a lifetime was requested by many in his country, Amponsah searched for traditional karate on the Internet and was attracted by the charms of Uechi-ryū karate.

In 2016, Amponsah visited Japan with four members of the national Ghanaian team and trained Shōtōkan, Wadō-ryū, and Uechi-ryū karate. The training in Uechi-ryū occurred at the Tōkyō Headquarters of the Okinawa Uechi-ryū Karatedō Association, a group that Amponsah contacted directly.

Sumida Hitoshi, who was involved in welcoming the African karateka remembers that "The purpose of their visit to Japan was to popularize Uechi-ryū karate in Ghana. In the future, we will cooperate with the headquarters of the association in Okinawa to provide them with necessary support and advices."

In order to deepen his research, Amponsah returned to Japan in October 2017 for two weeks of training at the Tōkyō Headquarters.

Currently, at his Nakayama Shōtōkan Karatedō dōjō, 52 members are practicing the mainland Japanese karate system while studying the technique of Uechi-ryū karate founded by Uechi Kanbun.

While instructing karate and making a living as a construction carpenter, Amponsah is also an official of the national Ghana Karate Federation, serving as chief referee, coach and technical committee member. He works on improving the national skills by teaching some 1,000 karateka in more than 50 dōjō.

As there are many requests for Uechi-ryū as a traditional karate in Ghana, Amponsah is deepening exchanges with the Tōkyō based group through video and email exchanges. Eager to accurately understand the essence of the Okinawan style, Amponsah proceeds step by step in his research of Okinawa karate.

2018年01月28日

03 カメルーン

平和の武 普及に情熱

沖縄小林流

中部アフリカに位置するカメルーンは日本の1.25倍の面積がある。フランス語と英語を公用語とするこの国は、日本のJリーグでプレーしたサッカーのパトリック・エムボマ選手や「不屈のライオン」の異名を持つ代表チームの活躍でも、よく知られている。

空手は1950年代のころ、柔道と共にフランス軍人によって紹介されたという。その後、地元の空手家の努力により、世界空手連盟の国順位でエジプトに次ぐアフリカ2番目の国となった。競技空手が盛んで、沖縄空手はあまり見られないが、剛柔流、小林流や古武道は普及している。

1977年カメルーンの商業都市、ドゥアラ市生まれのジュール・ウンゴリ氏は、12歳の時、父から松濤館空手や柔道を学んだ。3段になった2008年、沖縄小林流系を指導する同国人のゴドフロワ・クム氏と出会い、沖縄の空手と古武道の手ほどきを受けた。

スペインに留学し、情報技術修士号を取得したウンゴリ氏は、仕事を求め10年にイギリス北部のリーズ市に移住した。

武術への情熱がITより勝ったウンゴリ氏は同年に空手のプロとなった。道場や公民館などで小林流を指導しながら、健康・栄養などのカウンセリング活動も行っている。現在、知念賢祐氏が指揮するワールド王修会伝統沖縄小林流空手道古武道連盟の英国支部長を務め、70人に指南している。

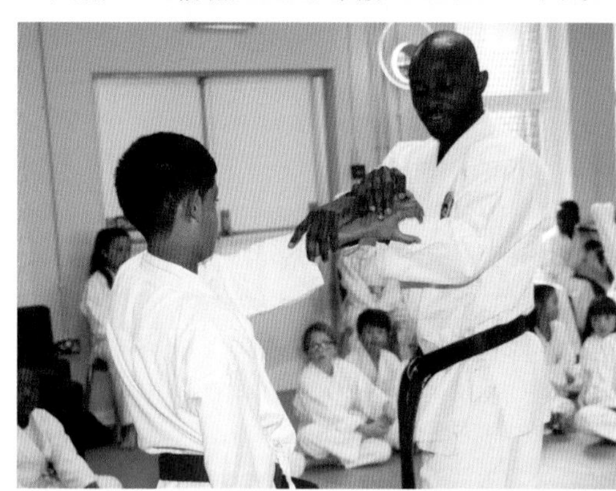
子どもたちに指導するウンゴリ氏(右)=提供
Ngoli (right) instructing children.

英国に住んでいても、心は生まれ故郷のカメルーンから離れることはない。毎年1~2回帰郷し、道場を巡って沖縄空手の指導に努めている。

17年12月15日ドゥアラ市で行われた武道祭にも積極的に関った。人種、宗教、政治の違いを超えて活動する「カメルーン武道の友人協会」が主催した、この演武会では世界18の武術が紹介された。催しの目標「人類のための格闘技・カメルーンの永続的な平和」は、「平和の武」である沖縄空手の目的と同様といえるだろう。

16年に初めて沖縄を訪れ、首里手中興の祖・松村宗棍(昆)の墓を参拝した。沖縄の人々の修養する姿に感激し、沖縄空手に対する熱情が改めて確認できたという。

「毎日の稽古を通して空手は、精神と身体の面で素晴らしい幸福をもたらしてくれる」と語るウンゴリ氏。故郷でも沖縄空手を広めたいと情熱を燃やすカメルーンの空手家は、沖縄空手の精神を胸に修練の道を進む。

Published on 2018/1/28

Okinawa Shōrin-ryū

A passion to spread a martial art of peace

Located in Central Africa, Cameroon is 1.25 times larger than Japan. With French and English as official languages, the country is also well known for Patrick Mboma, a soccer player who played in the Japanese J-League, and the national Cameroun team nicknamed “The Indomitable Lions.”

Karate is said to have been introduced in this country by French soldiers along with jūdō in the 1950s. Later, thanks to the efforts of local karateka, Cameroon became the second country in Africa after Egypt in the national ranking of the World Karate Federation. In this country, sport karate is popular and Okinawa karate is rare but yet, Gōjū-ryū, Shōrin-ryū and kobudō are present.

Born in 1977 in Douala, Jules Ngoli learned Shōtōkan karate and jūdō from his father from the age of twelve. After achieving 3rd dan in 2008, he met fellowman Godefroy Koum who was teaching Okinawan Shōrin-ryū and started learning Okinawa karate and kobudō.

After studying in Spain and obtaining a master’s degree in information technology, Ngoli moved to Leeds in northern England in 2010 in search of a job.

His passion for martial arts outweighing IT, he became a karate professional the same year. Today, while teaching Shōrin-ryū in dōjō and community centers, he also works as a consultant on health and nutrition. Currently, he is the head of the British branch of the World Ōshukai Traditional Okinawa Shōrin-ryū Karatedō Kobudō Federation under the direction of Chinen Kenyū and teaches some 70 people.

Even if living in the UK, Ngoli’s heart will never leave Cameroon. Once or twice every year, he returns home and strives to teach Okinawa karate in local dōjō.

In this spirit, he actively took part in the martial arts festival held in Douala on December 15, 2017. Organized by the Association of Friends of Martial Arts, a group that acts regardless of races, religions, and politics, the event showcased eighteen martial arts from around the world. In Ngoli’s mind, the goal of the event “Martial arts for humankind and the lasting peace in Cameroon” is similar to the purpose of Okinawa karate which is a “Martial art or Peace”.

In 2016, Ngoli travelled to Okinawa for the first time and visited the tomb of Matsumura Sōkon, the forefather of Shurite. Impressed by the Okinawans’ attitude towards mind’s cultivation, he says that he was able to reaffirm his passion for Okinawa karate.

He comments that, “Through daily practice, karate brings a great mental, spiritual and physical well-being.” A Cameroonian karateka passionate about spreading Okinawa karate in his homeland, Ngoli follows the path of training with the spirit of Okinawa karate in his heart.

2020年04月26日

04 ギニアビサウ

過酷な地 不屈の指導

小林流王修会

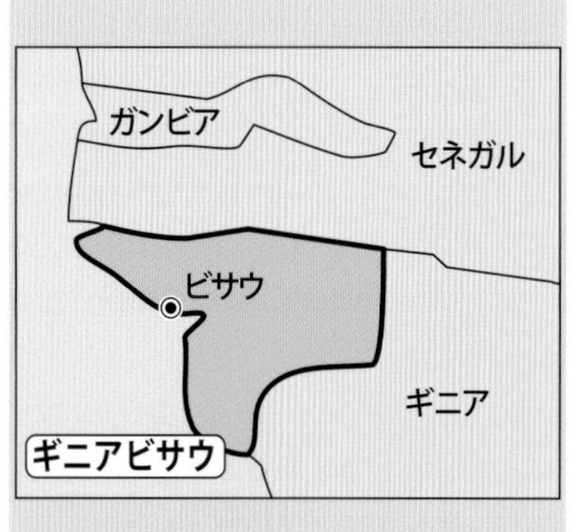

西アフリカに位置しポルトガル語圏の共和制国家ギニアビサウ(人口約180万人)は三重県の人口に相等し、九州とほぼ同じ面積を持つ。1973年の独立宣言後、旧フランス領であったギニアとの混同を防ぐため、首都ビサウの名が国名に追加された。

アフリカ大陸は54の主権国家で構成される。世界空手連盟にはその内50カ国の空手連盟が登録されているが、今のところギニアビサウの登録はない。

空手道場の存在さえ見えないこの国では、一人のフランス人が地道に沖縄空手を指導している。

67年パリ生まれのニコラ・ベルナロヤ氏は、8歳のころパリ17区にあった道場で空手を始めた。数年後、指導者が去ったところ、75年からフランスで小林流と古武道の普及に挑んでいた知念賢祐氏が指導するようになった。その流れからベルナロヤ氏は、81年から知念氏の直弟子になった。「当時、道場では10人しか稽古していなかった」とベルナロヤ氏は振り返る。

空手と同時にベルナロヤ氏は、ボクシングも鍛錬していた。知念氏の下で古武道の手ほどきを受けたが、稽古する時間がなく、武器術をあきらめ徒手空拳の道に専心した。空手とボクシングを磨き、ベルナロヤ氏は体育教師になった。

自宅で稽古に励むベルナロヤ氏（提供） Bernaroyat training at home.

しかし、新たな人生を歩みたいという希望を抱き、93年にアフリカ移住を決め、ギニアビサウへ旅立った。当地を選んだ理由について「特になかった。人生の偶然だ。でも当時も今日も、この国はすべてが可能な中間地帯だ」と答える。

移住直後から98年まで道場を開いたが、内戦が勃発し、道場閉鎖の事態に見舞われた。ギニアビサウはアフリカで最も貧しい国の一つでヨーロッパへの麻薬の中継地点であるとも言われる。「危険で暴力的なこの国でどう生きるかは非常に難しい」とベルナロヤ氏。

それでも、知念氏から4段の昇段を認められ、鍛錬を続けた。現在は家族と暮らし、銀行の警備と一般サービスの管理責任者として生計を立てている。勤務時間外に娘と息子や地域の子供に空手を指導し普及に努め、大人にはボクシングも教えている。「新たな夢は大きな道場の開設。少しずつ準備を進めているが、その日暮らしで生活しているため、その先は不透明だ」と胸の内を明かした。

肉体的および精神的に自信と自己制御を養う力を授けてくれる空手。ベルナロヤ氏は過酷な環境下、不屈の心で挑戦し続け、日々稽古で汗を流している。

Published on 2020/4/26

04 Guinea-Bissau

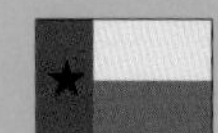

Shōrin-ryū Ōshūkai

Indomitable spirit of teaching in harsh ground

Located in West Africa, the Portuguese-speaking republic Guinea-Bissau declared its independence in 1973 and in order to prevent confusion with the former French territory Guinea, the name of the capital Bissau was added to the country's name.

Among the 54 sovereign states of the African Continent, fifty are registered with the World Karate Federation, but it is not the case of Guinea-Bissau.

In this country where karate is scarce, a Frenchman is steadily teaching the Okinawan art.

Born in Paris in 1967, Nicolas Bernaroyat started karate in a club located in the 17th arrondissement of Paris at the age of eight. A few years later, as the instructor left, Chinen Kenyū, who was trying to popularize Shōrin-ryū and kobudō in France since 1975, began to teach at the club. Bernaroyat became a direct student of Chinen in 1981 and recalls that "At that time, we were very few practicing at the dōjō, maybe 10 people."

Meanwhile, Bernaroyat also practiced boxing. Although he was taught kobudō by Chinen, he had not enough time to practice karate and weapons. He thus gave up kobudō and devoted himself to the path of empty hands. Polishing his karate and boxing skills, he became a physical education teacher.

Having the desire to live a new life, Bernaroyat decided to move to Africa in 1993 and set out for Guinea-Bissau. On the reason why he chose this destination, he replies "There is no particular reason, the chance of life, but especially at the time and still today, it is really a no man's land where everything is possible..."

Right after moving to the African nation and until 1998, he operated a dōjō but as civil war broke out, he had to close it.

Guinea-Bissau is one of the poorest countries in Africa and is also said to be a drug stopover to Europe. "It is very difficult to live in this dangerous and violent country," says Bernaroyat.

Even so, the Frenchman who was granted a 4th dan by Chinen continued to train. He now lives with his family and work as a person in charge for security and general services in a bank. During his off-hours, he teaches karate to his daughter and son and local children, and also teaches boxing to adults. "My new dream is to open a large dōjō. I'm preparing little by little, but as I'm living one day at a time, nothing is sure," he comments.

Karate gives one the power to develop self-confidence and self-control both physically and mentally. In the harsh environment he lives in, Bernaroyat continues to challenge life with an indomitable spirit and keeps practicing on a daily basis.

シルベスター・オニアンゴ・オダーアー氏は、ケニア南西部のシアヤ州で1984年に生まれた。16歳の時、兄弟が行う姿をまねてテコンドーを習ったが、2004年に松濤館の道場に入門し、日本の空手を学び始めた。

マサイなど多様な民族が集う、この国においての空手史は1970年前後にさかのぼるという。国際協力機構の隊員、田村良雄氏が同国で剛柔流空手道を紹介。今もこの国に住み続け、指導している。

オダーアー氏は8カ月間、松濤館の空手を稽古したが「稽古がきつくて昇段もなく、道場通いをやめた」。2010年まで個人で稽古を重ね、アフリカン拳法という雑種空手も2年間練習した。紫帯になり稽古に励んだが、学生だった師が離れ、オダーアー氏は再び、師無き身となった。

その後、仕事を求めケニアの首都ナイロビに移り、スポーツジムで指導員を務めた。後に同ジムで空手を指導するようになった。

転機が訪れたのは14年。ソーシャルメディアでさまざまな人たちと交流を深め、知り合ったマレーシア人のジョン・チェン氏に「世界一の空手家になりたい」と打ち明けた。その希望が、

型を繰り返し練習するオダーアー氏（手前）=提供
Oduor (front) practicing kata.

2019年12月22日

05 ケニア

研究に情熱 精進誓う

少林流

チェン氏より沖縄少林流聖武館に紹介されることになった。

15年8月に聖武館ドイツのジャマル・ミヤサラ氏が初めてケニアを訪問した。その際にオダーアー氏は、喜屋武朝徳氏の空手を継承する同系統の空手の手ほどきを受けるようになった。

ミヤサラ氏は、オダーアー氏の研究熱心さを認め、茶帯に昇段させた。それを受けたオダーアー氏は、聖武館の空手に専心することを決意した。「この沖縄空手は、これまで習った空手と違って新鮮で楽しく、気持ちよく習える空手と感じた」と振り返る。

現在ナイロビで暮らし、14年に開設した道場「ブラヴォ・フィットネス・センター」で15人に指導、このほか3道場にも弟子がいるという。

沖縄空手では無段者のオダーアー氏はボディーガードとフィットネスインストラクターとして生計を立てている。「いい人になることが空手の目的だと思う。健康を維持し、感情のコントロールに役立つ」と空手に取り組む意義を示した。

訪沖の経験はないが、「聖地」への思いを胸にミヤサラ氏の下で、動画などを活用して稽古と指導に励む日々を送る。「この世界では何も簡単に手に入らない。手に入れるには努力するしかない」。沖縄空手に魅せられたオダーアー氏はさらなる精進を誓った。

Published on 2019/12/22

05 Kenya

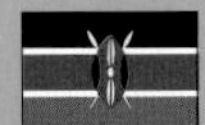

Shōrin-ryū

Passionate and devoted to research

Sylvester Onyango Oduor was born in 1984 in the Siaya County in southwestern Kenya. At the age of 16, he learned taekwondo by imitating his brother's moves, and entered a Shōtōkan dōjō in 2004.

It is said that the history of karate in this country dates back to the early 1970s when Tamura Yoshio, a member of the Japan International Cooperation Agency, introduced Gōjū-ryū in the country. Tamura still lives and teaches in Kenya.

Oduor studied for 8 months in the Shōtōkan dōjō but "because the training was so hard and there was no grading I stopped training there." After training on his own until 2010, he then studied African kenpō karate for 2 years, receiving a purple belt. Although serious about training, his teacher who was still a student left and Oduor became teacherless again.

Later on, Oduor moved to Nairobi, the capital of Kenya, in search of work and served as an instructor at a sports gym and along the way began teaching karate at the gym.

The turning point in his karate life came in 2014. As he interacted with various people on social media, he requested to a Malaysian friend by the name of John Cheng to help him reach his goal of becoming the best karateka in the world. Chen introduced him to his instructor Jamal Measara of the Okinawa Shōrin-ryū Seibukan.

In August 2015, Measara, the head of Seibukan Germany, visited Kenya for the first time. From this moment, Oduor began to receive instruction in the karate system of Kyan Chōtoku.

Measara acknowledged Oduor's zeal for research and promoted him to brown belt. In response, Oduor decided to devote himself to the karate of the Seibukan. He recalls, "I felt that, unlike the karate systems I had learned so far, this Okinawan karate was fresh, fun, and easy to learn."

Currently living in Nairobi, he teaches 15 people at the dōjō Bravo Fitness Center opened in 2014 while teaching in 3 other clubs.

Still not a black belt holder yet, Oduor makes a living as a bodyguard and a fitness instructor. On the significance of practicing karate, he says, "The purpose of karate is to become a good person. It also helps people control their emotions and become healthier persons."

Although he has not visited Okinawa yet, Oduor spends his days practicing and learning under Measara and keeps images of the birthplace of karate in his thoughts.

"Nothing good comes easy in this world; you have to struggle for it." Fascinated by Okinawa karate, the Kenyan karateka vows to devote himself to the art of the empty hand.

2020年09月13日

06 ジンバブエ

人格形成へ鍛錬積む

小林流小林館

ムテテレロ・モヨ氏(45)とテレンス・ブラウン氏(53)は、ブルガリアから移住したボジダー・イヴァノフ氏(49)と共に2002年から沖縄空手を学んでいる。現在は3人で「アセニウム小林流小林舘空手道場」を運営している。

モヨ氏は幼いころから空手に興味を持っていたが、空手を危険なスポーツとしていた両親の反対に遭い、1994年の大学入学の際にしか始められなかったという。5年間剛柔流を学び、大学卒業後、就職のため移った首都のハラレで極真系の道場に入門。2002年、沖縄空手を指導する日本人の道場広告を見て、千葉晴信氏(71)の道場の門をくぐった。

宮城県出身の千葉氏は大学で空手を始めた後、沖縄で小林流小林舘の仲里周五郎氏に師事。1978年以降青年海外協力隊員としてアフリカに渡りさまざまな国々で活動し、空手も指南した。80年にジンバブエに定住し、現在に至る。

イヴァノフ氏もモヨ氏と同時期に入門。道場移籍の理由について「他の流派になかった自然な動き、呼吸法、分解などが魅力的」と両氏。当時ブラウン氏はすでに千葉氏の弟子だった。

現在、人口160万人のハラレには千葉氏の道場のほか二つの小林舘の道場がある。その一つが、モヨ氏らが2019年4月に開設した「アセニウム小林流小林舘空手道場」。最初の頃は彼ら3人だけで練習をしていたが、現在では大人15人、子ども25人が共に汗を流している。

モヨ氏(3列目右)と笑顔を見せるブラウン氏(同左)、道場生たち(提供)
Moyo (3rd row right) and Brown (3rd row left) and some of their students.

1979年までローデシアと称されたジンバブエでの空手史は60年代までさかのぼるという。本土系の流派が人気だが、同小林舘と剛柔流の道場も存在し、普及に励んでいる。

「今では空手は、学校の正課として取り入れられるように検討されている。私たちはカリキュラム作成に協力し、そのカリキュラムがジンバブエ空手連盟から政府に提出された。近々、学校での小林流空手の導入が期待される。うれしい」とモヨ氏の心も弾む。

銀行の監査役のモヨ氏、国際タバコ会社輸出管理者のブラウン氏、歯科医のイヴァノフ氏は、3人とも小林舘の4段。「勝敗より、人格形成を目的とする空手」を座右の銘とする3人は、武道をセラピーとしてがん患者の子どもの痛みの緩和に取り組む組織や、少女、女性の力となって地域社会の強化を目標とするNGOにも参加している。

モヨ氏らは社会貢献も行い、沖縄空手の素晴らしさを伝え続けている。

Published on 2020/9/13

06 Zimbabwe

Shōrin-ryū Shōrinkan

Training for character building

Ntethelelo Moyo (45) and Terence Brown (53) have been studying Okinawa karate since 2002 together with Bozhidar Ivanov (49), a former Gōjū-ryū karateka who emigrated from Bulgaria. Currently, the three of them run the Atheneum Shōrin-ryū Shōrinkan Karatedō dōjō.

As a child, Moyo was interested in karate but he could only start practicing when he entered university in 1994 due to the opposition of his parents who regarded karate as a dangerous sport. For five years he studied Gōjū-ryū and after graduating from university, he entered a Kyokushin dōjō in Harare, the capital city where he moved to get a job. In 2002, after seeing an advert for Okinawa karate in a local newspaper, he entered the dōjō of Chiba Harunobu (71).

From Miyagi Prefecture, Chiba started karate at university and then studied under Nakazato Shūgorō, the founder of the Shōrin-ryū Shōrinkan. From 1978 on, Chiba travelled to various African countries as a Japan overseas cooperation volunteer and taught karate during his missions. He settled in Zimbabwe in 1980 and still lives there to this day.

Regarding why Moyo and Ivanov switched style, they say, “We enjoyed the focus on perfection of kata, natural movements, breathing and application techniques which were not found in other styles.” At that time, Brown was already a student of Chiba.

Today in Harare, there are two Shōrinkan dōjō in addition to Chiba’s dōjō. One of them is the Atheneum dōjō opened by the three men in April 2019. At the beginning, only the three of them practiced but now, 15 adults and 25 children are sweating together at the dōjō.

It is said that the history of karate in Zimbabwe dates back to the 1960s. While Mainland Japanese systems are popular, Shōrin-ryū and Gōjū-ryū dōjō also exist and are working hard to popularize Okinawa karate.

“It is worth noting that karate is now being considered to be part of the syllabus for learning in schools. To that end, our club participated in the development of the karate curriculum which was submitted by the Zimbabwe Karate Union to the government for their consideration. We are happy that the Shōrin-ryū’s syllabus was accepted and may soon be taught in schools,” says Moyo.

Moyo is an auditor in a bank while Terence is a shipping and export administration manager for an international tobacco company. Ivanov is a dental surgeon. They are all Shōrinkan 4th dan.

“More than victory or defeat, the ultimate aim of karate lies in the perfection of the character.” With this motto at heart, the three men work with various organizations that aim at strengthening the local community. They thus contribute to a better society conveying the splendor of Okinawa karate.

2018年04月22日

07 タンザニア

伝統の技 向上に意欲

ザナキ道場

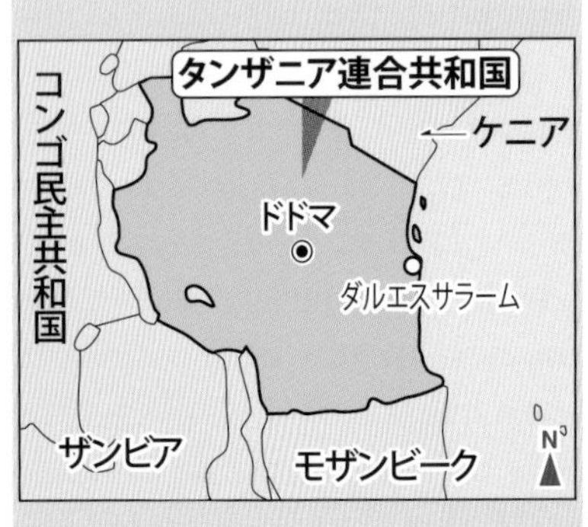

「人類発祥の地」「キリマンジャロの国」として知られているタンザニア。この国での空手の始まりは1970年にさかのぼるという。

米国籍タンザニア出身の同国の空手パイオニア故ナンタンブ=カマラ・ボマーニ氏は、68年に米兵として沖縄を訪れ、6カ月間、剛柔流の順道館館長宮里栄一氏に師事した。73年にボマーニ氏は、当時首都のダルエスサラーム市で「ザナキ道場」を開設し空手を普及させた。

65年同市生まれのフンディ・ルマダ氏は、78年にボマーニ氏のザナキ道場に入門した。空手とともに、インド式ヨガの修行も始めた。

3年後、インドのコルカタに招待されヨガをさらに学び、85年から2年間スウェーデンでもヨガの研究を深めた。88年には、米国テキサス州ヒューストンにヨガインストラクターとして派遣され、後にダラスに移住を決めた。ヨガを指導しながら米国で活躍した剛柔流の東恩納盛男氏や村松真孝氏らの指導を受け、空手の稽古を続けた。2015年からルマダ氏は、沖縄剛柔流空手道総本部順道館に所属する。

「人間にとって空気はすべて。空手を通して出会ったヨガで吸入と呼気は生命的で重要な機能」と気づいたルマダ氏は、ヘルスケアに興味を持つこととなった。医療業界での可能性を探る中、呼吸療法医に進んだ。現在、ダラス市にあるベイラー大学メディカルセンターの集中治療室で心肺呼吸ケアセラピストとして仕事をしている。

型サンセールーの稽古を見守るルマダ氏(中央)=提供　Ramudha (center) watching over the practice of the kata Sansērū.

「ストレスの多いこの職場で、冷静な行動を教わる空手は大いに助けとなっているが、それだけではない。毎日の空手の訓練で人生の生き方が導かれる。空手の道の途中で出会う人々も大きな恵み」とルマダ氏は明るい笑顔で語る。

毎年2回ほど母国を訪れるルマダ氏は、故郷での剛柔流空手の普及にも挑み続け、「ザナキ道場」と併せて3道場で定期的に指南している。

「タンザニアでは、空手は人気のスポーツ。日本出身の国際協力機構派遣員から空手を学ぶ機会もあるが多くの指導者は若くて質はまだ低い。歴史あるザナキ道場だけで5千人以上が開祖宮城長順氏の空手を体験した。ボマーニ先生の功績を守り、将来、本物の道場を築き、剛柔流の技術を高めたい」

ルマダ氏は現在4段。宮城氏の師匠で那覇手中興の祖東恩納寛量氏の遺訓「空手を修業する者は社会の為(ため)になれ」を心に刻み、世界を舞台に活動を続ける。

In Tanzania, known as "the cradle of humankind" and "the country of the Kilimanjaro," it is said that the beginning of karate dates back to 1970.

Karate pioneer in Tanzania, the late Nantambu Camara Bomani was a US citizen born in Tanzania. In 1968, he visited Okinawa as a US soldier and studied under Miyazato Eiichi, head of the Gōjū-ryū Jundōkan, for six months. In 1973, Mr. Bomani opened the Zanaki Dōjō in Dar-es-Salaam, the then capital of Tanzania, and popularized karate.

Born in the same city in 1965, Fundi Rumadha entered the Zanaki Dōjō in 1978. Along with karate, he also began practicing Indian yoga.

Published on 2018/4/22

Zanaki Dōjō

The will to improve traditional technique

Three years later, he was invited to Calcutta in India to further study yoga, and from 1985 he deepened his studies of yoga in Sweden for two years. In 1988, he was sent to Houston Texas as a yoga instructor and later decided to move to Dallas. While teaching yoga there, he continued to practice Gōjū-ryū karate under the guidance of Higaonna Morio and Muramatsu Masataka.

Since 2015, Rumadha is a member of the Okinawa Gōjū-ryū Karatedō Sōhonbu Jundōkan.

"Air is everything to all living beings. Inhalation and exhalation are vital and important functions in yoga." Having realized this, Rumadha was attracted to health care and started exploring the possibilities in the medical field, ending up becoming a respiratory therapist. Today, he works as a cardiopulmonary respiratory care therapist in the intensive care unit of the Baylor University Medical Center in Dallas.

"In such a stressful work environment, karate, which teaches calm behavior, is really helpful. But that's not all. Daily karate practice guides my entire way of life. The people I have met through karate are also a great blessing," says he.

As he visits Tanzania about twice a year, Rumadha takes upon himself to spread Gōjū-ryū karate in his homeland, regularly teaching at three dōjō among which the Zanaki Dōjō.

"Karate's popularity in Tanzania is high. There are some opportunities to learn karate from Japanese instructors who come as Japan International Cooperation Agency (JICA) specialists but most of local instructors are young and their teaching skills are still low. The Zanaki Dōjō, the mother of all dōjō in Tanzania, trained over 5,000 students in Miyagi Chōjūn's karate since its inception. Protecting the achievements of Bomani sensei, I want to build a real dōjō in the future, and improve Gōjū-ryū's technical level."

Rumadha holds currently a 4th dan. Keeping in mind the teaching of Higaonna Kanryō "Those who practice karate should serve the society", he continues his activities on the world stage.

1990年にナミビアは南アフリカから独立を果たした。ナミブ砂漠で知られるこの国での空手史は1970年代にさかのぼり、ナミビア空手連合が創立されたのは96年。現在は8団体で約900人が空手を学んでいるとカール・ヴァンデルメルヴァ氏は説明する。

ヴァンデルメルヴァ氏は61年南アフリカ生まれ、82年にナミビアに移った。2年後友人を通して商・工業の中心地ウィントフック市にある沖縄剛柔流の道場に入門した。

指導していたのはケープタウン出身のヘニ・デヴリス氏だった。デヴリス氏は78年にナミビアで剛柔流を普及するために招かれ、翌年に道場を開設。その後20年間にわたり指南した。

ヴァンデルメルヴァ氏は「少年時代は陸上競技とラグビーに熱中していたが、20代前半は昼間に仕事し、夜や週末に大学で勉強していたため、スポーツをする時間がなかった。その時空手に転向した。最初は週2回の稽古だったが、だんだん稽古量が増えて、クラスの指導も任されるようになった」と振り返る。

競技空手にも挑戦し、95年ジンバブエで開催された第6回全アフリカ選手権大会でナミビア国ナショナルチームのキャプテンも務めた。その2年後競技空手から引退、本格的に指導へとシフトした。

多くの門下生を指導しているヴァンデルメルヴァ氏（前列左から6人目）＝提供　Van Der Merwe (6th from the left in the front row) with some of the many students he teaches.

2020年01月12日

08 ナミビア

集中力養い武道追求

沖縄剛柔流空手本部道場

99年ヴァンデルメルヴァ氏は、デヴリス氏から首都ウィントフックの沖縄剛柔流空手ナミビア本部道場を譲り受け、国際沖縄剛柔流空手道連盟ナミビア支部長に任命された。

2016年に東恩納盛男氏から7段への昇段を認められた。現在、ナミビア本部道場において、ヴァンデルメルヴァ氏は5人の指導者と共に週5回の稽古を指揮している。そこでは5~60歳まで180~200人が沖縄の空手を学んでいる。そのほかの支部道場でも約50人が同統を学ぶ。

空手の一方、仕事として世界4大会計事務所・総合コンサルティングファームの一つで、公認会計士と監査役を務めている。

パレートの法則（80:20の法則）を信じるヴァンデルメルヴァ氏は「人生のほぼすべてにおいて結果の80%は20%の努力に由来する。稽古中に相手を傷つけたり、けがをすることもある。空手は集中力を向上させる優位なワークアウトだと思う。しかし、誰でも人体を駆使して動くので、すべての武道は本質的に同じ」と論理を説く。

今夏7月には本部道場創立40周年記念合宿が開催される。節目の合宿はナミビアの空手史に足跡を刻む画期的な出来事となるだろう。

Published on 2020/1/12

Okinawa Gōjū-ryū Karate Honbu Dōjō

The pursuit of martial arts that cultivate concentration

In Namibia, a country that gained its independence from South Africa in 1990, the history of karate dates back to the 1970s. Founded in 1996, the Namibian Karate Union has presently eight member organizations. Carl Van Der Merwe estimates that there are currently about 900 people studying karate in Namibia.

Born in South Africa in 1961, Van Der Merwe moved to Namibia in 1982. Two years later, through a friend, he entered an Okinawa Gōjū-ryū dōjō in Windhoek, the future capital. It was Hennie De Vries from Cape Town who was instructing. De Vries was invited to spread Gōjū-ryū in Namibia in 1978 and opened a dōjō the following year to teach in the country for 20 years.

"I started karate as I did not have time to do sports like athletics or rugby anymore. I was working during the day and studying at university at night and during the weekends. In the beginning, I trained twice a week but then the training amount gradually increased and later I started teaching karate," Van Der Merwe recalls.

While Van Der Merwe also participated in karate competitions, serving as the captain of the Namibian national team at the 6th All-Africa Championships held in Zimbabwe in 1995, he quickly retired of tournament to specialize in karate teaching.

In 1999, he was appointed as the head of the Namibia Branch of the International Okinawa Gōjū-ryū Karatedō Federation after receiving the keys of the Windhoek dōjō from De Vries.

Having received his 7th dan from Higaonna Morio in 2016, he now teaches 5 days a week with his five instructors at the Namibian headquarters. There, 180 to 200 people from 5 to 60 years old study Okinawa karate. At another branch dōjō, about 50 people follow the same tradition.

Next to karate, Van Der Merwe, who is a chartered accountant and a registered public accountant and auditor, works at one of the Big Four auditing firms in the world.

He explains, "I believe in the Pareto 80/20 principle: for almost everything in life 80% of results come from 20% of the effort. Karate forces you to concentrate as you are doing techniques that can hurt your training partner or you can get hurt. It is also a great physical workout. However, martial arts are inherently the same as we all work with the human body."

This July, a training camp will be held to commemorate the 40th anniversary of the founding of the Namibian honbu dōjō. The milestone event will definitely leave a trace in the history of karate in Namibia.

2021年12月12日

⓽ マダガスカル

修業の学び 生活に応用

国際剛柔流アカデミー

アフリカ大陸の南東海岸沖に浮かぶマダガスカル島は世界で4番目に大きな島で、バニラの世界生産量の約8割を占める国。沖縄とは熱帯林、ハイビスカス、マンゴー、パイナップルなど多くの類似点があり、毎年多くの台風が接近するのも共通している。

1960年にフランスから独立したこの共和国では、60年前半から空手の普及が始まった。64年に松濤館系の道場に入門したルネ・ラマニトランドラサナ氏(84)は、67年に行われた第1回マダガスカル選手権大会で組手の王者となった。77年に東京で開催された第4回世界空手道選手権大会の際に来日し、78年初期までさまざまな武術と剛柔流を学んだ。現在フランスに住む氏は、宮里善博氏が主席を務める順道館の支部長である。

58年マダガスカル生まれのツイヨリ・ランドリアニンドリナ氏は、70年に和道流の茶帯だった叔父2人から手ほどきを受け、6年後ラマニトランドラサナ氏の道場に入門した。その後師と共に剛柔流に転向した。

法学学問を続けるため、ランドリアニンドリナ氏は90年にフランスに移住し、再会した師と沖縄剛柔流の研究を深めた。

三戦(サンチン)の型の稽古をするランドリアニンドリナ氏(手前)と門弟たち=フランス(提供) Randrianindrina (front) and his students in France practicing the kata Sanchin.

35年間以上空手を稽古し研究してきたランドリアニンドリナ氏は、学んだ教えを分かち合うため、師匠の許可を得て、2008年に順道館に所属する国際剛柔流協会を設立した。公法と政治学で修士号を取得したが、空手の稽古と指導を存分にするためテキスタイル、衣料品等の貿易仲介会社を立ち上げ社長を務めている。

フランスの3道場の他、15年にマダガスカル首都アンタナナリボにも同会の「国際剛柔流アカデミー」を開設し、約50人が剛柔流を学んでいる。

「アカデミーでは数人の高段者が指導を担い、私も定期的に訪れ指導してきた。残念ながら、コロナ感染症とマダガスカルの非常に困難な健康状態を踏まえて、2年間故郷に行けていない」と氏は打ち明ける。

「願望が不可能なことを可能にする」と座右の銘を心に刻む氏は、現地と連絡を取り続け、早期のマダガスカル門弟との再会を楽しみにしている。

自身の経験を振り返って、空手で取得する尊重、努力の精神、意志、誠実さなどの価値観は、日常生活に応用すると必然的に成功につながると氏は信じる。17年に7段に昇段した氏は次の帰郷を待ちながら、妻、子息と娘2人を含む門下生たちと研究を続ける。氏いわく、空手は家族全員にとって人生そのものである。

Published on 2021/12/12

International Gōjū-ryū Association

Applying the lessons of training to daily life

Madagascar, which floats off the southeastern coast of the African continent, is the fourth largest island in the world and accounts for about 80% of the world's production of vanilla. It bears many similarities with Okinawa such as tropical forests, hibiscus, mangoes, pineapples, and the visit of typhoons.

In this republic, which became independent from France in 1960, the spread of karate began in the first half of the 1960s. René Ramanitrandrasana (84), who entered a Shōtōkan dōjō in 1964, became the kumite champion at the 1st Madagascar Championships in 1967. As he came to Japan in 1977 for the 4th World Karate Championships held in Tōkyō, he studied various martial arts and Gōjū-ryū until early 1978. Currently living in France, he represents the Jundōkan, chaired by Miyazato Yoshihiro.

Born in Madagascar in 1953, Tsiory Randrianindrina was taught the basics of karate by two uncles who were brown belts in Wado-ryū. In 1976, he entered the dōjō of Ramanitrandrasana and followed him on the path of Gōjū-ryū.

In order to continue his law studies, Randrianindrina moved to France in 1990 and started training again with his first mentor.

After over 35 years of practice, he established the International Gōjū-ryū Association in 2008 with the permission of his master to share what he had learned. Although he holds a master's degree in public law and political science, he has set up a trade brokerage company for textiles, clothing, etc. to be able to fully practice and teach karate.

In addition to the three dōjō it has in France, his association set up the International Gōjū-ryū Academy in Antananarivo, the capital of Madagascar, in 2015, and about 50 people are now learning karate there.

"Several seniors handle the training at the academy, and I have been visiting and instructing regularly. Unfortunately, I haven't been able to go home for two years because of the Covid-19 pandemic and the difficult health situation of Madagascar," he confesses.

Believing in the maxim "The fact of wanting makes the impossible possible," he keeps in touch with Madagascar and looks forward to an early reunion with his island students.

Looking back on his experience, Randrianindrina believes that values such as respect, sense of effort, will, honesty and humility acquired in karate will inevitably lead to success when they are applied to daily life. Promoted to 7th dan in 2017, he continues his research with his students which include his wife, son and two daughters. According to him, karate is life itself for his whole family.

2019年03月24日

⑩南アフリカ

本場の心 技学び錬磨

グレンビスタ空手アカデミー

首都プレトリアの南西に南アフリカの最大の都市ヨハネスブルクがある。

1947年その町で生まれたアーノルド・ドゥビア氏は若いころ、スプリングボード競技にまい進した。しかし、アパルトヘイトを理由に南アフリカはオリンピック参加禁止処分を受け、競技を断念した。

そして20歳のころ、この国の空手パイオニアの一人ジェームス・ルソー氏の下で沖縄空手を始めた。

南アフリカでの空手普及は、1950年代に始まった。柔道家が空手の本を手にしたのがスタートだという。60年代には数人の空手家が日本を訪れ指導を受けた。松濤館空手道の道を選んだスタン・シュミット氏やノーマン・ロビンソン氏と共に松濤館から沖縄剛柔流の道を選んだジェームス・ルソー氏もいた。

69年、空手歴2年のドゥビア氏は、師のルソー氏と共に日本を訪れた。東京の沖縄空手道協会代々木修練会で4カ月間、当時都内で指導していた東恩納盛男氏に師事した。帰国前にドゥビア氏は、初段に昇段。その後日本と沖縄を訪れながら研究を重ね、85年に自らの道場を開設した。89年からは専業の空手指導者になった。

弟子と共に写真に納まるドゥビア氏(前列左から4人目)=提供
De Beer (fourth from the left in the front row) with some of his students.

91年、合宿に参加するためドゥビア氏は沖縄を訪れた。その際、73年に知り合った上原米和氏の兄、沖縄昭霊武術協会・剛柔流直心館上原空手道場の故上原恒氏に出会った。上原恒氏に魅了され、ドゥビア氏は、国際昭霊武術協会と関わりを持ち活動を続けた。

那覇市にあったダイナハ(現ジュンク堂書店)裏にある上原空手道場を定期的に訪問し、剛柔流と古武道を学んだ。「ジェームス先生からは、サイとヌンチャクを習ったが、恒先生からは棒、サイ、トンファなどの型を教えてもらった」とドゥビア氏は振り返る。

南アフリカでは、長年空手を学んだ者が道場から離れないように古武道が計画的に導入された。独学で古武道を学んだ指導者は多かったが、門下生のレベルが上がると指導が難しくなったケースも出たという。

上原氏の許可を得て、ドゥビア氏は自尊心を抑え、白帯を締めて琉球古武道信武館の赤嶺浩氏に指導を求め、入門が認められた。現在グレンビスタ空手アカデミーでは高弟3人に琉球古武道の指導を任せている。

71歳で八段のドゥビア氏は、鍛錬の道に導かれた各指導者を尊敬しながら、本部道場で約80人、南アフリカとカメルーン、ポルトガルやオーストラリアにある15道場でも指南し続けている。

Arnold de Beer, who was born in Johannesburg in 1947, participated in springboard diving competitions when he was young. However, South Africa was banned from participating in the Olympics because of apartheid and seeing no point in continuing, he abandoned this sport.

It's at the age of twenty that he started karate under James Rousseau, one of the country's karate pioneers.

The spread of karate in South Africa began in the 1950s. It is said that jūdōka started karate by picking up books on the art. In the 1960s, several karateka visited Japan to learn karate. While Stan Schmidt and Norman Robinson chose the Shōtōkan path, James Rousseau switched from Funakoshi's karate to Okinawa Gōjū-ryū.

Published on 2019/3/24

⑩ South Africa

Glenvista Karate Academy

Polishing the technique in the spirit of the cradle

In 1969, de Beer, who had been training karate for two years, visited Tōkyō with his teacher James Rousseau and trained for four months at the Yoyogi Shūrenkai under Higaonna Morio. Returning home, de Beer was promoted to the rank of 1st dan. Continuing his research, he visited Japan and Okinawa and in 1985, he opened his own dōjō, becoming a full-time karate instructor in 1989.

In 1991, de Beer visited Okinawa to participate in a seminar. This is when he met the late Uehara Kō, the older brother of Uehara Yonekazu, who de Beer had met in 1973. Fascinated by the karate of the head of the Okinawa Shōrei Bujutsu Association - Gōjū-ryū Jikishinkan Uehara Karate Dōjō, de Beer started training with Uehara Kō.

After this encounter, he regularly visited the Uehara Karate Dōjō to learn Gōjū-ryū and kobudō. “We started kobudō with sai and nunchaku kata in the early days with James sensei, but afterwards Kō sensei taught me sai, bō and tonfa kata,” de Beer recalls. In South Africa, kobudō was systematically introduced so that those who had learned karate for many years would not leave the dōjō. Many instructors learned kobudō on their own but in many cases, it became difficult to teach as the level of the students increased.

With the permission of Uehara, de Beer swallowed his pride, tied a white belt, and asked Akamine Hiroshi, head of the Ryūkyū Kobudō Shinbukan, to teach him. Currently, at the Glenvista Karate Academy, three of his high-ranked assistants are entrusted with teaching Ryūkyū kobudō.

At the age of 71, de Beer, who holds an 8th dan, respects all the masters who have guided him on the path of karate. While teaching about 80 people at his main dōjō, he also instructs karateka in 15 dōjō in South Africa and overseas branches located in Cameroon, Portugal and Australia.

2022年3月27日

⑪南アフリカ

剛柔流普及に努める

ステレンボッシュ本部道場

1973年に那覇市民会館で「剛柔流空手道開祖宮城長順先生20年祭記念演武大会」が開催された。その時、25歳の南アフリカ出身のバッキーズ・ローブシャー氏は、当時剛柔流の東恩納盛男氏が指導していた東京代々木修練会のメンバーとして演武に参加した。氏は現在、東恩納氏が最高師範を務める国際沖縄剛柔流空手道連盟(IOGKF)の2人の9段のうちの一人。

48年生まれのローブシャー氏は、耳が大きく、いじめに苦しんでいたことから格闘技に目を向けた。「バッキーズは、“スープ碗”また“変な顔”を意味する」と氏は打ち明ける。

ボクシングを経て、14歳の時、近くにあった同国で最も古い大学ステレンボッシュ大学で極真系の空手を始めた。両親が指導料を支払う余裕がなかったため、氏は毎晩、母が経営していた下宿の下宿生の靴を磨き、得たお金で稽古を続けた。その後、松濤館に移り、65年に初段に合格した。

翌年、師であったジェームス・ルソー氏が剛柔流に転向し、ローブシャー氏は初めて剛柔流の型「セイユンチン」を習った。

当時ローブシャー氏は、型と組手の競技でも大活躍していて、72年、パリで行われた第2回世界空手道選手権大会に国の代表選手として参加した。その際、パリ経由で南アフリカに足を運んだ東恩納氏に初めて会ったことを深く記憶しているという。大会後、東恩納氏は6カ月間南アフリカで指導し、ローブシャー氏を東京へ誘った。25日間の船旅を終えて東京に到着した氏は、6カ月間代々木で剛柔流の鍛錬をした。

ローブシャー氏(前列左から4人目)と有段者(提供)　Laubscher (fourth from the left in the front row) with some of his senior students.

帰国後ローブシャー氏は学校教師を経て、国防軍に入隊し、スポーツと体育のシニアスタッフオフィサーを務めた。98年に退職し、夢だった「空手オンリーの人生」を満喫できるようになった。

19歳から指導するローブシャー氏は、82年に現在の道場を自身の農場に開設した。ブドウ畑に囲まれた道場で、氏は23人の有段者の指導を担い、高弟が70人余りの弟子に指南している。国内のIOGKF加盟37の支部道場を監修しながら、世界を飛び回り合宿も定期的に指導する。

「空手は自身の脆弱(ぜいじゃく)性と直接対峙(たいじ)させてくれる。真の指導者からの正しい指導を受ければ、空手はこれらの弱点を克服するのに役立ちます」とバッキーズ氏は考える。

しかし空手は武芸であることから、「完璧に達することは決してありません」とも言う。「完璧さを目指して努力することが空手の本質だ!」

In 1973, a demonstration to commemorate the 20th anniversary of the death of Gōjū-ryū's founder Miyagi Chōjun was held in Naha City. Among the demonstrators was 25-year-old South African Bakkies Laubscher, who participated as a member of the Tōkyō Yoyogi Shūrenkai run at that time by Higaonna Morio of Gōjū-ryū. Laubscher is today one of the only two 9th dan of the International Okinawa Gōjū-ryū Karatedō Federation that Higaonna heads.

Born in 1948, Laubscher turned his attention to martial arts because he had big ears and suffered from bullying. "'Bakkies means soup bowls or funny face" he confesses.

Published on 2022/3/27

Stellenbosch Honbu Dōjō

Striving to popularize Gōjū-ryū

After boxing, he started Kyokushin karate at the age of 14 at the nearby Stellenbosch University, the oldest university in the country. His parents not able to afford to pay tuition fees, he cleaned the shoes of the students that stayed at the boarding house managed by his mother and continued to practice with the money he earned. After that, he started training Shōtōkan karate and became a 1st dan in 1965. The following year, his teacher, James Rousseau switched to Gōjū-ryū, and Laubscher followed him and learned the Gōjū-ryū kata Seiyunchin for the first time.

At that time, Laubscher was also active in competing in kata and kumite. In 1972, he participated in the 2nd World Karate Championships held in Paris as a national team member. He remembers meeting for the first time Higaonna on that occasion. The Okinawan instructor was on his way via Paris to South Africa where he taught for six month after the world tournament. During his stay, Higaonna invited Laubscher to Tōkyō who, after a 25-day cruise to Japan, trained in the Yoyogi dōjō for six months.

Returning from Japan, Laubscher worked as a school teacher before joining the South African Defense Force where he served as a senior staff officer for sport and physical training. Retiring in 1998, he was finally able to "live his dream of only doing karate."

Laubscher, who has been teaching karate since the age of 19, opened his current dōjō in his farm in 1982. In this dōjō surrounded by vineyards, he teaches 23 black belts, while his senior students instruct more than 70 members. Within South Africa, he supervises 37 branch dōjō, and also travels around the world to teach seminars.

"Karate brings you in direct confrontation with your own vulnerability, your own weaknesses and if you use it and approach it correctly with correct guidance from a real teacher, it helps you to overcome these weaknesses and vulnerabilities," says he.

He goes on saying that since karate is an art, "One can never ever reach perfection. The striving for that perfection is the essence of karate!"

2017年4月30日

⑫ 南アフリカ

稽古通し 心と体鍛錬

順道館支部道場

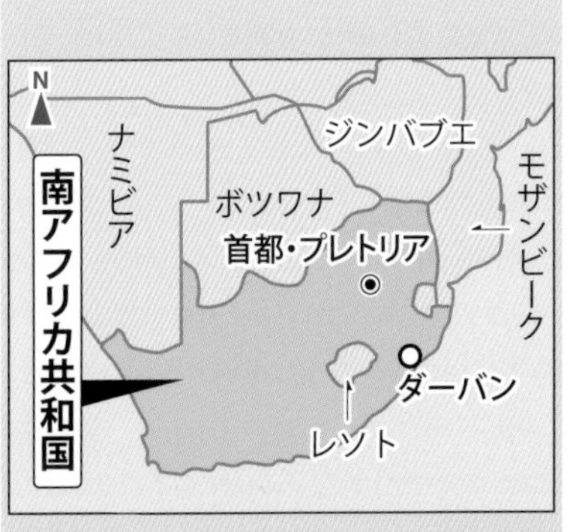

欧米で盛んとされる空手。沖縄が編み出したこの武術は世界中188カ国に普及している。各大陸に、様々な形で愛好家たちがおり、アフリカでも真剣に研究されている。

世界空手連盟によれば、アフリカの54カ国中、49カ国で空手が親しまれている。その中でも、南アフリカ共和国は長年にわたり沖縄との交流がある。同国には、本土の4大流派の一つの松濤館や極真系以外では、沖縄剛柔流が広まっている。

1966年に南アフリカ人としては初めてジェームス・ルソー氏=当時(23)=が沖縄を訪れ、那覇市安里にある名門「順道館」で稽古した。その記事が同年12月3日付の沖縄タイムスに掲載された。後の75年には、剛柔流の東恩納盛男氏ら数人がアフリカ大陸の最南端にあるこの共和国に渡り、演武と指導を行った。それ以降、今日まで多くの南アフリカ人が剛柔流を研究している。↗

バディ・ガーベンダー氏(57)もその一人だ。東海岸のダーバン市出身のガーベンダー氏は10歳のころ、山口剛玄氏の剛柔会の現地支部道場に入門した。当時はアパルトヘイト(人種隔離)の政策下であったため、白人の道場と黒人の道場があったと氏は記憶している。76年に初段となり指導を始めた。そして89年、知り合いを通じて沖縄剛柔流と出合った。97年に宮里栄一氏が開設した順道館を初めて訪れ、同年、支部長に任命された。

自宅道場で稽古に励むガーベンダー氏(前列右から3人目)と弟子たち=南アフリカ・ダーバン(提供)　Govender (3rd from the right on the front row) practicing hard at his home dōjō.

しかし、氏にはもう一つの「顔」がある。16歳、初段に昇段した年に、サッカーのセミプロになった。その後プロ選手となり、79年から87年まで、南アフリカ1部リーグのチームでゴールキーパーとして活躍した。

プロとしての練習とリーグ戦による遠征が多く、道場に通うことが一度は厳しくなったが、個人稽古は続けていた。「空手のおかげでサッカーがうまくなった」と本人は言う。そして、9年間のプロ選手としての活躍を終え、道場に戻った。

97年にはダーバンに沖縄剛柔流空手道総本部順道館南アフリカ道場を開設。2011年には自宅道場も開設した。空手競技と関わることなく、この道場では「稽古」と「研究」に集中しているという。

現在、250人が金曜日と日曜日を除く毎日、ガーベンダー氏の下で沖縄剛柔流に欠かせない補助運動、器具運動、型と組手を繰り返し、空手を通して体と精神を鍛えている。

初めて沖縄を訪れた際に氏は、言葉の壁を感じたが、唯一きちんと理解できた言葉は「Keiko」。文字通り、指導しながら、今も稽古に励んでいる。

Published on 2017/4/30

12 South Africa

Jundōkan Shibu Dōjō

Tempering the soul and body through training

Karate has spread in some 188 countries around the world and even in Africa, it is researched quite seriously. According to the World Karate Federation, karate is practiced in 49 of the 54 African countries.

In South Africa, next to Shōtōkan and Kyokushin, Okinawa Gōjū-ryū is extremely well widespread.

In 1966, James Rousseau (23 years old at the time) was the first South African to train at the Jundōkan in Asato, Naha City. An article on his visit was published in the Okinawa Times dated December 3rd of the same year. Later in 1975, Higaonna Morio and several karateka travelled to South Africa and since then, many South Africans have been studying Gōjū-ryū.

Buddy Govender (57) is one of them. Born in Durban, he entered at the age of 10 the local branch dōjō affiliated with the Gōjū-kai of Yamaguchi Gōgen. He remembers that there were dōjō for white people and others for colored people due to the apartheid policy at the time. He started teaching karate after becoming a black belt in 1976. Then, in 1989, he discovered Okinawa Gōjū-ryū through an acquaintance. In 1997, he visited for the first time the Jundōkan and was appointed as the country's representative the same year.

However, the karate devoted person that he is has another face. At the age of 16, the year he was promoted to black belt, Govender started soccer semi-professionally. He then became a professional football player playing as a goalkeeper for a team competing in the South African 1st division from 1979 till 1987.

Due to his training as a professional player and game travels, it became for a while difficult to attend dōjō practice but yet, he continued his personal karate training. He comments that, "Thanks to karate, I've become better at football." Finally, ending a nine years professional career, he returned to the dōjō.

In 1997, he established the South African branch of the Okinawa Gōjū-ryū Karatedō Sōhonbu Jundōkan in Durban. In 2011, he also set up a dōjō in his house. Staying away from competition, people in this dōjō focus on "Keikō - training" and "Kenkyū - research".

Currently, 250 people are training every day except Friday and Sunday.Under Govender, they repeat the supplementary exercises known as hojo-undō and kigu-undō, kata and kumite, all indispensable in the study of Okinawa Gōjū-ryū.

When he first visited Okinawa, Govender felt the language barrier. However, the one word that he clearly understood was "Keikō" and today still, he instructs and practice with fervor.

インド洋マダガスカル島の東に位置する小さな島国モーリシャス。熱帯地方にあるこの島は、ほぼ東京都と同じ面積の2千平方キロメートル余。人口約120万人。主な産業は観光、サトウキビ、繊維産業で沖縄との共通点は多い。

オランダ領からフランス領になったこの島は後にイギリス領となり、1968年に独立した。イギリス連邦加盟国の一つで92年には共和国となった。

国家スポーツであるサッカーと比べて、空手はマイナーな競技。モーリシャス空手連盟によると、65年ごろ、日本船が同島に入港し始めたことを機に空手が普及し始めたという。現在、50余の道場でおよそ1万人が空手を稽古している。そのほとんどを本土系の空手が占める中、小林流と又吉古武道を継承する道場や剛柔流を継承する道場もある。

1949年モーリシャスの首都ポートルイス生まれのヌーハメド・ドゥルー氏は、16歳のころ、柔道を習い、同島に転任した日本人エンジニアから松濤館空手の手ほどきも受けた。72年にインドのムンバイ大学に入学し、4年間、パーベス・ミストリ氏の武術アカデミーで剛柔流を学んだ。

技を確かめ指導するドゥルー氏（中央後方）＝提供　Dulloo (center rear) making sure the technique is correct.

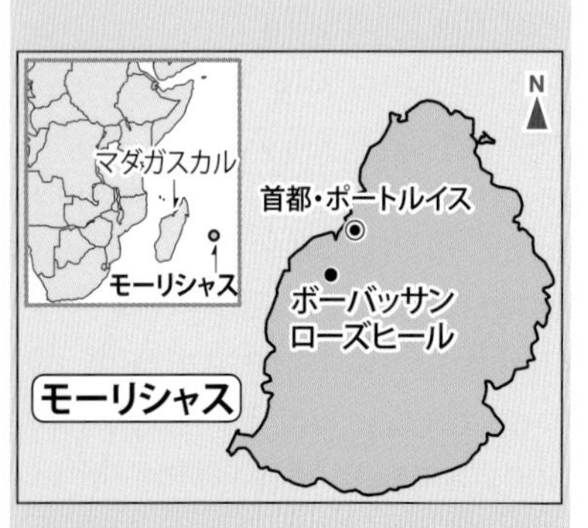

2018年09月23日

⑬モーリシャス

伝統の技 島々で指南

拳法会拳武館

その後、剛柔流開祖宮城長順氏の指導を受けた山口剛玄氏の三男山口剛史氏が最高師範を務める国際空手道剛柔会に入り、南西インド洋諸島の支部長に任命された。

長年、剛柔流のルーツを追求してきたドゥルー氏は、84年初めて沖縄を訪れ、2006年に空手発祥の地でセミナーにも参加した。14年に比嘉世幸や宮城氏の指導を受けた渡口政吉氏の弟子で沖縄空手道拳法会拳武館（沖縄市）の久場良男館長と出会い、弟子入りした。

ロレト大学で経済学、経営学、スポーツ管理の講師をしているドゥルー氏は、非営利にボーバッサンローズヒールでの本部道場と島内3支部で150人に剛柔流を指導している。同系統の普及のため、周辺のレユニオン島、マダガスカル、コモール、モルディブにも出かけ技術指南を行う。この島々では約90人が空手研究に挑んでいる。

「空手の哲学、道徳、倫理的価値は分け合えるものです。空手の実用性と現実性が普遍的に容認できるので、空手は地域社会やグローバル社会において重要な役割を果たす」とドゥルー氏の信念は揺るぎない。

現在、全モーリシャス空手連盟の副会長を務める教士7段。強い使命感に基づき、全アフリカ剛柔流空手連盟の代表として普及活動に力を尽くす。

Published on 2018/9/23

Kenpōkai Kenbukan

Teaching traditional technique in southern islands

In the Indian Ocean, Mauritius is a small island country located east of Madagascar that became a republic in 1992. A tropical island, it has an area of more than 2,000 km², which is almost the same as Tōkyō and a population of about 1.2 million. With many similarities with Okinawa, the main industries are tourism, sugar cane and textile industry.

Compared to the national sport soccer, karate is a minor activity. According to the Mauritius Karate Federation, karate began to spread around 1965 when Japanese ships started arriving to the island. Nowadays, about 10,000 people are practicing karate in more than 50 dōjō. While most are practicing mainland Japanese karate, there are a few dōjō that teach Shōrin-ryū, Matayoshi kobudō and Gōjū-ryū.

Born in 1949 in the capital of Mauritius Port Louis, Noorahmed Dulloo started learning jūdō at the age of 16 and later studied Shōtōkan karate from a Japanese engineer posted in Mauritius. He entered the University of Mumbai, India in 1972 and studied Gōjū-ryū at the Bujutsu Academy of Pervez Mistry for four years.

After that, Dulloo joined the International Karatedō Gōjū-kai led by Yamaguchi Gōshi, son of Yamaguchi Gōgen, a disciple of Miyagi Chōjun, the founder of Gōjū-ryū. He was also appointed as the branch manager of the Southwest Indian Ocean Islands.

In pursue of the roots of Gōjū-ryū, Dulloo visited Okinawa for the first time in 1984 and participated in a seminar in the birthplace of karate in 2006. In 2014, he met and became a student of Kuba Yoshio, director of the Okinawa Karatedō Kenpōkai Kenbukan in Okinawa City. Kuba was a disciple of Toguchi Seikichi, a student of Higa Sekō and Miyagi Chōjun.

Dulloo, a professor in economics and business and sports management at the Loreto College in Port Louis, teaches Gōjū-ryū to 150 people at his headquarters dōjō located in Beau-Bassin Rose-Hill and three other dōjō in the island. To spread this karate system, he also travels to nearby Reunion Island, Madagascar, the Comoros, and the Maldives to provide technical guidance. About 90 people are studying under him in these islands.

Dulloo's belief in karate is unwavering. "Because karate philosophy, moral and ethical values are undoubtedly transferable and universally acceptable as being pragmatic and realistic, karate has a vital role to play in any local society as well as the global world."

A 7th dan in karate, Dulloo is the Vice President of the All Mauritius Karate Federation. Moved by a strong sense of mission, he also devotes his time to disseminate karate as a representative of the All-Africa Gōjū-ryū Federation.

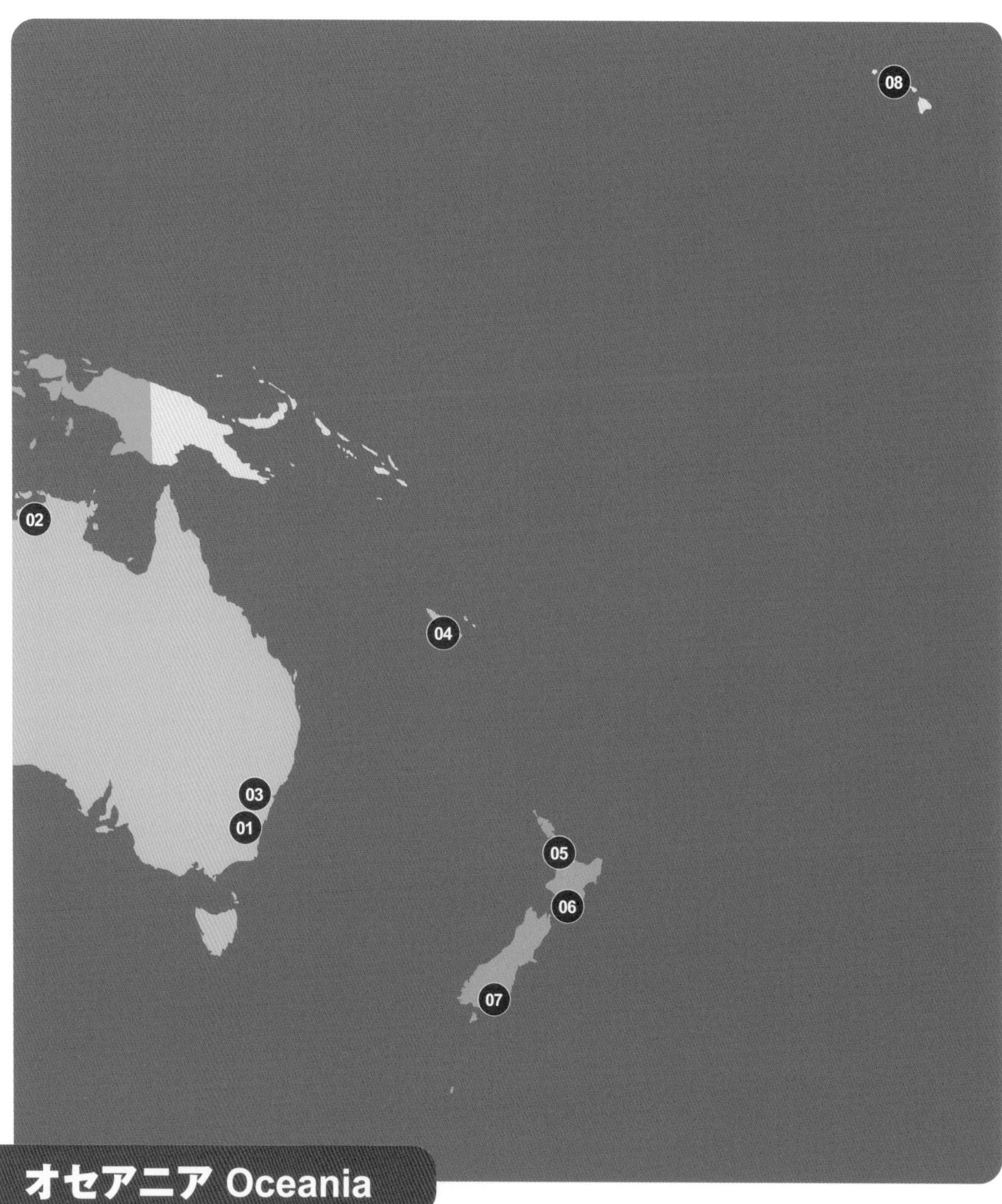

オセアニア Oceania

オセアニア
Oceania

1946年インドネシアマラン生まれのジョハネス・ウオン氏は、9歳から武術を習い始めた。極真系の空手を学び、13歳からほかの武術にも目を向けた。カンフー、柔道の手ほどきを受けても、初恋であった空手をやめず、武術探求に励んだ。17歳の時、インドネシアの特殊部隊に入隊し、後に経験を生かして4年間戦闘インストラクターを務めた。

74年に家族や子どもの将来を見据えたウオン氏は、オーストラリアに移住。ニューサウスウェールズ州で機械工学士として生計を立てた。定住後、ウオン氏は地元の大学や学校体育館で空手クラブを開き指導に励んだ。

空手人生の分岐点は82年、同州に短期留学に訪れた玉城吉樹氏との出会いだった。玉城氏は52年に剛柔流明武舘を開設し97年に県指定無形文化財「沖縄の空手・古武術」保持者に認定された故八木明徳氏の弟子、池宮城政明氏の門弟だった。玉城氏の協力を得てウオン氏は83年12月に訪沖し、沖縄市にある池宮城氏の道場の門をくぐった。

武器術にも興味を持つウオン氏は小林流の垣花恵春氏に古武道を習った後、孝武流孝武会の金城孝氏を紹介され、孝武会に入会している。

王道場でウオン氏（前列中央）と高段者たち=提供　Wong (center in the front row) and high-ranked members at the Wong's Dōjō.

2020年11月22日

01 オーストラリア

修練を重ね忍耐培う

王道場

現在ウオン氏は剛柔流8段と古武道9段。シドニー郊外にあるトゥンガビーに住む。1978年に道場を開設し、沖縄空手と古武道の師匠の技法と精神を追求しようと道場名を「沖縄空手道・古武道　王道場」に改名した。約50人が沖縄の武術を学び、国内に7道場、故郷インドネシアでも1道場で指南している。

王道場のウェブサイトに漢字で記されている「練習練習在練習」は、ウオン氏の武術に対する姿勢を示すモットーだ。「正しくなるまで練習をするのではなく、間違わないように練習をやり続けるのだ」とウオン氏は力説する。

仕事を退職したウオン氏は、技法だけに専心するのではなく、古武道の武具も自ら製作することが趣味だという。カラオケやギターも楽しんでいる。

「沖縄通」であるウオン氏は、2年に1回訪沖し、これまで25回以上沖縄を訪れた。流派を超えて武術交流を求め、県主催の世界大会や国際セミナーなどへ積極的に参加、何度も地元メディアに取り上げられた。

心技体の鍛錬を繰り返す空手道の神髄は忍耐にあると信念を抱く。池宮城、金城両師の教えを大切にしつつ武の道を追求し、愛する沖縄の武術の継承に励む。

Published on 2020/11/22

Wong's Dōjō

Practicing and cultivating endurance

Born in Malang, Indonesia in 1946, Johanes Wong began learning martial arts at the age of nine. Starting with Kyokushin karate, he switched to kungfu and jūdō from the age of 13 and continued to pursue the way of martial arts without abandoning his first love, karate. At the age of 17, he joined the Indonesian Special Forces and later used his experience to serve as a combat instructor for four years.

Thinking about the future of his children and family, he moved to Australia in 1974 and made a living as a mechanical engineer in New South Wales (NSW). After arriving in Australia, he also started his first dōjō and taught karate in a school gymnasium and a university hall.

The turning point in his karate life was the encounter with Tamaki Yoshiki, who visited NSW for a short-term study abroad program in 1982. Tamaki was a student of Ikemiyagi Masaaki, himself a disciple of the late Yagi Meitoku of the Gōjū-ryū Meibukan. With the cooperation of Tamaki, Wong visited Okinawa in December 1983 and entered the dōjō of Ikemiyagi in Okinawa City.

As Wong was also interested in weapons, he learned kobudō from Kakinohana Keishun of Shōrin-ryū before being introduced to Kinjō Takashi and joining his Kobu-ryū Kobukai.

Today, Wong is a Gōjū-ryū 8th dan and a kobudō 9th dan who lives in Toongabbie, NSW. The dōjō he opened in 1978 was renamed “Okinawa Karatedō & Kobudō Wong's Dōjō” in an attempt to pursue the techniques and spirit of his Okinawan masters. Approximately 50 people study there while Wong teaches at seven dōjō in Australia and one dōjō in Indonesia.

On his dōjō's website is mentioned a maxim that describes Wong's attitude towards martial arts: “Renshū, Renshū, Zai Renshū.” He explains it as “it is important to practice not until you get it right, but until you cannot get it wrong.”

As he is now retired, Wong says that his hobby is not only to concentrate on techniques, but also to make kobudō weapons while enjoying karaoke and guitar.

A deep Okinawa enthusiast, Wong has visited Okinawa once every two years for a total of more than 25 times so far. Seeking martial arts exchanges beyond systems, he actively participated in prefectural-sponsored events, and has been featured in the local Okinawan media many times.

Wong believes that the essence of karatedō, in which the spirit, technique and body are continuously conditioned, lies in endurance. Valuing the teachings of both Ikemiyagi and Kinjō, he pursues the way of the martial arts and strives to pass on the Okinawan martial arts of his beloved Okinawa.

2019年11月24日

02 オーストラリア

美徳の教え 胸に錬磨

ダーウィン直心館

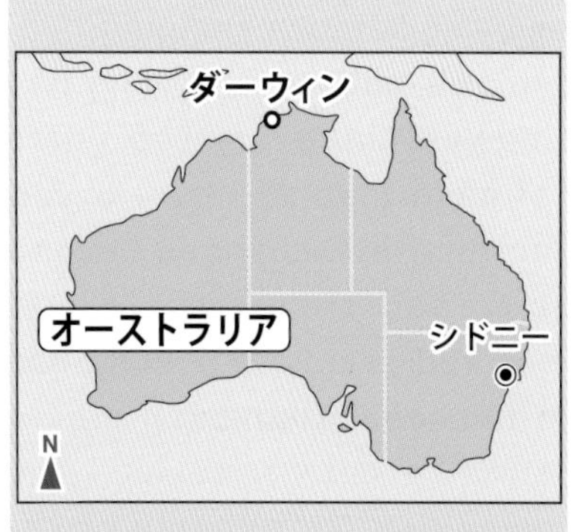

東ティモール生まれのラリ・ゴンカルベス氏(68)は、13歳の頃、カンフーを習い、2年後、本格的に空手を学びたいと極真系の道場に入門した。「当時の指導者はほとんどがマカオ出身の中国人でした」とゴンカルベス氏は思い返す。

18歳の時ゴンカルベス氏は、大学で建築を学ぶためオーストラリアに移住した。シドニーで入学後、フルコンタクト空手を普及する同国のパイオニアの一人ウオリー・スラヴォスキー氏に弟子入りした。

その後、1977年から指導に携わるゴンカルベス氏は、87年に、オーストラリアの北側にあるダーウィンに移った。そこで、建築家として生計を立てながら、空手の普及に励んだ。

しかし、フルコン系空手の限界を感じて90年代初めに沖縄空手を調べ、沖縄剛柔流を鍛錬する知り合いから上原恒氏を訪ねるよう勧められた。上原氏は、宮里栄一氏より剛柔流、平信賢氏の高弟赤嶺栄亮氏より琉球古武道を学んでいる。

ゴンカルベス氏はすぐに受け入れ許可を求め、歓迎された。93年、初めて那覇市のダイナハ(現ジュンク堂書店)の裏にある沖縄昭霊武術協会剛柔流直心館の門をくぐった。「上原先生の空手

型「サイファー」を稽古するゴンカルベス氏(手前)と門下生たち=提供
Goncalves (front) and his students practicing the kata Saifā.

の最も魅力的な側面は、個人指導です。それぞれの門下生が何をしているかを気付かせられること。私がこれまで通った大人数のコマーシャル道場と全く違う雰囲気でした」

それ以降、毎年沖縄を訪れ、上原氏の指導を受け続けた。2000年から剛柔流に完全に転向し、2014年からは直心館の支部として認められた。

18年に上原氏は他界。それでも今年も、2代目会長の宮里信光氏の指導を受けるためゴンカルベス氏は来沖した。「上原先生との出会いを言葉に表せれば『一期一会』が適切で、それは好きな言葉でもあります。上原先生は非常に厳しい師範でしたが、すごく思いやりのある人でした。先生との思い出は父と息子の関係と同様で、今もその関係を大切に保っていきたいと思っています」と25年間の交流を振り返る。

ゴンカルベス氏は、上原氏や宮里氏の指導方針をまねて、量より質を選び、少人数への指南を決めた。現在、ダーウィン直心館で8人が沖縄の空手と古武道を研究している。

「精神と身体修行を通して良い人になることが空手の目的。そして学んだ美徳を他人に分かち合うことも空手の魅力」と信念を抱く。20年余り座禅にも取り組み、物静かながらも選んだ道に妥協を許さないゴンカルベス氏。これからも師から受けた美徳の教えを地道に伝授していく。

Born in East Timor, Larry Goncalves (68) learned kungfu at the age of 13 and two years later, he entered a Kyokushin dōjō to seriously learn karate. He recalls that at that time, instructors were mainly Chinese from Macau.

When 18 years old, he migrated to Australia in order to attend university in Sydney to study architecture. While studying, he continued his full contact karate training with a pioneer in this system in Australia, Wally Szlagowski.

Goncalves, who has been teaching since 1977, moved to Darwin on the north side of Australia in 1987. There he made a living as an architect while promoting earnestly karate.

Published on 2019/11/24

02 Australia

Darwin Jikishinkan

Teaching and polishing virtues

However, feeling the limits of full contact karate, he started to investigate Okinawa karate in the early 90's and was recommended to visit Uehara Kō by an acquaintance who trained in Okinawa Gōjū-ryū. Losing no time, Goncalves immediately asked for permission to be accepted and as he was welcomed, he entered for the first time in 1993 the Okinawa Shōrei Bujutsu Association Jikishinkan in Naha City.

"The most attractive aspect of Uehara sensei's karate was that he made you think about what you were doing and the instruction was also very personalized. It was a completely different atmosphere from the commercial dōjō that I had attended so far."

From then on, Goncalves visited Okinawa every year to train under Uehara. Completely switching to Gōjū-ryū karate in 2000, he was recognized as a Jikishinkan branch in 2014.

In 2018, Uehara passed away. Nevertheless, Goncalves kept coming to Okinawa to receive tuition from Miyazato Nobumitsu, the second chairman of the association.

Looking back at 25 years of relationship with Uehara, he comments, "The expression Ichi-go Ichi-e - roughly translated as 'one chance in a lifetime'- symbolizes my encounter with Uehara sensei and it is one of my favorite proverb. He was a very stern teacher but he was also a very caring person. My memories of Kō sensei are of a relationship of father and son and I still cherish this relationship."

Following the teaching policies of Uehara and Miyazato, Goncalves chose quality over quantity and therefore teaches only a small number of people. Currently, eight persons are studying Okinawa karate and kobudō at the Darwin Jikishinkan.

On the charms of karate, he believes that "Becoming a better person through mental and physical training is the purpose of karate and then sharing those qualities with the general community is its charm." Having also practiced zazen for more than 20 years, Goncalves is a quiet person who does not allow compromise on his chosen path. He will continue to steadily transmit the precepts of virtues received from his teachers.

2017年06月11日

03 オーストラリア

上地流の指導法基盤

アーサー・モラス武道センター

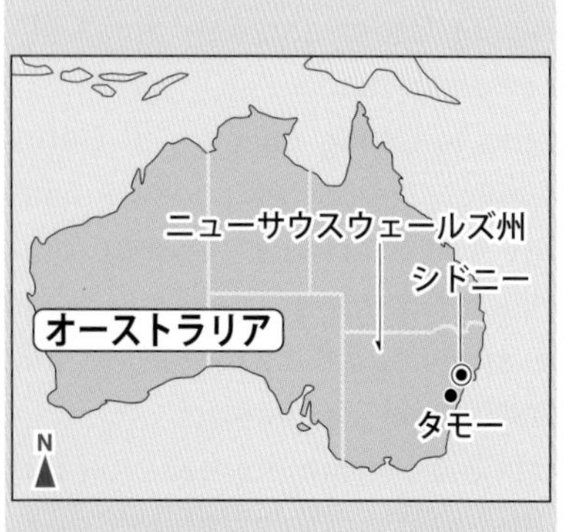

オーストラリアにおいて空手が初めて紹介されたのは1960年初期のこと。本土系の剛柔流、松濤館、極真系が最初の流派で、70年設立されたオーストラリア空手連盟には現在、157の流会派が登録されており、その10カ所余は沖縄空手・古武道の支部である。なお同連盟に非加盟の沖縄空手系の支部道場も多くある。

66年、上地流を習い、指導していたエストニア出身のアティ・カエント氏がオーストラリアに渡り同流派を普及した。それが、沖縄空手の同国での始まりだ。カエント氏の多くの門弟の中に、アーサー・モラス氏がいた。

現在、沖縄空手を愛好する外国空手家の多くは、まず最初に、本土系の流派から空手に入り、その後沖縄空手を指導する者と出会い移行するケースが主だが、モラス氏の場合は、最初から上地流を習い始めた。その理由を聞くと、「それしかなかったから」と笑顔で率直に答える。

52年生まれの氏は、69年からこの道に入り、74年にバンクスタウンに道場を開設した。そして、85年に初めての訪沖を果たしたモラス氏は、2代目宗家の上地完英氏に師事。「カエント先生に本物の上地流を指導されたが、やはり沖縄での小手鍛えなどは激しかった」と思い出す氏。あれから20回以上訪沖している。いまも、世界空手連盟の世界大会に出場経験がある競技選手を育てたモラス氏は、上地流の伝統指導法を稽古の基盤としている。

セミナーで指導するモラス氏＝右（トーマス　ポジェルニー氏提供）　Moulas (right) teaching a seminar (photo from Thomas Podzelny).

99年、ニューサウスウェールズ州にある小さな町のタモーに移転して本部道場を立ち上げ、全国にある9の支部道場500人余りに指南するモラス氏。「オーストラリアでは格闘技も非常に盛んだが、空手の人気も絶大。特に子どもたちに」。モラス氏の門弟の3分の2は子どもたちである。

言葉遣いの穏やかな氏は現在、首席師範を務める高良信徳氏の沖縄上地流唐手道協会の9段、伊敷秀忠氏から習う沖縄古武道の6段として沖縄の武術を普及するが、沖縄を訪れる際に上地流の各会派長との技術交流と親睦を深めている。

数年前、複数の給油所のオーナー業を引退したモラス氏は、空手のほか羊240匹の世話をすることが趣味という。「近隣の数千の羊を飼っている農場主に比べると、私は小さなファーマー」と微笑みながら語る。でも、ものを育てるのは、「量より質が大事」。空手も同様である。そして、上地宗家に教えられた空手の秘訣（ひけつ）である「稽古」を信じて汗を流し続ける。

Published on 2017/6/11

03 Australia 

Arthur Moulas Martial Arts

The Uechi-ryū teaching method as a foundation

Karate was first introduced in Australia in the early 1960s, the first systems being mainland Gōjū-ryū, Shōtōkan, and Kyokushin. Established in 1970, the Australian Karate Federation currently has 157 styles and systems registered, of which more than 10 are Okinawa karate and kobudō branches. There are also many Okinawa karate branch dōjō that are not registered with the federation.

In 1966, Ahti Kaend, an Estonian Uechi-ryū instructor, travelled to Australia to spread the style. It is said to be the beginning of Okinawa karate in the country. Among Kaend's many disciples was Arthur Moulas.

Many foreign karateka who love Okinawa karate first started with a mainland style and then, meeting an Okinawa karate expert, switched system. In the case of Moulas, he first started learning Uechi-ryū. When asked why, he answered frankly, "Because that's all there was."

Born in 1952, Moulas entered the way of karate in 1969 and opened a dōjō in Bankstown in 1974. Making his first trip to Okinawa in 1985, he studied under Uechi Kanei, the second Sōke. "While I was taught real Uechi-ryū by Kaend sensei, forearm conditioning in Okinawa was still extreme," he recalls. Since then, he has visited Okinawa more than 20 times. Even now, Moulas, who has trained athletes who have participated in the World Karate Federation's world championships, uses the traditional Uechi-ryū teaching method as the basis for his training.

In 1999, Moulas relocated to Tahmoor, a small town in New South Wales, and set up his honbu dōjō from which he guides more than 500 people training in 9 branch dōjō nationwide. "Martial arts and karate are extremely popular in Australia, especially with children." Two-thirds of Moulas' students are children.

A gentle speaking man, he currently spreads the martial arts of Okinawa as a 9th dan with the Okinawa Uechi-ryū Karatedō Association led by Takara Shintoku, and a kobudō 6th dan, studying with Ishiki Hidetada. Yet, when visiting Okinawa, he trains and socializes with all the leaders of each Uechi-ryū school.

Having retired from the gas station owning business a few years ago, Moulas says his hobby, next to karate, is to take care of his 240 sheep. "Compared to farmers who own thousands of sheep in the neighborhood, I'm a small farmer." However, when it comes to raising, "Quality is more important than quantity". The same is true for karate. At the end, believing as taught by Uechi Sōke that "training" is the secret of karate, he continues to train hard.

昨年12月、独立の是非を問う住民投票を実施し、フランスにとどまることを決めた南太平洋に浮かぶフランス領のニューカレドニア(NC)と沖縄の交流は1905年にさかのぼる。

当時、800人余りのウチナーンチュが労働移民を決めこの島に渡り、ニッケル鉱山の炭鉱員として働いた。今も、沖縄系2世、3世などがこの島で暮らす。

空手が盛んなこの島は、フランスの形の王者ミン・ダック選手を生んだ。首都ヌメア出身の氏は、糸東流の空手家で、2019年にオセアニア選手権大会で優勝を果たした。

1964年パリ生まれのエリック・ルグルメレック氏は、フランス大手建設会社で機材責任者として働く。仕事柄、アフリカやドバイなどで長年の転勤生活を続けてきた。

空手は21歳の時から始め、和道流や松濤會の空手を習った。仕事の関係で94年にアフリカとマダガスカルの間に浮かぶ仏海外県のマヨットに転勤した際に剛柔流と出合った。

同島には、県出身の渡口政吉氏が開設した尚礼会系列の道場があった。フランスにおいて尚礼会は1970年代後半から普及し、先駆者のウイリ・フル

門下生の指導に励むルグルメレック夫妻=ニューカレドニア・パイタの道場(提供) Mr. and Mrs. Le Grumelec in the Paita dōjō.

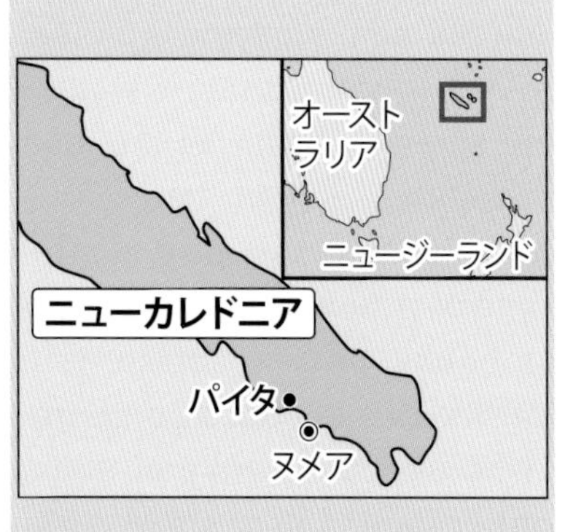

2022年4月3日

04 ニューカレドニア

剛柔流の神髄を追求

拳武会

シュ氏は渡口氏や高弟の内藤末吉氏に師事し、現在内藤氏の雄武館の副館長を務めている。

剛柔流に魅了されたルグルメレック氏は、97年に初段を授かり、転勤先のガボンで尚礼館道場を開設。13年間、指南した。2008年に3段に昇段した。

稽古に励みながら、氏は渡口氏のルーツを追求し沖縄に目を向け、沖縄市にある沖縄空手道拳法会拳武館の久場良男氏へ受け入れを求めた。

念願がかない、ルグルメレック氏は19年11月に2週間、訪沖し、渡口氏の弟子久場氏に師事した。「久場先生の空手は奥深い。これは、私が尚礼館空手の延長として求めていたものだ」と氏は拳武館への転向の理由を述べる。

勤める会社が世界各地域に拠点を有することを活用し、空手3段でもある妻と次の転勤先をニューカレドニアに決めた。同島とパリを結ぶ便は必ず日本を経由することから、「定期的に久場先生の指導を受けたい」との希望を氏は持っている。

21年からルグルメレック夫妻は仕事の傍ら、ヌメア郊外パイタに道場「沖縄空手剛柔流拳武会NC」を開設し、現在10人に指導している。

渡口氏の言葉「空手の神髄とは、どのような状況にあっても笑っていられることである」。ルグルメレック氏は、日々の練習を通して、この言葉の意味を感じているという。その教えを弟子に分かち合いたくて、研究と指導に励む。

New Caledonia, a French special collectivity in the South Pacific Ocean, has a history with Okinawa that dates back to 1905.

From that year, more than 800 Okinawans immigrated to this island to work as coal miners in nickel mines. Even now, Okinawan second and third generations live in New Caledonia.

An island where karate is popular, NC has given birth to kata champion Minh Dack who was born in the capital Noumea.

Born in Paris in 1964, Eric Le Grumelec works as an equipment director in a major French construction company. Through his profession, he has lived for many years in Africa and Dubai among other locations.

Published on 2022/4/3

04 New Caledonia 

Kenbukai

Pursuing the essence of Gōjū-ryū

Le Grumelec started Japanese karate when he was 21. Due to his work, he was transferred in 1994 to Mayotte, an overseas French department which floats between Africa and Madagascar. This is where he discovered Gōjū-ryū.

In Mayotte, there was a dōjō affiliated with the Shōreikai of Okinawan Toguchi Seikichi. This system had spread in France since the latter half of the 1970s through French pioneer Willy Fruchout who studied with Toguchi and one of his top students Naito Suekichi.

Charmed by Gōjū-ryū, Le Grumelec was awarded the 1st dan in 1997 and opened a Shōreikan dōjō in Gabon where he was transferred, teaching there for thirteen years.

As he kept practicing earnestly, he also started looking for the roots of Gōjū-ryū and turning his attention to Okinawa, he asked Kuba Yoshio of the Okinawa Karatedō Kenpōkai Kenbukan to accept him as a student.

His request approved, Le Grumelec visited Okinawa in November 2019 for two weeks and studied under Kuba, a disciple of late Toguchi. "Kuba sensei's karate is profound. This is what I was looking for as an extension of Shōreikan's karate," he comments.

Taking advantage of the fact that his company has bases in various regions of the world, he decided to move to New Caledonia with his wife, who is also a 3rd dan karateka. Since flights connecting Noumea and Paris always go through Japan, he hopes to visit Kuba on a regular basis.

In 2021, the Le Grumelec have opened a dōjō in Paita, a suburb of Noumea. Having named it "Okinawa Karate Gōjū-ryū Kenbukai NC", they currently instruct 10 people.

According to Toguchi, "The quintessence of karate is the ability to smile on any occasion." Le Grumelec says that he starts feeling the meaning of these words through his daily practice. As he hopes to share this principle with his disciples, he strives to research and teach the art of karate.

ニュージーランドと空手といえば、今年3月、2020年東京オリンピックの事前合宿で沖縄県、沖縄市と協定を結んだ同国空手連盟の存在が思い浮かぶ。

オランダのゼーラント州にちなんで名づけられたこの島国での最初の空手道場は、1958年に柔道家によって開設されたという。その後ニュージーランド人が日本で修業し、極真系、松濤館や剛柔流が普及した。

56年ファンガレイ市生まれのケビン・プレステッド氏は75年19歳の時、同町で松濤館を指導していたボッブ・ダルトン氏の静空館に入門し、3年で初段に昇段した。

79年プレステッド氏は警察に入り、特殊部隊や警察犬ハンドラーとして任務を果たした。同時に競技空手の世界で活躍し、全国組手チャンピオンになった。86年シドニーで行われた世界空手道選手権大会にも出場している。↗

しかし、88年に三段の氏は警察をやめて、富山県にある静空館本部道場で3カ月の間、技を磨いた。帰国後89年にスタンモアベイで現在の道場を開設し、鍼治療の道にも進んだ。92年から自宅で鍼院を開業し、警察の銃器ライセンス調査官にも任命された。

サイの稽古をするプレステッド氏(右)と弟子入りして25年のティム・ヒローヒ氏(提供)　Plaisted (right) training the Sai with Tim Herlihy, his student for 25 years.

2017年12月10日

05 ニュージーランド 

発祥の地で心技刻む

ファンガパラオア本部道場

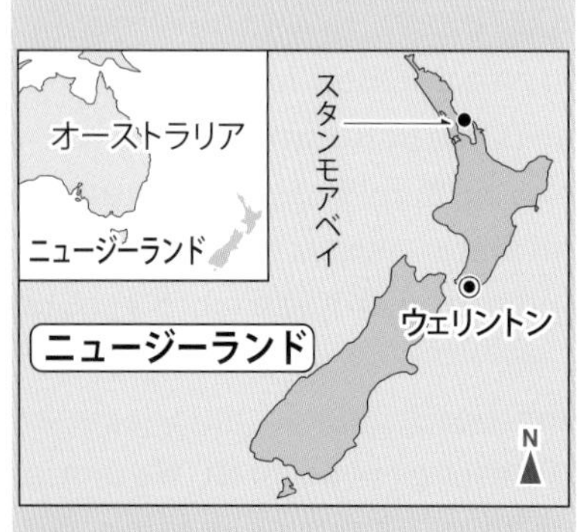

95年沖縄空手・古武道世界大会のプロモーションで派遣されたキャラバン団がニュージーランドを訪れた。自身の空手の将来を熟考していた氏は関連のセミナーに参加し、指導員の一人、松林流の平良慶孝氏と出会った。真の沖縄空手の流派との出合いを求めていた時期にその幸運を逃がさず、本場の空手に身と心を向けた。

プレステッド氏は「以前から空手の本場と先人に興味を持っていた。また、弟子を含めて古武道にも関心があった。私の空手と共通点のある松林流と出合えた事は運命だ」と振り返る。

97年に初来沖し、興道館平良空手道場で汗を流した。滞在中の11月2日、流祖長嶺将真氏が亡くなり、葬儀にも参列した。プレステッド氏にとってこの旅は新たな人生の始まりとなり、滞在中は山根流の古武道も学び始めた。

あれから二十回余沖縄を訪れ、段位は現在7段。本部道場で25人、国内合計3カ所60人に指導。警察の業務、針術と空手の指導で充実した人生を送っている。伝統空手、古武道、競技空手のバランスを保ちつつ、取り組んでいる。

ニュージーランド空手連盟の役員として2020年東京五輪に向けた準備に余念はないが、来夏開催される第1回沖縄空手国際大会にも特別な思いを抱いている。南の国の空手家は、「空手発祥の地」で本場の技と魂を改めて心身に刻む。

Published on 2017/12/10

05 New Zealand

Whangaparoa Honbu Dōjō

Shaping the spirit and technic in the birthplace

Some Okinawans may remember of the agreement signed between the New Zealand Karate Federation, the Okinawa Prefecture and Okinawa City for a pre-camp in relation with the 2020 Tōkyō Olympics.

In this nation, the first karate dōjō is said to have been opened by a jūdōka in 1958. After that, New Zealanders trained in Japan and the Kyokushin, Shōtōkan and Gōjū-ryū styles became popular.

Born in Whangarei in 1956, Kevin Plaisted started training at the age of 19 years old at the Seikūkan, a Shōtōkan club run by Bob Dalton. After 3 years, Plaisted was graded 1st dan black belt.

Joining the police in 1979, he worked in the armed offenders squad before becoming a dog handler. Simultaneously, he participated in competitions and, becoming a national kumite champion, was selected to attend the 1986 World Karate Championships held in Sydney.

Leaving the police in 1988, Plaisted visited the Seikūkan honbu dōjō in Tōyama Prefecture and for 3 months, polished his skills. Back home in 89, he established his present dōjō in Stanmore Bay, opened an acupuncture clinic in his home in 1992 and rejoined the police serving as a firearms licensing manager.

In 1995, a karate delegation visited New Zealand to promote the first Okinawan world tournament. Considering the future of his karate, Plaisted attended a seminar taught by Taira Yoshitaka of Matsubayashi-ryū. Having found a true Okinawan karate style, Plaisted turned his heart and soul to the karate of Okinawa. "A number of things brought me to Okinawa. The fact that it was the origin of karate and the close connection to the early masters. I and my students also had an interest in kobudō. It was a fate to meet Matsubayashi-ryū, a style that has many similarities with my former style."

Visiting Okinawa for the first time in 1997, he trained at the Kōdōkan Taira Karate Dōjō. During his stay, the founder of the style Nagamine Shōshin passed away and he attended the funeral. According to him, this trip was the start of a new life as he also started to learn Yamanni-ryū kobudō.

After more than 20 visits to Okinawa, he is presently ranked 7th dan. 25 people train in his dōjō while some 60 more people train in 3 other dōjō.

Maintaining a good balance between tradition and competition, Plaisted is eagerly awaiting for the 2020 Tōkyō Olympics as well as the 1st Okinawa Karate International Tournament to be held next summer. During his next visit to Okinawa, he will make sure that the technic and spirit of the birthplace of karate are correctly engraved in his mind and body.

2019年12月29日

06 ニュージーランド 

逆境越え 普及と交流

剛柔流と琉球古武道

ハカで有名なラグビー代表オールブラックスの国、ニュージーランド。北島にあるハミルトン市は先住民マオリの村々があった場所だ。マオリの父を持つデレク・イングリッシュ氏(50)は18歳の頃、空手に入門した。

イングリッシュ氏が入った道場は、通学するワイカト大学のスポーツセンターにあった。当時の館長は剛柔流の東恩納盛男氏の組織に加盟していたテリー・ヒール氏。現在ヒール氏は、独立した団体「剛柔流空手道ニュージーランド」の代表として空手と格闘技を指導し、国内の剛柔流関係者と技術交流を深めている。

国際関係学アジア研究を学んだイングリッシュ氏は、1992年に英語指導助手に採用され、沖縄に滞在することになった。

師のヒール氏の紹介状を手に那覇市の東恩納道場を訪れたが、当時東恩納氏は不在。後日、同道場関係者の神村武之氏の協力で上原恒氏の道場に案内され、本場での稽古が始まった。

「最初の頃は上原道場で稽古していた神村先生の三段技と型だけで心身ともに消耗した」とイングリッシュ氏。後に館長の上原氏に預けられたが、「当初、上原先生は私の空手が貧弱だと感じ、古武道を教えることにした。私の動きをより流動的にすること、腰と丹田の使い方への意識と理解を発展させることが目的でした。私にとって未知のことでした」と振り返る。

組手を研究するイングリッシュ氏(左)=提供　English (left) studying kumite.

それから12年間、沖縄に住み稽古に励んだ。2004年の帰国後、剛柔流と古武道の指導に挑戦。08年には上原氏から師範免許を授与された。公認道場にも認められ、沖縄昭霊武術協会直心館NZが誕生した。

だが、母国での普及は容易ではなかった。「ニュージーランドの空手界は、他流会派や新たなアイデアに対して閉鎖的でした」。イングリッシュ氏は逆境にもめげず、ヒール氏の協力を受けて古武道の普及から名を作り、その後剛柔流の指導に戻った。「このプロセスを通し、多くの永続的な友情が生まれた」という。

父子家庭になり、6歳の娘を育てる、つらい時期もあった。電気技師として生計を立て、多くの苦労を乗り越えた。安定した暮らしを送る今、「当時は娘を育てることと武術が人生のすべてだった」と述懐する。

イングリッシュ氏は、剛柔流・琉球古武道信武館の6段。現在は自身の道場以外、ヒール氏の道場で空手・古武道、関連する2道場で空手、4道場で古武道を指導している。精力的な武術交流を通じ、これからも武術の真の価値である尊敬と友情を伝えていく。

Born in the city of Hamilton, on a Maori land located in the North Island, Derek English (50), whose father was Maori, began karate at the age of 18.

The dōjō that he joined was at the sports center of the University of Waikato where he studied. The instructor was Terry Hill, a former member of Higaonna Morio's Gōjū-ryū organization. Today, Hill continues to teach Gōjū-ryū and martial arts independently.

After studying international relations and Asian studies, English went to work and live in Okinawa in 1992 as an English language teacher. Upon his arrival in Naha City, he visited the Higaonna Dōjō in Makishi, Naha, with a letter of introduction from Hill, but Higaonna was not on the island at that time. Later, with the cooperation of Kamimura Takeshi, he was introduced to Uehara Kō's dōjō and started practicing in the birthplace of karate.

Published on 2019/12/29

06 New Zealand

Gōjū-ryū & Ryūkyū kobudō

Promotion and exchange after overcoming adversity

"First, Kamimura sensei, who did his personal training at the Uehara Karate Dōjō, proceeded to take me through sandangi and kata and I was completely exhausted at the end of the session," he recalls. Later, he was entrusted to Uehara sensei but "Uehara sensei thought my karate was poor and began to teach me kobudō instead. This was to make my movement more fluid and to develop my understanding and use of koshi (waist) and tanden (core); both very alien concepts to me at that time."

English lived in Okinawa for 12 years and deepened his practice. After returning home in 2004, he strived to teach Gōjū-ryū and kobudō as he was awarded a teaching license by Uehara. Being also recognized as an official dōjō, the Okinawa Shōrei Bujutsu Association – Gōjū-ryū Jikishinkan NZ was born.

However, it was not easy to spread his art in his motherland. "Initially, teaching karate in NZ was very difficult. The schools here are closed to different styles and ideas." In spite of adversity, English made a name for himself teaching kobudō with the cooperation of Hill and then started teaching Gōjū-ryū. "Doing so has created many lasting friendships" he says.

Becoming a solo parent and raising a 6-year-old daughter, there were difficult times. Making a living as an electrician, he overcame many hardships and now lives a stable life recalling that "At that time, raising my daughter and martial arts was my life."

English is now a 6th dan in Gōjū-ryū and has the same rank in Ryūkyū kobudō Shinbukan. Currently, in addition to his own dōjō, he teaches karate and kobudō at Hill's dōjō, karate at two other clubs and kobudō at four others. Through energetic martial arts exchanges, he continues to convey the true value of martial arts that are respect and friendship.

2018年11月25日

07 ニュージーランド

障がい超え 稽古励む

ダニーデン伝統空手研究所

喜友名諒選手らが金メダルを獲得したスペインの世界空手道選手権大会の同会場では、第3回パラ空手世界選手権大会も開催された。

健常者の第24回目の大会に比べ、パラ空手の競技大会は歴史が浅いかもしれない。だが、ハンディキャップを持ちながらも空手に真剣に取り込む人々は少なくない。

そんな中ニュージーランドには、障がいを乗り越えて、スポーツと沖縄空手を通して人生を謳歌(おうか)する男がいる。

1956年英国生まれのジョン・マラブル氏は11歳の時、外壁を登った際に落下した。結果的に脊髄の胸椎レベルを折り、下半身不随の障がい者となった。脊髄治療の名門病院で9カ月間入院し、アーチェリー、卓球、水泳を教わった。退院後は、学校に通いながら陸上競技や水泳に励んだ。

自己の身を守るには不利な境遇にいることを感じたマラブル氏は、イギリスの数道場を訪れ、入門を求めたが受け入れられず、書籍から護身術を学んだ。74年に家族と共にニュージーランドに移住し、下半身不随障がい者同志のスポーツに参加し続けた。そして、76年に極真系の空手道場への入門を果たした。

数年後、国際沖縄剛柔流空手道連盟(IOGKF)の東恩納盛男氏がニュージーランドを訪れた際に、3級だったマラブル氏は初めて沖縄空手を体験した。厳しい稽古の後、東恩納氏が自らの黒帯を外し、マラブル氏を呼んだ。昇段という意味ではなく、稽古に励む精神と決心に対する尊敬の表しとして帯が渡された。「帯を壁にかけて、継続を促すように」と言われた。

車いすに乗りながら指導するマラブル氏(左)=提供　Marrable (left) teaching while riding his wheelchair.

属する道場がIOGKFに加盟し、マラブル氏は80年に初段を取得した。その際に東恩納氏から「もう、私の帯を着けなさい」と言われ、涙を止めるのに苦労したという。

空手と同様に、ニュージーランドのパラ選手団代表としてフルマラソンや卓球に挑んでいた氏は84年に引退。しかし、再びチャレンジしようと2000年、スキー競技の実践と普及に挑んだ。06年に肩の大けがにより、再び手術を受けた。しかし、若い頃にいろいろな人に聞かされた「できない」という言葉は、全く浮かぶことなく回復することができたという。

10年前に行われた剛柔流の「世界武道祭」で、東恩納氏より招待され、見事な演武で観客に感動を与えた。そして16年に、発祥の地で尊敬する師より六段を授かった。

「充実した人生を生きる!」をモットーにマラブル氏は、漢(おとこ)としての道を歩み、多くの人に夢と希望を与え続ける。

Published on 2018/11/25

07 New Zealand

Dunedin Institute of Traditional Karate

Overcoming obstacles and training eagerly

At the same venue of the World Karate Championships in Spain, where Kiyuna Ryō won a gold medal, the 3rd Para-Karate World Championships were also held.

Compared to the 24th edition of senior championships, the para-karate competition may have a shorter history but yet, many people with disabilities practice and compete in karate very seriously.

Among them, there is a man in New Zealand who overcame obstacles and enjoys life through sports and Okinawa karate.

Born in England in 1956, John Marrable fell while climbing a cliff when he was 11 years old and, breaking his back, became a paraplegic. Hospitalized for nine months at a prestigious hospital for spinal cord treatment, he was taught archery, table tennis and swimming. After leaving the institution, he competed in athletics and swimming while attending school.

Feeling disadvantaged in regards to protecting himself, Marrable visited several karate clubs in England but was turned down and had to learn self-defense from books. In 1974, he moved to New Zealand with his family and continued to practice sports with people with lower body disabilities. Then, in 1976, he was allowed to join a Kyokushin karate dōjō.

A few years later, Marrable, who was still a 3rd kyū, experienced Okinawa karate for the first time on the occasion of Higaonna Morio's visit to New Zealand for a seminar. After a rigorous training session, Higaonna removed his own black belt and called Marrable. Although not meant as a promotion, he handed his belt to Marrable as an acknowledgement of his spirit and determination shown in practice. He was told to "put the belt on his wall and use it as a source of inspiration to keep practicing".

As the dōjō he belonged to joined Higaonna's organization, Marrable was promoted to 1st dan in 1980. At that time, Higaonna told him "Now you can wear my belt," and Marrable had a hard time controlling his emotions.

Along with karate, Marrable has been a member of the New Zealand paraplegic team for full marathon and table tennis before retiring in 1984. However, eager to challenge himself, he got into competitive skiing in 2000. In 2006, due to a serious shoulder injury, he underwent surgery again. However, as he believes there is no such word as "can't", he recovered.

At the "World Budōsai" held 10 years ago in Naha City, Marrable was invited by Higaonna and impressed the audience with a splendid demonstration. And in 2016, he was promoted to 6th dan in the birthplace of karate.

With the motto "Live life to the fullest", Marrable follows a man's path providing dreams and hopes to many other people.

2017年05月28日

08 ハワイ

精神修養 段位厳格に

ハワイ聖武館

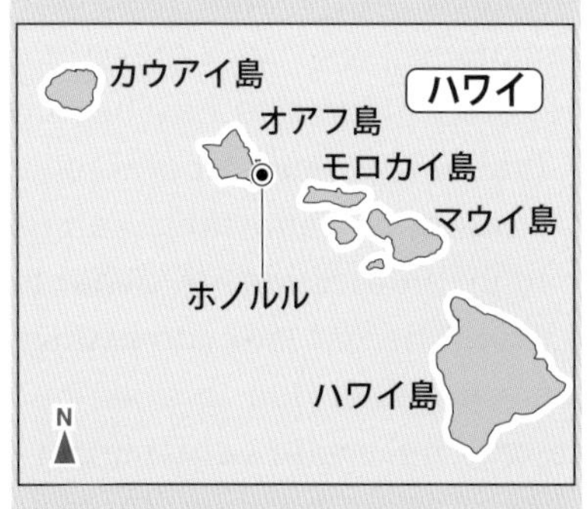

空手が初めてハワイで紹介されたのは1927年のこと。ハワイを訪れた首里手の大家、屋部憲通氏はホノルルとカウアイで指導し、海軍の漢那憲和氏と共にマウイ島も訪れ、演武を披露した。後に32年~34年、本部朝基や宮城長順の各氏などもこの島々を訪問し、指南した。

今日もハワイで空手は盛ん。だが、多くの流会派が存在するなか、移民し現在まで残って指導している日本人はたった2人。糸東流で兵庫県出身の小高忠三氏と沖縄県出身の照屋正一氏だ。

45年北谷生まれの照屋氏は、12歳のとき、極真の大山倍達氏の映画『猛牛と戦う空手』を見て、自宅近くに無償で指導していた島袋栄三氏から手ほどきを受けた。師が本島北部に移住したため、15歳で北谷町吉原に「聖武館」を開設した喜屋武朝徳氏の後継者の一人島袋善良氏の門をたたき、10年間修行に励んだ。伝統の型と共に組手も研究した。「当時流派を超えて、たくさんの人と組手の練習ができた。道場に米兵も多かったから、いろいろ試せた」と笑いながら思い出す照屋氏。

琉球大学卒業後、氏は琉球銀行に入行したが、2年後の70年にハワイに渡った。最初の頃は個人観光タクシーなどさまざまな仕事を行い、その後、総菜屋を設立し、ハワイ全島のスーパーマーケットに日本食のデリバリーをする会社の経営者となり、フード業界で成功した。

セミナーで突きの指導をする照屋正一氏(右)=提供　Teruya (right) instructing in a seminar

仕事の傍ら、ハワイに到着してからすぐにモイリイリコミュニティーセンターで空手の指導も始めた。現在、少林流ハワイ聖武館の館長として師の島袋善良氏の空手を継承している。師範代には、小児科の医師で長女のニーナ氏と実業家の長男の正樹氏がいる。

空手は、精神を育てる人間形成の道と信じる照屋氏。85年、段位にこだわるハワイ関係者と一線を画す氏は、ハワイ聖武館において階級形態を変えた。氏は「館長」のみを名乗り、道場では五段を最高段位とし、その後は錬士、教士、範士の称号のみと決めた。弟子には、ホノルル最高裁判所長、弁護士、成功した実業家や政治家などがいる。

2015年11月1日、45年間のコミュニティーに対する貢献が認められ、ハワイ沖縄連合会より「レガシーアワード賞」を受賞した。師の教え「芸は身を助くなり」を信じる照屋氏は、ハワイ2カ所、名古屋数カ所の支部道場を通して地道に頑張り続ける。

Hawaii Seibukan

Spiritual training and strictness regarding ranks

Karate was first introduced in Hawaii in 1927 when Shurite expert Yabu Kentsū instructed in Honolulu and Kauai. Later, from 1932 to 1934, Motobu Chōki and Miyagi Chōjun also visited these islands to teach karate.

Today, while karate is still popular in Hawaii, only two Japanese immigrants are still instructing there. They are Kodaka Chūzō, a Shitō-ryū master from Hyōgo prefecture, and Teruya Masakazu from Okinawa.

Born in Chatan in 1945, Teruya started karate with Shimabukuro Eizō, who was teaching free of charge near his home, after watching a movie with Ōyama Masutatsu. He was 12 years old. At 15 years old, after his master moved to the northern part of Okinawa's main island, he joined the Seibukan in Yoshihara, Chatan, the dōjō of Shimabukuro Zenryō. Training hard for 10 years, he studied kumite as well as traditional kata. "At that time, I was able to practice kumite with many people from other styles. As there were many American soldiers in the dōjō, I was able to try various techniques," recalls Teruya with a laugh.

After graduating from the University of the Ryūkyūs, he joined the Bank of the Ryūkyūs, but moved to Hawaii two years later in 1970. In his early days, he did a variety of jobs and then founded a delicatessen store to become the owner of a company that delivers Japanese food to supermarkets across Hawaii, thus succeeding in the food industry.

Since his arrival, he also started teaching karate at the Moiliili Community Center. Currently, as the director of the Shōrin-ryū Hawaii Seibukan, he teaches the karate of his master. His assistant instructors include his eldest daughter Nina and eldest son Masaki, respectively pediatrician and businessman.

Teruya believes that karate is a way of human formation that nurtures the spirit. In 1985, in order to separate himself from the Hawaiian karate world which was attaching too much importance to ranks, he changed his school's rank system. In this process, he chose to use only the name "kanchō" for himself, decided that the 5th dan would be the highest rank and that after 5th dan, titles would be only Renshi, Kyōshi, and Hanshi. Among his disciples can be found the Honolulu Chief Justice, lawyers, successful businessmen and politicians.

On November 1, 2015, Teruya received the "Legacy Award" from the Hawaii United Okinawa Association for his contribution to the community for 45 years. Believing in his teacher's saying "Art brings bread," he continues to teach diligently in his two Hawaiian dōjō and several branch dōjō in Nagoya.

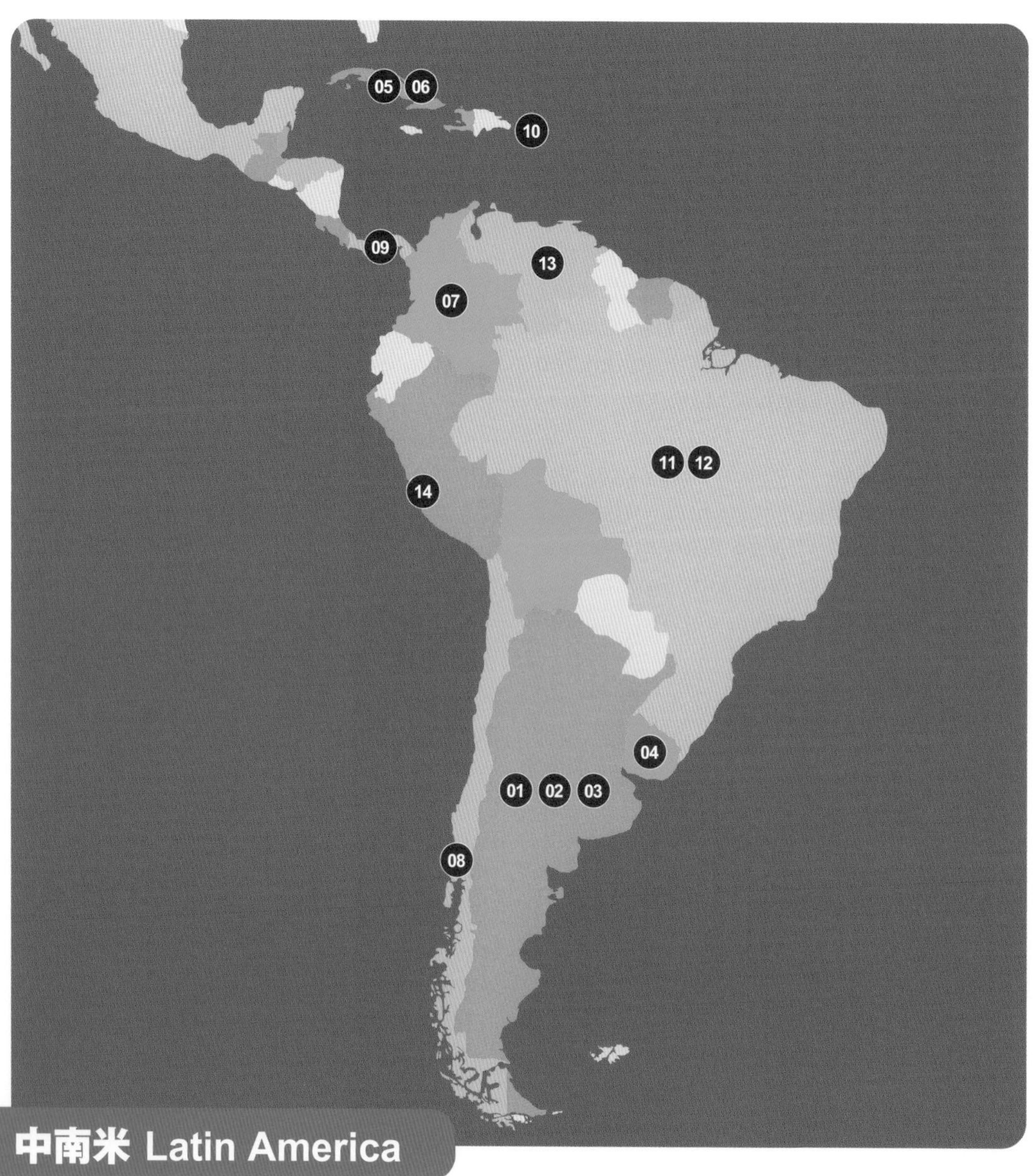

中南米 Latin America

中南米
Latin America

2017年04月09日

01 アルゼンチン

弟子7万人に技継承

宮里道場

南米において、アルゼンチンは見逃すことのできない空手王国の一つだ。タンゴの国として知られているこの国への沖縄系の移民は1918年から始まり、現在、約3万5千人の沖縄系の人たちが暮らしている。

約100年の間、多くの空手家もこの国へ移民した。この中には歴史を刻んだ人として、24年に移民した武士松村宗棍(昆)の唐手を引く祖堅方範氏、38年に移民した小林流の比嘉仁達氏と、県指定無形文化財保持者故宮平勝哉氏の右腕で59年に移民した宮里昌栄氏がいる。

28年西原町生まれの宮里氏は、13歳のころ、空手に入門し、47年に小林流志道館の宮平勝哉氏に師事した。そして、59年、家族と共に南米へ移民した。

当時31歳の宮里氏は、コルドバ市でクリーニング店を経営しながら自宅で稽古を続けた。本人いわく、「指導をするつもりはなかったが、ある日系人の行事で演武をしたら、指導するよう頼まれた」という。

その催し物とは、59年5月25日、コルドバ市日系人協会が主催した演武で、これが宮里氏の空手活動展開の原点だった。63年から道場を開き、日系人以外にも多くの地元の人に指導し、小林流志道館の技と理念の本格的な普及に努めた。78年、同市で現在の「宮里道場」を開設。巨大なこの道場は675平方メートルの広さで、100人以上が同時に稽古できる施設である。そこから、育った多くの指導者がさらに道場を開設し、宮里道場協会で空手を習った弟子の総数は7万人以上にも上る。

1959年、アルゼンチン・コルドバで演武する故宮里昌栄氏(左)=提供
Miyazato Shōei demonstrating in Cordoba in 1959.

宮里氏の功績を認めたコルドバ市は「市民に必要な組織」として、2007年に記念モニュメントを建てた。

地元メディアでインタビューされた宮里氏は、このように語っていた。「明日死んでもいい。しかし、間違いなく、私が行ってきた何かが弟子の良心に残る、何かが受け継がれる。だから、うれしい」。最後まで指導し続けた宮里氏は、13年7月2日に85歳で亡くなった。

宮里道場協会の会長だった氏を引き継いだのは次男の宮里昌利氏(63)。現在の組織は、アルゼンチン24州のうち13州に73道場を持ち、海外には6カ国に14の支部がある。本場沖縄との交流を深めながら宮里道場は、小林流志道館の空手を同国と海外で継承し続けている。

(右)アルゼンチンの道場で指導する宮里昌利氏(提供)　Miyazato Masatoshi instructing.

Published on 2017/4/9

01 Argentina

Miyazato Dōjō

Passing on the art to 70,000 students

Within South America, Argentina is unmistakably one of the karate kingdoms. Okinawan immigration to the country of tango began in 1918 and today, some 35,000 Okinawans live there.

During a 100 years span, many karateka also immigrated to this country. Among those who paved the way are Soken Hōhan, who learned the martial art of Bushi Matsumura Sōkon and emigrated in 1924, Higa Jintatsu of Shōrin-ryū who immigrated in 1938 and Miyazato Shōei, who immigrated in 1959 as the right-hand man of late Miyahira Katsuya.

At that time, 31-year-old Miyazato continued to practice at his home while running a laundry shop in Cordoba. According to him, "I didn't intend to teach, but when I performed at a Nikkei event, I was asked to instruct."

This particular event was a demonstration hosted by the Cordoba City Nikkei (Japanese descendants) Association on May 25th, 1959. It was the origin of Miyazato's karate activities in Argentina. After opening a dōjō in 1963, he instructed many Japanese descendants and locals, and earnestly strived to spread the techniques and ideas of the Shōrin-ryū Shidōkan.

In 1978, he opened the current Miyazato Dōjō in Cordoba. This huge dōjō of 675 square meters allows more than 100 people to practice at the same time. From there, many instructors started opening their own dōjō, and the total number of disciples who have learned karate within the Miyazato Dōjō Association rises to more than 70,000.

Acknowledging Miyazato's achievements, the city of Cordoba built a commemorative monument in 2007, emphasizing that his association is "an organization necessary for citizens." In addition, two years later, during the 50th anniversary of the opening of the dōjō, the Argentine government declared that it was "a celebration of national interest." On the Japanese side, in 2011, Miyazato Shōei received a certificate of commendation from the Minister of Foreign Affairs.

Interviewed by the local media, Miyazato said: "I can die tomorrow. But with no doubt, something I've done will remain in the conscience of my disciples, something will be inherited. Therefore, I'm happy." Miyazato, who continued to teach until the end, died on July 2, 2013 at the age of 85.

His second son, Miyazato Masatoshi (63), inherited the chairmanship of the Miyazato Dōjō Association. The current organization has 73 dōjō in 13 of the 24 Argentine states and 14 branches in 6 countries abroad. While deepening exchanges with Okinawa, the Miyazato Dōjō continues to inherit the karate of the Shōrin-ryū Shidōkan both in Argentina and overseas.

2018年12月09日

02 アルゼンチン

伝統の技と精神守る

小林流武徳館

今年の夏、ブラジル、アルゼンチン、ボリビアの3カ国で沖縄県人移民110周年記念式典が行われた。アルゼンチンの会場となったブエノスアイレスでも空手は盛んだが、首都から350キロ北西にあるサンタフェ州ロサリオ市でも沖縄空手が継承されている。

1960年ロサリオ生まれのカルロス・マグナバッチ氏は、11歳の時テコンドーに入門した。3カ月後、クラスが中止となり空手に転向した。「ロサリオには、空手道場は二つしかなく、その一つであった究道館に入門した」。

青年時代は、大工屋で働いていた。79年仕事中に人さし指と親指の指骨を失った。その事故による障害を乗り越えて稽古に励んだ。80年代初期、職を変えたマグナバッチ氏は郵便配達員になった。そして、大好きな空手の指導にも挑んだ。現在、生まれ故郷のロサリオで毎日、仕事を終えて空手の技と精神を伝えている。現在50人余りが沖縄空手を学んでいる。

マグナバッチ氏の空手の足跡には、さまざまな空手家たちとの出会いが刻まれている。首里手系の空手を南米で普及したホルヘ・ブリンクマン氏に弟子入りした。「ブリンクマン氏は（アルゼンチン国民で）初の黒帯を締めた男。彼の下で89年に亡くなるまで師事した」と振り返る。90年には沖縄を訪れ、ブリンクマン氏にも師事した少林流拳真館の喜瀬富盛氏の指導も受けた。

門下生と共に稽古に打ち込んでいるマグナバッチ氏（後列左から4人目）＝提供　Magnavachi (fourth from the left in the back row) with his students.

96年に沖縄を訪れた際に、沖縄市にある武徳館コザ道場の泉久氏を通じ、故儀武息一氏を紹介された。「運命的な出会いだった。1カ月間、儀武先生の下で教わり、弟子入りが認められた」。現在沖縄を除いて世界で米国、南アフリカ、アルゼンチンの3カ国しか沖縄空手道小林流武徳館協会の支部は存在しない。

「今日アルゼンチンでは、高段が売買され、新たな流派が作られ、稽古よりお金を中心に活動する組織も少なくない。この環境の中、自分に合う指導者を見つけることが不可欠。正しく教わった空手は、良い人をつくる」と説く。

マグナバッチ氏自身、人生のすべてが空手に関連付けられているという。「空手は武芸であり、その学習と訓練は決して終わらない。各段階で成熟すれば、空手を理解することになると信じている」。

これまで7度、沖縄を訪れているマグナバッチ氏は、2011年に故儀武氏から8段を授与された。入門を許され、道に導いた亡き師の姿を胸に、2代目会長の儀武誠氏の下で誇り高く小林流武徳館の空手を守り続けている。

This summer, ceremonies to commemorate the 110th anniversary of Okinawan immigration were held in Brazil, Argentina and Bolivia. 350 km northwest of the Argentinean capital, Rosario in the Santa Fe Province was a venue for the ceremonies. There, Okinawa karate is also being passed on.

Born in Rosario in 1960, Carlos Magnavachi began his martial career with taekwondo at the age of 11. Three months later, his class being canceled, he switched to karate. "There were only two dōjō in Rosario, and I chose to enter one of them, a Kyūdōkan dōjō."

During his youth, Magnavachi worked at a carpenter's shop. In 1979, he lost

Published on 2018/12/9

02 Argentina

Shōrin-ryū Butokukan

Protecting traditional skills and spirit

his index finger and thumb phalanges while working but overcame the obstacles caused by the accident and kept training hard. In the early 80's, he changed his job to become a postman and kept teaching his passion, karate. Today, in his hometown of Rosario, he daily conveys the skills and spirit of karate after his work to more than 50 people.

Along his karate path, Magnavachi has encountered various karateka. He became a disciple of Jorge Brinkmann, a pioneer of Shōrin-ryū in South America. "Mr. Brinkman was the first man to wear a black belt in Argentina. I studied under him until his death in 1989," he recalls. In 1990, he visited Okinawa and trained under Kise Fusei of the Shōrin-ryū Kenshinkan, an instructor of Brinkmann.

When he visited Okinawa in 1996, he was introduced to the late Gibu Sokuichi through Izumi Hisashi, head of the Butokukan Koza Dōjō in Okinawa City. "It was a predestined encounter. I was taught by Gibu sensei for a month and was allowed to become his student." Today, except for Okinawa, there are only three branches of the Shōrin-ryū Butokukan Association in the world: the USA, South Africa and Argentina.

"Today in Argentina, high-ranking grades are bought and sold, new systems are created, and there are many organizations that focus on money rather than practice. In such a world, it is essential to find a leader who suits you. Correctly taught, karate nurtures good people," Magnavachi explains.

In his case, he says that everything in life is associated with karate. "Karate is a martial art, and its study and practice never end. I believe that as someone matures at each stage, he/she will better understand karate."

Having visited Okinawa seven times so far, Magnavachi was awarded the 8th dan by Gibu Sokuichi in 2011. With the spirit of his deceased master who accepted him in his school and led him on the path, he is proudly protecting the karate of the Butokukan under the guidance of its second chairman, Gibu Makoto.

2021年03月28日

03 アルゼンチン

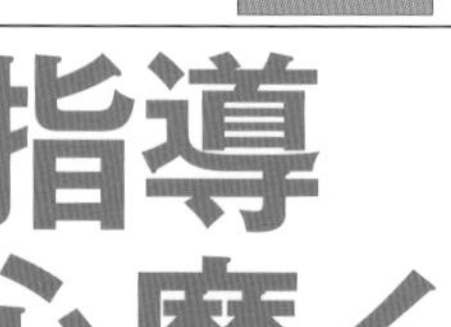

連日指導 技と心磨く

マルティネス道場

沖縄に本部を置く空手・古武道の支部道場は世界各国に広がっているが、支部道場が自国内で一つにまとまって全国組織として活動する国はアルゼンチンとインドの2カ国のみだ。

長い移民の歴史を有すアルゼンチンには15の沖縄空手・古武道の流会派で組織する沖縄空手古武道の協会がある。初代会長は県出身でブエノスアイレス都市圏に道場を構え、松林流を指導する赤嶺茂秀氏。現在は小林流のルイス・レモス氏が代表を引き継いでいる。

1970年ブエノスアイレス生まれのラモン・マルティネス氏は松林流大田会の代表として活動し、協会組織に加盟している。12歳の頃に空手を始め、糸東流と琉球古武道の道場に入門した。

仕事で移動が増えたため、道場の多い小林流志道館系の道場で稽古を続けたマルティネス氏。分岐点となったのは99年だ。松林流系を指導するカルロス・アマロ氏の道場に入門し、基本を学んだ。その時「伝統と技術の多様性のあるこの流派に魅了された」という。

松林流々祖・長嶺将真氏の空手の研究を重ねるマルティネス氏は、2012年に松林流を指南する米在住の大田栄八氏に会い、弟子入りした。「先生の気取ったところがないこと、優れた技術

稽古を終え、充実した表情のマルティネス氏（後列右端）と門下生＝提供
Martinez (far right in the back row) after the lesson.

力、そして指導法が魅力的でした。先生と交流を深めると、素晴らしい人に出会えたことが分かる」と喜びを明かす。

現在、北部のサンタフェ州にあるプエルト・ヘネラル・サン・マルティンに住む。その名の由来はアルゼンチンなどの国々をスペインから独立させた軍人ホセ・デ・サン・マルティンだという。

2001年4月に開設した道場では5歳から64歳の男女80人が稽古に励んでいる。マルティネス氏は建設会社の管理職として働きながら毎日指導。「仕事や勉強のため平日に来られない人もいるので週末にもクラスを開く」。大田氏が指揮する大田会亜国の代表として国内の4支部道場で空手と古武道も指導している。

キャリア35年のマルティネス氏は6段。2017年、夢だった空手の本場への旅を実現し、第5回沖縄空手国際セミナーに参加した。「言葉の壁を何とか乗り越え、素晴らしい経験だった。また間違いなく沖縄に行く」と充実した稽古を振り返り、次回の訪沖に胸を躍らせる。

今年はマルティネス道場開設20周年。妻、2人の子どもも稽古に励んでいるという。マルティネス氏は空手が友情を育むと信じ、仲間たちと技法や精神面を磨き、精進の道を歩む。

Published on 2021/3/28

03 Argentina

Martinez Dōjō

Teaching every day to polish the skills and mind

Dōjō of karate and kobudō that follow a headquarters located in Okinawa are present all over the world, but there are only two countries in the world where many of these branches are united and operate as a national organization: Argentina and India.

Argentina is home to an Okinawa karate and kobudō association which gathers 15 groups with honbu dōjō in Okinawa. The first chairman was Akamine Shigehide, an Okinawan who teaches Matsubayashi-ryū in the Buenos Aires metropolitan area. Currently, Shōrin-ryū Luis Lemos has succeeded him as the chair person.

Born in Buenos Aires in 1970, Ramon Martinez is the representative of the Matsubayashi-ryū Ōta-kai and a member of the national association. He started karate at the age of twelve by entering a Shitō-ryū and Ryūkyū kobudō dōjō.

Because of his work and the many business trips involved, Martinez continued to practice in Shōrin-ryū Shidōkan dōjō that were well spread all over the country.

The turning point occurred in 1999 when he entered the dōjō of Carlos Amaro who had practiced Matsubayashi-ryū with Akamine. Learning the basics of this style, Martinez was "fascinated by this system rich of a long tradition and a wide variety of techniques."

Having researched the karate of the founder Nagamine Shōshin, Martinez met Ōta Eihachi, a Matsubayashi-ryū instructor living in the USA, and became his student in 2012. "Sensei's simplicity, great technical prowess and ability to transmit was fascinating. When I got to know him more deeply, I realized I had met a great person."

Currently, Martinez lives in Puerto General San Martin in the northern province of Santa Fe. The name comes from General Don José de San Martín, considered the Father of the Nation in Argentina.

At the dōjō he opened in April 2001, 80 men and women between the ages of 5 to 64 are training together. While working as an administrator in a construction company, Martinez teaches every day. "Even Saturdays and Sundays, since some adults can only train on weekends due to work or studies," he says.

With 35 years of karate, Martinez is now a 6th dan. In 2017, he realized his dream of travelling to the birthplace of karate and participated in the 5th Okinawa Karate International Seminar. He says, "Despite the language barrier, thanks to the good disposition of the Okinawan people, it was a wonderful experience. I will definitely go to Okinawa again."

This year marks the 20th anniversary of the opening of the Martinez Dōjō. Together with his wife and two children who also practice with him, Martinez believes that karate fosters friendship and thus goes on refining the technique and spirit of karate with his dōjō members.

2018年02月25日

04 ウルグアイ

武術交流 友情を育む

空手古武道協会

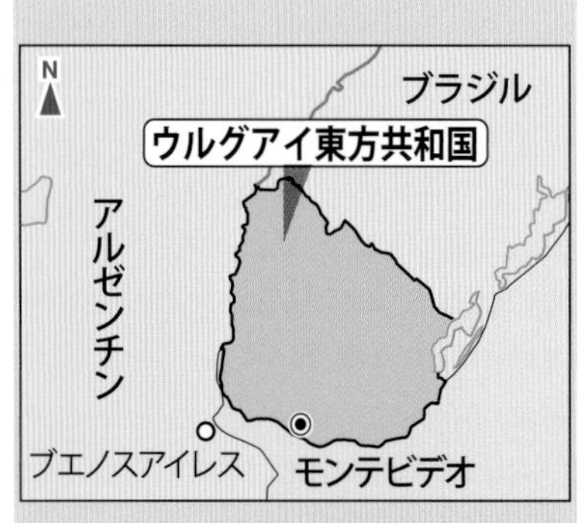

アルゼンチンとブラジルに囲まれたウルグアイは1828年に誕生し、ヨーロッパ系白人が総人口の85%余を占めるといわれる。

この国で空手を広めた人物は、南米に剛柔流の普及に努めた那覇出身の赤嶺誠一氏。戦前、剛柔流の比嘉世幸氏の指導を受け、57年にブラジルに移り「健心館」を開設。62年にはウルグアイにも空手を紹介している。

ラドコ・バルカー氏は、スロバキア(旧チェコスロバキア)で1953年に生まれた。父は農業用原子力エネルギーの科学者で研究開発のため、68年に家族と共にウルグアイを訪れた。4年間の契約終了後バルカー家は、同国への移住を決意した。

17歳のころ、バルカー氏は知り合いの薦めで健心館に入門した。78~86年、ブラジルのサンパウロ市を訪れ、赤嶺氏にも師事した。その後、首都モンテビデオで本部道場を開設した。↗

しかし、バルカー氏は、さらなる技の向上と空手のルーツを探し求めていた。07年に、剛柔流国際空手古武道連盟(比嘉世幸氏創設)に所属するスロバキア人ラディスラブ・クレメンティス氏と出会い、新たな研究が始まった。

型の技を解説するバルカー氏(中央)=提供　Balcar (center) explaining a kata's technique.

その後、ウルグアイに同連盟の高段者を招いて講習会を開き、世界各地で行われるセミナーにも参加した。本場沖縄には4回訪れ、又吉清徳氏、喜友名朝有氏に師事した。バルカー氏の熱心な取り組みが認められ、16年に空手8段・古武道3段に昇段した。

現在ウルグアイの本部道場で50人が練習し、国内の7支部のほか、チリ、スペイン、ブラジル、メキシコでも指南している。「ウルグアイでは、スポーツ系やフルコンタクト系の空手が非常に多い。しかし人間・精神・論理性の価値ある伝統空手も保たれている。系統や流派より大切なのは、武術交流を通じて生まれる友情」と説く。

多くの武術家が文武両道で精進するように、モンテビデオ市の土木技師として働くバルカー氏は、50年前からギター演奏も続けるアーティストでもある。これまでクラシック音楽や、ボサノバ・タンゴなどのラテン音楽のCD14作品をリリースしている。

「世界中の多くの人々と出会い、文化と習慣に接触することは大きな恵み。武道から学んだ自制心と忍耐力も同様です」。自身の活動すべてを愛し、多忙な日々を送る中、空手は究道無限と信じ、研究と指導の道を歩み続ける。

Surrounded by Argentina and Brazil, Uruguay was born in 1828, and it is said that white Europeans make up more than 85% of the total population.

The person who spread karate in this country and South America is Akamine Seiichi. From Naha, he studied under Higa Sekō before WWII, moved to Brazil in 1957, opened the Kenshinkan and introduced karate to Uruguay in 1962.

Radko Balcar was born in Slovakia (former Czechoslovakia) in 1953. A scientist expert in nuclear energy for agronomy, his father was sent to Uruguay in 1968 for research development and the Balcar family followed. After four years, the family decided to stay in Uruguay.

Published on 2018/2/25

04 Uruguay

Association of Karate and Kobudō

Martial arts exchanges fostering friendship

At the age of seventeen, Radko Balcar entered the Kenshinkan on the recommendation of a friend. From 1978 to 1986, he also visited São Paulo in Brazil to study under Akamine Seiichi. Later, he opened the national honbu dōjō in the capital Montevideo.

However, Balcar was looking for further improvements in his technique and the roots of karate. In 2007, he met Slovakian Ladislav Klementis who belonged to the Gōjū-ryū International Karate Kobudō Federation founded by Higa Sekō. That was the beginning of new researches.

After that, Balcar invited high-ranking instructors of the federation to Uruguay to hold seminars and also participated in seminars held all over the world. Visiting Okinawa four times, he studied under Matayoshi Seitoku and Kiyuna Chōyū and in recognition of his enthusiastic efforts, he was promoted to 8th dan in karate and 3rd dan in kobudō in 2016.

Currently, 50 people practice at the Uruguayan honbu dōjō, and in addition to the seven branches in the country, Balcar also instructs in Chile, Spain, Brazil and Mexico. He points out that, "In Uruguay, competitive and full contact karate are extremely popular. However, traditional karate is maintained for its high human, spiritual and ethical values. More than style, what is important is the friendship created through martial arts exchanges."

Like many martial artists devote themselves to Bunbu Ryōdō, Balcar, who works as a civil engineer in Montevideo, is also an artist who has been playing the guitar for 50 years. He has edited 14 CDs of classical music and Latin rhythms.

"Karate brought me many friends in many countries and discovering their culture and customs is a blessing. And so are discipline and patience that I was able to develop through martial arts." While loving all his activities and living a busy life, he believes that karate is endless, and continues his research and guidance.

沖縄県出身のキューバへの移民は、110年前の1907年にさかのぼるという。アンティル諸島の真珠と呼ばれる同国では、1930年代に中国系の武術が紹介されたといわれているが、空手の導入は65年とされている。64年、漁業指導のためキューバを訪れた那覇市出身で松林流の門下生小波蔵政昭氏が翌年空手指導を始めた。その後、喜屋武朝徳氏の流れをくむ本土系空手の常心門もキューバに広く普及した。

59年キューバ革命後、スポーツを行うことは国民の権利という政策が実施され、スポーツのように空手も盛んに楽しまれるようになった。

54年生まれ、愛称"フレッディー"で知られているアルフレド=ハシント・ロジャス=タマヨ氏は、22歳の時、多くのキューバ人のように常心門に入門した。79年に道場を開設し指導に当たった。その後98年、剛柔流の比嘉世幸氏の指導を受けたキモ・ウオール氏の弟子、プエルトリコ出身の5段ハイメ・アコスト氏がキューバに剛柔流を紹介し、ロジャス=タマヨ氏も宮城長順氏を開祖とする剛柔流に転向した。

後に、本場の剛柔流を学びたいキューバ人は自

2016年にキューバで開催されたセミナーで。指導した瀬名波重敏氏(右から2人目)とロジャス=タマヨ氏(同3人目)=提供　In Cuba in 2016, Freddy (3rd from the right) with Senaha Shigetoshi (2nd from the right).

2017年11月26日

05 キューバ

病乗り越え若者指導

剛柔館

然と小波蔵氏に相談した。2000年、小波蔵氏は、那覇中学校の同級生で剛柔流琉翔会会長の瀬名波重敏氏を伴いキューバを訪れ、ロジャス=タマヨ氏は琉翔会に弟子入りし、道場の看板も変えた。02年、1997年に創立されたキューバ剛柔流空手協会の会長に就任し、現在に至っている。

ロジャス=タマヨ氏にとって、本場との交流を実現したのは奇跡でもあるが、ある意味、嵐の前の静けさだったとも言える。

2006年52歳の時、心血管虚脱にあった氏は、左足と左手が不自由になりてんかん病もかかった。現在では、ほぼ完全回復を果たしたが、木工職人で左利きの氏は、まだうまく絵を描けない。しかし、空手をやめず、投薬中であっても、琉翔会加盟23道場で約2千人に指導を続けている。また、キューバ国立芸術大学においても空手を指南している。

「息子2人の誕生という幸せな一時期を除いて、空手は私の人生に最高の瞬間を与え続けてくれた。病の中、空手はリハビリに大いなる助けとなった」と語る"フレッディー"。

日々の人生に感謝しながら、いかなる苦しみも乗り越えられるよう若者たちの体と精神を築くことを使命に、空手の素晴らしさを伝え続けている。

Published on 2017/11/26

05 Cuba

Gōjū-Kan

Teaching the youth while overcoming illness

Immigration from Okinawa to Cuba dates back to 1907. In the country called the Pearl of the Antilles, it is said that Chinese martial arts were introduced in the 1930s, but the introduction of karate started in 1965. In 1964, Kohagura Masaaki, a Matsubayashi-ryū karateka from Naha City who visited Cuba to teach fisheries techniques, started instructing karate the following year. After that, the mainland karate system of Jōshinmon widely spread in the island.

After the Cuban Revolution in 1959, the policy that practicing sports was the right of the people was implemented and karate became popular among other sports.

Born in 1954 and known by the nickname "Freddy," Alfredo Jacinto Roja Tamayo began his career in karate at the age of 22 by joining - like many other Cubans - a Jōshinmon dōjō. He opened his own dōjō in 1979 and started teaching. In 1998, Gōjū-ryū expert Kimo Wall's student 5th dan Jaime Acosta, from Puerto Rico, came to Cuba to introduce Gōjū-ryū and Freddy decided to switch to the style founded by Miyagi Chōjun.

Along the way, as Cubans wanted to learn Gōjū-ryū from the source, they naturally consulted with Kohagura. In 2000, Kohagura visited Cuba with Senaha Shigetoshi, his classmate from Naha Junior High School and the chairman of the Gōjū-ryū Ryūshōkai. Having decided to join the Ryūshōkai, Freddy changed the signboard of his dōjō. In 2002, he became the chairman of the Cuban Association of Gōjū-ryū Karate, which was founded in 1997, and holds this post to this day.

For Freddy, it was a miracle to be able to develop a relation with the cradle of karate, but in another way, like the expression says, it was "the calm before the storm".

At the age of 52 in 2006, Freddy suffered from a cardiovascular accident. Today, he has almost fully recovered, but the woodworker and left-handed man he is still can't paint well. However, he has not stopped karate, and even while taking medication, he continues to teach about 2,000 people at the 23 Ryūshōkai dōjō in the country. He also teaches karate at the National University of Arts in Cuba.

"Except for the happy moments that were the birth of my two sons, karate continues to give me the best moments in life. In my illness, karate was also a great help for my rehabilitation," says Freddy.

While appreciating daily life, Freddy continues to convey the charms of karate with the mission of building the body and spirit of the youth so that they can overcome any kind of suffering.

2019年08月11日

06 キューバ

次世代へ魂 信念貫く

セリマル道場

キューバに初めて空手を紹介したのは、那覇市出身で松林流の小波蔵政昭氏。しかし1969年の帰国以降、喜屋武朝徳氏の流れをくむ本土系少林流常心門の空手が拡大、普及した。

72年ハバナ生まれのエルネスト・グズマン氏は、6歳から常心門の道場に入門し、80年に同系のエウスタキオ・ロハス氏に師事した。「沖縄空手に興味が湧いたのは、87年頃、映画『ベストキッド』を見たとき。その後、欧州の雑誌を通して喜屋武朝徳や松林流流祖の長嶺将真先生のことを知り、発祥の地沖縄に目を向けた」と振り返る。

89年に稽古場のセリマル道場を開き、翌年から故ラウル・リソ氏の下でも研さんを積んだ。リソ氏は日本で空手を学んだキューバの空手の父の一人だ。常心門に所属しつつ当初は小波蔵氏に手ほどきを受けていた。リソ氏はグズマン氏に長嶺氏の著作を渡し、沖縄空手の追求を勧めた。↗

グズマン氏は師のロハス氏と共に松林流の原理と稽古法を研究し、少しずつ少林流である常心門から松林流系の空手に移り変わっていった。

2002年に行われた長嶺宗家追悼演武大会の際に、グズマン氏は初めて来沖し、本場で稽古した。

大田栄八氏（前列右から3人目）とグズマン氏（同4人目）を囲む協会のメンバー＝提供　Ōta Eihachi (third from the right in the front row) and Guzmán (fourth from the right) surrounded by the members of the association.

翌年、キューバ松林流空手道協会が設立され、グズマン氏は技術責任者、ロハス氏は有段者会々長に任命された。08年以降は米在住で同系統の大田栄八氏に師事している。

キューバでは、スポーツ、文化、武道は無料で教えられるケースが多い。錬士7段のグズマン氏は、陶磁器産業の協同組合経営者兼陶磁器士として生計を立てながら、空手と古武道をボランティアで指導する。メンバーは年間60数ペソ（日本円で300円位）で空手を学べる。

同協会本部のセリマル道場には、有段者135人、5歳から50人余りの少年少女が登録。さらに20年間に渡り、同協会は国内50の市町村で137の小中高や大学で空手を教え、現在16地方中13地方58道場で1068人が同系統を学ぶ。その内80%は児童という。

「空手道は自身の人生のすべての行動と側面を導く月明かりです。礼儀、清廉潔白、努力と『平和の武』である空手の精神を普及することが次世代への大きな贈り物」とグズマン氏は信じる。

今年の11月、道場開設30周年記念行事が行われる。「普及が進んでいても決して満足できません。社会の幸福と調和のためにもっと努力すべきです」と決意を新たにしている。

Published on 2019/8/11

06 Cuba

Celimar Dōjō

Passing on the spirit to the next generation

A Matsubayashi-ryū karateka from Naha City, Kohagura Masaaki was the first to introduce karate to Cuba. After his return to Japan in 1969, the mainland Japanese karate system of Jōshinmon spread in the country.

Born in La Havana in 1972, Ernesto Guzmán entered a Jōshinmon dōjō at the age of six, studying under Eustaquio Rojas in 1980. He recalls, "I became interested in Okinawa karate when I saw the movie 'The Karate Kid' around 1987. After that, I learned about Kyan Chōtoku and Nagamine Shōshin, the founder of Matsubayashi-ryū, through a western magazine and turned my attention to Okinawa."

Opening the Celimar Dōjō in 1989, he also studied under the late Raúl Rizo, one of the fathers of Cuban karate. Although he belonged to Jōshinmon, Rizo was initially taught by Kohagura. Rizo handed over Nagamine's book to Guzmán and recommended to him the pursuit of Okinawa karate.

Together with Rojas, Guzmán studied the principles and training methods of Matsubayashi-ryū, and gradually changed from the Shōrin-ryū system of Jōshinmon to the karate of Nagamine Shōshin.

On the occasion of the 2002 Nagamine Sōke Memorial, Guzmán visited Okinawa for the first time and trained in the birthplace of karate.

The following year, the Cuban Matsubayashi-ryū Karatedō Association was established, with Guzmán in charge of technical matters and Rojas as the head of black belts association. Since 2008, the group trains under Ōta Eihachi, an Okinawan instructor who lived in the USA.

In Cuba, sports, culture and martial arts are often taught free of charge. Guzmán, a 7th dan Renshi, volunteers to teach karate and kobudō while earning a living as a ceramist. Members can learn karate for 60 pesos a year.

At the Celimar Dōjō, 135 black belt holders and about 50 members from the age of 5 to 50 are registered. For the last 20 years, the association has taught karate at 137 elementary, junior high and senior high schools and universities, and currently 1068 people are studying Matsubayashi-ryū in 58 dōjō located in 13 of the 16 Cuban regions. 80% of them are children.

Guzmán believes that "Karatedō is the moonlight that guides all the actions and aspects of my life. The popularization of courtesy, cleanliness, the sense of effort and the spirit of karate, a 'martial art of peace' is a great gift for the next generations."

This November, an event will commemorate the 30th anniversary of the opening of the Celimar dōjō. As a renewal of his determination, he says "I am very happy with the development of our school in Cuba, although never satisfied. We can do more for the happiness and harmony of our society."

2020年10月25日

07 コロンビア

礼を重んじ 文武両道

マコト道場

南米において日本人移民が少なかった国はチリ、ウルグアイ、ベネズエラ、エクアドルとコロンビアなどがあると言われている。

コロンビアの場合、1954年に、いったん中断した日本との外交関係が再開。翌年、柔道が初めて国内で指導されたという。

空手については、医者のハイメ・フルナンデス・ガルソン氏が、アルゼンチンに進学した際、沖縄小林流空手を習い、1963年の帰国時、空手を初めて披露したと記録されている。67年に首都ボゴタで同国初の道場も開設されている。

その3年後にカリブ海に面するカルタヘナ生まれのロベルト・ザパタ氏は、14歳のころ、空手道場に入門した。同道場は74年同国で支部を設置した本土系の剛柔流拳昌会に加盟していたため、ザパタ氏は最初から剛柔流開祖・宮城長順氏の流れをくむ空手を学んだことになる。↗

約16年間剛柔流を修練したザパタ氏は2000年ごろ、東恩納盛男氏の存在を知り、3年後沖縄剛柔流に転向した。08年には国際沖縄剛柔流空手道連盟のコロンビア支部長に任命されている。

現在、ザパタ氏はサンティアゴ・デ・カリ(通称カリ)に住んでいる。その地で03年に「マコト道場」を開き、空手家でもある妻と共に剛柔流を指導している。「道場名は、武士道の誠の意味が好きで

道場で型「セイユンチン」を指導するザパタ氏(中央)=提供　Zapata (center) teaching the kata Seyunchin in his dōjō.

決めた。人は、言葉と行動において真実であるべきだと思う。要するに正直に生きること」と説明する。国内にある5支部道場でも指南している。19年に2度目の来沖の際、5段に昇段した。

ザパタ氏は、デザイン会社を立ち上げグラフィックデザイナーとして生計を立てている。長年折り紙を学んできた妻は、商品開発を務め、道場生と保護者向けに折り紙のワークショップも開催している。

当初ザパタ氏は護身術を求め空手を習い始めたという。「今はさまざまな理由で稽古に励む者がいる。私は護身術としての空手を究めながら、稽古を通して得られる健康が空手のもう一つのメリットと感じている。その両側面を中心に指導したい」と意気込む。

居合道にも取り組むザパタ氏は究道無限という理念を大切にする。「多様な知識は成長に役立つ。居合道は空手とは目的の異なる武道だが、技を行う際の呼吸、残心、演武中の着眼など空手との類似点もある」

ザパタ氏は武道と芸術に人生を託し、礼を重んじる伝統空手が自己啓発に導くことを信じて、文武両道の活動に専心する。

Published on 2020/10/25

07 Colombia

Makoto Dōjō

Bunbu Ryōdō and the value of etiquette

In South America, Chile, Uruguay, Venezuela, Ecuador and Colombia are considered countries with few Japanese immigrants.

In the case of Colombia, diplomatic relations with Japan, which had been suspended once, resumed in 1954. The following year, jūdō was taught there for the first time.

Regarding karate, it is recorded that Doctor Jaime Fernández Garzón learned Shōtōkan in Argentina and arrived in Colombia in 1963, opening the first dōjō in the capital Bogotá in 1967.

Born in Cartagena three years later, Roberto Zapata entered a karate dōjō at the age of 14. As the dōjō was a chapter of the mainland Gōjū-ryū Kenshōkai organization, which was established in the country in 1974, Zapata learned Gōjū-ryū karate from the beginning.

After 16 years of training, he heard of Higaonna Morio around 2000 and switched to Okinawa Gōjū-ryū three years later. In 2008, he was appointed as the head of the Colombian branch of the International Okinawan Gōjū-ryū Karatedō Federation.

Currently, Zapata lives in Santiago de Cali, commonly known as Cali. There, in 2003, he opened the Makoto Dōjō, where he teaches karate with his wife, who also practices the art. "I chose that name based on the Bushidō Code. I liked 'Makoto' for what it means: Sincerity or True Heart. Use the truth in words and actions. In short, be honest". Today, next to the main dōjō, there are five branch dōjō in the country who train under Zapata, who was promoted 5th dan when he visited Okinawa for the second time in 2019.

Zapata started a design company and earns a living as a graphic designer. His wife, who has studied origami – the art of folding paper into figures - for many years, has developed origami related products and also holds origami workshops for dōjō members and their parents.

Initially, Zapata began to learn karate for self-defense purposes. "Motivated students come to my dōjō for many reasons. But even so, for me, it is still the self-defense aspect which matters, to which can be added the fact of staying healthy through practice. I want to teach mainly these two aspects of karate" says he.

Zapata, who also train in iaidō, values the concept of infinite research. "All knowledge helps to grow. Karate and iaidō have different objectives but they have similarities as martial arts such as breathing during the execution of the techniques, zanchin - alertness, or the eyes focus while rendering a kata among others."

Living a life based on martial arts and graphic art, Zapata believes that traditional karate, that values gratitude, leads to self-development. Thus he keeps on walking the path of Bunbu Ryōdō, the way of art and martial arts.

2018年10月28日

08 チリ

伝統学び 地道に鍛錬

神武館ミラソル

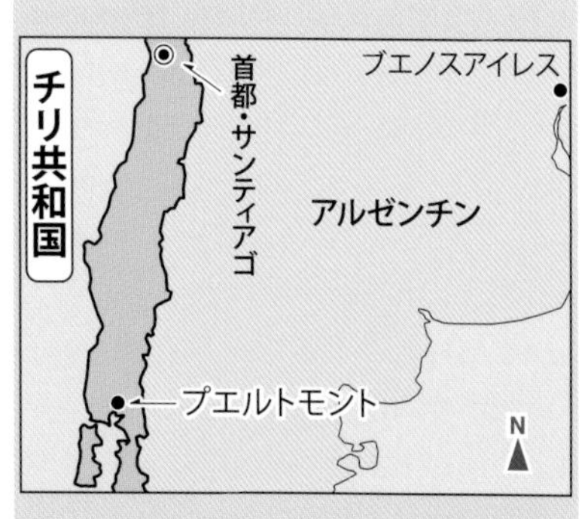

ノーベル賞詩人パブロ・ネルーダらを生んだ詩人の国、チリ。チリと言えば、イースター島のモアイ像と日本でも人気のチリワインが思い浮かぶ。チリと日本の交流は1800年代後半にさかのぼるが、近隣国のアルゼンチン、ブラジル、ペルーと違って移民契約が結ばれず、日本からの移民は非常に少ない。

チリにおける日本武道の普及は1935年にドイツ人の柔術家カート・ゴロノヴ氏の移民までさかのぼるという。ゴロノヴ氏の弟子のヘルナン・モンカダ氏が60年代初期に米国人から空手を習い、初の道場「アンデス流空手」を開設し、空手の普及に努めた。また、60年初期に空手を習ったアルトウロ・プティ氏もパイオニアの一人という。

今日広く普及する流派として松濤館、糸東流と剛柔流がある。伝統空手のほか競技空手も盛んだ。今年9月に南米で唯一の世界空手連盟主催のKARATE1シリーズA大会が、首都のサンティアゴで開催された。

1964年、チリ南部の都市プエルトモントで生まれたミルゾン・ザンブラノ氏は、1982年にギド・アラルコン氏が指導する剛柔流の道場に入門した。91年サンティアゴで開催された故諸見里安憲氏の指導する国際セミナーに参加し、初段に昇段した。諸見里氏は、60年代からペルーを拠点に、沖縄市にある神武館の故兼井勝良氏の剛柔流と古武道を隣国のベネズエラ、アルゼンチン、ブラジルなどに普及させていた。魅了されたザンブラノ氏は、2007年に諸見里氏が亡くなるまで技術指導を受けた。

神武館ミラソルで稽古を終えたザンブラノ氏(右から6人目)=提供
Zambrano (sixth from the right) after a training session at Jinbukan Mirasol.

1996年故郷で道場「神武館ミラソル」を開設し、神武会チリ支部長を務める。国内の4道場で100人余りに沖縄の武術を指導するほか、道場の門を超えて、教育施設や大学で若者の育成を支える手段としても空手の普及に励んでいる。

今年8月に行われた第1回沖縄空手国際大会を機に、ザンブラノ氏は3度目の訪沖を果たし、弟子3人と共に大会に参加した。滞在期間中、沖縄剛柔流空手古武道神武会神武館総本部で2代目館長の兼井斉氏から技術指導を受け、親睦を深めた。

「私の人生において空手は、普遍的な概念であるチームワーク、連帯、規律、尊敬、健康的な生活を強化するもの。空手は、沖縄の文化の一つとして地域に強く根付いている。そこから学び、私自身の文化への理解を強化することにつながると感じる」と意義を示す。

アンデス山脈を望む国でザンブラノ氏は、地道に沖縄生まれの空手と古武道を継承し続ける。

(ミルゾン・ザンブラノ氏は2022年1月15日に亡くなりました。ご冥福をお祈りいたします。)

When speaking of Chile in Japan, Easter Island's Moai statues and popular Chilean wine come to mind. Relations between Chile and Japan date back to the late 1800s, but unlike neighboring countries Argentina, Brazil and Peru, immigration contracts were not signed and Japanese immigrants are very few.

The spread of Japanese martial arts in the country dates back to 1935 when German Jūjutsu artist Curt Gronow immigrated to Chile. Hernan Moncada, one of his disciples, learned karate from Americans in the early 1960s and opened the first Chilean dōjō, "Andes Ryu Karate", in an effort to popularize karate. Arturo Petit, who learned karate in the early 1960s,

Published on 2018/10/28

08 Chile

Jinbukan Mirasol

Learning from tradition and training steadily

is said to be another karate pioneer.

Today, in addition to Shōtōkan, Shitō-ryū and Gōjū-ryū, competitive karate is quite popular. Last September, the only Karate 1 Series A tournament sponsored by the World Karate Federation in South America was held in the capital Santiago.

Born in Puerto Montt, a city in southern Chile in 1964, Mirson Zambrano entered the Gōjū-ryū dōjō of Guido Alarcón in 1982. He was promoted to 1st dan black belt in 1991 when he participated in a seminar held in Santiago led by the late Moromizato Anken. Based in Peru since the 1960s, Moromizato spread the Gōjū-ryū karate and kobudō of the Jinbukan to neighboring countries such as Venezuela, Argentina, and Brazil. The Jinbukan, at that time led by late Kanei Katsuyoshi, is located in Okinawa City. Fascinated, Zambrano studied under Moromizato until his passing in 2007.

In 1996, Zambrano opened the dōjō Jinbukan Mirasol in his hometown and served as the director of the Jinbukai Chile branch. In addition to teaching Okinawan martial arts to more than 100 people in four dōjō in the country, he strives to popularize karate as a means to support the development of young people in various educational institutions and universities.

On the occasion of the 1st Okinawa Karate International Tournament held last August, Zambrano made his third visit to Okinawa and participated in the tournament with three students. During his stay, he received instruction from Kanei Hitoshi, the second director of the Jinbukan Honbu Dōjō, and deepened friendship with local karateka.

"In my life, karate strengthens the universal concepts of teamwork, solidarity, discipline, respect and a healthy life. Karate is strongly rooted in the community as one of Okinawan cultural assets. Learning from this, I feel that it will help me deepen my understanding of my own culture."

In a country overlooked by the Andes, Zambrano continues to pass on Okinawan karate and kobudō.

(Mirson Zambrano passed away on January 15, 2022. May he rest in peace.)

2021年04月25日

09 パナマ

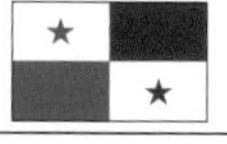

沖縄でルーツ再確認

ドラゴン拳法

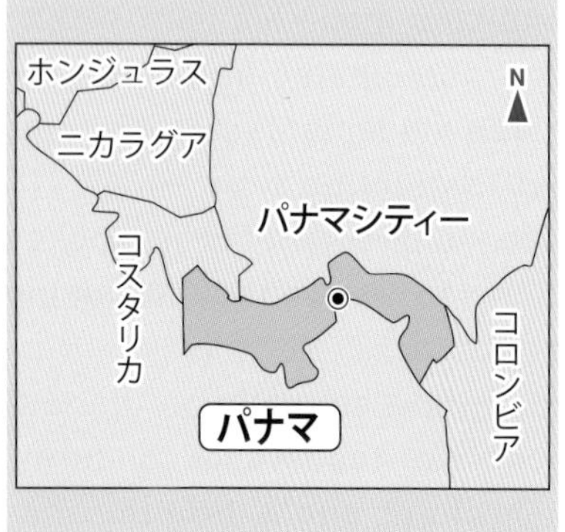

1914年に開通したパナマ運河は、パナマ共和国のパナマ地峡を切り開き、大西洋と太平洋を結ぶ。この国での空手普及は、1960年初期にさかのぼる。米軍が運河地帯を占領していた時代に、運河のカリブ海側にある港町コロンで、地元の人々が米兵に空手を学んだのが始まりだという。

解説するのは、7年続けてナショナルチームの組手選手として活躍したクリスチャン=アンソニ・エンジ氏(46)。氏の曽祖父母は、運河の労働者として香港から移民し、コロンに定住した。エンジ氏は、15歳のある日、拳法の稽古を見てすぐに入門したと振り返る。

沖縄で拳法といえば、中村茂氏を開祖とする沖縄拳法が思い浮かぶが、中国拳法以外に独自で展開した日本拳法やアメリカン拳法も存在する。

「血のつながりのない初代の故ジィミ・エンジ氏も1958年頃に香港から移民し、コロンを拠点に拳法空手を普及させた。どこで誰から空手を習ったのかは不明だが、伝授した型はセーサン、ワンシュー、パッサイなど」と自身の系統を紹介するエンジ氏。地元の道場で基本を学び、90年代後半、首都パナマシティに移り、2代目でパナマ空手連盟の会長も務めたルイス・ペレイラ氏に師事した。

ペレイラ氏(後列右から3人目)、エンジ氏(同4人目)と昇級審査を終えた生徒の皆さん=提供　Pereira (3rd from the right in the back row), Ng (4th from the right) and some students who have completed a promotion test.

拳法を続けながら、エンジ氏はプエルトリコで少林流空手と古武道を指導するウイリアム・ソラノ氏に出会い、98年から沖縄空手も研究した。

沖縄への関心が高まり、発祥の地への旅という夢を2020年にかなえた。県主催の沖縄空手国際セミナーに参加すると同時に、西原町に道場を構え、喜屋武朝徳氏に師事した故仲里常延氏の弟子で、少林寺流と古武道を指導する親川仁志氏に師事した。「稽古中、先生は私の系統の型を演武するように頼まれた。驚いたことに、型は非常に似ていた」とエンジ氏は語る。

エンジ氏は99年に4人で道場「ドラゴン拳法」を首都に開設し、現在、40人余りが空手と古武道を学ぶ。沖縄から帰り、親川氏に習った型と棒を取り入れているという。

保険業界で働き25年のキャリアを持つエンジ氏、今日、中南米の22か国以上に支店を有する米国の保険会社で地域セールスディレクターを務める。忙しい毎日に日々の空手の稽古は欠かせないという。「バランスの取れた心と体を発達させ、暴力を防ぎ、社会に尽くせる人間を育てることが空手の最大の目的」とエンジ氏は信じる。

沖縄訪問で自身の空手のルーツを再発見できたエンジ氏は、すべての出会いを大切に自己の鍛錬と門下生の指導に励む。

Published on 2021/4/25

Dragon Kenpō

Reconfirming his karate roots in Okinawa

In the country of the Panama Canal, which was opened in 1914, the diffusion of karate dates back to the early 1960s. It is said that locals learned karate from US soldiers in the port town of Colón on the Caribbean side of the canal at a time when the US military occupied the canal's zone.

So says Christian Anthony Ng (46), a former Panama national team kumite athlete for seven consecutive years. His great-grandparents emigrated from Hong Kong as canal workers and settled in Colón. Ng recalls that one day when he was 15 years old, he saw some people practicing kenpō and immediately joined.

"While we are not connected, first generation Jaime Wai Ng also emigrated from Hong Kong around 1958 and spread kenpō karate from Colón. It is unknown where and from whom he learned karate, but the kata he taught were Sēsan, Wanshū and Passai among others," Ng explains.

Later, Anthony Ng moved to the capital Panama City in the late 90's and started studying under Luis Pereira, a man who served as the second president of the Panama Karate Federation.

While continuing his kenpō practice, Ng met William Solando, an instructor of Shōrin-ryū karate and kobudō in Puerto Rico, and started his study of Okinawa karate in 1998.

As his interest for Okinawa was increasing, his dream of travelling to the birthplace of karate was fulfilled in 2020. While participating to the Okinawa Prefecture sponsored Okinawa Karate International Seminar, he also trained under Oyakawa Hitoshi, a Shōrinji-ryū and kobudō instructor with a dōjō in Nishihara and who is a disciple of the late Nakazato Jōen, who himself studied under Kyan Chōtoku. "During the training, Oyakawa sensei asked me to perform some of the kata of my style and to our great surprise, they were very similar," Ng recalls.

Ng opened his dōjō the "Dragon Kenpō" in the capital in 1999 with four people. Today, more than 40 people study karate and kobudō with him. He says that after his return from Okinawa, he has incorporated the kata and bō techniques that he learned from Oyakawa.

Ng has been working in the insurance industry for 25 years and currently serves as a regional sales director for a US insurance company with branches in more than 22 countries in Latin America and the Caribbean. He says that daily karate training is indispensable in his busy life. "For me, the main purpose of karate is to develop a well-balanced mind and body, prevent violence and forge better individuals for our society."

Having rediscovered the roots of his own karate during his visit to Okinawa, Ng cherishes all encounters and strives to persevere while guiding correctly his students.

2021年11月14日

⑩プエルトリコ

規律や忍耐 最も重要

プエルトリコ武術センター

アメリカ合衆国
キューバ
ドミニカ共和国
プエルトリコ
サンフアン
バヤモン

俳優のベニチオ・デル・トロや歌手のリッキー・マーティンを生んだ島、プエルトリコ。

美しいビーチで知られ、沖縄と同じ温暖な気候を誇るカリブ海に浮かぶリゾート地での空手普及は、1960年半ばから始まったといわれている。米兵から学んだ同島出身の空手家が指導に努め、現在は空手が非常に盛んだ。

「島の78の自治体には少なくともそれぞれ一つの空手道場がある」。このように話すのは、45年同島生まれのルイス・クワドラド氏。青年時代自ら体を鍛えていた氏は、18歳の頃に首都のサンフアンにあった松濤館系の道場に入門した。

プエルトリコ財務省の会計士として生計を立てながら空手の稽古に励んだ氏は、1722年にスペイン人によって設立された街バヤモンで1972年に武術センターを開設した。

稽古を始めて17年後、沖縄の古武道に出合った。「全くの偶然でした。80年に通りすがりにキモ先生の道場に入り、彼が亡くなるまで一緒に過ごした」

1960年代前半、海兵隊のキモ・ウオール氏は沖縄に駐留し、剛柔流を比嘉世幸氏、古武道を又吉真豊氏に師事した。65年からはプエルトリコ

ルイス・クワドラド氏(中央)、子息のイヴァン氏(右から2人目)と高弟たち(提供)
From right to left Jesus Miguel Jimenez, Iván Cuadrado, Luis Cuadrado, Efrain Rivera and Natalio Debs.

を拠点に世界各地で空手と古武道を指南し、71年に同島で光道館道場(後に「古道館」に改名)を開設。2018年に死去した。

5年間ウオール氏の指導を受けたクワドラド氏は、又吉家の古武道を道場のカリキュラムに加えた。自宅敷地内にある氏の道場の他、二つの支部道場で古武道を監督する。2010年にクワドラド氏は、指導者であり兄のような存在でもあったウオール氏より古武道の6段を允許(いんきょ)された。

「キモ先生は沖縄を愛し、いつも『好きなことをやっている。それは沖縄空手を稽古すること』と常に言っていた。又吉先生と比嘉先生に深く影響され、沖縄と空手のさまざまな側面を教わった」

その教えを受けたクワドラド氏は、規律、忍耐力と共感が空手の最も重要な真価だという。素朴ではない、より良い人になるための必要な資質だと解釈する。

武具作りの他、氏はクラシック音楽と読書が好きだという。「人は毎日何かを学ばないといけないことを理解しないといけない。死ぬ日まで、生涯学習が大切」

武術をこの島の美しい自然に例えれば、将来の木となるには小さな種を植えなければならないという。心と体を鍛え、知恵を分かち合い、弟子が自身を超えていくことが指導者の最大の誇りだと考えて、クワドラド氏は指導に専心する。

Puerto Rico, the island that gave birth to actor Benicio del Toro and singer Ricky Martin. It is said that karate appeared on this Caribbean island that boasts the same warm climate as Okinawa in the middle of 1960s, when Puerto Ricans learned karate from US soldiers. Today, karate is extremely popular in this island.

"In each of the 78 towns of the island, there is at least one karate school." He who says so is Luis Cuadrado, who was born on the island in 1945. As a young man, he used to train on his own to stay in shape and at the age of eighteen, he entered a Shōtōkan dōjō in the capital city San Juan.

Published on 2021/11/14

⑩ Puerto Rico 

Puerto Rico Bujutsu Center

Valuing discipline and perseverance above all

Practicing karate while working as an accountant in the Puerto Rico Treasury Department, Cuadrado opened a martial arts center in 1972 in Bayamon, a city founded by Spaniards in 1722.

After seventeen years of karate practice, he encountered Okinawa kobudō. "It was mere chance. In 1980, I passed in front and entered the dōjō of Kimo sensei and stayed with him until the last day of his life."

In the early 1960s, while stationed in Okinawa as a US Marine, Kimo Wall studied Gōjū-ryū under Higa Sekō and kobudō under Matayoshi Shinpō. From 1965, based in Puerto Rico, he taught karate and kobudō all over the world and in 1971, he opened the Kōdōkan Dōjō on the island. He passed away in 2018.

After training with Wall for five years, Cuadrado added Matayoshi kobudō to the curriculum of his dōjō located in his house. Meanwhile, he supervises kobudō at two other karate dōjō. In 2010, he was promoted to the 6th dan by Wall, who he considers his teacher and older brother.

"Kimo sensei loved Okinawa. He always told us 'I do what I love, I practice Okinawan karate.' Being a direct student of Matayoshi sensei and Higa sensei had a huge influence on him and he had a lot of knowledge to share."

According to Cuadrado, the charms of karate are discipline, perseverance and empathy. They are qualities that are necessary to become a better person but not a naive one.

Besides making weapons, Cuadrado likes classical music and reading. "One must understand that one learns something every day. The day you stop learning is because you are dead."

Comparing martial arts to the beautiful nature of the island, he says that people must plant a small seed to have a tree in the future. Training mind and body and sharing his wisdom, he believes that it is the greatest pride of a teacher to be outdone by his student and thus devotes himself to teaching.

2018年09月09日

⑪ブラジル

守礼の武道普及に力

新秀館 アカデミア・マトリス

ブラジル沖縄県人移民110周年記念式典が8月5日、同国のジアデマ市で開かれた。4日には前夜祭パレードが行われ、エイサーとサンバのほか空手も披露された。

ブラジルで空手が紹介されたのは1956年。その2年前にブラジル移住を決めた南風原出身の新里善秀氏(当時28歳)は、54年1月に親、兄弟3人、妻、子ども2人と共に、1500年にポルトガル人に発見されたこの地を踏んだ。新里氏は、住み着いた沖縄出身の農民入植地で若者に空手の指導を始めた。

1927年生まれの新里氏は中学校時代、糸洲安恒氏の高弟、徳田安文氏の下で空手を習った。徳田氏が終戦の年に亡くなり、新里氏は徳田氏の兄弟弟子の知花朝信氏と空手を続けた。69年から知花氏の後継者で同門の宮平勝哉氏と交流を持った。古武道では赤嶺誠一、仲本政博、兼井勝良の各氏に師事した。

新里氏は1962年にサントス市で道場を開設し、2008年に亡くなるまで多くの人たちに空手と古武道を教えた。組織が大きくなり、道場も移転し、道場名も変わったが、「新秀館」の名で親しまれている「アカデミア・マトリス」は今もサントス市にある。ポルトガル語で同道場名は、本部道場と意味する。ブラジルでは約150支部で、7500人が新里氏の空手を習う。その他、11カ国にも新秀館の技と精神が継承されている。

新里昌弘氏(後列右から4人目)と光秀氏(同5人目)=サントスの本部道場(提供) Shinzato Masahiro (4th from the right in the back row) and Mitsuhide (5th from the right) at the Santos Dōjō.

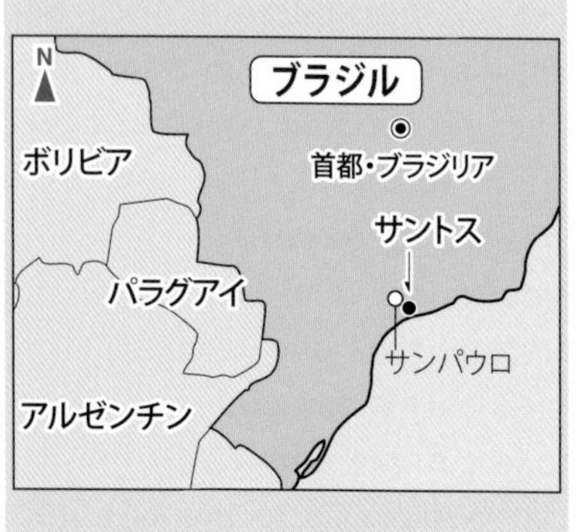

創始者が亡くなった後、1950年南風原生まれの長男、昌弘氏(9段)が館長を継ぎ、60年サン・ヴィセンテ生まれの兄弟・ネルソン光秀氏(7段)が技術指導者として兄を支える。兄は弁護士、弟は航空技術者として生計を立てていたが、現在は空手の指導に集中している。

週3日午前と夕方の空手、週2日の古武道を指導するほか、新里兄弟は年間30余のセミナーを週末に開き、競技大会、運動会、忘年会、空手の日記念行事も開催している。

8月にあった第1回沖縄空手国際大会には新秀館のブラジル、アルゼンチン、チリ、スペイン支部などから約100人が来沖した。参加した新里光秀氏は「新秀館は、空手がもたらす健康上の恩恵、空手に含まれる哲学、空手のすべてを楽しむ大きな家族」と語る。父・善秀氏からは「常に、空手のチャンピオンを育てるよりも、社会に役立つ市民のチャンピオンを育てることが大切」と教え込まれたという。

新里兄弟は、空手の徳で魅力でもある「礼儀・姿勢・努力・責任・明朗」を守りながら、父と同じ目標を追求し、沖縄が生んだ「守礼の武道」を世界に普及している。

Published on 2018/9/9

11 Brazil

Shinshūkan Academia Matriz

Striving to popularize the martial art of courtesy

A ceremony to commemorate the 110th anniversary of immigration from Okinawa to Brazil was held on August 5th in the city of Diadema, Brazil. During the eve parade, in addition to Eisa and Samba, karate was also demonstrated.

Karate was introduced in Brazil in 1956. From Haebaru in Okinawa, Shinzato Yoshihide (28 years old at the time) decided to move to Brazil in 1954 with his whole family, composed at the time by his parents, his 3 brothers, his wife and 2 children. Living in a colony of Japanese and Okinawan farmers, he began to teach karate to the youth.

Born in 1927, Shinzato learned karate under Tokuda Anbun, a student of Itosu Ankō when he was in junior high school. As Tokuda passed away in 1945, Shinzato continued karate with Chibana Chōshin, a fellow disciple of Tokuda. After 1969, he maintained exchanges with Miyahira Katsuya, a successor to Chibana. He also studied kobudō under Akamine Seiichi, Nakamoto Masahiro, and Kanei Katsuyoshi.

Shinzato founded a dōjō in Santos in 1962 and taught karate and kobudō to many until his passing in 2008. Today, the headquarters for Shinshūkan, the Academia Matriz is still in Santos. In Brazil, there are about 150 branches, and 7,500 people study Shinzato's karate. In addition, the technique and spirit of the Shinshūkan are being inherited in 11 countries.

After the decease of the founder, Masahiro (9th dan), the eldest son born in Haebaru in 1950, succeeded as the kanchō, and Mitsuhide Nelson (7th dan), his brother born in São Vicente in 1960, is responsible for the technical matters. While Masahiro made a living as a lawyer, Mitsuhide was an aeronautical engineer but now they concentrate on teaching karate.

In addition to instructing karate and kobudō five days a week, the Shinzato brothers hold more than 30 weekend seminars a year, and also organize various competitions and gatherings year-round.

About 100 Shinshūkan members from Brazil, Argentina, Chile, Spain, etc. travelled to the 1st Okinawa Karate International Tournament in August. Shinzato Mitsuhide who participated said, "At our Shinshūkan, we enjoy karate for it brings health benefits, for the philosophical content in the practice, but mainly for being a family." His father Yoshihide used to say, "Rather than raise karate champions, always nurture champions of citizenship, that is, to help in the formation of people who will be useful to the society".

Preserving the virtues and charms of karate that are "Courtesy, attitude, effort, responsibility and brightness," the Shinzato brothers pursue the same goal as their father and strive to spread karate, a martial art of courtesy born in Okinawa, to the world.

中南米の最大国ブラジルへの日本と沖縄からの移民は、1908年にさかのぼる。戦前空手が指導されたという説もあるが、戦後、船越義珍氏の直弟子の原田満祐氏が56年、銀行の仕事で同国に移住し、初めての空手道場を開設したとされる。原田氏は63年にヨーロッパに移ったが、氏のように多くの指導者がブラジルに移民した。中には沖縄出身の空手家で58年に移民した剛柔流の赤嶺誠一氏と54年に移民した小林流の新里善秀氏もいる。現在、故新里氏の新秀館は、国内に多くの道場を登録し、アルゼンチンとウルグアイにも支部を持つ。

73年生まれのフラビオ・ビセンテ・デ・ソウザ氏は、10歳の頃に剛柔流に入門し、後に新里氏の小林流に転向した。2006年に師の承認を得て故兼井勝良氏の神武会の古武道を習い始めた。08年、師の死去後、沖縄小林流空手道協会所属重礼館の石橋満雄氏の友となり、同館に加盟した。

デ・ソウザ氏は武術のほか、沖縄の民謡と踊りにも興味を持ち、ブラジル沖縄県人会で文武両道の研究を続けた。1993年に故郷のサンパウロ市にある同会本部で道場を開設し、自宅にも小さ

稽古会で指導するデ・ソウザ氏（中央）＝提供　De Souza (center) instructing during a training session (photo from Ricardo Yukawa).

2017年10月22日

⑫ブラジル

空手の神髄伝承に力

重礼館フラビオ道場

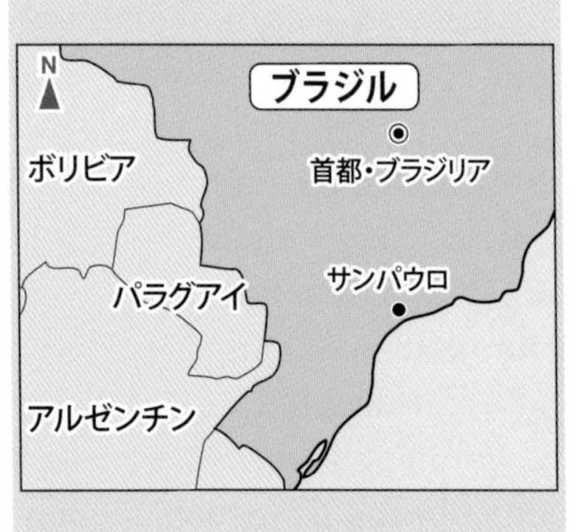

な道場を設置。現在は本部で60人、全国12の道場で300人余が稽古する。2014年に、デ・ソウザ氏は7段に昇段した。

弟子が競技に参加できるように、デ・ソウザ氏の道場は競技連盟に登録している。「ブラジルでは、40万人余の空手家がいるといわれている。その内25万人は世界空手連盟に所属するブラジル空手連合に加盟している。競技は若者にとって大切だが、沖縄の空手と古武道の伝統を守ることが私たちの最も重要な目的」と確信をもって語る。

デ・ソウザ氏は、毎日、人のために命を懸ける仕事もしている。1990年に空軍に入隊し、92年サンパウロ市消防隊に入隊。危険と隣り合わせのこの仕事では、空手で学んだ自制心が活かされていると言う。仕事のほかに、貧しい子どもたちの教育を支援する道具として空手も活用している。「好意的な結果が出ることが多く、沖縄空手のすごさをいつも感じる」と話す。

沖縄の武と芸に魅了されたデ・ソウザ氏。今年10月22日（日本とブラジルの時差は11時間）にブラジル沖縄文化センターで「第2回沖縄空手道古武道演武会」が行われる。イベントの考案者でもあるデ・ソウザ氏は門弟と参加する。「10月25日・空手の日」を記念し、来年の第1回沖縄空手国際大会のPRも兼ね、そして何よりも、沖縄空手の神髄を伝えるために。

Published on 2017/10/22

Jūreikan Flavio Dōjō

Striving to pass on the essence and tradition

Immigration from Japan and Okinawa to Brazil dates back to 1908. While there are theories that karate was taught prior WWII, Harada Mitsusuke, a direct disciple of Funakoshi Gichin who moved to Brazil in 1956, opened the first karate dōjō there. While Harada relocated to Europe in 1963, other karate experts moved to Brazil, like Gōjū-ryū Akamine Seiichi and Shōrin-ryū Shinzato Yoshihide, who immigrated respectively in 1953 and 1954. Today, Shinzato's Shinshūkan has many dōjō in Brazil and branches overseas.

Born in 1973, Flavio Vicente de Souza first started with Gōjū-ryū karate at the age of 10 and later switched to Shinshūkan. In 2006, with the approval of his teacher, he began learning Kanei Katsuyoshi's kobudō. In 2008, after the passing of Shinzato, he befriended Ishibashi Mitsuo of the Jūreikan and joined this group affiliated to the Okinawa Shōrin-ryū Karatedō Association.

In addition to martial arts, De Souza also became interested in Okinawan folk songs and dances, and study both at the Okinawa Association of Brazil.

In 1993, he opened a dōjō at the association's center in his hometown of São Paulo, and also set up a small dōjō at his home. Currently, 60 people are practicing with him and more than 300 people train in the 12 dōjō located in the country. In 2014, De Souza was promoted to 7th dan.

In order for his students to enter competitions, De Souza's dōjō is registered with the national sport oriented federation. "It is believed that in Brazil there are more than 400,000 practitioners. Among those, 250,000 people are registered with the Brazilian Confederation of Karate that is affiliated to the WKF. Competition is important for the youth, but preserving the tradition of Okinawan karate and kobudō is our most important purpose."

Every day, De Souza put his life in danger to save others. After serving in the Brazilian air force until 1992, he then joined the fire department of the State of São Paulo where he works today. He says that the self-control that he learned through karate was useful in his line of work. "Achieving positive results, I feel the greatness of Okinawa karate."

This October 22nd, the 2nd Okinawa Karatedō Kobudō Enbukai will be held at the center where he teaches. The originator of the event, De Souza will participate with his disciples to commemorate "October 25th, the Day of Karate", to promote the 1st Okinawa Karate International Tournament and above all, to convey the essence of Okinawa karate.

2020年12月13日

⑬ベネズエラ 

鍛錬と社会貢献に力

心武館

競技空手界においてベネズエラと言えば、2010年代に個人形の世界王者になったアントニオ・ディアズ氏の名が浮かぶ。この国で空手の歴史は1960年代に移住した日本人によって始まったと言われる。

エルネスト・アグレダ氏は62年にマラカイボ湖に面するカビマスに生まれた。10歳の時、日本人が首都カラカスで開設した道場「錬武館」の門をくぐり、松濤館系の空手道を学んだ。

83年に全沖縄古武道連盟の演武団が南米に派遣された。アグレダ氏は、団員の兼井勝良、真栄城守成、金城孝ら諸氏の演武を見て発祥の地の武術に惹(ひ)かれたという。後に沖縄剛柔流誠武会の空手を米国人に習い、87年からベネズエラに移住した平松義人氏の弟子になった。

長野生まれの平松氏は沖縄県出身の遠山寛賢氏、兼井勝良氏や又吉眞豊氏らに師事し、77年からベネズエラで剛柔流と又吉系の古武道の普及に励んだ。

アグレダ氏は86年に小林流と出合った。故郷で開催された大会においてブラジルで空手の普及に貢献した新秀館開祖・新里善秀氏に初めて会った。

空手の鍛錬に励んでいるアグレダ氏(前列左から3人目)と門弟ら=提供　Agreda (third from the left in the front row) and his disciples training hard.

後に国内のセミナーを企画したが、ベネズエラの治安状況もあって開催に至らなかった。しかし、不屈のアグレダ氏は2005年に新里氏を招き小林流と古武道のセミナー開催にこぎ着けた。これが、同国における小林流普及の始まりとなった。

「空手キャリアの中で多くの師範に出会うことができた。新里先生は武道と人間性の面で高い資質を持った人。私にとって先生は過去、現在、未来、一生の師」と特別な思いを抱く。

アグレダ氏は1982年に故郷のカビマスに道場「心武館」を開設した。現在小林流6段。国内にある計4道場150人を指導している。指導モットーは「劣等感をぬぐい、困難を乗り越えていく力を学ぶ」だという。

2009年に誠武会から脱会し、新秀館に加盟。南米各国に活動を広げる国際新秀館のベネズエラ支部長も務めている。また、2代目新里昌弘氏や同会アルゼンチン代表のヘクトール・セバジョス氏に師事し、鍛錬を積んでいる。

長年、大学で数学教授として教壇に立ったアグレダ氏は「学んだことは何かに生かさないと意味がない」と指摘する。経済危機真っただ中にある地元では、自ら代表を務める大学の貯蓄銀行を通して最貧地域へ食糧配達を定期的に行い、社会貢献にも努めている。これからも空手の鍛錬と共に活動に励む決意を示した。

When speaking of Venezuela in the world of sport karate, the name of Antonio Díaz, who became kata world champion in the 2010s, comes to mind. It is said that the history of karate in this country was started by Japanese immigrants in the 1960s.

Ernesto Agreda was born in 1962 in Cabimas, a city that faces Lake Maracaibo. When he was 10 years old, he entered a dōjō in the capital Caracas and learned Shōtōkan karate.

In 1983, a group of the All Okinawa Kobudō Federation was dispatched to South America for a series of demonstrations. Seeing the performances of Kanei Katsuyoshi, Maeshiro Shusei and Kinjō

Published on 2020/12/13

13 Venezuela

Shinbukan

Dedication to training and serving the society

Takashi, Agreda was attracted by the original karate of Okinawa. After training with an American member of the Okinawa Gōjū-ryū Seibukai, he became in 1987 a student of Hiramatsu Yoshihito.

Born in Nagano, Hiramatsu studied karate under Okinawan masters Tōyama Kanken, Kanei Katsuyoshi and Matayoshi Shinpō. Since 1977, he was teaching Gōjū-ryū and Matayoshi kobudō in Venezuela.

In 1986, Agreda discovered Shōrin-ryū when he met Shinzato Yoshihide, the founder of Shinshūkan, who largely contributed to the spread of karate in Brazil. Later, Agreda planned a seminar in his country, but it was not held due to political disturbances in Venezuela at that time. However, not giving up, Agreda invited Shinzato in 2005 for a seminar which marked the beginning of the spread of Shōrin-ryū in the country.

“Although I met many masters in my career, when it comes to martial arts and humanity, Shinzato sensei is a person of high quality. For me, he is my teacher of the past, present, future, and will stay in my heart forever.”

Agreda, now a 6th dan in Shōrin-ryū, opened the dōjō Shinbukan in Cabimas in 1982. He teaches a total of 150 people in four clubs in the country with the motto “To learn to live without complexes, nurturing the power to overcome difficulties.”

In 2009, he left the Seibukai and joined the Shinshūkan and now serves as the Venezuelan representative for the International Shinshūkan. Presently, he keeps training under the second heir of the system Shinzato Masahiro and the Argentine national head Hector Ceballos.

Agreda, a university professor of mathematics, points out that “what you have learned is meaningless unless you apply it to something.” Amid the economic crisis that undergoes Venezuela, he organizes food delivery days for the humblest sectors of his town through the university savings bank of which he is the current president. Next to training diligently in martial arts, he is determined to contribute to the society through various means inside and outside the dōjō.

2019年01月13日

⑭ペルー

伝統見つめ武芸追求

神人武館サンタアニタ

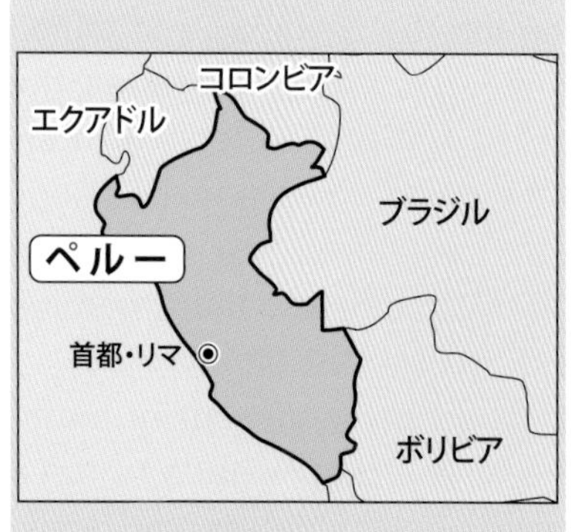

ペルーといえば、サイモン＆ガーファンクルによってカバーされた名曲「コンドルは飛んでいく」が思い浮かぶ。インカ帝国の遺跡マチュ・ピチュを誇るこの国に日本人は1899年、沖縄県出身は1906年に移民した。

1960年代後半に日本人より空手が紹介され、75年にペルー空手連盟が発足したという。現在、本土系の空手に加えて、東恩納盛男氏の沖縄剛柔流、上江洲安儀氏の一心流と小林流が継承されている。

50年旧知念村生まれの新里善彦氏は、15歳の頃、小林流の翁長良光氏と琉球古武道の赤嶺栄亮氏に師事し、78年にペルーに渡った。到着後、日本ペルー文化センターで同国において初めて小林流のクラスを開設し、2001年までに沖縄の武術の普及に努めた。後に米国フロリダに移住した。↗

1965年首都リマ生まれのリチャード・ヴァルディヴィエゾ＝カマッチョ氏は、82年に新里氏の道場に入門した。師の渡米後、新里氏が発足した「ペルー沖縄空手古武道協会」の代表になり、ペルー神人武館支部長に認証された。

電子工学技術者の生涯を送りながらカマッチョ氏は、小林流の普及に励んだ。88年から日本ペルー文化センターでの指導のほか、現在、7支部道場を監修し、180人に技術指導を行う。2016年にはサンタアニタ道場を開設した。同道場では25人が汗を流し、空手と古武道の研究に精進している。

サイを指導するヴァルディヴィエゾ＝カマッチョ氏（左）＝提供
Camacho (left) teaching sai.

17年10月に国際神人武館空手道協会の翁長良光会長がペルーを訪れ、合宿で指導した。その際にカマッチョ氏は、翁長氏から空手の4段を授与された。

「空手は、稽古や仕事において前進する方法だと思う。多くの人が真の道を知らない中で、優れた歴史と哲学を有する神人武館に所属することは誇りです。私にとって、新里先生と翁長先生に出会えたことは、とてもラッキーだと思う」と振り返る。

競技空手が盛んなペルーは、多くの選手の活躍により世界の舞台で好成績を残している。少年にとって競技がいい体験であると理解するカマッチョ氏も、道場生の競技大会への参加を勧めている。「翁長先生は、競技空手にあまり目を向けないが、チャンピオンになった弟子を祝福してくれる」と喜ぶ。

競技の一方で、まだ沖縄を訪れたことのないカマッチョ氏は、古代の技法と型の分解を研究し続けている。ペルーのことわざ「打たれた金は輝く」を信じて、真の武芸を求め行く。

Published on 2019/1/13

14 Peru

Shinjinbukan Santa Anita

Pursuing martial arts with a focus on tradition

In Peru, home of the Machu Picchu, Japanese and Okinawans immigrated respectively in 1899 and in 1906.

Karate is said to have been introduced by Japanese in the latter half of the 1960s, and the Peruvian Karate Federation was established in 1975. Currently, in addition to mainland karate styles, Higaonna Morio's Okinawa Gōjū-ryū, Uezu Angi's Isshin-ryū and Shōrin-ryū are being taught.

Born in the former Chinen village in 1950, Shinzato Yoshihiko studied Shōrin-ryū under Ōnaga Yoshimitsu and Ryūkyū kobudō under Akamine Eisuke from the age of 15, and moved to Peru in 1978. Upon his arrival, he opened the first Shōrin-ryū class in the country at the Japanese Peruvian Cultural Center and strived to popularize Okinawan martial arts until 2001 when he emigrated to Florida, USA.

Born in Lima in 1965, Richard Valdivieso Camacho entered Shinzato's dōjō in 1982. After his teacher left, he became the representative of the "Peruvian Association of Okinawa karate and kobudō" established by Shinzato, and was recognized as the head of the Peruvian Shinjinbukan school.

While making a living as an electronic engineering technician, Camacho worked hard to popularize Shōrin-ryū. In addition to teaching at the Japanese Peruvian Cultural Center since 1988, he currently supervises 7 branch dōjō and provides technical guidance to 180 people. In 2016, the Santa Anita dōjō was opened where today twenty-five people study karate and kobudō.

In October 2017, Ōnaga Yoshimitsu, chairman of the International Shinjinbukan Karatedō Association visited Peru and taught a seminar. On that occasion, Camacho was awarded the 4th dan in karate by Ōnaga.

Looking back at his career, he says "I think karate is a way to move forward in training and work. While many people don't know the true path of karate, I'm proud to belong to the Shinjinbukan which has an excellent history and philosophy. I think I was very lucky to meet both Shinzato sensei and Ōnaga sensei."

Peru, where competitive karate is popular, has achieved good results on the world stage. Camacho, who understands that competition is a good experience for young karateka, also encourages his students to participate in competitions. "Ōnaga sensei doesn't pay much attention to competitive karate, but he congratulates students who have become champions," he happily comments.

Although allowing competition, Camacho, who has never visited Okinawa, continues to study ancient techniques and the applications of kata. Believing in the Peruvian saying "Gold, when beaten, shines", he perseveres seeking the way of true martial arts.

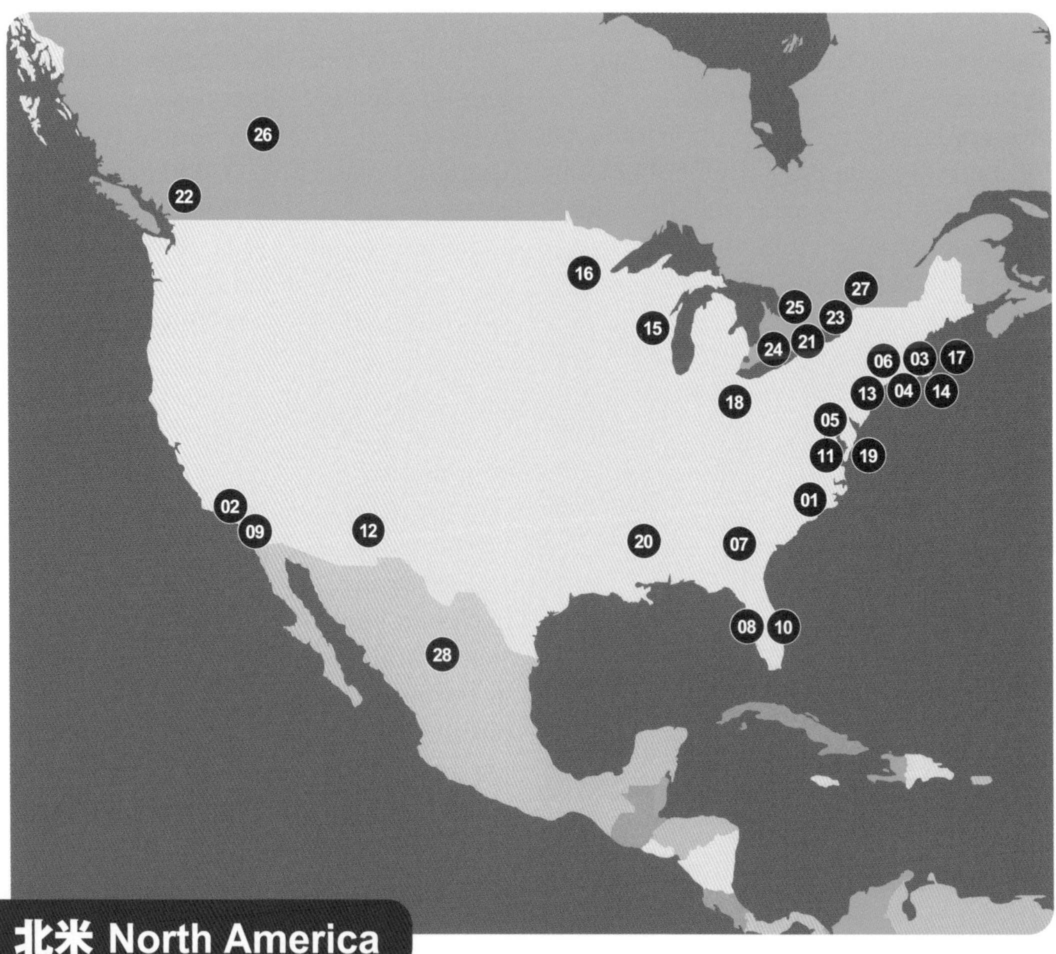

北米 North America

北米
North America

2019年12月08日

01 米国

流派超え技術交流

沖縄小林流研鑽会

1937年、米国ノースカロライナ生まれのドグ・ペリー氏は子どものころから、当時人気だったボクシングに専心し、140余りの試合に出場した。

56年、海兵隊に入隊。基地内で練習する沖縄帰りの兵隊を見て、空手と出合った。「あの頃、柔道は人気でしたが、空手は言葉さえ未知の武術でした」とペリー氏は語る。沖縄で一心流を習った米兵らを通して空手の基本を習い、後に沖縄に駐留し、同系流祖の島袋龍夫氏に師事した。

仕事の関係で定期的に沖縄を訪れることのできたペリー氏は、ひたすら稽古に励んだ。ベトナム戦争中、休暇を利用し、人気の行き先であったバンコクやマニラではなく、沖縄に戻り鍛錬を重ねた。

70年ごろ、同じ兵員のビール・ヘイズ氏と共に道場を開設し指導を始めた。

75年再び沖縄に配属された際に、仲里周五郎氏の弟子で宜野湾市普天間にあった城間次郎氏(現在は米在住)の道場に入門。「仲里先生の小林流のほか、ムエタイの経験者でもある城間先生は、厳しい鍛錬と組手中心の指導で門弟を鍛えていた。何回もほかの道場を訪れ組手に参加した。かなり粗い稽古法でしたが、いい思い出もいっぱいです」と振り返る。

セミナーで技術指導を行うペリー氏(中央赤帯)=ポランダーアカデミー提供
Perry (center with the red belt) teaching at a seminar (photo from the Polander Academy).

80年代初めに軍隊を退役したペリー氏は故郷で道場を開設。合宿のため訪米した仲里氏と交流を深め、小林流小林舘米国支部の代表までになった。

長年の研さんの成果として、2008年に仲里氏より9段の称号が与えられた。12年に沖縄小林流研鑽会を立ち上げ、引き続き故仲里周五郎氏の小林流を指南している。

若いころ多くの競技大会に出場したペリー氏は、スポーツとしての空手を批判しない。しかし「自制心と護身の武芸である空手はスポーツではない。今日と違って、かつては競技大会のための練習はしていなかった」とこだわりは強い。

空手の国際化に伴い、今では複数の指導者から手ほどきが受けられなくなったことに危機感を感じるペリー氏。流派を超えた技術交流を復活させようと、米国で長年沖縄空手の普及に取り組んできた高段者と共に定期的にセミナーを開いて指導している。

小林流の流祖・知花朝信氏は「美しい手は切れる。強い手は美しい」という言葉を残した。範士10段のペリー氏は「自然でなければ正しくない。実行するなら、優雅にやれ」をモットーに沖縄空手の「極意」を伝え続ける。

Published on 2019/12/8

01 United States 

Okinawa Shōrin-ryū Kensankai

Martial exchanges transcending styles

Born in North Carolina in 1937, Doug Perry devoted himself to boxing, which was popular at the time, and participated in more than 140 matches.

Joining the Marine Corps in 1956, Perry saw a fellow service man who had returned from Okinawa practicing karate on base. That was his encounter with karate. "At that time, jūdō was popular, but karate was an unknown martial art," says Perry. He learned the basics through an American who had learned Isshin-ryū in Okinawa and later, as he was stationed in Okinawa, trained under the founder Shimabuku Tatsuo.

As he was able to visit Okinawa on a regular basis due to his work, Perry practiced eagerly. During the Vietnam War, he used his vacations to return to Okinawa for training instead of choosing the popular destinations that were Bangkok and Manila.

Around 1970, Perry opened a dōjō with a fellow Marine, Bill Hayes, and began instructing.

When he was assigned to Okinawa again in 1975, Perry entered the dōjō of Shiroma Jirō (currently living in the USA), a student of Nakazato Shūgorō. At that time, the dōjō was in Futenma, Ginowan City. "In addition to Nakazato sensei's Shōrin-ryū, Shiroma sensei was also experienced in Muay Thai and trained his students strictly with an emphasize on kumite. We visited other dōjō many times and practiced kumite. It was a fairly rough method of training, but I have a lot of good memories," Perry recalls.

Perry, who retired in the early 1980s, opened a dōjō in his hometown, Hendersonville. Deepening his relation with Nakazato, who visited the USA for training camps, he later became the national representative of the Shōrin-ryū Shōrinkan.

As a result of many years of practice, he was promoted to 9th dan by Nakazato in 2008. Establishing the Okinawa Shōrin-ryū Kensankai in 2012, he continues to teach the karate of late Nakazato.

Perry, who participated in many competitions when he was young, does not criticize karate as a sport. However, he points out that "Karate, which is a martial art of self-control and self-defense, is not a sport. Unlike today, we didn't practice for competitions."

With the internationalization of karate, Perry feels a sense of crisis as people are no longer able to receive tuition from multiple instructors. In order to revive technical exchanges that transcend styles and schools, he regularly participates in seminars with high-ranked teachers of Okinawa karate.

The founder of Shōrin-ryū, Chibana Chōshin, left these words to posterity: "Beautiful hands can cut. Strong hands are beautiful." Now a Hanshi 10th dan, Perry continues to convey the "inner secrets" of Okinawa karate with the motto "If it is not natural, it is not right. If you do something, do it with style."

米国において活発に展開している沖縄空手の流派の一つ、一心流。具志川(現うるま市)出身の創始者島袋龍夫氏は、喜屋武朝徳や宮城長順各氏等に師事し、1946年に道場を開設。55年に米海兵隊に空手指導者として採用され、56年に一心流と命名した。

2年後の58年11月下旬、当時20歳のアルシンョ・アドベンクラ氏が沖縄に駐在した。フィリピン系で38年アラスカ生まれのアドベンクラ氏は、8歳からフィリピン武術のエスクリマの手ほどきを受け、武の道に進んだ。

来沖直後、米軍キャンプ・バトラーの同僚に誘われ12月1日、島袋氏の安慶名道場に入門した。61年に沖縄婿になり、空手のみならず沖縄の文化にもなじんだ。2回もベトナム戦争に派遣された氏は20年間、米国と沖縄を行き渡り、81年に米軍の役務から退いた。

75年に他界した島袋氏から受け継いだ一心流空手の研究・継承に努めながら同年、具志川田場にある琉棍会に入門し、伊波光太郎氏の下で本格的に古武道を習い始めた。

2000年代初期、アドベンクラ氏は、海兵隊のマーシャルアーツプログラム立ち上げに大きく貢献した。「海兵隊に人殺し技を教えると使ってしまう恐れがあると多くの人は信じていた。しかし、武道が教える自制と礼儀の取得を通して、逆に良い効果が生まれた。戦う術を学べば、戦いたくない

門下生と稽古を行うアルシンョ・アドベンクラ氏=提供
Advincula training with a student.

2017年09月24日

02 米国

心技継承 強い使命感

女神ガーデン道場

心を養う」と説明する。

1994年に町道場を閉館したアドベンクラ氏は現在、カリフォルニア・オーシャンサイドの自宅内に設けた「女神ガーデン道場」で指導している。氏の「一心会」には、北米だけで30余りの道場がある。明るい性格で快活な人柄のアドベンクラ氏は、元曹長ということもあり、79歳に見えない身体を持つ。70年余りの武術の鍛錬で自信と知識を身に付けた。

一方で、歴史も調べる使命感も強く、94年から弟子を連れて毎年沖縄を訪れ、同系統の関係者のインタビューを行っている。

「龍夫先生は、動きのまねをするのではなく、コンセプトを指導していたが、言葉の壁があったから多くの米兵には通じなかった」と振り返るアドベンクラ氏。〈空手は健康とフィットネスのためにある/備えあれば憂いなし/空手は護身術である〉。島袋氏から直接教わった「考え」を今も大切にしている。

米国では現在、無数の一心流の組織が存在する。しかし、一期生で生涯武道として一心流空手を継承した人物は少なく、アドベンクラ氏はその一人。笑顔が輝く見事な保持者だ。

Isshin-ryū is one of the Okinawan karate styles that is widely spread in the USA. The founder, Shimabuku Tatsuo, was hired by the US Marine Corps as a karate instructor in 1955.

In November 1958, a twenty years old Arcenio J. Advincula was stationed on Okinawa. Born in Alaska in 1938 with Filipino roots, he started his martial journey being taught the Filipino art of escrima at the age of eight.

After his arrival, he was taken to Shimabuku's Agena Dōjō on December 1st. Becoming uchināmuku, a son-in-law of an Okinawan family in 1961, he deepened his understanding of Okinawan culture and karate. Doing two tours to Vietnam

Published on 2017/9/24

02 United States 

Megami Garden Dōjō

Inheriting the spirit and skills with a firm sense of mission

during the war, he travelled back and forth between the USA and Okinawa for 20 years, and retired from the Marine Corps in 1981.

In 1975, Advincula started learning kobudō at the Ryūkonkai dōjō of Iha Kōtarō located in Taba Gushikawa, while striving to research and inherit the Isshin-ryū karate of Shimabuku who passed away the same year.

In the early 2000s, Advincula contributed significantly by pioneering the Marine Corps Martial Arts program. "Many people believed that it was risky to teach murderous techniques to Marines as they might use these techniques. However, by acquiring the self-control and etiquette taught by martial arts, an opposite positive effect is nurtured. By learning fighting skills, one nourishes the will to not fight."

Having closed his dōjō in 1994, Advincula is currently teaching at the Megami Garden Dōjō established in his home in Oceanside, California. His group Isshin-kai counts more than 30 dōjō in North America alone. A man of cheerful personality, Advincula has a body that does not look his age, partly because he is a former master sergeant. Through more than 70 years of martial arts training, he has gained confidence and knowledge.

On the other hand, he has a firm sense of mission to study history and since 1994, he has been visiting Okinawa with his students every year and has interviewed people who belong to the same style.

"Rather than teaching by movement imitation, Tatsuo sensei taught concepts. But due to the language barrier, many American soldiers didn't understand." [Karate is for health and fitness and for self-defense. If one is prepared through karate, he has nothing to worry about.] Today he still cherishes the lessons he learned directly from Shimabuku.

There are currently innumerable Isshin-ryū organizations in the USA. However, there are few first-generation students left who have inherited this karate as a lifelong martial art. Advincula is one of them. A wonderful holder with a shining smile.

2018年04月08日

03 米国

技磨き 道徳と心育む

ウォルター・マットソン道場会

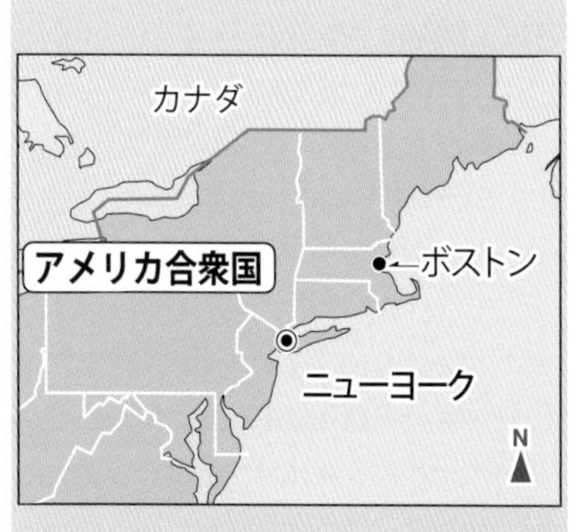

毎年4月第三月曜日に行われるボストンマラソンの開催市ボストン。米マサチューセッツ州北東部にある大都市は、沖縄空手3大流派の一つ上地流の米国における発祥の地でもある。

1957年から沖縄で上地流を学んだジョージ・マットソン氏は、58年にボストンに帰郷し道場を開いた。それが米国での上地流普及の始まりだ。

39年同市生まれのウォルター・マットソン氏(前述のジョージ氏とは親類ではない)は、20歳の頃、米国駐在海兵隊の時に少林流を指導していたチャールズ・ベーゲル氏に師事した。60年にはジョージ氏の上地流道場に入門した。

マットソン氏は62年に指導を始めたが、空手のプロにはならず、タクシー乗務員やセールスマンなど様々な仕事をしながら空手を続けた。81年にフレイミングハム町で道場を開設し、06年まで毎日指導を行ってきた。

その後、冬季をフロリダ州サラソータ市、夏季をマサチューセッツ州のサンドウィッチ町で妻と共に過ごすマットソン氏は、「ウォルター・マットソン道場会」というグループを立ち上げた。現在、両州を中心に4段以上の空手家に指南している。

弟子たちとマットソン氏(前列左から3人目)=提供
Mattson (front row third from the left) with some of his students.

沖縄を初めて訪れたのは、1970年のとき。当時、2代目宗家上地完英氏や高弟の面々から直接、技術指導を受けた。その後20回以上沖縄を訪れ、武術の基礎である先輩後輩の関係を深めた。86年には高良信徳氏に正式に弟子入りし、上地流の各会派長とも交流を大切に続けている。

約60年の武歴を有するマットソン氏は、どの武術でも、師は弟子に稽古法を教えることしかできないと考える。「那覇に行くのに様々な道があるように、空手の稽古法も様々ある。すべての人に正しい道がある。しかし、三戦や小手鍛えは必須。餅をこねるように、毎日体を鍛え、より高い可能性に達することが空手の道です」。

友情と協力を大切に武術の道を進むマットソン氏は「空手に引きつけられたのは、最初の指導者ベーゲル氏の人格」と振り返る。現在は、身体能力より人格を慎重に考慮して弟子入りを決めているという。

4月21日には本部町で行われる上地完文氏の銅像建立除幕式に出席する。「空手の大家は、道徳と心を優先する。上地先生や高良先生の技を研究することは、単なる突きと受けを学ぶことではない。両師の人間性を研究し、彼らのような人間に近づくことが最も大切」と説く。

Boston, the host city of the Boston Marathon which is held on the third Monday of April every year. When it comes to karate, this huge city is also the birthplace of Uechi-ryū in the USA. Indeed, George Mattson, who studied Uechi-ryū in Okinawa in 1957, returned to Boston in 1958 and opened a dōjō there. This was the beginning of the spread of Uechi-ryū in the country.

Walter Mattson (not related to George Mattson) was born in Boston in 1939. At the age of 20, while he was a US Marine, he studied under Charles Berger, who had received some instructing in Shōrin-ryū. In 1960, Mattson entered the Uechi-ryū dōjō of George Mattson.

Published on 2018/4/8

03 United States 

Walter Mattson Dōjō-kai

Polishing the technique and nurturing values

Walter Mattson began teaching in 1962, but he didn't become a karate professional and continued to practice and teach karate while doing various jobs such as taxi driver and salesman. Later, he opened a dōjō in Framingham Massachusetts in 1981 and taught daily until 2006.

From then on, Mattson has been living with his wife in Sarasota, Florida from October to May and in Sandwich, Massachusetts from May to October. He has set up a group called the Walter Mattson Dōjō-kai and currently instructs 4th dan and above karateka mainly in both states.

Mattson first visited Okinawa in 1970. At that time, he received technical guidance directly from Uechi Kanei and his high-ranking disciples. Following this first visit, he travelled to Okinawa more than 20 times, deepening senior-junior relationships, which is the basis of martial arts. In 1986, he officially became a disciple of Takara Shintoku, but continues to cherish exchanges with the leaders of each Uechi-ryū organization.

With about 60 years of martial experience, Mattson believes that in any martial art, a teacher can only teach the student how to practice. "Just as there are several roads to get to Naha, there are several methods to learn karate. There is a right way for every student. But Sanchin and kote-kitae are essential. The way of karate is like making mochi - rice cake: the rice has to be worked every day in order to make mochi. We all aspire to reach our full potential thus we have to work our bodies every day!"

Walking on the path of martial arts valuing friendship and cooperation, Mattson recalls that, "It was Mr. Berger's character that I found appealing." Currently, he accepts new students by carefully considering his/her personality rather than physical ability.

"The priority of karate masters is helping people to develop good moral character and good hearts. Researching the techniques of masters Uechi and Takara is not simply about learning their punches and blocks. We need to study the human nature of these masters in the hope of becoming the kind of men they are".

米国東海岸では、剛柔流空手のパイオニアとして、日本本土の山口剛玄氏に教わったアメリカン剛柔流の創始者ピター・アーバン氏、1950年代前半から渡口政吉氏や八木明徳氏に師事したアンソニ・ミラキャン氏、60年前後、比嘉世幸氏と渡口政吉氏に師事し、当時コザ市八重島区に尚武館を開設した新城正信氏の指導を受けたフランク・ヴァン=レンテン氏が足跡を残す。

帰国後、剛柔流、少林流、上地流を習ったフランク・ヴァン=レンテン氏は、三つの流派を統合し「護身道空手道協会」を立ち上げたが、83年同協会を高弟のジョン・ポルタ氏にゆずり、元師匠の新城氏の下に戻った。

ニュージャージー州生まれのポルタ氏(79)は、54年に武道の道に入り、後に、レンテン氏の下で剛柔流空手を学び始めた。59~66年に、米国財務省で護身術を指導し、66年に今の道場「ポルタ空手・古武道アカデミー」を開設した。

84年に護身道協会の解散を決断したポルタ氏も、八重島の尚武館を訪れ、新城氏の指導を求めた。稽古と普及に励み、ポルタ氏は90年、第一回世界のウチナーンチュ大会の武芸祭に参加するため来沖した。

門下生たちとポルタ氏(3列目右から4人目)=提供　Porta (4th from the right in the 3rd row) with some students.

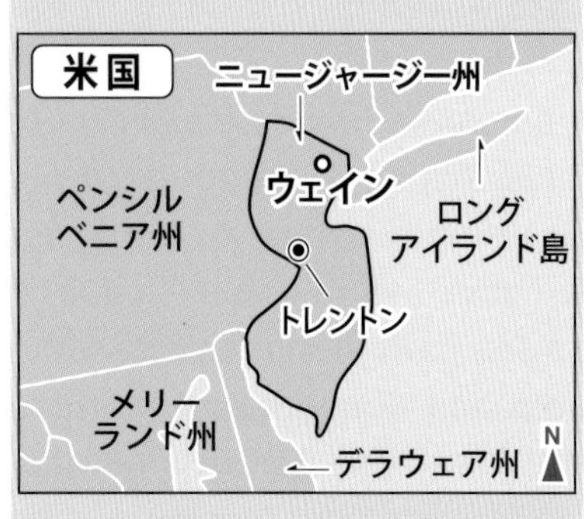

2019年10月13日

04 米国

伝統の心技守り鍛錬

ポルタ空手・古武道アカデミー

演武中、型サンセイルーの集団演武の指揮を任されたポルタ氏の研究熱心さと功績が認められ、新城氏より教士7段に昇段、沖縄剛柔流尚武館空手協会の米国代表に任命された。

道場外の活動としてポルタ氏は、74年に聖書哲学学士号を取得し、牧師に任命された。96年にベリアン大学で青少年専門牧師になり、キリスト教黒帯協会の牧師にもなった。現在も、空手で学んだ護身術を生かし、教会の環境において信者や関係者の安全を保障するためのプログラムを開発・指導する。同時にキリスト教の牧師として奉仕に努めている。

2006年、尚武館2代目新城正史氏より範士9段の証を授与されたポルタ氏は、今日も、新城家の剛柔流空手と又吉眞豊氏の古武道を本部道場で60人、このほか4道場で門弟たちを指導している。

道場訓「錬心尚武」の心を持って鍛錬へと導かれたポルタ氏は、正信氏の言葉「空手は心の中あり」を胸に刻む。「新城先生は、とても親切で、謙虚で思慮深い強い空手家でした。先生は“空手は個々の個人的な旅。従来の伝統価値を守り、厳しく頻繁に訓練することが大切”と仰っていた」。今もその教えを大切に、沖縄の武術を指南している。

Among the Gōjū-ryū pioneers on the east coast are Peter Urban, the founder of American Gōjū-ryū, who was a student of Yamaguchi Gōgen, Anthony Mirakian, who studied under Toguchi Seikichi and Yagi Meitoku in the early 1950s, and Frank Van Lenten who studied under Shinjō Masanobu in the early 1960s. At that time, Shinjō, a student of Higa Sekō and Toguchi Seikichi, operated the Shōbukan dōjō in the Yaeshima district of Koza City, today's Okinawa City.

After returning home, Van Lenten, who had learned Gōjū-ryū, Shōrin-ryū, and Uechi-ryū, integrated the three systems and launched the "Goshindō Karatedō Association". In 1983, he left the group

Published on 2019/10/13

04 United States 

Porta Karate Kobudō Academy

Training while preserving traditional spirit and technique

to his student John Porta and returned to train with his former master, Shinjō.

Born in New Jersey, Porta (79) entered the martial arts path in 1954 and later began studying Gōjū-ryū karate under Van Lenten. From 1959 to 1966, he taught self-defense at the US Treasury Department, and in 1966 he opened the current Porta Karate Kobudō Academy.

In 1984, Porta decided to dissolve the Goshindō organization and travelled to the Shōbukan to ask for Shinjō's guidance. Encouraged in his training and popularization activities, Porta visited Okinawa in 1990 to participate in the martial arts demonstration of the 1st World Uchinānchu Festival.

After the event, during which he conducted a group demonstration, he was appointed, in recognition of his zeal for research and his achievements, as the American representative of the Shōbukan association and promoted to 7th dan by Shinjō.

Outside of his academy, Porta received a bachelor's degree in biblical studies in 1974 and was appointed pastor. He then became a minister with specialization in youth ministry at Berean University in 1996 and a pastor of the Christian Black Belt Association. He still uses self-defense techniques he learned in karate to develop and guide programs to ensure the safety of believers and pastors in the church environment while ministering as a Christian pastor.

In 2006, Porta was promoted to Hanshi 9th dan by Shinjō Masashi, the second chairman of the Shōbukan. He still teaches karate and kobudō to 60 people at his dōjō and to more members in four other locations in the USA.

Porta keeps training and instructing with the words of his late master engraved in his soul: "karate is in the heart". "Shinjō sensei was very kind, humble and thoughtful, and very strong in his karate. He used to say that karate is an individual journey. Keep traditional values and train hard and often." Cherishing these teachings, Porta continues to pass on the martial arts of Okinawa.

アジア・中東
アフリカ
オセアニア
中南米
北米
ヨーロッパ
米国

リリー小林流空手道場

2018年11月11日

05 米国

技の反復 神髄を追求

リリー小林流空手道場

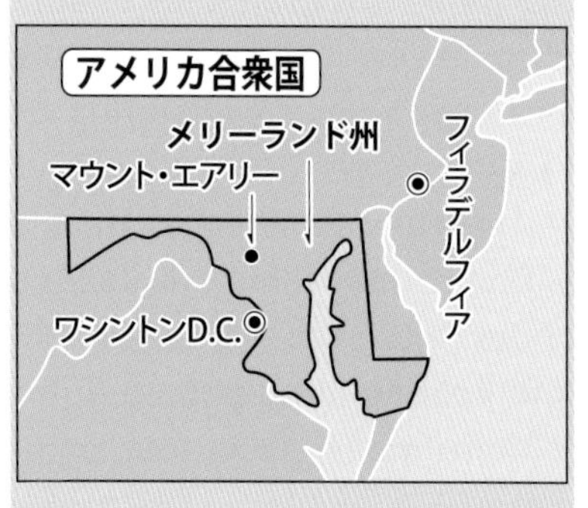

2014年に発行された『沖縄小林流空手道協会誌』の第一章「範士横顔」に、唯一米国人として紹介されているのはジェームス・リリー氏。

1942年、メリーランド州ボルチモア生まれのリリー氏は、63年海兵隊員として沖縄に配属された。ケネディ大統領が暗殺された11月22日から数日後、米軍基地から出て空手道場を求めた。友人のレン・ネイダート氏と共にタクシーに乗り、「一番強い道場に連れてってください」と運転手にお願いした。すると、浦添市城間にある宮城驍氏が指導する宮城道場に案内された。

歓迎の言葉として、稽古が厳しくこれまで米軍人で3カ月以上稽古した人はいない、昇段は望んでも期待できないと警告された。それでもすぐに入門した二人は、空手に打ち込んだ。小手鍛え、基本、型の繰り返しという稽古の後、お茶タイムが始まり、宮城氏や先輩の仲西豊氏や高良名勇氏との親睦が始まった。

95年訪沖した際に、「厳しい鍛錬に耐えられないと道場の皆さんは思っていた。しかし、休まず稽古に挑んだ貴方に対して、皆が敬意を払い始めた」と宮城氏は打ち明けた。

65年に帰国し、警察官として勤めながら空手の指導に挑んだ。宮城氏とも連絡を常に取り合い、ほどなく初段に昇段した。76年同州マウント・エアリーに移り、道場「リリー小林流空手道場」を開設。現在20数人の弟子と共に、宮城驍氏の小林流と古武道を継承している。

宮城驍氏（前列左から3人目）の道場で汗を流したリリー氏（同2人目）＝提供
Lilley (front row 2nd from the left) next to Miyagi (3rd from the left) in the Miyagi Dōjō.

範士9段であるリリー氏は、著者として出版もしている。25年間、警察官の職で得た経験を生かし、10数冊の諸説等を著した。その内の2冊は、警察関連著者団よりベストブックとして高い評価も受けた。

「宮城道場の門をくぐった時は、護身術を習うつもりだったが、単なる戦う術以上のものが学べた。空手は、生き方であり、すべての行動に空手がある。空手は、熱心な物の習い方、人にものを伝えること、忍耐などをその道を歩む人に教え込んでくれる。また、じっくりと人を見る力も学べる」と言う。

自己規律と心技体の統一というコンセプトに導かれたリリー氏は、型を使うときに自身の世界にいるかのように感じるという。「ある意味、型の精神性が表れる。技の繰り返しで空手のエネルギーと精神を感じる。演武が終わると、安らかな心の状態でいられる」と解説する。

沖縄と米国の空手界にとって父親、リリー氏にとって兄のような存在である宮城氏が指導する空手を大切にして伝え続ける。

In the book "Okinawa Shōrin-ryū Karatedō Kyokai Shi" published in 2014, James Lilley is the only American Hanshi introduced.

Born in Baltimore, Maryland in 1942, Lilley was assigned to Okinawa as a Marine in 1963. After his arrival, he went out with his friend Len Neidert and sought a karate dōjō. Asking the taxi driver to take them to the best karate club, they were driven to the Miyagi Dōjō of Miyagi Takeshi in Gusukuma, Urasoe City.

As a welcome word, they were warned that the training was strict and that no U.S. military personnel had practiced for more than three months, and that they could not expect a promotion. Even so,

Published on 2018/11/11

05 United States 

Lilley Shōrin-ryū Karate Dōjō

Repeating techniques in the pursuit of the essence

the two men joined and trained hard. After the practice of kote-kitae, basics and kata repetition, it was time for tea time. Along the way, friendship with Miyagi and the seniors deepened.

When he visited Okinawa in 1995, Miyagi confessed to him, "Everyone at the dōjō thought that you would not stand the rigorous training. However, you came back and soon everyone started gaining great respect for you."

After returning to the USA in 1965, he taught karate while working as a police officer. Constantly in contact with Miyagi, he was soon promoted to 1st dan black belt. In 1976, he moved to Mt. Airy, Maryland and established the Lilley Shōrin-ryū Karate Dōjō. Nowadays, with some 20 students, he is preserving the karate and kobudō of Miyagi.

Today a 9th dan, Lilley is also a published author who has written a dozen books based on his 25 years of experience with the police force. Among these, two books were highly praised by the police-related authors association.

"When I entered the Miyagi Dōjō, the original reason was to learn self-defense. But as time went on, I learned there was much more than just fighting to be learned. I found karate to be a Way of Life. In truth karate is a part of everything I do. Karate instills the disciples to work hard, study hard, teach others and to be patient. And through karate, one can also learn to see others for who they are."

Guided by the concepts of building self-discipline and the unification of mind and body as one, Lilley says he feels as if he is in his own world when performing kata. He explains, "In a sense, the spirit of the kata reveals itself. By repeating the technique, one can feel the energy and spirit of karate. After the performance, one can be in a peaceful state of mind."

Lilley will continue to cherish and convey the karate taught by Miyagi, who is for him like a father to the Okinawa and the USA karate worlds and to him like an elder brother.

1950年代後半、沖縄で上地流空手を習ったジョージ・マットソン氏は、帰国後の63年に『THE WAY OF KARATE』を発刊した。ベストセラーになったこの書で、空手が一気に有名になったことが北米における上地流空手の普及の原点とされている。

同本を読んだフランク・ゴーマン氏は、著者のマットソン氏に連絡し、ロードアイランドで道場を構えていたチャールス・アール氏を紹介された。これが20歳のゴーマン氏の上地流空手の始まりとなった。同系統を選んだ理由を問うと「マットソン先生の本は当時他の空手本と異なっていた。単なる突きや蹴りの教本ではなく、空手の哲学と人間形成の側面が紹介され、魅力的でした」と氏は答える。

1942年同州ポータケット生まれのゴーマン氏は、3年間鍛えられ65年に初めて沖縄を訪れた。上地流2代目上地完英氏に受け入れられ、21年間上地氏のもとで空手を学んだ。上地氏の86年の指導引退に伴い、ゴーマン氏は仲松健氏に師事するようになった。「78年、沖縄で稽古をしていたとき、上地先生は五つの上地流道場で稽古できるように調整してくれた。その後感想を聞かれ、各

ハムデンの道場で指導をしているゴーマン氏(右から2人目)=米国コネティカット州(提供)　Gorman (second from right) teaching at Hamden's dōjō.

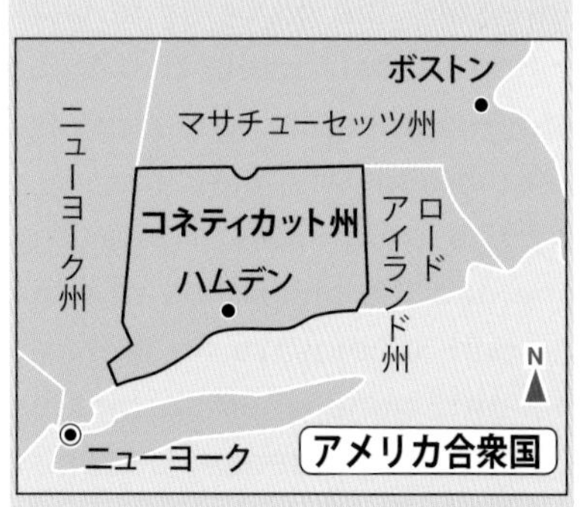

2021年9月26日

06 米国

自己実現 目指し稽古

北米自適塾

高段者の稽古法が違うので混乱していると伝えた。先生の意見を求めたところ、『仲松を見ろ!』と返答をもらった」と当時のいきさつを振り返る。

地元YMCAの数会場で指導したゴーマン氏は、73年にマサチューセッツ州、後に87年にフロリダ州に移り道場を開設した。現在、氏が住むコネティカット州ハムデンで弟子のブルース・トゥルガン氏の道場で指南する。そこで、十数人が稽古し、米国各州やアルゼンチンからの空手家も定期的に学びに来るという。

80年代に空手のプロ指導者になる前に、ゴーマン氏はワイヤとケーブル業界で機械エンジニアとして働いていた。職業から得られた分解能力を空手に応用し、氏はきめ細かい指導で知られている。

「自我は稽古する者の邪魔になる可能性がある。だれでもゆっくりと稽古をするべきだと思う。一気にすべてを学ぶことはしない方がいい。空手の鍛錬で得られる無限の教えを学び、理解するには、長い時間と厳しい練習が必要不可欠だ」と氏は指摘する。

ゴーマン氏は、『自己の改善と実現』が空手で最も重要な目的と信じる。日々、沖縄で得られた知恵を習いたい者と気持ちを分かち合いながら、それぞれの空手も自身の道作りもすべてが“進行中”であることを理解しつつ、研究と指導に励む。

George Mattson, who learned Uechi-ryū karate in Okinawa in the latter half of the 1950s, published "The Way of Karate" in 1963 after returning from Japan. This best-selling book, with which karate became famous right away, is considered to be the origin of the spread of Uechi-ryū in North America.

After reading the book, Frank Gorman contacted the author and was introduced to Charles Earl, who had a dōjō on Rhode Island. This was the beginning of 20-year-old Gorman's walk on the Uechi-ryū path. When asked why he chose this system, Gorman replies, "Mattson's book was different from other karate books at that time. It wasn't so much a

Published on 2021/9/26

06 United States 

North American Jiteki Juku

Training for self-actualization

book about punching and kicking. For me it was more about philosophy and personal development."

Born in Pawtuckit, Rhode Island in 1942, Gorman trained for three years and visited Okinawa for the first time in 1965. He was welcome by Uechi Kanei, the second heir of Uechi-ryū, and studied karate under him for 21 years.

When Uechi retired in 1986, Gorman began to study under Nakamatsu Ken. "When I was training in Okinawa in 1978, Uechi sensei arranged for me to train at five different dōjō with five different senior masters." When asked by Uechi what he thought about the experience, he replied he was confused because all of the masters seemed to practice Uechi-ryū differently. Asking for Uechi's advice, he was told "Watch Nakamatsu!"

Gorman, who taught at several YMCA locations, moved to Massachusetts in 1973 and later to Florida in 1987 where he opened a dōjō. Now living in Hamden, Connecticut, he is currently instructing at the dōjō of his student Bruce Tulgan. There, more than a dozen people practice together, and karateka from other states and Argentina also come to practice occasionally.

Prior to becoming a professional karate instructor in the 1980s, Gorman worked as a mechanical engineer in the wire and cable industry. Applying the analyzing skills gained from his profession to karate, he is well known for his detailed instruction.

He stresses, "Our egos can get in the way of us learning and advancing. I think everyone should take their training slowly. Do not try to learn everything right away. It takes a lot of time and hard practice to learn and understand the infinite lessons karate training can teach us."

For Gorman, the most important purposes in karate are "self-improvement and self-actualization." Every day, while sharing with those who want to learn the wisdom gained in Okinawa, he keeps researching and guiding others, making them understand that everyone's karate and path building are "a work in progress".

アメリカの最初の空手道場が設立されたのは1945年のころという。館長は、中国拳法と空手の技を習ったロバート・トライアス氏であり、後に沖縄で聞きなれない首里流を名乗った。

50年代以降、日本人指導者や沖縄で空手を習い、帰国した多くの米兵によって空手が全米に普及した。現在、あらゆる形で空手が人気の格闘技になったが、本場とはかなり違った方式で指導されているのも事実だ。

そんな中、沖縄空手を伝統的に普及してきたパイオニアといえば、剛柔流の故アンソニー・ミラキャンやマイケル・マンキューソ(73)、小林流の伊波清吉(85)、上地流のジョージ・マットソン(80)やウオルター・マットソン(78)、松林流の故宇江城安盛、一心流のアルセニオ・アドビンクラ(79)らの各氏がいる。現在、沖縄の組織の直接的な支部は40余あり、その下には数え切れない町道場がある。なお、分裂した道場もきわめて多いそうだ。

沖縄とその空手に憧れる米国人が多い中、1946年生まれのダン・スミス氏は特別な存在だ。16歳のころ本土系の松濤館と出合い2段の腕前になった。

当時、それまで沖縄空手と縁のなかったスミス氏の空手に新たな風が吹いた。大学の軍事奨学金を

ダン・スミス氏(後列右から4人目)と息子のアラン・スミス氏(同3人目)。前列中央は島袋善保氏　Dan Smith (4th from the right) with his son Alan (3rd from the right) and Shimabukuro Zenpō in the center.

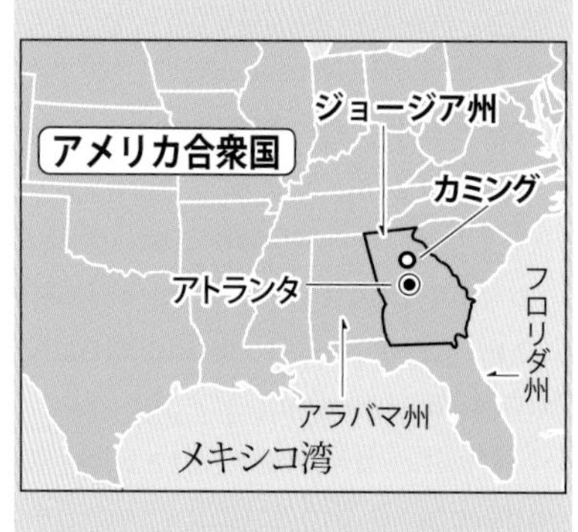

2017年07月23日

07 米国

聖地への恩返し胸に

コールマウンテン空手道場

受け、68年の卒業後、軍に任官され、3年間沖縄に赴任した。

松濤館系の道場を求めて氏は、いろんな道場を見学したが、その系統の道場は存在しなかった。ある日、北谷町謝苅で指導していた島袋善良・善保各氏の「聖武館」に入門した。「この道場では、私がこれまでやってきた空手とは異なっていたが、稽古法が魅力的」と氏は思い出す。

帰国後、無線通信業界で仕事をしながら、喜屋武朝徳氏の手(ティー)を継ぐ島袋家の空手を磨きつつ指導の道に入った。75年に聖武館米国を創立し92年、ジョージア州カミング市に現在の道場を開設した。

これまで、40回以上沖縄を訪れ、ビジネスのノウハウも活かし、氏は多くの空手の催しを後押ししてきた。その一つに、96年アトランタ五輪での喜納昌吉氏による「全ての武器を楽器に」という舞台に参加した県出身空手家40人はスミス氏の大きなサポートを受けたという。後に2001年、米国で沖縄空手の世界大会も開催した。

流派を問わない全面的支援について、09年範士9段に昇段した氏は「島袋家と沖縄の友人に対する愛情が私の原動力。1968年に温かい心で迎えられ、今日までウチナーンチュとして優しくされてきた。ある意味で恩返し」と説明する。間違いなくスミス氏は、アメリカにおける沖縄空手の恩人だ。

The first American karate dōjō was founded around 1945 by Robert Trias, who had learned Chinese martial arts and karate, and later called his style Shuri-ryū, an unfamiliar name in Okinawa.

From the 1950s, karate spread throughout the entire country due to the endeavor of Japanese instructors and many US soldiers who had learned karate in Okinawa.

Meanwhile, some pioneers have popularized Okinawa karate the traditional way. Among them are the late Anthony Mirakian and Michael Mancuso of Gōjū-ryū, Shōrin-ryū Iha Seikichi, George Mattson and Walter Mattson of Uechi-ryū, the late Matsubayashi-ryū Ueshiro Ansei, and Isshin-ryū Arcenio Advincula. Currently, there are more than 40 direct branches of Okinawan organizations with countless dōjō under them. There are also quite a lot of groups that broke out.

Published on 2017/7/23

07 United States 

Coal Mountain Karate Dōjō

Repaying the kindness of the birthplace

Born in 1946, Dan Smith stands out among the many Americans who yearn for Okinawa and its karate. At the age of 16, he started Shōtōkan and earned a 2nd dan black belt.

At that time, a new wind blew in Smith's karate, a man who had no connection so far with Okinawa karate. With a military scholarship for college, he graduated from university in 1968 and was stationed to Okinawa for three years.

In search of a Shōtōkan dōjō but finding none, he entered the Seibukan of Shimabukuro Zenryō and Zenpō in Jagaru, Chatan Town. "I was excited to join because the methods and training were very attractive," he recalls.

After returning to the USA, while working in the wireless industry, he continued to deepen his knowledge and started teaching Kyan Chōtoku's karate as inherited by the Shimabukuro. He founded Seibukan USA in 1975 and opened his current dōjō in Cumming, Georgia in 1992.

Smith has visited Okinawa more than 40 times and has supported many karate events by making the best of his business know-how. For example, a delegation of 40 Okinawan karate experts who showcased their skills during Kina Shōkichi's performance at the 1996 Atlanta Olympics received a huge amount of support from him. Later, in 2001, he also held the Okinawa Karate World Championships in the USA.

Regarding his full support regardless of style, Smith, who was promoted to 9th dan in 2009 says, "My love for the Shimabukuro family and friends in Okinawa is my driving force. I was warmheartedly welcomed in 1968 and have been treated kindly as an Uchinānchu to this day. In a sense, it is a way to repay this kindness." Without a doubt, Dan Smith is a great benefactor of Okinawa karate in the USA.

2020年12月27日

08 米国

疑問と考察 鍛錬の源

裏庭道場

アメリカ合衆国
アラバマ州
ジョージア州
ミシシッピ州
ルイジアナ州
フロリダ州
ブレイデントン
メキシコ湾

米国カリフォルニア生まれのジョン・ロード氏(70)は24歳の時、家族と移り住んだフロリダ州でアメリカン拳法を習った。

翌年カロライナに移り、フレッド・ラビ氏に弟子入りした。ラビ氏はベトナム戦争で従軍し、キャンプハンセンに駐留した際に島袋栄三氏に師事した。島袋栄三氏は一心流開祖・島袋龍夫氏の弟。戦前剛柔流の宮城長順氏や首里手・泊手の喜屋武朝徳氏に師事した。

「ラビ先生の動きを見て、これまで習った空手と違うものを見つけたと感じた」とロード氏。1979年4月に金武町を訪れ、4カ月間、島袋氏の少林流空手の指導を受けた。

この年の末、多くの米軍人の指導に当たった島袋栄三氏は8カ月間、ロード氏のいる米国に滞在した。「先生と一緒に暮らせて光栄でした。29歳の私には、この運命の機会を十分に理解できなかったかもしれませんが、前向きに異国で暮らす先生を見て、すごく勉強になった」と振り返る。

若者に空手の魅力を伝えるロード氏(中央)=提供
Lohde (center) conveying the charms of karate to young people.

80年にロード氏はノースカロライナ州で道場を開設した。81年に国立公園局のパーク・レンジャー(自然保護官)になり、さまざまな公園で任務を果たした。時には動物園でのハンドラーやパフォーマーの仕事も引き受けた。トラやジャガー、ヒョウを扱い、勤務では心の持ち方など沖縄空手の知識が役立ったという。

勤務先の地域で危険にさらされている若者たちにも空手を指導した。「プログラムの目標は良いロールモデル、人格形成、自己規律をもって子どもの生活に介入すること。この目標の達成に向けても、沖縄伝統空手の精神はふさわしいものがある」と強調する。

2014年まで指導に励んだロード氏は道場を高弟に譲り、現在はフロリダ州ブレイデントンの自宅内の「裏庭道場」で指導に努めている。師が他界する2年前の15年にロード氏は宜野座で8段を授与された。

この年から島袋氏にも師事した妻のパムさんと共にハリケーンシーズン中は故郷フロリダで、冬は暖かい沖縄で過ごしている。

空手の魅力は「静かな力を養う過程」にあり、「年を取ると同時に気付かされた」とロード氏。そこにたどり着くため、常に疑問を持ち、考察する作業の重要性も指摘した。

ロード氏は組織に加盟せず、師から伝授された技と教えを胸に、空手を追究する意義を日々見つめながら稽古に取り組んでいる。

Born in California, John Lohde (70) studied American kenpō at the age of 24 in Florida.

The following year, he moved to Carolina and became a student of Fred Raby, who served in the Vietnam War and trained with Shimabukuro Eizō when he was stationed at Camp Hansen. Shimabukuro Eizō was the younger brother of Shimabukuro Tatsuo, the founder of Isshin-ryū. Before WWII, he studied with Miyagi Chōjun of Gōjū-ryū and Kyan Chōtoku, an expert of Shurite and Tomarite.

"As I watched Raby workout with his small class, I knew his karate was significantly different from what I had been learning in Florida," says Lohde. Ultimately, he visited Kin Town in April 1979 and practiced Shimabukuro's Shōrin-ryū karate for four months.

Published on 2020/12/27

08 United States 

Ura Niwa Dōjō

Examination as a source of discipline

At the end of the year, Shimabukuro, who taught many US military personnel in Okinawa, decided to live for eight months in the USA, staying close by where Lohde was living. "I was honored to help and to live with Shimabukuro Eizō sensei. I was only 29 and possibly not prepared to fully appreciate the opportunity. Still, it was educational to watch a karate master navigate a complex culture with only a basic understanding of a language," Lohde recalls.

Opening a dōjō in North Carolina in 1980, Lohde became a law enforcement park ranger and worked at numerous national parks. He also did work as a handler and performer working at zoos, handling tigers, jaguars and leopards. He recalls that karate came in handy in both professions.

He also taught karate to "at-risk" youth. "The goal of these 'At Risk programs' is to intervene in the child's life with positive role models, character development and self-discipline. The spirit of Okinawa traditional karate is appropriate for achieving this goal," he emphasizes.

Having taught until 2014, Lohde handed over his dōjō to his senior student and now teaches at his backyard "Ura Niwa Dōjō" in his home in Bradenton, Florida. In 2015, two years before his teacher passed away, he was awarded the 8th dan in Ginoza.

From this year, together with his wife Pam who also studied with Shimabukuro, he spends his time in Florida during the hurricane season while living in Okinawa during winter.

Lohde believes that the charm of karate is "the process for developing quiet strength," something he noticed "as he matured as a person". In order to get there, as his favorite saying is "what is the real question?" he points out the importance of examination.

Affiliated with no organization, Lohde focuses on the significance of pursuing karate every day, keeping in mind the skills and teachings his master taught him.

2020年01月26日

09 米国

技の研さん重ね指南

小林流小林館

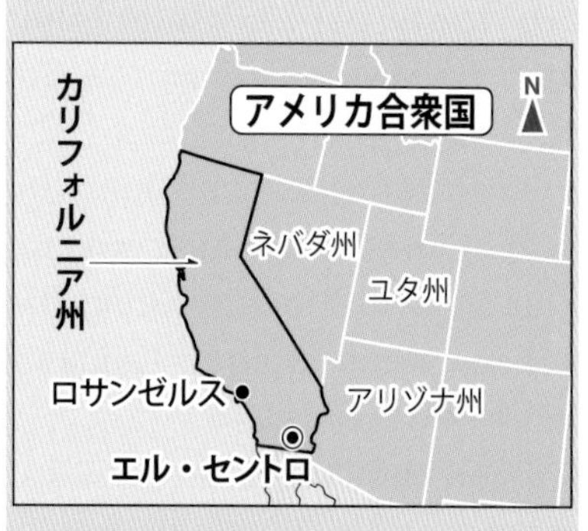

1919年から首里手の屋部憲通氏は8年間、米カリフォルニアに滞在した。指導した記録はないが、今日米国では首里手系の空手が広く普及している。

その中でも、小林流始祖・知花朝信氏の高弟故仲里周五郎氏の小林流小林舘について、カリフォルニア州のナビル・ヌージャン教士は「米国をはじめ世界で活発に活動している。小林舘のカリキュラムに従う道場は世界に100以上あり、評判も非常に良い」と説明する。同州で同系の空手は、66年から仲里氏に師事したシド・キャンベル氏により普及したという。

50年イスラエル生まれのヌージャン氏は、19歳の時、さらなる進学のため米国に移住した。大学でサッカーチームに所属し、72年に、チーム仲間のロバート・サベッラ氏と共に空手を始めた。後に日本航空のパイロットにもなったサベッラ氏は、当時日本本土系の空手を稽古していたという。ヌージャン氏も76年から指導にも携わり、道場を開館させた。

キャンベル氏と出会った両氏は、88年に沖縄を訪れ、仲里氏が開設した那覇市安謝の小林舘道場で汗を流した。「忘れられない体験になった。仲里先生の性格、リーダーシップ、空手の手腕に感銘を受けた。先生はとてもタフでした!」とヌージャン氏は振り返る。すっかり発祥の地の空手と仲里氏に魅了され、同年小林舘に正式に入門した。

道場で型を指導するヌージャン氏(手前左)=提供
Noujaim (front left) teaching kata at his dōjō.

あれからヌージャン氏は、船越義珍氏の空手二十箇条にある「空手は湯の如し、絶えず熱度を与えなければ元の水に還へる」という教えに従い、毎年数回沖縄を訪れ、研さんを積む。

本場沖縄で学んだものは、カリフォルニア州エル・セントロの道場に通う60人に伝授する。米国内のほかイスラエル、ヨルダン、デンマーク、英国、チリ、アルゼンチン、メキシコ、バミューダ、インドなど15支部でも指南する。

中学校のスピーチ言語病理学者であるヌージャン氏は、24年前から沖縄の指導者を招いて恒例の小林舘キャンプを開催している。

2009年、仲里氏から8段を授与されたヌージャン氏は「小さなことをやれない人は、大きなことはやれない」と謙遜する。

沖縄の伝統、社会、人々、文化、そして武道に関われることをとても幸運なことと感じているというヌージャン氏は「チムグクル」を胸に沖縄空手の普及に努め、感謝の思いを形にし続けていく。

Published on 2020/1/26

09 United States 

Shōrin-ryū Shōrinkan

Mastering the technique and teaching

From 1919 and for 8 years, Shurite expert Yabu Kentsū resided in California. Although there is no record of him teaching karate during his stay, today, Shurite related karate is widely spread in the USA.

Among the various systems, Californian Nabil Noujaim describes the Shōrin-ryū Shōrinkan founded by the late Nakazato Shūgorō, a student of the founder of Shōrin-ryū Chibana Chōshin, in the following words. "Shōrinkan is well represented in the US and the world. There are more than a hundred dōjō following the Shōrinkan curriculum in the world and they all have a very good reputation."

Shōrinkan was popularized in the Californian state from 1966 by Sid Campbell who studied directly under Nakazato.

Born in Israel in 1950, Noujaim moved to the USA at the age of 19 to further his education. A member of the soccer team at college, he started karate in 1972 with his teammate Robert Sabella. Sabella, who later became a Japan Airlines pilot, was practicing mainland Japanese karate at that time. Noujaim also became involved with teaching karate and in 1976, he opened his own dōjō.

Sabella and Noujaim met Campbell and visited Okinawa in 1988, training at Nakazato's Shōrinkan in Aja, Naha City. "It was an experience that I will never forget. I was heavily impressed with Nakazato sensei's character, leadership, and karate skills. He was very tough!" remembers Noujaim. Charmed by Nakazato and Okinawa, he officially became a member of the Shōrinkan the same year.

Since then, following one the 20 karate principles of Funakoshi Gichin that says, "Karate is like hot water; without continuous heat it will cool down," Noujaim has been visiting Okinawa several times every year to deepen his karate knowledge.

What he learns in Okinawa, he teaches it to 60 people who train at his dōjō in El Centro, California, the Okinawa Karatedō Shōrin-ryū Shōrinkan. In addition to the USA, he also teaches in 15 branches located in Israel, Jordan, Denmark, the UK, Chile, Argentina, Mexico, Bermuda and India among others.

A high school speech language pathologist who also officiated collegiate and professional football, Noujaim has hosted Shōrinkan camps in Southern California for the past 24 years.

Promoted to 8th dan by Nakazato in 2009, he humbly believes that "If you can't do the little things right, you will never do the big things right."

As he feels very fortunate to be involved with Okinawa's traditions, society, people, culture and martial arts, Noujaim strives to popularize Okinawa karate the Okinawan way in order to express the gratitude he has for Okinawa.

2018年12月30日

⑩ 米国

絆と魂育む女性館長

ジェンセンビーチ上地流空手道場

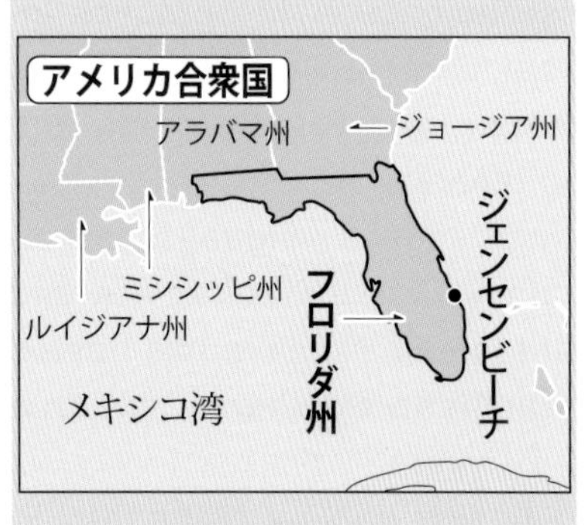

「親善と団結の力、国際理解と寛容の促進、人間同士の平和な関係と友情を育むこと。このすべてを通して、互いの生活様式へのより良い理解がもたらされ、世界平和が築かれるでしょう」。この言葉を発信するのは、上地流八段のペギー・ヘス氏(66)。

ヘス氏は、プロボクサー、ロッキー・マルシアノ氏とマービン・ハグラー氏を生んだマサチューセッツ州ブロックトンで生まれた。1974年、22歳の時、元兵隊で友人のステフェン・バンチック氏と共に米国で上地流の源泉といえるマットソン空手アカデミーに入門した。

157センチと小柄だが、その存在はビッグな女性空手家といえる。教員養成大学卒のヘス氏は、空手の道に進む前から指導者の才があった。上地流の魅力にはまり、先輩から導かれ、本場沖縄を訪ねることを決めた。↗

1978年2月、宜野湾市普天間にある上地流の本部道場の門をたたいた。ヘス氏を歓迎し、2カ月間に渡り指導したのは、上地流2代目の上地完英氏。滞在の良い思い出は山ほどあるが、上地氏の人格が分かるある出来事が記憶に残っているという。「私が帰国する前に、上地先生が恩師のジャック・サマーズ氏に電報を送り、私が初段の審査を受けられるように許可を求めた。想像してみてください…上地先生が許可を求めたなんて!」

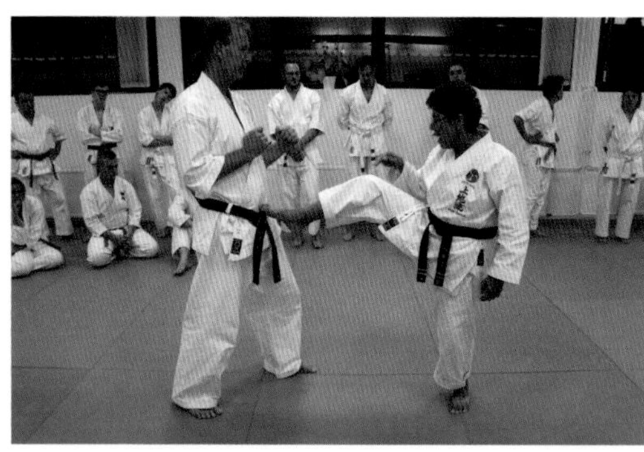

セミナーで足先蹴りを指導するヘス氏(右)=提供　Hess (right) teaching toe kicking at a seminar.

空手の奥深さに感銘を受け、初段に合格したヘス氏はさらに稽古に励み、82年、指導員になった。翌年、フロリダのジェンセンビーチに移り、自宅で道場を開設。これまで130人余りの弟子を育てた。世界に飛び回って指導してもヘス氏は、教士である前に学ぶ者であることを常に忘れない。

空手の目的を問うと、「米社会では、誰でも銃は持てる。銃には勝てない。男女問わず、空手を学ぶ理由はけんかに強くなるためではない。強い体を築き、自信を持って自己認識を育み、姿勢と健康を改善するのが目的です。そして何よりも新しい友情を築きながら楽しい時間を過ごすこと」と力強い。

その言葉通り、明るさ、自信と強い体がヘス氏の武器だ。家事、料理、講演など“何でもできるペギ”といわれるヘス氏は、道場でも自ら示して指導するというスタイルを貫き、きめ細かく弟子に技を伝えている。

「(私は)上地流の一流の指導者に師事した。それぞれの特徴と性格から学び、贈ってくれた恵と祝福を次世代に伝えたい」。空手を通じて世界中の人々と末変わらぬ友情を持てるよう、ヘス氏は揺るぎない決意を抱いている。

Published on 2018/12/30

⑩ United States 

Uechi-ryū Karatedō Dōjō of Jensen Beach

A female kanchō nurturing bonds and souls

"Through the power of goodwill and unity; by promoting international understanding and tolerance; by developing peaceful relations and friendships among people, a better understanding of one's way of life will result and world peace will be built." These are the words of Peggy Hess (66), a 8th Dan in Uechi-ryū.

Hess was born in Brockton, Massachusetts, the home of Rocky Marciano and Marvin Hagler. In 1974, at the age of 22 and together with her friend Stephen Banchick, she enrolled in the local Mattson Academy, the cradle of Uechi-ryū in the USA.

Although she is 157 cm tall, she has a huge presence as a karateka. Graduated from a teacher's college, she had a talent as a teacher even before she started walking the path of karate.

Having felt in love with Uechi-ryū, she decided to visit Okinawa and in February 1978, she entered the Uechi-ryū Honbu Dōjō in Futenma, Ginowan City. Uechi Kanei, the second heir of the style welcomed her and taught her for two months. Among the many good memories she has, she remembers an event that reveals Uechi's personality. "When I found out that Master Uechi had sent a telegram to my teacher Jack Summers asking permission to test me for Shōdan before I left the island. Imagine ... he asked for permission!"

Impressed by the depth of karate, Hess trained harder and became an instructor in 1982. The following year, she moved to Jensen Beach, Florida and opened a dōjō at her home. She has raised more than 130 disciples so far. As she often flies around the world to teach Uechi-ryū, she always remembers that she is first a student and then a teacher.

When asked the purpose of karate, she says, "I tell male or female that the reason they should be studying karate is not to learn how to fight because everyone has a gun, and no one can bite a bullet. The purpose of their study should be to build their bodies strong, to foster self-awareness with confidence, to improve their posture and general health, and above all to have fun while building new friendships."

In this spirit, brightness, self-confidence and a strong body are Hess's weapons. Known as "do it all Peg!" in the dōjō, she sticks to the style of showing and teaching by herself, carefully conveying the art to her students.

"I have studied under the best masters of Uechi-ryū. Learning from their characteristics and personalities, I want to pass on their wisdom and blessings to the next generation."

Through karate, Peggy Hess has an unwavering determination to create and maintain a lasting friendship with people all over the world.

日本で拳法と言えば、中国の武術や香川県に総本山を有し1947年に創始された日本の武道「少林寺拳法」が思い浮かぶ。

中国語からの訳語で武術を意味する言葉「拳法」は、琉球の武術、いわゆる空手を紹介するために船越義珍氏の『琉球拳法唐手』(22年上梓)にも使用された。

現在世界中には、各国のさまざまな武術の他に、日本で32年に発足した日本拳法、エド・パーカー氏が創始したアメリカン拳法など、多くの拳法が存在する。

沖縄では、首里・泊手の型と実践組手を基本とする沖縄拳法が知られている。「沖縄の手(ティ)=沖縄拳法」という構想で60年ごろ、故中村茂氏によって命名された沖縄空手の流派の一つである。

米国での沖縄拳法の普及は、沖縄で空手を習った多くの米兵のほか、72年以降、ニューヨークを拠点に指導する県出身の比嘉照行氏や77年以降、米国に移住した故親田清勇氏によって行われた。

55年ニュージャージー州ブリッジトン生まれのビル・ベリー氏は、17歳の時、警察官が指導していた近所のテコンドーの道場に入門した。

84年から87年、海兵隊員になった妻が沖縄に駐留するよう命じられた。同行したベリー氏は、嘉手納基地内のスーパーで働き始め、空手発祥の

セミナーでのベリー氏(前列右から3人目)と喜屋武徹氏(同4人目)=米国ジョージア州　Berry (third from the right in the front row) and Kyan (to his right) at a seminar in Georgia, USA.

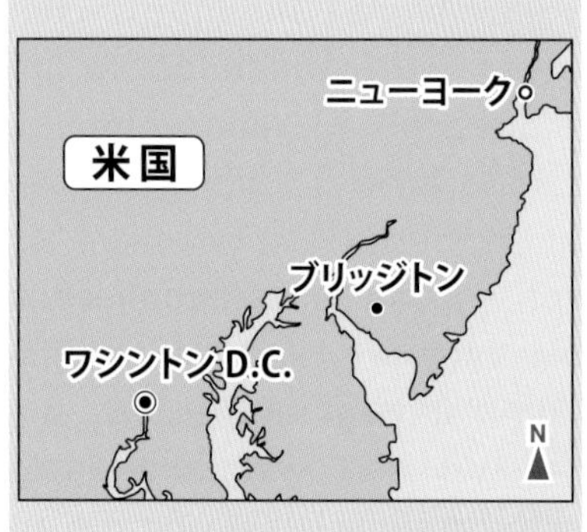

2022年1月9日

⑪米国

技術向上 研修重ねる

沖縄拳法

地での指導者を求めた。

85年、米軍基地で勤務していた沖縄拳法空手道協会・拳友会の喜屋武徹氏の下で、ベリー氏は沖縄拳法を習い始めた。

97年に妻が再び沖縄に駐留するようになり、ベリー氏も2003年まで沖縄に滞在し、喜屋武氏の下で研究を重ねた。その後も、技術向上の検証のため2、3年おきに訪沖をしたという。氏は「沖縄に戻り続けた理由は、周囲の人々を鼓舞するリーダーで友人でもある喜屋武先生とその家族を訪ね、訓練を続け、できる限り多くのことを学びたかった」と説明する。

21年6月に喜屋武氏の師である中村氏の高弟で同協会の喜納敏光会長より6段への昇段を認められたベリー氏は、現在、妻と一緒にバージニア州に住み、請負会社で予算アナリストとして働きつつ、自身の道場「ポトマックショアズ拳友会」と米国内の3支部道場で指導をしている。

「沖縄は空手の発祥の地。空手着を身に着けて帯を締める時、沖縄と深いつながりを感じる。深く掘り下げて、諦めない心が沖縄空手の精神であり、この奥深さが私にとって何より魅力的だ」とベリー氏は言う。ロータリークラブの会員でもある氏は、道場内外で社会貢献も目指す。これも沖縄空手の神髄なのだ。

Speaking of kenpō in Japan, people think of Chinese martial arts and Shōrinji Kenpō which was founded in 1947 with headquarters in Kagawa Prefecture.

The term "kenpō," a translation of a Chinese word meaning martial arts, was used by Funakoshi Gichin in his 1922 published book "Ryūkyū Kenpō Karate" in order to introduce the Ryūkyūan martial art that is karate.

Today, next to the many martial arts using this term, Nihon Kenpō, established in Japan in 1923, and American Kenpō, founded by Ed Parker in the USA, come to mind.

Okinawa Kenpō is a karate style based on Shurite and Tomarite kata and the practice of sparring. It is a system that was named around 1960 by the late Nakamura Shigeru on the concept that "Okinawa tī (the original karate) equals Okinawa Kenpō".

Published on 2022/1/9

⓫ United States 

Okinawa Kenpō

No end towards technical improvement

The spread of Okinawa Kenpō in the USA is due to the many servicemen who learned karate in Okinawa, as well as Okinawans Higa Teruyuki, who has been teaching in New York since 1972, and the late Oyata Seiyū, who moved to the USA in 1977.

Born in Bridgeton, New Jersey in 1955, Bill Berry entered a nearby Taekwondo dōjō at the age of 17. From 1984 to 1987, his wife, who was a Marine, was stationed in Okinawa. Accompanying her, Berry worked at a supermarket on Kadena Air Base and sought a karate instructor.

In 1985, he started training Okinawa Kenpō under Kyan Tōru, head of the Kenyūkai within the Okinawa Kenpō Karatedō Association who was also working on base.

In 1997, as his wife was once again stationed in Okinawa, Berry came along and deepened his practice with Kyan until 2003. After that, he visited Okinawa every 2-3 years to verify the quality of his technique's improvement. He says, "The reasons why I have continued to return to Okinawa are to visit Kyan sensei and his family, to continue my training and learn as much as I can."

In 2021, Berry was promoted to 6th dan by Kina Toshimitsu, a senior student of Nakamura Shigeru and chairman of the Okinawa Kenpō Karatedō Association. He now lives in Virginia with his wife and is a budget analyst while working for a contracting corporation. He teaches Okinawa Kenpō karate at his Potomac Shores Kenyūkai and in 3 other branches.

"When I put my uniform on and tie up my belt, I feel a strong sense of connection with Okinawa. To dig deep and never give up is the essence of Okinawa karate and its depth is its greatest charm." A member of the Rotary Club, Berry also aims to contribute to society outside the dōjō. This is also the essence of Okinawa karate.

米国で沖縄空手の多くの流派の普及は、帰国した米兵により行われた。しかし、長嶺将真氏が1947年に命名した松林流の普及に関して、60~70年代に渡米したウチナーンチュの功績は大きい。その中には、宇江城安盛氏、長嶺高兆氏、大嶺朝徳氏などの空手家がいる。

55年、当時那覇市美栄橋町(現久茂地)にある長嶺道場で師事した海兵隊員のジェムス・ワクス氏は、帰国後オハイオ州で道場を開設。沖縄の本部に指導者要請をしたところ、62年に長嶺道場の宇江城氏(当時30歳)が派遣され、2002年の死去まで、多くの弟子を育てた。

宇江城氏の門弟の一人ジョセフ・キング氏は、1960年代に最初の黒帯の一人になり、ニューヨーク州ロングアイランドのグレートネック村で「沖縄空手道場」を開き指導にあたった。

56年同村生まれのフレッド・スレシンジャー氏は13歳の頃キング氏の道場に入門し、空手の手ほどきを受けた。

22年間稽古に励み、91年に、長嶺将真氏85歳生年祝賀会を機に行われた世界大会の際に初めて沖縄を訪れた。「当時、2代目の長嶺高兆先生

信武館道場で技を鍛錬するスレシンジャー氏(中央)=提供
Schlesinger (center) training at the Shinbukan.

2021年07月11日

⑫米国

沖縄武術 世界に発信

真武館

から受けた温かいおもてなしは今でも忘れられない」と氏は語る。

2003年にスレシンジャー家は、ニューメキシコ州のリオランチョに移住した。4年後、獣医師を務めながら、氏は67坪の道場「真武館道場リオランチョ」を開設した。14年に同所で自身のクリニックを開き、鍼術(しんじゅつ)を含む中国の伝統的な獣医学を専門とした。しかし17年に道場を閉鎖し、「真武館」を自宅敷地内に移動し後世の指導を続けた。

「真武館」では、松林流の空手の他にも、古武道の達人でもあった参院議員の喜屋武真栄氏が長嶺道場に伝授した古武道や琉球古武術保存振興会の古武道の研究を手掛けている。

仕事と武術指導の他、09年からは本部の指示のもとで15カ国に支部、米国内に35余りの道場を有する世界松林流空手道連盟(平良慶孝会長)の英語ウェブサイトの運営を行っている。

19年、空手歴50年の節目の年に来沖したスレシンジャー氏は、松林流の6段に昇段した。

昨年に予定されていた那覇市泊新屋敷公園での長嶺将真氏の顕彰碑除幕式が、今年の11月に延期された。スレシンジャー氏は「われわれが持っているのは今だけだ」という格言を信じて参加を希望し、本部からの連絡を待つ。その間、地道に沖縄の武術の研究と指導に努める。

Many schools of Okinawa karate were popularized in the USA by returning military servicemen. However, when it comes to Matsubayashi-ryū, some Okinawans have made great contributions to the spread of the style in the 1960s and 1970s. Among them are Ueshiro Ansei, Nagamine Takayoshi and Ōmine Chōtoku.

Former Marine James Wax, who studied at the Nagamine dōjō in Naha City in 1955, opened a dōjō in Ohio after returning home. Requesting an instructor from Okinawa, Ueshiro Ansei (30 years old at that time) of the Nagamine dōjō was dispatched in 1962 and trained many students until his death in 2002.

A student of Ueshiro, Joseph King was one of the first American black belts under Ueshiro during the 1960s. He opened the "Okinawan Karate Dōjō" in Great Neck village, Long Island, New York.

Published on 2021/7/11

⑫ United States 

Shinbukan

Promoting Okinawan martial arts worldwide

Born in the same village in 1956, Fred Schlesinger entered King's dōjō at the age of 13 and started learning karate.

After 22 years of practice, he visited Okinawa for the first time in 1991 for Nagamine Shōshin's 85th birthday celebration event. "I still can't forget his son Nagamine Takayoshi's very warm hospitality toward our group," he recalls.

In 2003, the Schlesinger family moved to Rio Rancho, New Mexico. While working as a veterinarian, Schlesinger established in 2007 a 2400 square foot dōjō in Rio Rancho that he named the Shinbukan Dōjō of Rio Rancho. In 2014, he opened his own clinic in the same city, specializing in traditional Chinese veterinary medicine. However, he closed his dōjō three years later and moved the Shinbukan to his home premises to continue teaching his students.

At the Shinbukan, people study Matsubayashi-ryū karate, some of the kobudō taught at the Nagamine dōjō by Kyan Shinei, a kobudō expert and a member of the House of Representatives, as well as the kobudō of the Ryūkyū Kobujutsu Hozon Shinkōkai.

In addition to his work and martial tuition, since 2009, Schlesinger manages under the direction of the headquarters the English website of the World Matsubayashi-ryū Karatedō Association headed by Taira Yoshitaka. The organization has branches in 15 countries and more than 35 dōjō operated in the USA.

Schlesinger was promoted to karate 6th dan in 2019, a milestone year marking his 50 years of karate practice.

The unveiling ceremony of Nagamine Shōshin's praising monument at Tomari Shinyashiki Park in Naha City, which was scheduled for last year, has been postponed to November this year.

Schlesinger, who believes in the maxim "All we ever have is now" hopes to participate and awaits information from the headquarters in Okinawa. Meanwhile, he steadily strives to study and teach Okinawan martial arts.

2021年05月23日

⑬ 米国

鍛錬通し 剛柔流追求

武道クエスト

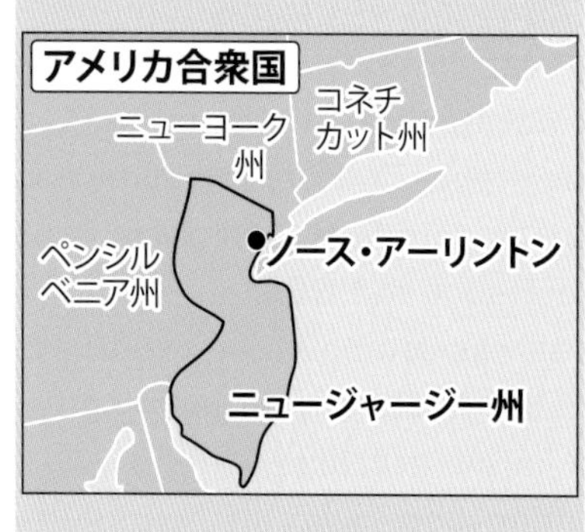

フランク・シナトラの名曲「ニューヨーク・ニューヨーク」で「眠らない街」と歌われたニューヨーク市での空手の始まりは、1950年代にさかのぼる。52年、極真会館館長の大山倍達氏が渡米し、同市などで演武を披露した。その後、松濤館系や当時、「韓国空手」と名付けられていたテコンドーなどが普及した。

58年、同市ブロンクス区生まれのルイス・モラレス氏は、12歳のころ、テコンドーを経て空手の道を歩み始めた。70年代のブロンクスはギャングの多い街として知られていた。生まれ育った環境の影響を受けて、モラレス氏は空手を通して効果的な護身術を身に付けたかったと振り返る。

氏が通った剛柔流の道場では、渡口政吉氏の尚礼館系の型と本土系剛柔会の組手を学んだ。82年に両系統の発祥の地での稽古を体験したくて、日本本土と沖縄を訪ねた。帰国後、米在住で剛柔流を指導する故知念輝夫氏を紹介され、約16年間師事した。「知念先生の型の演技にほれ込んだ」と氏は述べる。

99年2回目の訪沖の際、DVDを通して存在を知った西原町で沖縄剛柔流拳志會を構える外間

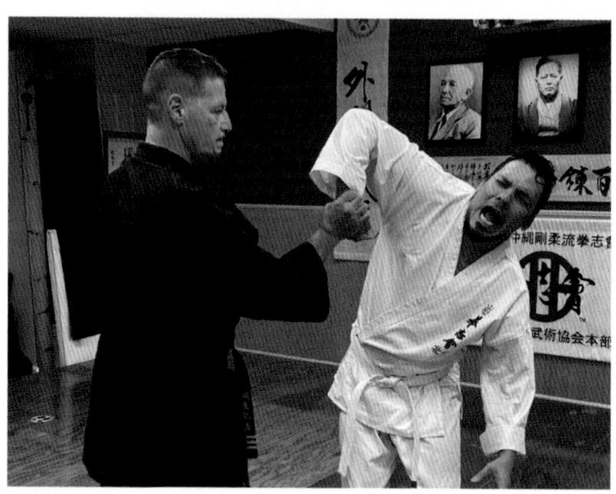

分解を指導するルイス・モラレス氏（左）＝米国ニュージャージー州（提供）
Morales (left) instructing an application in New Jersey.

哲弘氏に面会し、翌年拳志會に正式に加盟した。

モラレス氏は加盟の動機を「外間先生に会ったとき、本当に目を見張るようなものだった。先生の空手は、剛柔流の神髄である剛法と柔法を体現する」と語る。

20代から空手の指導をするモラレス氏は、80年代に初の道場をブロンクス区で開いた。2005年、隣州ニュージャージーのノース・アーリントンに移住し道場「武道クエスト」を開設。ニューヨーク州ヨンカーズ市にも子どものクラスを指導し、コロナ禍前には約200人が稽古に励んでいた。

09年には、拳志會の北米支部長に任命され、米国8支部、カナダ4支部で剛柔流、古武道、急所術などを指南している。

「武道の本当の意味は、戈（ほこ）を止める、すなわち争いを止める」とモラレス氏は強調する。ブロンクス等でさまざまな経験に直面した氏は鍛錬を通して自信を養い、口頭での空手スキルも発達させ、身体的な技法より言葉のスキルを生かして身を守れたという。

空手は単なる護身の武ではなく、歴史、古来の鍛錬法、分解、健康上の利点、多くの側面から学ぶことができ、人に「学びを止めないことと、可能な限り最高の自分になろうとする憧れ」を与えてくれる。モラレス氏はこれが空手の魅力だと信じて今も指導をする。

Published on 2021/5/23

⑬ United States 

Budō Quest

Pursuing Gōjū-ryū through training

The beginning of karate in the "City that never sleeps" dates back to the 1950s. In 1952, Ōyama Masutatsu, the head of Kyokushin Kaikan, travelled through the USA and performed in New York. Later on, Shōtōkan and Taekwondo, which at that time was called "Korean karate", became popular.

Born in the Bronx in 1958, Luis Morales first started with Taekwondo at the age of twelve before entering a karate club. The Bronx in the 70's was known as a borough of gangsters. Influenced by this environment, Morales recalls that he wanted to learn an effective self-defense method through karate.

At the Gōjū-ryū dōjō he joined, he practiced Toguchi Seikichi's Shōreikan kata and mainland Japanese Gōjū-kai kumite. In 1982, eager to experience training in the birthplaces of both systems, he visited mainland Japan and Okinawa. After returning home, he was introduced to the late Chinen Teruo, who lived in the USA and taught Okinawan Gōjū-ryū, and studied for about 16 years with him. As he says, he felt in love with the way Chinen performed his kata. When he travelled to Okinawa for the second time in 1999, Morales met Hokama Tetsuhiro, head of the Kenshikai in Nishihara Town. The year following that trip, he officially joined Hokama's organization.

About the motive for joining, he says, "When I met Hokama sensei, it was a real eye opener. Sensei's karate completely embodies the essence of Gōjū-ryū that is hard and soft."

Having taught karate since his twenties, Morales opened his first dōjō in the Bronx in the 1980s. In 2005, he moved to North Arlington, New Jersey, and opened the dōjō Budō Quest, budō meaning martial art in Japanese. He also has a satellite dōjō in Yonkers, NY, where he teaches children. Prior to the Covid-19 pandemic, he taught 200 students between the two locations.

In 2009, he was appointed Kenshikai's head for North America and since has been teaching Gōjū-ryū, kobudō, etc. in 8 branch dōjō in the USA and 4 in Canada.

He stresses that, "As the kanji is written, the real meaning of bu in budō is to stop a spear, meaning to stop a conflict." Following this philosophy, he cultivated self-confidence through training and was able to use his verbal skills rather than physical ones to protect himself.

Karate is not simply an art of self-defense and many aspects like history, ancient training methods, kata applications and health benefits can be studied. It gives you a "yearning to never stop learning, a yearning of trying to be the best possible you." Because of all this, Morales keeps teaching karate as he believes in all its charms.

高校時代、ジェリー・フィジャニー氏は米フットボールの選手としてプロのキャリアを目指したが、大学1年目にけがをしたことから空手の道を選んだ。

1960年ニューヨーク生まれのフィジャニー氏は17歳の時、米国で松林流空手の普及に励んだ宇江城安盛氏の弟子が指導していた近隣の道場に入門した。後に、宇江城氏、大嶺朝徳氏、長嶺高兆氏に師事した故ジョセフ・カルボナーラ氏らの指導を受け、88年から空手のプロとして指導を始めた。

現在、氏はロングアイランドの東側にあるミドル・アイランドの道場「東海岸黒帯アカデミー・ザ武道館」で指導している。90年に開設したこの道場では200人が一貫して松林流系の空手を学ぶ。カルボナーラ氏の薦めで2009年に設立させた「松林流空手道国際協会」は海外10カ国と米国合わせて25以上の加盟道場を有する。

09年訪沖の際に、フィジャニー氏は開祖長嶺将真氏の高弟である田場兼靖氏に再会した。「北米のセミナーで1度お会いした田場先生と交流を深め、先生の空手と生き方に感銘を受けた」と氏は言う。本場沖縄との連携を求めフィジャニー氏は後に、田場氏の空手を継ぐ国際松源流空手道協会(玉城剛会長)と協力協定を結んだ。

東海岸黒帯アカデミーで児童と稽古するフィジャニー氏(中央)＝提供
Figgiani (center) practicing with children in his academy.

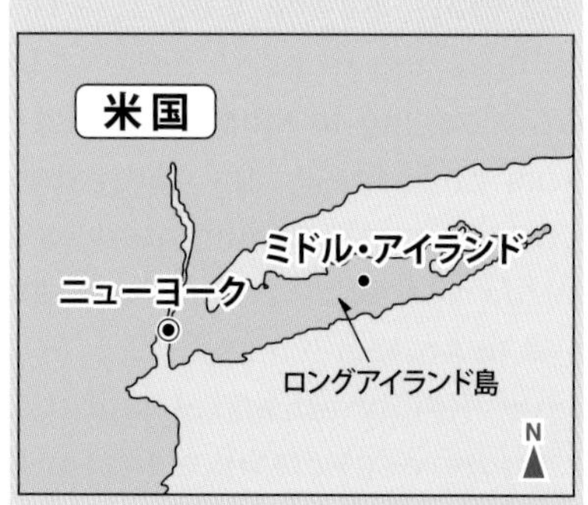

2021年12月26日

⑭米国

武道の哲学で人格形成

松林流空手道国際協会

1991年の訪沖の帰国後、社会貢献ができないかと考えた氏は、地域の児童を対象とした空手を通した人格形成プログラムを考案。10年間の構想でロングアイランド州のハイスクールと警察の協力を受け、2003年に『REACH』(英語で「教育を尊重し常により高く登る」との意味)と名付けられたプログラムが誕生した。「伝統空手を通したリーダーシップスキルや非暴力の解決方法を指導することが特徴。ギャングやいじめ対策プログラムでもある」とフィジャニー氏は強調する。

ロングアイランド州や警察体育協会の資金提供を受ける『REACH』は新型コロナウイルス感染症の拡大前、活動の範囲を17の学校に広げ、社会的に高く評価されている。12年に全国警察体育協会より表彰されたフィジャニー氏は、「空手ほど一人一人の人間の可能性を伸ばすのに良いものはないと心から信じている」と活動の裏付けになる思いを語る。

武道の哲学を日常生活に取り入れるためユニークな方法を開発した氏は、前進することを楽しみにしている。これまで数冊の書籍を執筆し、障がいを持つ子ども向けのプログラムなど、多方面で活動を広げる。これらすべての活動は、道場のマットでの稽古に基づいている。

In high school, Jerry Figgiani sought a professional career as an American football player but started karate after suffering an injury during his first year of college.

Born in New York in 1960, Figgiani entered a nearby dōjō at the age of 17. The dōjō was run by a student of Ueshiro Ansei, a pioneer of Matsubayashi-ryū (also readable as Shōrin-ryū) in the USA. Later, he trained under the late Joseph Carbonara, who had studied with Ueshiro, Omine Chōtoku and Nagamine Takayoshi and began teaching as a karate professional in 1988.

Today, he teaches at the "East Coast Black Belt Academy, the Budōkan" in Middle Island, New York. At this dōjō, which was opened in 1990, 200 people focus on practicing Matsubayashi-ryū karate. The Shōrin-ryū Karatedō International Association, which he established in 2009 on the recommendation of Carbonara, has more than 25 affiliated chapters in 10 foreign countries and the USA.

Published on 2021/12/26

⑭ United States 

Shōrin-ryū Karatedō International Association

Character building through martial arts philosophy

During his visit to Okinawa in 2009, Figgiani met again with Taba Kensei, a senior student of Nagamine Shōshin and founder of Shōgen-ryū. Having first met him during a US seminar, Figgiani wrote in one of his books, "I was not only impressed with his karate but with the way he conducted himself." Aiming at connecting with an organization in the birthplace of karate, Figgiani later signed a cooperation agreement with the International Shōgen-ryū Karatedō Association, chaired by Tamaki Takeshi.

After a trip to Okinawa in 1991, Figgiani started wondering how he could contribute to society. He then devised a character building program for local children. The "REACH" program, which stands for "Respect Education and Always Climb Higher," was born in 2003 with the cooperation of the local high schools and the Long Island police. Figgiani stresses that, "We teach leadership skills and non-violent resolution to conflict using traditional martial arts as the vehicle. It is also an anti-gang and anti-bullying program."

Funded by local governments and the Police Athletic League and highly regarded within the society, the REACH program had expanded its range of activities to 17 schools before the Covid-19 pandemic. Figgiani, who was commended by the National Police Athletic Association in 2012, says, "I truly believe that there is nothing better to develop human potential in each and every person than karatedō."

Having developed a unique method to incorporate the philosophy of martial arts into everyday life, Figgiani looks forward to advancing in his journey and has written several books and expanded his activities in many fields, including programs for children with disabilities. Yet, all his endeavors are based on training on the mats at the dōjō.

2020年02月09日

⑮ 米国

平和の武 継承に努力

オーセンティック古武術 空手・古武道スタジオ

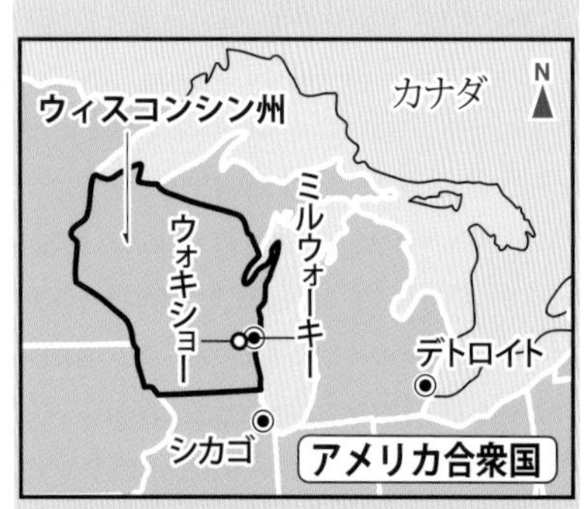

米国ウィスコンシン州ラクロス生まれのニール・ストルスマーク氏(58)は、16歳で空手の手ほどきを受け、翌年、沖縄小林流の道場に入門した。道場長のダニエル・シュローダー氏は山下忠氏に師事した空手家だった。山下氏は小林流を仲里周五郎氏、古武道を又吉眞豊氏からそれぞれ指導を受けている。

米国の古武道のパイオニアには、糸東流系の空手と琉球古武道の出村文男氏、そして山下氏がいる。両氏は1960年代後半に渡米、空手古武道の普及に励んだ。出村氏は映画『ベスト・キッド』でミスター・ミヤギを演じたパット・モリタ氏のスタント役も務めた。

ストルスマーク氏は、84年に山下氏の直弟子になった。翌年、師のシュローダー氏の道場(69年開設)を受け継ぎ指導を始めた。今年3月でストルスマーク氏は、道場運営35周年を迎える。↗

90年に行われた第1回世界のウチナーンチュ大会の武芸祭に参加したストルスマーク氏は、当時初めて我喜屋良章氏に出会った。「我喜屋先生は又吉先生の右腕でした。空港へ出迎えに来て、滞在中、運転手となってくれた。先生の振る舞いと、信じられないほどの武術のスキルに魅了された」とストルスマーク氏は振り返る。

本部道場で棒を指導するストルスマーク氏(左)=提供
Stolsmark (left) teaching at his headquarters dōjō.

97年に又吉氏が他界した後、我喜屋氏は又吉家の道場『光道館』の館長兼理事長を務めた。2002年に独立し、沖縄古武道同志錬成会として指導を続けた。その時、ストルスマーク氏は北米地区本部長に指名された。2011年に健康上、指導ができなくなった我喜屋氏は、ストルスマーク氏を同錬成会の代表に任命した。

現在ストルスマーク氏は、故郷のウィスコンシン州ウォキショーにある本部道場とワタータウンの道場で指南する。両道場では60人の黒帯を含む約120人が沖縄の武術を学ぶ。国内外の30数道場でも監督している。

ハーレーダビッドソンに乗るのが趣味のストルスマーク氏は過去、大工の仕事で生計を立てていたが、現在は空手と古武道に人生をささげている。

12年に仲里氏から8段、昨年、沖縄古武道9段を授与された。それでも毎年発祥の地を訪れ、古武道を與儀助盛氏、古武道と又吉家の金硬流唐手を伊敷秀忠氏に師事する。空手は01年から所属する小林流小林舘の仲里稔氏にも学んでいる。

「平和」という言葉を好み「沖縄人とこの島のライフスタイルが好き」というストルスマーク氏。稽古の徳として「健康とフィットネス、心の良い状態、他人との調和」を掲げ、今後も沖縄と世界の懸け橋として活動し続ける。

Born in Lacrosse, Wisconsin, Neil Stolsmark (58) started karate at the age of 16 and entered a Shōrin-ryū dōjō the following year. The head of the dōjō was Daniel Schroeder, a karateka who studied under Yamashita Tadashi, who himself trained under Nakazato Shūgorō for Shōrin-ryū and Matayoshi Shinpō for kobudō.

Among the pioneers of kobudō in the USA are Shitō-ryū master Demura Fumio and Yamashita. Both men immigrated in the latter half of the 1960s and worked on popularizing karate and Okinawan weaponry systems. Demura is remembered for he acted as the stunt for Pat Noriyuki Morita, who played the role of Mr. Miyagi in the movie "The Karate Kid".

Published on 2020/2/9

⑮ United States 

Authentic Ancient Arts Karate & Kobudō Studios

Diligently passing on martial arts of peace

Stolsmark became a direct student of Yamashita in 1984. The following year, he took over Schroeder's dōjō, which was opened in 1969, and began teaching. This March, Stolsmark will celebrate the 35th anniversary of him operating the dōjō.

In 1990, as he participated in the 1st World Uchinānchu Festival, he met for the first time Gakiya Yoshiaki. "Gakiya sensei was Matayoshi sensei's right hand man. He picked us up at the airport and drove us around during our stay. I was attracted to Gakiya sensei by both his demeanor and incredible skills," he remembers.

After Matayoshi's passing in 1997, Gakiya served as the head of the Matayoshi family's dōjō Kōdōkan. Becoming independent in 2002, he continued to teach as the head of the Okinawa Kobudō Dōshi Renseikai of which Stolsmark was appointed head for North America. In 2011, Gakiya, unable to instruct due to health reasons, appointed Stolsmark as the representative of the Renseikai.

Today, Stolsmark instructs at the headquarters dōjō in Waukesha and another location in Watertown, Wisconsin. At both places, about 120 people, including 60 black belts, learn Okinawan martial arts. He also supervises more than 30 dōjō in the USA and overseas.

While Stolsmark used to make a living as a carpenter, he now devotes his life to martial arts. Promoted to 8th dan by Nakazato in 2012, he is also a 9th dan in Okinawa kobudō. Nevertheless, he visits the birthplace of karate every year and polishes his skills with kobudō experts Yogi Josei and Ishiki Hidetada. He also trains karate with the present head of the Shōrinkan, Nakazato Minoru.

As his favorite word is peace, Stolsmark also stresses that, "besides the training, I often come because I love the people and the Okinawan lifestyle." Valuing training as he feels that karate and kobudō offer the practitioner many positive things such as "good health and fitness, good state of mind and harmony with others," he wishes to continue to stand as a bridge between Okinawa and the world.

米国ミネソタ州生まれのティム・ユルギンス氏(53)は、1985年に軍でのキャリアを求めて海兵隊に入隊した。

ユルギンス氏は最初に配属されたカリフォルニア基地で沖縄空手と出合った。そこで松村少林流の空手を指導していた隊員から手ほどきを受けた。

2年後、沖縄の基地に異動し、祖堅方範氏の空手を継いだ喜瀬富盛氏に少林流、小渡世吉氏に古武道を2年間師事した。

以降、仕事に伴いさまざまな地域を回ったが、94年2度目の訪沖の際、琉球古武道信武館の赤嶺栄亮氏の紹介で琉球古武術の道を歩み始めた。「信武館で見た古武道の力と集中力に驚いた」と当時を振り返る。

96年に海兵隊を辞めたユルギンス氏は東京に移った。請負業者や米国連邦職員として働きながら、メリーランド大学で情報システム管理学を学び、経営学修士を取得した。東京在住中には稽古とともに指導も行った。現在も都内には大森と多摩に信武館の支部がある。

2006年に帰郷したユルギンス氏は、ミネソタ州福祉局のITスーパーバイザーを務めた。3年後、ロンズデール市で信武館の支部道場を開設し、10

セミナーで指導するユルギンス氏(中央)=トーマス・ポジェルニー氏提供
Jurgens (center) teaching at a seminar (photo from Thomas Podzelny).

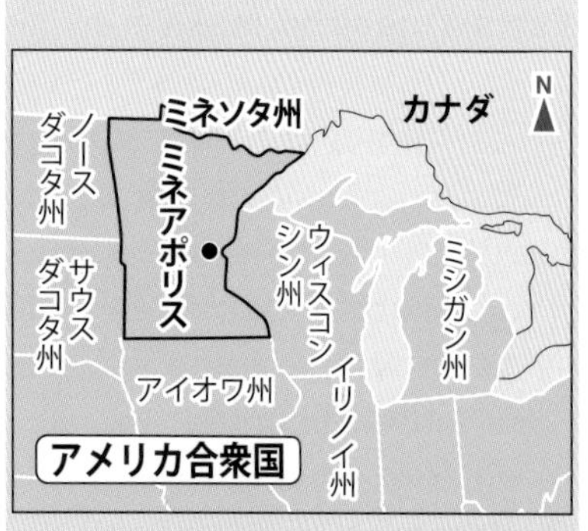

2020年07月12日

⑯ 米国

礼儀順守 普及に努力

琉球古武道信武館

年間空手と古武道の指導に当たった。ミネソタの道場は19年に閉鎖したが、弟子が自らの道場で普及活動を続けている。

11年には米海軍から将校に任命され、再び米軍人となったユルギンス氏。これまで日本、ジブチ、バーレーン、レバノン、UAE、エジプトに駐在し、現在はシンガポールで任務に当たっている。

ユルギンス氏は古武道7段、信武館2代目赤嶺浩氏が会長を務める沖縄小林流空手道無拳会の8段で、同系の北米最高指導者として活動する。「米国7道場、カナダ3道場のメンバーが赤嶺先生の武術を習っている。道場訪問やセミナーの開催を通じ、私も普及活動に力を尽くしたい」と思いは熱い。

空手と古武道の魅力を問うと「人として成長するためには、人は物事にチャレンジしていく必要がある。その意味で空手と古武道は生涯にわたるチャレンジを与えてくれる」と答えた。

ユルギンス氏が特に大切にしているのは礼儀作法という。「最初と最後の礼は大事。常に尊敬と自身の洗練を心に留めておけば、より良い人間になると信じている」。日本語能力試験では3級を取得。沖縄、日本そして世界各地で得た知識と経験を生かし、沖縄の武術の普及に努めていく。

Published on 2020/7/12

⑯ United States 

Ryūkyū Kobudō Shinbukan

Striving to popularize the art while maintaining etiquette

Born in Minnesota, Tim Jurgens (53) enlisted in the Marine Corps in 1985 and encountered Okinawa karate at his first assignment in California, training with fellow servicemen who taught Matsumura Shōrin-ryū karate.

Two years later, he was stationed in Okinawa and studied Shōrin-ryū with Kise Fusei, a disciple of Soken Hōhan, and kobudō with Odo Seikichi for two years.

From this time, he has travelled to various areas in the world for his work. It is when he visited Okinawa for the second time in 1994 that he began to follow the path led by Akamine Eisuke, head of the Ryūkyū Kobudō Shinbukan. He recalls, "I was amazed at the power and focus of the kobudō I saw there."

Leaving the Marine Corps in 1996, Jurgens moved to Tōkyō and while working as a contractor and then US federal employee, he studied information systems management at the University of Maryland and earned a MBA. While in the capital, Jurgens taught while practicing and even today, there are branches of Shinbukan in Ōmori and Tama.

Returning to the USA in 2006, Jurgens worked as an IT supervisor at the Minnesota State Welfare Department. Three years later, he opened a Shinbukan branch dōjō in Lonsdale, where he taught karate and kobudō for 10 years. The Minnesota dōjō was closed in 2019, but his students continue to run their own dōjō.

As he re-enlisted as an officer in the US Navy in 2011, Jurgens has been stationed in Japan, Djibouti, Bahrain, Lebanon, UAE, Egypt, and is currently on duty in Singapore.

A 7th dan in kobudō and a 8th dan in Okinawa Shōrin-ryū Karatedō Mukenkai, headed by Akamine Hiroshi, the second heir of the Shinbukan, Jurgens serves as the senior instructor in North America for both systems. He comments, "We have seven dōjō in the US and three in Canada that practice Akamine sensei's martial arts. Visiting the dōjō and holding seminars, I do my best to promote the association's activities."

When asked about the charms of karate and kobudō, he answered, "In order to grow as a person, people need to face challenges. Karate and kobudō can provide a lifelong challenge, through which people can continue to grow."

Fluent in Japanese, Jurgens especially values etiquette. "I often say to my students that everything starts and ends with a bow. If we are always considering respect and our own refinement in mind, we can hope to become better people." Making the best of the knowledge and experience gained in Okinawa, Japan and other parts of the world, he strives to popularize Okinawan martial arts.

全米の州で最小面積のロードアイランドに生まれたマーク・スピア氏(53)は7歳の頃、柔道の手ほどきを受けた後、ハワイアン拳法を習った。

沖縄空手を始めたのは1984年。拳法の師が交通事故で亡くなり、州内の故郷ウェスタリーにあったロバート・セリコ氏の道場に入門した。道場は故仲里周五郎氏が開設した小林流小林舘の加盟道場だった。

80年代後半に道場が閉鎖し、スピア氏は同系統の空手を求め、ロバート・ヘーテン氏の道場に移った。2008年まで小林流を続け、剛柔流等も研究した。

小林流流祖・知花朝信氏に師事した空手家を求めたスピア氏は2007年に阿波根直信氏を紹介された。仲介したのは武徳館の米国支部長マーク・スペンス氏だった。スペンス氏は同館初代会長の故儀武息一氏の弟子。儀武氏は仲里氏の高弟にあたる。

流祖に直接習った阿波根氏は、儀武氏と同様に長く仲里周五郎氏の指導を受け、1991年に沖縄空手・古武道小林流礼邦館協会を立ち上げた。

翌年、スピア氏は初めて沖縄を訪れ、阿波根氏

門下生と稽古に励んでいるスピア氏(右端)=提供 Spear (far right) with his students after a practice.

2021年3月14日

⑰ 米国

魂伝え 護身術を指南

礼邦館 ブラックベア道場

と会った。1年後入門が認められ、以降2年に一度をめどに訪沖。これまで14回、空手発祥の地・沖縄で汗を流している。

40歳の時、24年間の空手歴を数えたスピア氏はコネティカット州ストニントンで「ブラックベア道場」を開設した。新型コロナウイルス禍前には週6回、70人を指導していた。その8割は大人だという。

指導目的を問うと「沖縄空手の素晴らしさを伝えたいから」とスピア氏。88年からロードアイランドで警察官として勤務しているスピア氏は、さらに指導の目的として「護身術の重要性を知り、人々に自分自身と家族を守るためのツールを提供すること」と強調した。勤務の一環で法執行機関員や女性向けに護身術も指導しているという。

技術面のほかスピア氏は、小林流の研究に励み、流祖の歩みをたどっている。知花氏は大日本武徳會沖縄武徳殿開殿式記念演武会(1939年)の際に型「チントウ」を演武し、高く評価されたという。興味を抱いたスピア氏は同団体の国際部に加盟し、師範免許も有している。

現在米国東海岸の礼邦館ディレクター空手7段、古武道5段。「空手とは単なる技法ではなく、人の完成を表すものである」。道場も家族も大切とするスピア氏は、阿波根氏から継ぐ教えを弟子たちに伝え、沖縄の武術の普及に励んでいる。

Born on Rhode Island, Mark Spear (53) first learned jūdō as a kid before getting into Hawaiian kenpō. Following his teacher's death in a car accident, Spear entered the dōjō of Robert Celico in his hometown of Westerly in 1984, dōjō that was part of the Shōrin-ryū Shōrinkan founded by the late Nakazato Shūgorō.

As the dōjō closed in the late 80's, Spear looked for a similar place to train and entered Robert Herten's dōjō. He continued training there until 2008, while also experiencing Gōjū-ryū.

Seeking a karateka who had studied directly under Chibana Chōshin, the founder of Shōrin-ryū, Spear was introduced to Ahagon Naonobu in 2007. The mediator

Published on 2021/3/14

17 United States

Reihōkan Black Bear Dōjō

Transmitting the spirit while teaching self-defense

was Mark Spence, the director of the US branch of the Butokukan founded by Gibu Sokuichi, a senior student of Nakazato.

A direct student of Chibana and fellow practitioner of Gibu under Nakazato, Ahagon established the Okinawa Karate Kobudō Shōrin-ryū Reihōkan Association in 1991.

In 2008, Spear visited Okinawa for the first time and met Ahagon. Being officially accepted as a member the following year, he has visited Okinawa 14 times so far.

Reaching 40, Spear, who had practiced karate for 24 years, opened the Black Bear Dōjō in Stonington, Connecticut. Before the Covid-19 pandemic, he was instructing 70 people six times a week, of which 80% were adults.

Asked his goal as a teacher, he answers, "I like to share information and expose people to the beauty of Okinawa karate." As a police officer on Rhode Island since 1988, he further emphasizes saying, "I know the importance of self-defense and it is our goal to provide instruction to people so that they have the tools to take care of themselves and their families." As part of his work, he also teaches self-defense for law enforcement officers and women.

In addition to the technical aspects, Spear also researches the history of Chibana. For example, he found out that Chibana had performed the kata Chintō at the commemorative demonstration for the opening of the Dai Nippon Butoku Kai (DNKB) Okinawa Butokuden in 1939 and was praised for his performance. His interest being piqued, Spear chose to associate with the DNKB's international division and now holds a teacher license from this organization.

Today, Spear is a karate 7th dan and a kobudō 5th dan and represents the Reihōkan on the East Coast. "Karate is not what we do - it is what we are. It's not about kicking and punching, there is just so much more." Spear strives to popularize Okinawan martial arts by spreading the teachings passed on to him by Ahagon Naonobu.

沖縄空手の歴史において、来琉した中国福建省出身の白鶴拳の達人・呉賢貴（ごけんき）や五祖拳の達人・唐大基（とうたいき）は、大正年間に沖縄の空手界に影響を与えたと高宮城繁氏は『沖縄空手古武道事典』に記した。

高宮城氏の親戚で、名嘉真朝増氏と高弟の仲村安吉氏から首里手を習った故高宮城宏氏は、1980年代半ば中国系シンガポール人から五祖拳のうち九つの型を取得した。その後、同武術が盛んなシンガポールやフィリピンを訪れ研究を続けた。88年に自身の武術を「南少林五祖拳法・沖縄首里手」と名付け、北谷町の「沖縄五首館」で指導に励んだ。

米国ジョージア州生まれのゲアリ・パーカー氏（52）は、90年に米空軍兵として沖縄に配置された。上地流の道場を経て、高宮城氏に紹介され入門した。↗

6年間沖縄に滞在したパーカー氏にとって高宮城氏は、メンターで父親のような存在となり、帰国後も師弟関係は続き、親睦が深まっていった。

96年から地元で公務員になり、警察官に空手を指導。3年後、故郷のコロンバス市に「沖縄五首館流全米本部道場・コロンバス道場」を開設した。

ゲアリ・パーカー氏（右から4人目）の弟子と家族＝米国ジョージア州・コロンバス
Parker (fourth from right) with his family and students.

2021年08月22日

⑱ 米国

沖縄五首館流を継承

コロンバス道場

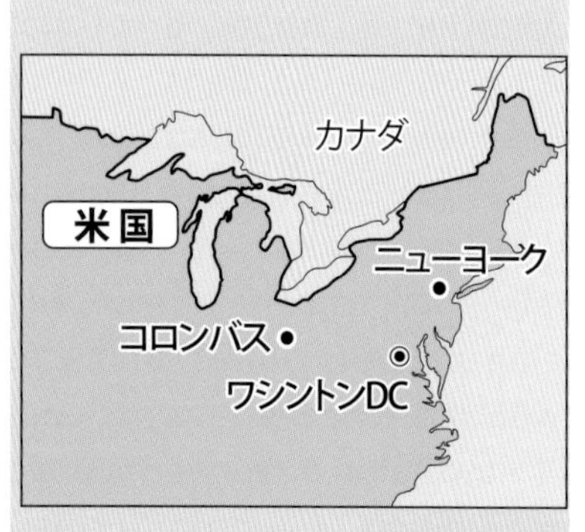

現在、宜野湾出身の妻泉さんと息子の賢治さんと共に40人ほどの門弟に指導し、他3州にも支部道場がある。

道場開設15周年を機に、高宮城氏は2014年に訪米。五首館流が熱心に稽古されていることを見て感銘を受けたという。翌年、パーカー氏は25年間の師と沖縄との交流を『チャンプルー』と題する本にまとめ出版した。

13年に高宮城宏氏が著した「五祖拳法備忘録」には、空手と五祖拳の根本的な違いが解説されている。著書によると、空手は「受け」から始まる型や「先手なし」に昇華した理念が打ち立てられているのに対し、五祖拳の型の大部分は「攻撃」から始まり、中国人の硬軟自在のアグレッシブな現実主義で拳法が発展してきたとのこと。

これまで、多くの空手研究者は空手のルーツを調べるため中国を訪れた。高宮城氏も五祖拳の研究に専心し、首里手と並行で探求したとパーカー氏は分析する。「五首館流において分けられて指導されている両武術は、一見反対に見えるが実に補完的である。空手とその型は優雅でありながら、中には暴力的な要素もある」と氏は追加する。

現在、高宮城氏の子息直樹氏が北谷の道場を継いでいる。パーカー氏は高宮城家との交流を保ち、師への義理を立てて、実用的で功利主義の五首館流を広く紹介していきたいと考えている。

Takamiyagi Shigeru wrote in the "Okinawa Karate Kobudō Encyclopedia" that Chinese Fujian masters Go Kenki of white crane fist and Tō Taiki of Wu Zu Quan (Goso-ken in Japanese / Five ancestor fist) have influenced the Okinawa karate world during the Taishō era.

The late Takamiyagi Hiroshi, a relative of the author, learned Shurite from Nakama Chōzō and his student Nakamura Ankichi, and nine forms of Wu Zu Quan from Chinese Singaporeans in the mid-1980s. He continued his research visiting Singapore and the Philippines where Wu Zu Quan is popular. In 1988, he named his system "Minami Shōrin Goso Kenpō / Okinawa Shurite" and taught it at his "Okinawa Goshukan" dōjō in Chatan Town.

Published on 2021/8/22

18 United States 

Columbus Dōjō

Preserving Okinawa Goshukan-ryū

Born in Georgia, Garry Parker (52) was assigned to Kadena Airbase in 1990. Introduced to Takamiyagi Hiroshi, he started training with him. Staying in Okinawa for 6 years, Takamiyagi became a mentor and a father figure and even after returning home, the teacher-student relationship continued.

Becoming a civil servant in 1996, Parker also started instructing karate to police officers. Three years later, he opened the US Okinawa Goshukan-ryū headquarters Columbus Dōjō in his hometown. Today, he teaches about 40 people with his wife Izumi from Ginowan and his son Kenji. There are also branch dōjō in three other states.

On the occasion of the 15th anniversary of the dōjō, Takamiyagi visited the USA in 2014. He was genuinely happy to see that his art was being taught and practiced diligently. The following year, Parker published "Chanpuru", a book about his 25 years of interaction with Okinawa and his teacher.

In 2013, in his book "Goso Kenpō - Memorandum", Takamiyagi explains the fundamental difference between karate and Wu Zu Quan. According to the author, while karate has kata that start with "uke (the act of receiving an attack)" and a philosophy of "not attacking first", most of the kata of Wu Zu Quan start with "kōgeki (an attack)". He also stresses that Chinese kenpō was developed according to the flexible and aggressive realism of the Chinese people.

So far, many researchers have travelled to China in search of the roots of karate. Parkers explains that Takamiyagi committed to learning Wu Zu Quan and then began teaching it along with Shurite. "In Goshukan-ryū, the parent systems that are Shurite and Wu Zu Quan are seemingly opposite, but they are really complementary. And while karate and its kata are graceful, they contain violent elements too," adds Parker.

Today, Takamiyagi's son Naoki has inherited the dōjō in Chatan. Parker keeps in touch with the Takamiyagi family and, as a duty towards his master, wishes to introduce widely the pragmatic and utilitarian martial art that is Goshukan-ryū.

米国バージニア州のハンプトン生まれのブライアン・ホブソン氏はハンプトン大学を卒業後、少年拘置カウンセラーや未成年者の保護観察官、仮釈放担当官を勤めたほか、イベント、スポーツやレクリエーション施設のマネジャーとして働いた経験を持つ。

ホブソン氏は12歳で沖縄空手を始めた。1982年、沖縄小林流小林舘の故仲里周五郎氏に師事した米国人フランク・ハーグローブ氏(75)の道場に入門。15年余り空手を学び、99年には退職した父と「鉄騎館空手スタジオ」を開設した。「さまざまな勤務経験がプロ意識を持った道場運営や、ほかとは違う空手指導者となることに役立った」と振り返る。

道場開設から2年後、ホブソン氏は空手大会に出場して優勝した。グランプリ賞金は沖縄への無料往復航空運賃。その切符を手に初の訪沖をしたホブソン氏は仲里氏に師事したほか、85年小林舘の米国空手キャンプで指導を受けた仲座清栄氏と再会も果たした。

42年東風平生まれの仲座氏は少林寺流や剛柔流を学んだ後、66年に仲里氏の道場に入門。後に2008年まで金城憲保氏が館長を務める小林舘八重瀬支部道場の副館長を務めた。

米国バージニア州を拠点に鍛錬を積んでいるホブソン氏(右端)と門下生ら=提供　Hobson (far right) and his students in Virginia.

2020年07月26日

⑲米国

首里手の奥義を探究

沖縄小林流清武館

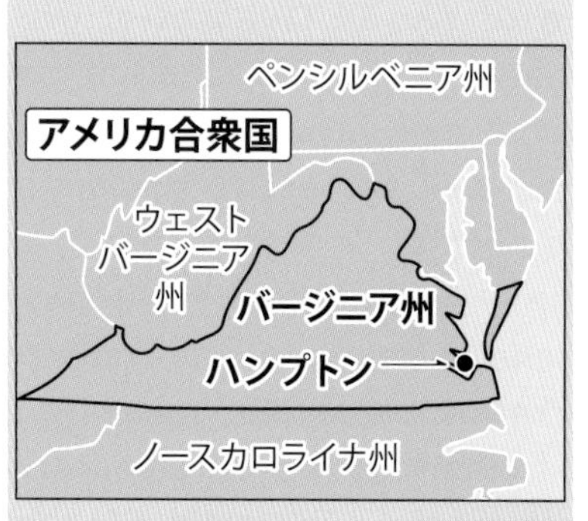

ホブソン氏の仲座氏との交流は続き、06年に沖縄への一人旅を決めたホブソン氏は、仲座氏を訪ね、個人指導を受けるようになった。

09年に仲座氏は小林舘協会から独立し沖縄小林流清武館協会を設立。誘われたホブソン氏は同協会への加盟を決めた。2013年に師である仲座氏の他界時にホブソン氏は、清武館協会の2代目会長という重大な役職を任命された。

現在、清武館協会は米国、カナダ、南アフリカで9支部道場を有する。ハンプトンの本部道場で約120人、近隣のヨークタウン道場で約50人が米国の清武館総本部長でもあるホブソン氏の指導を受けている。

「道場で泣き、戦場で笑う」をモットーに指南するホブソン氏は、知花朝信氏の空手を継承する沖縄や北米空手家との武術交流を大切にしている。「空手を学べば学ぶほど、知らないことがどれだけあるか分かることが魅力的。一生一型を学んでも、ある出会いによって考えたことのない異なる視点を解説され、研究が無限であると感じる」と説明した。

仲座氏が考案した清武館の紋章の中心には赤い「首里手」の文字が刻まれている。ホブソン氏は、小林流のルーツである「首里手」の歴史や技を深く見つめ、探求し続けていく。

Born in Hampton, Virginia, Brian Hobson worked as a juvenile detention counselor and a probation and parole officer for juveniles within the foster care system. After completing his graduate degree, he also worked as an event and recreational facility manager.

He started Okinawa karate at the age of 12 in 1982, entering the dōjō of Frank Hargrove (75), who studied under the late Nakazato Shūgorō, head of the Shōrin-ryū Shōrinkan.

After training for more than 15 years, he opened the Tekkikan Karate Studio in 1999 with his retired father. Looking back, he comments, "I have a wide array of job experiences, all of which I believe assisted me in being a different karate instructor as well as being able to provide a professional dōjō experience."

Published on 2020/7/26

19 United States 

Okinawa Shōrin-ryū Kiyobukan

Exploring the mysteries of Shurite

Two years after the Tekkikan opening, Hobson participated in a karate tournament and won the championship. The Grand Prix prize was a free round-trip airfare to Okinawa. As he visited Okinawa for the first time, he trained under Nakazato while reuniting with Nakaza Seiei, who taught him during a camp in 1985.

Born in Kochinda in 1942, Nakaza first studied Shōrinji-ryū and Gōjū-ryū before entering the dōjō of Nakazato in 1966. He later served as the vice director of the Shōrinkan Yaese dōjō of Kinjō Kenpō until 2008.

Maintaining his relation with Nakaza, Hobson decided to travel alone to Okinawa in 2006 and began to receive personal tuition from Nakaza. In 2009, Nakaza left the Shōrinkan association and established the Okinawa Shōrin-ryū Kiyobukan Association. Hobson was invited to join and so did he. When Nakaza passed away in 2013, Hobson was appointed second chairman of the Kiyobukan.

Currently, the association has nine branches in the USA, Canada and South Africa. About 120 people at the headquarters in Hampton and about 50 people at the nearby Yorktown dōjō train under Hobson, who stands as the general manager of the US Kiyobukan.

With the motto "Cry in the dōjō, laugh on the battlefield," Hobson values martial arts exchanges with Okinawan and North American karateka who studied Chibana Chōshin's karate. "I like the entire idea that the more you learn about karate, the more you find out how much you do not know. The learning is truly endless if you are open to it. You can train a lifetime on a single kata and someone can give you a different perspective that you have never considered that makes total sense and is very practical."

The coat of arms of the Seibukan devised by Nakaza has the characters "Shurite" in red in the center. Hobson continues to explore the history and techniques of Shurite, which is the roots of Shōrin-ryū.

2020年04月12日

⑳ 米国

ルーツ尊び 武術研究

少林流松村正統

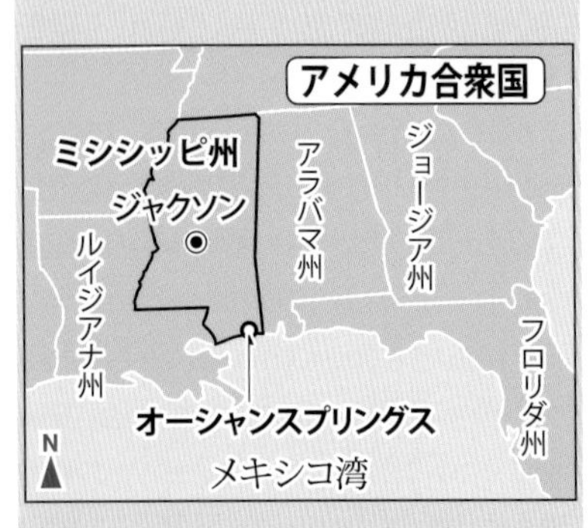

沖縄空手3大流派の一つ「しょうりん流」には、少林流、小林流、松林流等の系譜がある。少林流には、喜屋武朝徳氏の系統もあれば、祖堅方範氏の少林流松村正統もある。

米ジョージア州生まれのウォルト・ヤング氏(44)は13歳の頃、父の勧めで空手を始め、二十歳の海軍入隊まで本土系の空手を習った。2000年にジョージア大学に進学。ある日、少林流松村正統を指南するジョイス・ステツ氏についての記事を見た。その後、約4年間ステツ氏の下で少林流の手ほどきを受けた。

海軍将校の任を受けたヤング氏はメリーランド州に移った。その時、松村正統の空手を求め、祖堅氏に師事した赤嶺喜松氏の門弟に学んだ。

一大転機になったのは、05年末のリキ・ローズ氏との出会いだ。ローズ氏は1972年から84年まで、親と共にそして軍人として沖縄で生活。喜瀬富盛氏、師の祖堅氏や祖堅氏の高弟の西平向盛氏に師事。帰国後、沖縄少林流松村正統粋拳武芸会を立ち上げ、祖堅氏の武術の継承に努めた。

ヤング氏はローズ氏の弟子になり、空手の研究を深めた。「祖堅先生は1902年から武士松村の孫にあたるナビータンメーに武術を習った。その中には『三戦(さんちん)』と『白鶴(はくつる)』や武士松村の妻の『ウメークーサンクー』という型もある。27年まで稽古を重ね、以降52年までアルゼンチンに移り住んでいた。先生は帰郷後、指導に励んだ」と武芸会の副会長を務めるヤング氏は会のルーツを説明する。異動でヤング氏は2011年~14年沖縄に滞在。その際、23年間祖堅氏に師事した當間勲氏に空手、伊佐海舟氏に古武道を学んだ。

稽古後のヤング氏(中央)と門下生=提供　Young (center) and some students after training.

現在ミシシッピ州に住むヤング氏は、海軍気象学・海洋学官を務める。転勤が多く、固定した道場を保つのは厳しいという。自宅で稽古に励みつつ、ケンタッキー州ルイビルにある本部道場でも汗を流している。

米大統領ルーズベルトの外交政策「棍棒(こんぼう)を携え、穏やかに話す」という言葉を好むヤング氏は、武術研究に導かれ自身の道場のキーコンセプトとして武士松村の「人常敬恭　則心常光明也」を座右の銘とする。

空手が人生のすべてという空手家が多いと感じているヤング氏。「ルーツを尊重し、人格形成、他人への関心、そして謙虚さの維持は大切」とする。「だが、空手は、人生の一部であるべきだ」というスタンスも併せ持ち、光明な空手人生を歩み続ける。

Published on 2020/4/12

20 United States 

Shōrin-ryū Matsumura Seitō

Martial arts research while respecting the roots

One of the three major styles of Okinawa karate, Shōrin-ryū, includes the karate of Kyan Chōtoku and Shōrin-ryū Matsumura Seitō of Soken Hōhan.

Born in Georgia, Walt Young (44) started karate when he was 13 and learned mainland Japanese karate until he joined the Navy at the age of 20. Returning to the University of Georgia in 2000, he once read an article about Joyce Stech, who was teaching Shōrin-ryū Matsumura Seitō, and went on studying with her for about four years.

Commissioned as a Navy officer and transferred to Maryland, Young sought the same style of karate and trained with a student of Akamine Yoshimatsu, a direct student of Soken.

The turning point was his encounter with Ricky Rose in the late 2005. Rose lived in Okinawa from 1972 to 1984 with his parents and then as a serviceman. He studied under Kise Fusei, Kise's teacher Soken Hōhan and a senior student of Soken, Nishihira Kōsei. After returning to the USA, he set up the Okinawan Shōrin-ryū Matsumura Seitō Suiken Bugei Kai and strived to pass on Soken's martial arts.

Becoming Rose's student, Young deepened his research on karate. "Soken sensei began training under Nabe Tanmē, the grandson of Bushi Matsumura Sōkon, in 1902. Originally, the system included the kata 'Sanchin' and 'Hakutsuru' as well as 'Umē Kūsankū,' or the Kūsankū of Matsumura's wife. Soken continued his training until 1927 when he left for Argentina, not returning until around 1952," tells Young, who acts as vice chairman of the Bugei Kai.

From 2011 to 2014, Young stayed in Okinawa and trained with Toma Isao, a 23 years old student of Soken, as well as with Isa Kaishū in kobudō.

Today, he lives in Mississippi and serves as a US Navy meteorology and oceanography officer. As he is often transferred, it is difficult to operate a dōjō. Therefore, he practices at home and visits the Suiken hombu dōjō located in Louisville, Kentucky, when he can.

While President Theodore Roosevelt's foreign policy to "Walk quietly and carry a big stick" has always been Young's favorite quote, he has, for his dōjō, adopted Bushi Matsumura's favorite motto explained as "One should always be respectful and humble, and that as a rule the heart should be bright shining to those around you."

Young feels that there are many karateka for who karate becomes all consuming. "I think it is important to respect the roots, build a good personality, be interested in others, and maintain humility. But karate should be a part of your life, not your entire life." Keeping this stance at heart, Young continues to live a bright karate life.

2018年04月29日

㉑ カナダ

鍛錬で培う強い精神

松林流

1939年ドイツ・ベルリン生まれのフランク・ベアー氏は、56年にカナダに移住し、5年後カナダの空手の父と称される鶴岡政己氏の下で空手を始めた。63年に日系人3人の空手家と共に道場を開設し、指導の道に挑んだ。

空手のルーツを探し求めたベアー氏は、日本への旅を企画した。65年8月、日本に向かう途中、ハワイで指南していた松林流のトミー・森田氏から指導を受けた。日本に行きたいと話すと、「本土の空手はたった45年の歴史しかない。それより、発祥の地・沖縄に行った方がよい」と森田氏に言われ、本場に向かった。

同年10月沖縄の地を踏み、松林流開祖長嶺将真氏の門をたたいた。その後8カ月間、内弟子となり、長嶺氏宅でも暮らした。当時26歳。「復帰前の沖縄で、アメリカ人ではなくカナダ人であること、自国の文化のすばらしさの普及ではなく沖縄の文化を学ぶために来たと説明すると、沖縄人は受け入れてくれた。長嶺先生も、厳しい指導のほか、史跡や芝居にも案内してくれた」とベアー氏は懐かしく思い出す。

「長嶺先生の空手に対する自然と現実な対応が魅力的だった。禅を修業し、道場の中と外で区別してはいけないことも教わった」。地元新聞にもカナダの青年の来沖は紹介された。

セミナーで指導するフランク・ベアー氏(左)=提供
Baehr (left) teaching during seminar.

67年にベアー氏は成長した姿で帰国した。69年カナダを訪れた長嶺氏は、ベアー氏の父に会った。父ハンス氏は「息子は二人の父を持つ。生物学的父親の私と、精神的父親である長嶺氏」と語ったという。

ベアー氏はその後、電子工学の技術者として勤めながらトロント東部にあるスカーバローに道場を開設し、40年間普及に励んだ。北米に派遣された大嶺朝徳と長嶺高兆各氏にも師事した。

長嶺将真氏との会話の中、師匠が日本本土と欧米の空手の方向性に非常に不満を持っていたとベアー氏は振り返る。現代の人々は、肉体的の攻撃に耐える能力より、強い精神を必要とする。長嶺氏は、精神を鍛えることが現代空手の重点であるべきだと感じていて、弟子にそのメッセージを伝え続けたという。後にベアー氏は、空手を通して得られた精神力で、離婚や二つのがんという人生の危機を乗り越えた。

2017年、世界松林流空手道連盟の平良慶孝会長から八段を授与された。ベアー氏は、一番弟子のスティーブ・トロンブレイ氏の道場で指南役として、師から教わった沖縄空手とその理念を次世代に伝え続けている。

（フランク・ベアー氏は2021年12月4日に亡くなりました。ご冥福をお祈りいたします。）

Born in Berlin, Germany in 1939, Frank Baehr moved to Canada in 1956 and started karate five years later under Tsuruoka Masami, the "father of Canadian karate". In 1963, he opened a dōjō with three Japanese American karateka and started teaching karate.

In search of the roots of karate, Baehr planned a trip to Japan. In August 1965, on his way to Japan, he met Morita Tomotsuga of Matsubayashi-ryū, who was teaching karate in Hawaii. Explaining his travel's purpose, Morita told him, "You should go to Okinawa instead where karate was born rather than Japan where it is only 45 years old."

In October, Baehr stepped on the land of Okinawa and entered the dōjō of Nagamine Shōshin, the founder of Matsubayashi-ryū. For the next eight months, he became a live-in student living with the Nagamine family. He was 26 years old. He recalls, "At a time when Okinawa had not been returned to Japan yet, I explained to locals that I was not an American but a Canadian, and that I was there to learn about their culture and not to tell how much better our way was, and they warmed up very quickly. Next to training, Nagamine sensei took me on tours to historic sites and classical Okinawan plays".

Published on 2018/4/29

21 Canada 

Matsubayashi-ryū

A strong spirit cultivated through training

"Nagamine sensei's very natural and down-to-earth approach to the art was fascinating. Practicing zen, he also always stressed that there was no division between the dōjō and the street."

In 1967, he had returned home a grown man. When Nagamine visited Canada in 1969, he met Baehr's father who told the master, "My son really has two fathers: me, the physical father and you, his spiritual father."

From then on, Baehr worked as an electronics engineering technologist while teaching for 40 years at the dōjō he established in Scarborough, Toronto. Along the way, he received instruction from Ōmine Chōtoku and Nagamine Takayoshi who were dispatched to North America.

From his conversations with Nagamine, Baehr recalls that the master was very unhappy with the direction karate was taking in Japan and the West. He felt that modern times required a strong spirit and not as much the ability to deal with physical attacks. He felt that training the spirit should be the emphasis of modern karate. Later, karate gave Baehr the spiritual strength to deal with a divorce and facing and defeating cancer twice.

In 2017, Baehr was awarded the 8th dan by Taira Yoshitaka, Chairman of the World Matsubayashi-ryū Karatedō Association. He continues to pass on Okinawa karate and its philosophy learned from his master to the next generation at the dōjō of his top disciple, Steve Trombley.

(Frank Baehr passed away on December 4th, 2021. May he rest in peace.)

1946年オンタリオ州生まれのドン・シャプラン氏は、日系カナダ人の子どもたちと共に育ち、7歳の頃から柔道や柔術をして遊んだ。短いプロホッケーのキャリアを経て、氏は65年頃に米国のデトロイトの一心流空手道場に通い始めた。

当時のカナダでは空手道場はまだ珍しいものだった。師に勧められ、空手を始めて2年で一級になったシャプラン氏はオンタリオ州ウィンザー市で道場を開設した。

69年の夏、沖縄を訪れたシャプラン氏は、同系流祖の島袋龍夫氏に師事した。「一カ月間、刺激的な毎日を過ごした」と氏は語る。

20年間にわたり赤いユニホームで知られている王立カナダ騎馬警察や刑務所の警備員らに逮捕、抑制、手錠を指導するインストラクターを勤める間、氏は数回沖縄に出向き、90年に移住を決めた。

英語教師をしつつ、沖縄県立武道館が建設される前に、奥武山公園の入り口にあった米軍福利厚生施設「シーメンズクラブ」でも働いた。

第2次世界大戦の海兵隊員、平泳ぎの名水泳選手で、66年に琉球米国民政府教育局長として赴任した故ゴードン・ワーナー博士は、毎週水曜日にランチとスロットマシンの娯楽のため同クラブを訪れていた。シャプラン氏は剣道教士七段のワーナー氏に琉球古武道保存振興会の2代目会

セミナーで指導するシャプラン氏=中央右(提供)
Shapland (center right) teaching at a seminar.

2021年10月24日

㉒カナダ

武歴60年 地道に普及

琉球古武道哲心館

長・赤嶺栄亮氏のことを教わった。

93年に振興会総本部(信武舘)の道場に入門し、赤嶺氏や同館高弟の一人の玉寄英美氏に師事した。2年後に沖縄婿(ウチナームーク)となり、2002年まで沖縄生活を楽しんだ。

赤嶺氏の没年99年に、玉寄氏は琉球古武道哲心館協会を創立し、シャプラン氏は同会に加盟した。帰国後、バンクーバー近くのチリワックで道場を開設し指導を再開した。

現在、琉球古武道八段のシャプラン氏の下で、二段の息子と娘や高段者6人が週3回指導を受けるほか、カナダと米国で16の支部道場のメンバーが沖縄の武術の研究に励んでいる。

長年の大工の経験を活かし、和名“弾・砂風蘭”を持つ氏は古武術の武具を作るようになり、今日では世界各地から手作りのサイ、トンファー、ムーゲー(馬具のハミ)ヌンチャクなどの注文を受けている。

経験豊富である氏はいつも赤嶺氏の座右の銘「世間の手や上(しきんぬてぃやうい)」を心に留めている。「世のなかには必ず自分よりも上手な人がいるから、私は『初心、常に向上心を!』をモットーにしている」と氏は言う。

武歴60年間での素晴らしい出会いに感謝し、頂いた恩恵と友情を維持し沖縄の武術の普及に地道に努める。(ドン・シャプラン氏は2022年6月19日にお亡くなりになりました。ご冥福をお祈りいたします。)

Published on 2021/10/24

22 Canada

Ryūkyū kobudō Tesshinkan

60 years of practice and promotion

Born in Ontario in 1946, Donald Shapland grew up with Japanese Canadian children and practiced jūdō and jūjutsu from the age of seven. After a short professional hockey career, he began training at an Isshin-ryū karate dōjō in Detroit, USA, around 1965.

Karate clubs were still rare in Canada at the time. Encouraged by his teacher, Shapland, now a 2nd dan after two years or practice, opened a dōjō in Windsor, Ontario, Canada.

During the summer of 1969, he visited Okinawa and studied under Shimabukuro Tatsuo. “What I saw in one month was just as exciting as I had expected” he recalls.

While serving as an instructor for the Royal Canadian Mounted Police and prison guards for 20 years, he travelled to Okinawa several times and decided to move to the birthplace of karate in 1990.

Along to teaching English, he also worked at the US military welfare facility, the Seamen’s Club, which was then located at the entrance of the Ōnoyama Park.

The late Doctor Gordon Warrener, a World War II veteran and famed breaststroke swimmer who was appointed director of education for the U.S. Civil Administration of the Ryūkyūs in 1966, visited the club every Wednesday for lunch and slot machines. From Warrener, who was also a kendō 7th dan, Shapland learned about Akamine Eisuke of Ryūkyū kobudō.

In 1993, Shapland entered Akamine’s dōjō, the Shinbukan, and trained under him and Tamayose Hidemi, one of the seniors. Two years later, he married an Okinawan woman and enjoyed living in Okinawa until 2002.

When Akamine passed away in 1999, Tamayose founded the Ryūkyū Kobudō Tesshinkan Association, and Shapland joined the organization. After his return to Canada, he opened a dōjō in Chilliwack near Vancouver and resumed teaching.

Currently an 8th dan in Ryūkyū kobudō, Shapland teaches his son and daughter and 6 senior members three times a week. In addition, there are 16 Tesshinkan chapters in Canada and the USA that study Okinawan weaponry.

Using his many years of carpentry, Shapland began to make kobudō weapons such as tonfā, nunchaku and the likes and has been receiving orders from all around the world.

A man with a wealth of experiences, Shapland keeps in mind Akamine’s motto “No matter how good you are, there is always someone better.” That is why he cherishes the spirit of “Shoshin - always maintain a beginner’s mind - and never stop learning!”

Grateful for the wonderful encounters he has had in 60 years of martial arts, he tries to maintain the benefits and friendships he has received and strives to steadily spread Okinawan martial arts.

(Donald Shapland passed away on June 19th, 2022. May he rest in peace.)

カナダ空手連盟は1万6千人のメンバー、地方連盟は500余りの道場を公表している。オンタリオ州には107の道場があるとされるが、競技団体に加盟しない道場も多く、「空手家の人口と道場実数は倍以上に上る」とスコット・ホーガス氏は解説する。

1952年トロント生まれのホーガス氏は少年の頃ボクシングを体験し、73年に藪中勲氏の本土系剛柔流の道場に入門した。当時の映画『ビリー・ジャック』の鑑賞がきっかけだという。「武術達人の主人公が罪のない者を助ける役を演じ、すごく魅力的でした」。その後、首里手系の空手やさまざまな武術を習い、4段まで昇段した。

89年、ある大会の会場で小林流の故仲里周五郎氏に師事した米国人フランク・ハーグローブ氏に会った。「あなたは良い空手家だが、やっているのは本物ではない！　沖縄に行って本物を習うべきだ」と言われ、ハーグローブ氏と稽古し一緒に訪沖した。滞在中、剛柔流の指導者を求め、心治館の當山全秋氏を紹介された。

そこから、残りの滞在日数11日間指導を受け、7つの型を習った。帰国する前の最後の昼食時に當山氏へ弟子入りを求めたが断られた。しかし帰る直前に當山氏は心変わりし、弟子入りが

弟子と共に鍛錬に励んでいるホーガス氏（最後列左から3人目）＝提供Hogarth with his students (third from the left in the last row).

2021年02月28日

㉓カナダ

「善行」胸に人を育む

心治館会

許された。

當山氏との食事中、ホーガス氏は地面に落とした食べ物をすぐに拾って食べた。沖縄では戦時中も終戦後も食べ物や水は貴重だった。通訳者を介し、師の思いを探ったホーガス氏は、物を大切にする姿を師が目の当たりにし、弟子入りが許されたのでは、とみている。あれから30年たった今も、ホーガス氏は弟子として空手の普及に励んでいる。

78年に開設された道場「ファイティング・グリフィン・マーシャルアーツ」は後に心治館会カナダ国本部道場になった。2つの支部道場と合わせて500人ほどが剛柔流、沖縄の古武道などを学ぶ。

自身の英国のルーツを忘れず、道場名のグリフィンは「正義」を表す伝説上の生物だという。武術の指導を通して社会貢献のほか、20代の時にはイギリスで消防士になり、帰国後は救急救命士も務めた。

座右の銘「できる限りの善を行う」を胸に刻み、人を助けて人間形成に尽くすのが宿命とするホーガス氏。「武道は普遍的なイコライザー。決して戦わないように武術を習うというパラドックスが空手の最も重要な奥義」と強調した。

The Canadian Karate Federation is said to have 16,000 members and more than 500 clubs. In the Ontario province, there are 107 member clubs but many dōjō that do not participate in competition are not registered. "The population of karateka and the actual number of dōjō are more than double," says Scott Hogarth.

Born in Toronto in 1952, Hogarth entered the Japanese Gōjū-ryū dōjō of Yabunaka Isao in 1973 after watching the movie "Billy Jack". "A martial art expert, the hero's purpose was to protect the innocent and downtrodden, and it was very attractive." Later on, Hogarth practiced Shurite related karate and was promoted to 4th dan.

Published on 2021/2/28

23 Canada

Shinjikan Association

Raising people as a good deed

In 1989 at a tournament venue, Hogarth met Frank Hargrove, an American who studied under the late Nakazato Shūgorō of Shōrin-ryū. Hargrove told him, "You are a good karateka but too bad it's not real! You should go to Okinawa to learn real karate." Hogarth started to practice with him and even went to Okinawa. During his stay, he sought Gōjū-ryū and was introduced to Tōyama Zenshū of the Shinjikan.

After the introduction, he trained for the remaining 11 days of his stay and learned 7 kata. At the last lunch before his return home, Hogarth asked Tōyama if he would accept him as a student but was turned down. However, just before his departure, Tōyama had a change of heart and he was allowed to become his student.

A few years ago, Hogarth was told that the reason Tōyama liked him was because at their luncheon, he had dropped a piece of food on the ground and immediately picked it up and ate it. The master explained that during the war and after, food and clean water were very scarce! So from his point of view, the fact that Hogarth valued the food and preparation meant that he had value for all things.

The dōjō Fighting Griffin Martial Arts, which was established in 1978, later became the Shinjikan Canada Headquarters. About 500 people train Gōjū-ryū and kobudō at the two clubs of the association.

The "Griffin" in the dōjō's name stands for Justice and is a nod to Hogarth's British heritage. In his twenties, Hogarth became a firefighter in England, and served as a firefighter and an EMT on the ambulances after returning to Canada.

His motto being "To do as much good as I can," Hogarth believes it is his destiny to help people grow as humans. He emphasizes "Martial Arts is the universal equalizer! It is a paradox in that it teaches to fight really well, so one never has to! That is the most important aspect of karate."

2019年06月23日

㉔カナダ

忍の魂刻み 普及に力

琉球空手センター

1930年に宮城長順氏によって名付けられた沖縄空手三大流派の一つ剛柔流は、世界中で多くの愛好家によって継承されている。

1959年英国コベントリー生まれのカール・ウィラー氏は、14歳の時、故大塚博紀氏が創始した和道流系の道場に入門した。75年に、家族と共にカナダのケベック州に移り住み、本土系の剛柔会の道場に入門した。

当時剛柔会の指導者だったのはケン・タラック氏。同氏は85年に訪沖し、那覇市久米にある明武舘の館長で宮城長順氏の高弟故八木明徳氏に指導を受けた。同年、明武舘剛柔流に転向している。

その3年後、ウィラー氏も沖縄を訪れた。那覇市の明武舘本部道場で県指定無形文化財「沖縄の空手・古武術」保持者、八木明徳氏の指導を受けた。

同年ウィラー氏は、オンタリオ州にある人口2万人の風光明媚(めいび)な小さな町ダンダスに移った。次男の誕生後、妻が仕事に復帰し、「主夫」をしながら本格的な道場の経営に専念した。

子どもが進学すると2000年に本業である板金整備士に戻り、週3回の地元のコミュニティーセンターでの指導に変えた。現在も、約20人の門下生と汗を流し、八木家の空手と古武道を研究する。

剛柔流の普及に励むウィラー氏(中央)と八木明人氏(右)、八木明広氏(左)=提供　Wheeler (center) with Yagi Akihito (right) and Yagi Akihiro (left), grandsons of Yagi Meitoku.

「現段階では、大規模なクラスには興味がありません」とウィラー氏。退職時期をふまえて、専業の空手指導を考えているが、時が来たときに決断するという。

96年に八木明徳氏より5段、13年に初代の長男である国際明武舘剛柔流空手道連盟総本部・八木明達氏により教士8段を取得した。同連盟はカナダで28の道場、180の公認有段者を登録している。

初の訪沖以降20回も沖縄を訪れたウィラー氏は、その時々を思い起こす。「沖縄の人たちは温かい。八木明徳先生は、私の好きな言葉になった『忍』などを書にすることが好きで、多くの弟子に書を贈った」と亡き師をしのぶ。

2003年に亡くなった明徳氏の大切な教えは「空手において、主な目的として物理的な技術だけを学ぶことにするな。人生の教訓も学びなさい。人格の良い人になるべきだ。道場のみの空手と思うな」。

流派を超えてウィラー氏は、武道に関する読書が好きで、近代空手の父と称される船越義珍氏の著書も大切にしている。

競技空手界と接触を持たないウィラー氏は、海外の先導役として、八木家の空手の普及に地道に励み続けている。

Gōjū-ryū, one of the three major Okinawa karate styles, was named by Miyagi Chojūn in 1930 and has since been practiced by many martial arts enthusiasts around the world.

Born in Coventry, England, in 1959, Carl Wheeler entered a Wadō-ryū karate club at the age of 14. In 1975, he moved to Quebec, Canada, with his family and joined a mainland Japanese Gōjū-kai dōjō.

At that time, the Gōjū-kai instructor was Ken Tallack. Tallack visited Okinawa in 1985 and was instructed by the late Yagi Meitoku, the head of the Meibukan in Kume, Naha City, and a direct student of the founder, Miyagi Chōjun. The same year, Tallack switched to Meibukan Gōjū-ryū karate.

Published on 2019/6/23

24 Canada

Ryūkyū Karate Center

Spreading the spirit of "Nin"

Three years later in 1988, Wheeler also travelled to Okinawa and was taught by Yagi Meitoku.

That same year, Wheeler moved to Dundas, a small scenic town with a population of 20,000 located in Ontario. After the birth of his second son, his wife returned to work and Wheeler devoted himself to the management of a full-fledged dōjō while being a stay-at-home parent.

In 2000, when the children went on to higher studies, he returned to his main business, sheet metal mechanic, and transitioned to teaching karate at a local community center three times a week. Today, about 20 people train with him researching the karate and kobudō of the Yagi family.

"At this stage, I do not teach full time as I did in the past," Wheeler says. When he retires, maybe he will think of it but he will decide when the time comes.

In 1996, Wheeler was promoted 5th dan by Yagi Meitoku and in 2013, he was awarded the 8th dan by Yagi's eldest son Meitatsu, the head of the International Meibukan Gōjū-ryū Karatedō Association headquarters. In Canada, this organization has 29 registered dōjō and 180 certified black belts.

Having visited Okinawa 20 times since his first trip, Wheeler remembers that first time. "The people of Okinawa are very welcoming. One of my favorite sayings comes from master Yagi Meitoku: 'NIN' or 'ENDURE'. He liked to paint calligraphy and give them out to his students," he says recalling his late master.

Some of the teachings of Yagi are, "Do not put your main purpose in learning only physical technique in karate. Learn lessons of life, too. Be a good person of character. Karatedō is not only in the dōjō."

Regardless of styles, Wheeler loves reading martial arts books and the books of Funakoshi Gichin, the father of modern karate, are also on his shelves.

While having no contact with the sport karate circles, he continues to diligently popularize the Yagi family's karate as one of its leaders overseas.

2017年09月10日

㉕カナダ

誇り高く名を守る

究道館支部長道場

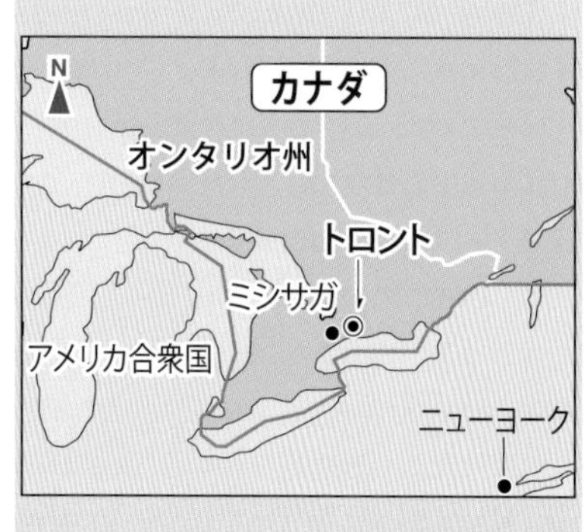

1959年ウルグアイモンテビデオ生まれのヘラルド・バルベス氏(58歳)は2010年から、カナダオンタリオ州のミシサガに住んでいる。沖縄小林流究道館の7段の腕前。

8歳で柔道、11歳の時に空手を習い始めた。しかし同国で空手が紹介されたのは1964年で、「全く新しい、未知でエキゾチックなものでした」とバルベス氏は振り返る。

本土系の松濤館や極真会系を修練したバルベス氏は、76年にアルゼンチン在住の宮里昌栄氏の弟子であった故ホルヘ・ブリンクマン氏と出会い、87年まで小林流志道館での稽古に励み、競技空手にも携わった。

修業のためアルゼンチンを頻繁に訪れ、81年に初めて究道館創始者の比嘉佑直氏の実弟、南米で空手普及に大きな足跡を残した比嘉仁達氏と息子の比嘉ベニト、オスカル各氏の演武を見た。彼らの素早い動きと腰使いに魅了され、87年からオスカル氏に師事した。

2000年に故郷を離れ、米国とスペインを経て8年前に、妻のマリエッラさんがエアーカナダに勤めていた関係でカナダに移住した。現在は体育教授をしながら小林流を指導している。カナダのほか、滞在した国々で副支部道場を開設し、年間4回ほど南米、ヨーロッパなどに出掛け、空手を教えている。

セミナーで指導するバルベス氏(左)=提供
Balves (left) teaching a seminar.

本土系と沖縄空手が極めて盛んなカナダでの指導活動開始は簡単ではなかった。当初建築の仕事をしながら、この国の最初の弟子と公園で稽古した。厳しい冬に耐えられずある商店の地下に移り、稽古を続けた。後に弟子が増え、トロントの公民館で稽古会を持つことができた。そして今年、8年間の努力の結果として正式に道場を開設した。現在、100人余がバルベス氏の指導を受けている。

南米人らしい明るい人物だが、空手を語り始めると顔は真剣そのものに変わる。「数より質を大切にしたい。究道館という名は誇り高く、守らなければならない」と語る。それには理由があった。

1994年、比嘉佑直氏の84歳を祝うために沖縄を訪れたバルベス氏は、入院中だった比嘉氏と初めて顔を合わせ、「頑張って」との言葉を受けた。その言葉の贈り物を「究道館の空手を継承するべし」と解釈し、普及に全力で挑んでいる。

2014年、那覇市壺屋にある究道館本部道場の直系組織「究道館究道無限会」の代表として究道館連合会の比嘉稔会長に認められ、ウルグアイ、カナダ、スペイン、チリ、米国、ドイツで弟子と共に、比嘉家の技と心を研究している。

Published on 2017/9/10

25 Canada

Kyūdōkan Shibuchō Dōjō

Proudly protecting his style's name

Born in Montevideo, Uruguay in 1959, Gerardo Balves (58), has been living in Mississauga, Ontario since 2010. He is a 7th dan expert in Okinawa Shōrin-ryū Kyūdōkan.

He started learning jūdō at the age of 8 and karate at the age of 11. But as karate was introduced in the country in 1964, "It was something totally new, unknown and exotic," Balves recalls.

Having studied Shōtōkan and Kyokushin, Balves met Jorge Brinkmann in 1975. Through this student of Miyazato Shoei, he trained in Shōrin-ryū Shidōkan karate until 1987.

Frequently visiting Argentina for training, he saw for the first time in 1981 a demonstration by Higa Jintatsu and his sons Benito and Oscar. The younger brother of Higa Yūchoku, the founder of the Kyūdōkan, Higa Jintatsu, was greatly involved with the spreading of karate in Argentina. Fascinated by their quick movements and the use of the hips, Balves started studying under Oscar in 1987.

Leaving Uruguay in 2000 to live in the USA and Spain, he moved to Canada 8 years ago as his wife Mariela worked for Air Canada. Today a teacher of physical education, he teaches karate in Canada while visiting the branch dōjō he established in South America and Europe.

It was not easy to start teaching karate in Canada, where mainland and Okinawa karate are extremely popular. He initially practiced in a park with his first Canadian students, while working in construction. Later, the number of students increasing, he was able to hold classes in a community center in Toronto. And in 2017, as a result of eight years of hard work, his dōjō was officially opened and more than 100 people are training under him today. He stresses, "I want to value quality over number. I am proud of the name Kyūdōkan and it must be protected."

The reason for such a belief is that in 1994, when Balves visited Okinawa to celebrate Higa Yūchoku's 84th anniversary, he met the master in the hospital for the first time and received the following words: "Do your best". For him, it was like an order to persevere in inheriting Kyūdōkan's karate. Since then, he has done his best to popularize the art.

In 2014, Balves was recognized by Higa Minoru, head of the Okinawa Shōrin-ryū Karatedō Kyūdōkan Federation, as the representative - shibuchō - of the Kyūdōkan Kyūdō Mugenkai, a group directly related to the Kyūdōkan honbu dōjō in Tsuboya, Naha City. Together with his students in Uruguay, Canada, Spain, Chile, Germany and the USA, Balves continues to study the skills and spirit of the Higa family.

2017年10月29日

㉖ カナダ

伝統誇り 交流を重視

デサ空手スクール

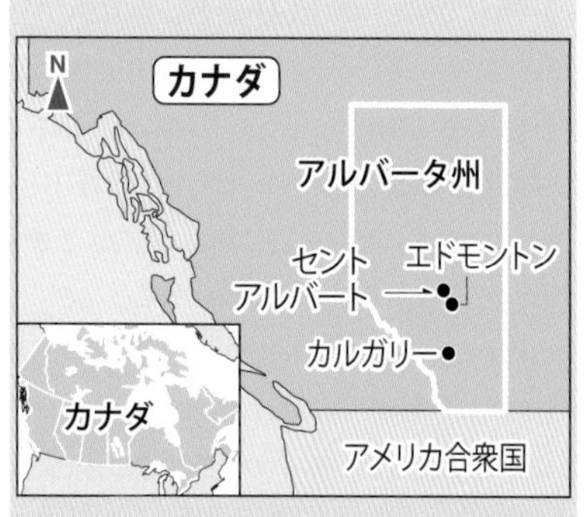

カナダで空手が紹介されたのは、同国で「空手の父」として知られている鶴岡政己氏によって1957年のこと。63年に現在のカナダ空手連盟の母体が設立され、現在、競技空手の国別ランキングでは15位となっている。競技空手が盛んな中、沖縄空手の支部は25余りある。

沖縄空手三大流派の一つである上地流を指導するマニュエル・デサ氏は、1964年ポルトガルで生まれ、5歳のころ両親と共にカナダ・アルバータ州エドモントン市に移民した。

デサ氏は、若いころから武術に興味を示したが、父母は課外活動以外を許さず、アルバータ大学入学の際に、本土系の空手和道流の道場に入門した。

そして、90年に上地流と出合った。町道場で指導していたのは、仲程力氏に師事するニール・ダニガン氏。上地流という強い空手とその系統が伝える哲学に魅了され研究に励み、93年に米国で上地流の第一人者である拳優会のアレン・ダーラ氏、またリック・マーチン氏に師事した。

空手に自らの可能性を感じたデサ氏は、少年カウンセラーの仕事をしながら公民館で空手の指導を始めた。96年にセントアルバート市で看板を掲げ、空手のプロの道を選んだ。

弟子と共に型の練習をするデサ氏(前列中央)=提供
Desa (center, front row) practicing kata with his students.

最初のころはラグビーセンターで指南した。そして、2003年に、妻と門下生の激励を受け、170坪の立派な空手スクールを開設した。増築をし、現在では約250坪の道場で350人に指導している。

08年に、読谷村渡具知を拠点とする新城清秀氏が会長を務める上地流空手道拳優会へ正式に入門が許され、15年に空手7段に昇段した。古武道は、金城政和氏が指揮する琉球古武道保存会に加盟している。しかし、空手の指導で毎日忙しい日々を送るデサ氏は、今古武道を少し中断しているという。

16年からデサ氏は、20人の指導者、1500人余の会員を登録する北米拳優会会長を務める。「新城会長の下、拳優会は、伝統を重んじ高い基準を維持すると共に、競技空手を積極的に取り込めるユニークな組織。メンバーは誇り高く、力強く活動している」と言う。

10回以上沖縄を訪れているデサ氏は、毎年本部道場の指導者を招き、講習会も実施している。「沖縄空手を鍛錬するそれぞれの世代の交流が重要。発祥の地に行くことも、沖縄の空手人がやってくることも、両方にとって有意義だ」

鍛錬を積み、充実した日々にも甘んじることなくデサ氏は現在、空手カナダ連盟で講習も重ねる。そして、発祥の地の空手を受け継ぐことの責任を忘れず、本場と幸運な交流を何よりも大切にしている。

Published on 2017/10/29

26 

Desa Karate School

Proud of the tradition and valuing exchange

Karate was introduced in Canada in 1957 by Tsuruoka Masami, the “father of karate” in this country and the parent body of the current Canadian karate federation was established in 1963. While competitive karate is popular, there are more than 25 branches of Okinawa karate in Canada.

Manuel Desa, was born in Portugal in 1964 and immigrated with his parents to Edmonton, Alberta at the age of five.

Ever since he was a small kid, he had a strong passion for martial arts. However, his parents did not believe in extracurricular activities and it is while in university that he started training Wadō-ryū karate.

Encountering Uechi-ryū in 1990, he first joined the dōjō of Neil Dunnigan, a student of Nakahodo Tsutomu. Impressed by this strong style of karate and the philosophy it conveys, he trained hard and in 1993 studied with Kenyūkai members Allan Dollar and Ric Martin, two prominent Uechi-ryū leaders in the USA.

Realizing his potential in karate, Desa began teaching karate in a few community centers while working as a youth counsellor. In 1996, he opened his dōjō in St. Albert choosing to dedicate himself completely to the path of karate.

Desa started teaching in a rented space in the basement of a rugby club building. In 2003, with the support of his wife and students, he decided to build his own 6000 square foot dōjō. Today, the dōjō having been expanded, approximately 350 students train regularly under his leadership.

Becoming officially a member of the Uechi-ryū Karatedō Kenyūkai headed by Shinjō Kiyohide, Desa was promoted to 7th dan in 2015. He is also a member of Kinjō Masakazu's Ryūkyū Kobudō Hozonkai.

In 2016, Desa served as the president of the Kenyūkai North America Organization that includes more than 20 instructors and 1500 students across the USA and Canada. “Under Shinjō sensei, we have the best of both karate worlds - a strong traditional karate curriculum that sets and maintains high standards while being able to actively engage in competitive karate. Our members are proud of this and are extremely active.”

Having visited Okinawa more than 10 times, he also welcomes every year instructors from the honbu dōjō in Yomitan. “Exchanges are important for each generation of karateka. Going to the birthplace and welcoming Okinawan karateka are meaningful for both sides.”

Not satisfying himself with his daily training, Desa is currently undergoing training courses with the Canadian national karate body. Remembering his responsibility of inheriting traditional karate, he values above all the fortunate relation he has developed with Okinawa.

1957年フランス人のエメ・ファヴル氏は、カナダに移住し、東部に位置し面積でカナダ最大の州ケベック州のモントリオールを拠点に望月拡雄氏の養正館空手の普及に努め、多くの弟子を育てた。

1966年生まれのシャンタル・ヴァヤンクール氏は、6歳に親の勧めで養正館系の道場に入門させられた。「少し落ち着かない少女だったらしい」と彼女は入門の理由を打ち明ける。21歳まで道場で心技体を磨き、指導方法も学んだ。師から道場を譲られ、ヴァヤンクール氏は道場主となった。

空手を始めたころから、彼女は空手のルーツを求め、発祥の地沖縄に行きたいという希望があった。

2000年に、当時、小林流守武館の空手を鍛錬していたアンドレ・レモン氏と共に沖縄を訪れ、那覇市首里鳥堀町にある守武館上間道場の上間康弘氏に出会った。すぐに上間氏の空手ときめ細かい指導や道場の家族ぐるみの雰囲気に魅了された彼女は、小林流への転向を決め、上間家の空手と古武道に専任した。

「流派を変えることは、私の人生で最も素晴らしい決断でした」と彼女は振り返る。

一部の道場生とヴァヤンクール氏（前列左から4人目） Some dōjō students with Vaillancourt (fourth from the left in the front row).

2022年3月13日

㉗ カナダ

高校で空手指導実現

小林流守武館ボワブリヤン

現在、モントリオールの北部にある人口約3万5千人の小さな町ボワブリヤンに住む彼女は、昼間は、高校で空手を指導し、夕方には週5回自身の道場で沖縄空手を指南する。道場には147人が所属し、その内11歳以下の少年少女が85人。

なお、カナダの学校において普段空手は取り入れられていない。地元の高校でレクリエーション活動技術士を勤めていたヴァヤンクール氏は、空手のプログラムを提案し特別に導入された。今日では15~16歳の生徒に空手の身体的と精神的のメリットを強調して教えているという。

2011年、レモン氏の脱会に伴い、ヴァヤンクール氏は「守武館カナダ」の代表に任命された。本質的にスポーツが大好きなヴァヤンクール氏は、空手の他に5歳からスキーをたしなむ。年の半分が冬のケベックで、彼女は週末にスキー場で滑り、春と夏は、マウンテインバイクでアドレナリンラッシュ（興奮状態）を満喫する。

黒帯4人家族の妻と母として、彼女は、空手のおかげで自分があるという。「空手を始めたころから、決して諦めないこと、忍耐力などを学んだ。目標を達成するために努力しなければなりません。謙虚な気持ちを保ち、敗北や落とし穴にもかかわらず勇気と決意を!」。これも空手の大切な教えの一つであり、技法と共に弟子に伝えていきたいという。

In 1957, Frenchman Aymé Favre moved to Montreal, Quebec and popularized Mochizuki Hiroo's Yōseikan karate.

Born in 1966, Chantal Vaillancourt entered a Yōseikan dōjō at the age of six. On the reason why she was taken to a karate club, she confesses, "It seems that I was a little turbulent." Until the age of 21, she honed mental, technical and physical skills at the dōjō and also learned how to teach. After her club being handed over to her by her instructor, she became a dōjō owner.

From the time she started karate, she wanted to go to Okinawa, the birthplace of karate, in search of its roots.

In 2000, she visited Okinawa with André Raymond, who was a member of the Shōrin-ryū Shūbukan at that time, and met Uema Yasuhiro of the Shūbukan Uema Dōjō in Shuri Torihori, Naha City. Immediately fascinated by Uema's karate and detailed instruction as well as the family atmosphere of the dōjō, she decided to switch to Shōrin-ryū and devoted herself to the study of the Uema family's karate and kobudō.

Looking back, she comments, "By changing style, I made the most beautiful decision of my life."

Published on 2022/3/13

27 Canada

Shōrin-ryū Shūbukan Boisbriand

Including karate in high school's programs

Today living in Boisbriand, a small town in the northern part of Montreal, she teaches karate in a high school during the day and teaches Okinawa karate five times a week at her dōjō in the evening. There are 147 members in the dōjō, of which 85 are boys and girls under the age of 11.

Karate is not usually adopted in Canadian schools. As Vaillancourt was a leisure technician responsible for all extracurricular activities for the students in a senior high school, she proposed and succeeded in incorporating a karate program. Today, she teaches karate emphasizing its physical and mental benefits to students aged 15 to 16 years old.

In 2011, as Raymond left the Shūbukan, Vaillancourt was appointed as the representative of "Shūbukan Canada".

A sports aficionado, she has been skiing since the age of five, in addition to practicing karate. In the Quebec's winter that lasts almost 6 months, she skis on weekends and enjoys adrenaline rushes on a mountain bike in spring and summer.

As a wife and mother of three black belts, she says she is who she is thanks to karate. "Since I started karate, I have learned to never give up and to be patient. You have to work hard to reach your goals. Staying humble, you have to be courageous and determined despite defeats and pitfalls!" This is also an important teaching of karate, and she wants to convey this to her students along with the technique of Shōrin-ryū.

2021年07月25日

㉘ メキシコ

少林流の技受け継ぐ

聖武館メキシコ

コアウイラ州トレオン出身のハイメ・メンデス氏(72)とヘリベルト・メンデス氏(67)の兄弟は、1970年代前半、空手に興味を持つようになった。いくつかの道場を見学したが、72年に出会った米国人のセテフェン・ウォータース氏に導かれ、沖縄空手に専心することを決めた。

元米陸軍特殊部隊兵のウォータース氏は、沖縄駐留の際に3年間ほど、空手を習った。師は、首里・泊手の喜屋武朝徳氏の空手を受け継ぎ、62年に北谷町で少林流聖武館を築いた故島袋善良氏と子息の善保氏だった。

その出会いから生まれた運を見逃さず、メンデス兄弟は20人ほどを集め、ウォータース氏の下で2年間師事した。

帰国する前に、ウォータース氏はメンデス兄弟と島袋善保氏をつないだ。76年に少林流の国際協会を設立した善保氏は、同年トレオンを訪れセミナーを指導した。

これまで市立の体育館で稽古していたメンデス兄弟は、善保氏の基準に従って道場を77年に開設。落成式の前に善保氏と相談の上、沖縄から当時空手2段で聖武館の高弟伊差川昇氏が派遣された。技術向上に伴い、道場生が競技大会で多く

道場の正門前のヘリベルト氏(左)とハイメ氏＝メキシコ(提供) Heriberto (left) and Jaime Méndez at the entrance of their dōjō.

のメダルを獲得し、聖武館メキシコの評判が広がり、79年に同系の空手がコアウイラ州大学に導入されるようになった。さらに、第2の道場も隣州のゴメスパラシオに開設された。

鍛錬に励みながら、メンデス兄弟は社会においても成功した。ハイメ氏は1940年スペイン移民に創立されたセルバンテス・デ・トレオン学園の代表になり、ヘリベルト氏は小児科医になった。

90年にハイメ氏ら3人が初めて沖縄の本部で稽古を体験した。その後、メンデス兄弟は、沖縄や米国などで善保氏の指導を受け続けたが、空手の人気に応えるため、そして技術のレベルを保つために、新たに指導者の派遣を求めた。

2001年に、北谷の本部道場で15年間鍛えられた座喜味秀明氏(当時21歳)はメキシコに渡り14年の米国への移住まで少林流空手の技術向上に努めた。座喜味氏は現在、ワシントン州でオークハーバー支部を開き、指導を続けている。

約50年間一筋の系統の研究と普及に努めるメンデス兄弟は現在、共に5段。メキシコ支部長を務めるのは弟のヘリベルト氏。道場の門弟40人と国内各地に住む弟子と共にメンデス兄弟は今日も、島袋家の空手を一本の道として向き合い汗を流す。

Published on 2021/7/25

28 Mexico

Seibukan Mexico

Inheriting Shōrin-ryū techniques

The brothers Jaime Méndez (72) and Heriberto Méndez (67) from Torreon, Coahuila, became interested in karate in the early 1970s. After visiting several karate clubs, they met Stephen Waters in 1972 and after watching his demonstration, decided to start Okinawa karate with him.

A former US green beret, Stephen Waters studied karate in Okinawa for more than three years with Shimabukuro Zenryō, a student of Kyan Chōtoku and founder of the Shōrin-ryū Seibukan in Chatan Town and his son Zenpō.

Following this lucky encounter, the Méndez brothers gathered about 20 people and studied under Waters for two years.

Before returning home, Waters connected the Méndez brothers with Shimabukuro Zenpō. In 1976, the year Shimabukuro established an international Shōrin-ryū association, he visited Torreon and taught a seminar.

The Méndez brothers, who had been practicing at a municipal gymnasium, opened a dōjō in 1977 according to Shimabukuro's standards. After consulting with Shimabukuro before the inauguration ceremony, Isagawa Noboru, a high-ranked Seibukan student, was dispatched from Okinawa to Mexico. As their technique improved, members of the dōjō won many medals at local competitions and the reputation of Seibukan Mexico spread. In 1979, a branch was established at the Autonomous University of Coahuila and a second dōjō was opened in Gómez Palacio in the neighboring state of Durango.

While diligently training, the Méndez brothers have also succeeded in life. Jaime became the director of the Colegio Cervantes de Torreón, an educational institution founded by Spanish immigrants in 1940, while Heriberto is a pediatrician.

In 1990, Jaime along with two of his students travelled to Okinawa and trained at the Seibukan in Chatan for the first time. Later on, the Méndez brothers continued to receive guidance from Shimabukuro in Okinawa and the USA, but also requested the dispatch of a new instructor in order to respond to the popularity of karate and to maintain the level of skill.

In 2001, Zakimi Hideaki (21 years old at the time), who had been training for 15 years at the Chatan dōjō, moved to Mexico and worked to improve the technique of Shōrin-ryū in the country. Relocating to the USA in 2014, he currently operates the Seibukan Oak Harbor branch in Washington.

The Méndez brothers, who have researched and promoted the same style for about 50 years, are currently 5th dan and Heriberto is the head of the Mexican Seibukan. Together with 40 students at the dōjō and members living in various parts of the country, the Méndez brothers continue to follow a one way path that is the karate of the Shimabukuro family.

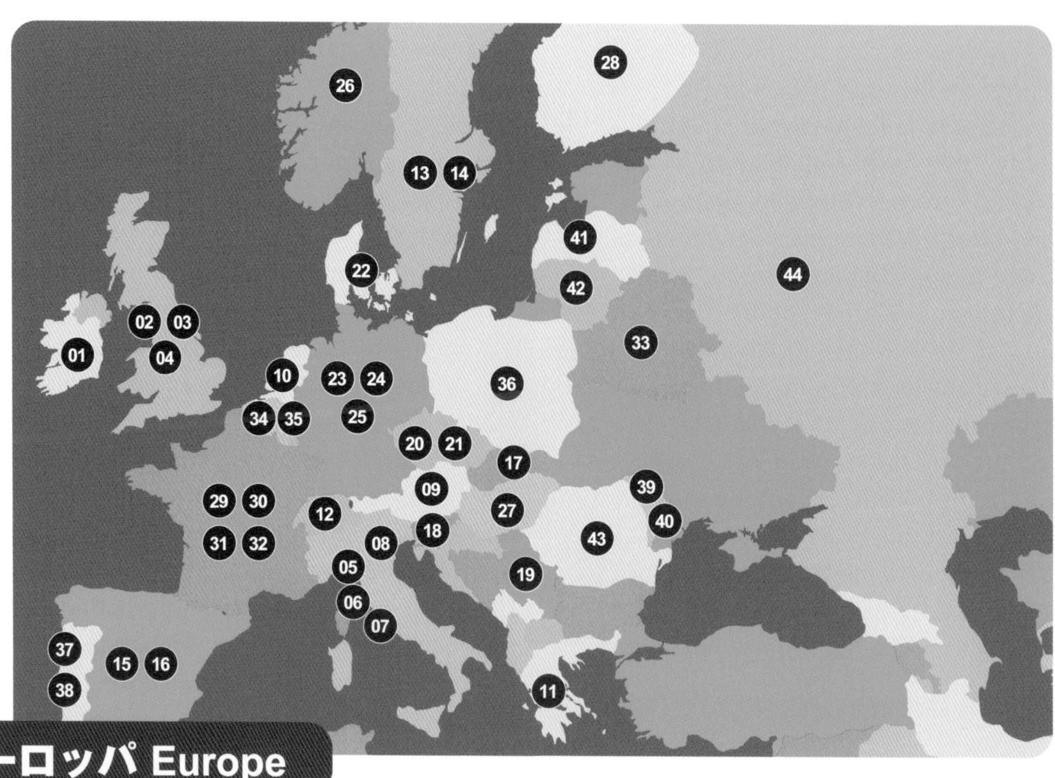

ヨーロッパ Europe

ヨーロッパ
Europe

2019年06月30日

01 アイルランド

日々鍛錬 人生の支え

松源流誠道場

アイルランドのドニゴール州バリーボフィー生まれのマイケル・クイン氏(48)は、24歳から約13年間、ナイトクラブの「用心棒」を勤めた。危険な仕事だが、これが沖縄空手との出合いにつながった。

1996年から、島袋栄三氏の少林流空手をアメリカ人を通じて学んだという仕事の同僚エドリアン・ロワン氏の手ほどきを受けた。「彼が攻撃に容易に対応し、相手を傷つけず拘束するところが魅力的でした」と当時を振り返る。

2010年までに近隣の松林流系の道場に入門。しかし、仕事の関係で空手に専心することが困難と感じたクイン氏は11年に大学に戻り、ソーシャルワークの学位取得へ向け勉強に励んだ。同年、自宅で道場を開設。道場名の「誠」について「他人、弟子、自身に対し正直で誠実であるべきだと信じて名付けた」と説明する。

15年にソーシャルワーカーの資格を取得したクイン氏は現在、児童保護の分野で働いている。「肉体的、性的、感情的等に虐待された子どもたちのケアに携わっている。挑戦的な仕事だが、やりがいがある。自宅に道場があるから稽古を通して職場のストレスから解放され、仕事の恐ろしさを家に持ち込むこともない」。家族と空手は、精神的なバランスの源だという。

真の沖縄空手と師を求め続けたクイン氏は、米国で松源流の普及に励むトニー・パートロウ氏と知り合い、糸満市で指導する前田清正氏を紹介された。

道場で稽古を終えたクイン氏(後列左から4人目)と門下生=提供
Quinn (fourth from the left in the back row) and his students after a training session at the dōjō.

松源流の始祖は、松林流初代長嶺将真氏の高弟故田場兼靖氏。2002年に沖縄松源流空手道協会を設立し、前田氏は2代目会長を務めている。

15年に沖縄を訪れたクイン氏は、前田氏に師事・弟子入りした。以降、5回沖縄を訪れている。現在5段のクイン氏は、同協会のヨーロッパ支部長にも任命された。道場で子どもから大人まで約50人を指導し、数カ国の組織と武術交流を行っている。

クイン家では、さまざまな知識を深めるため読書を大切にしているという。

〈慢心はすべての成長をはばんでしまいます。何事にも謙虚で反省を怠らず、進む方向を定めてそれに向かい、ただまっしぐらに進むことあるのみです。それこそ沖縄伝統の空手に生きる男子の本懐と申すべきでありましょう〉

クイン氏にとって、剛柔流の渡口政吉著『空手の心』に残されたこの言葉は、「誠」の意味を要約したものであり、空手の最も重要な側面を示している。

Born in Ballybofey, County Donegal, Michael Quinn (48) was a nightclub bouncer from the age of 24 and worked in this field for about 13 years. Although it was a dangerous job, it led to his encounter with Okinawa karate.

In 1996, he was introduced to Shōrin-ryū by Adrian Rowan, a fellow bouncer who had studied the system of Shimabukuro Eizō from an American practitioner. Quinn recalls that, "I admired how he could easily respond to attacks and restrain people without hurting or injuring them."

Although he studied Matsubayashi-ryū in a nearby dōjō, Quinn found it difficult to concentrate on karate because of his work. He thus returned to university in 2011 to acquire a degree in social work. The same year, he opened a dōjō at his home which he named "Makoto", which means sincerity or honesty in Japanese. "I am a firm believer in being honest and sincere with other people, with my students, and especially with myself."

Becoming a qualified social worker in 2015, Quinn is now working full time as a child protection social worker. "This involves working with children who are abused physically, sexually, emotionally or are neglected. It is a really mentally challenging job but rewarding too. As my dōjō is at my house, I can train anytime I want and forget about the work and problems of life." He also says that family and karate are his sources of spiritual balance.

As he continued to seek true Okinawa karate and teachers, Quinn became acquainted with Tony Partlow, a Shōgen-ryū instructor in the USA. Through him, Quinn was introduced to Itoman City based Maeda Kiyomasa.

The founder of Shōgen-ryū was late Taba Kensei, a high-ranked disciple of the founder of Matsubayashi-ryū Nagamine Shōshin. Taba established the Okinawa Shōgen-ryū Karatedō Association in 2002, and Maeda serves as the second chairman.

Quinn, who visited Okinawa in 2015, studied under Maeda and became his student. Since then, he has travelled to Okinawa five times and as a 5th dan, he has also been appointed as the head of the European branch of the association. He teaches about 50 people from children to adults at his dōjō while interacting with overseas organizations.

"Strong conceit prevents the growth of one's character or ability. To reach any goal, one must be modest, always maintain self-control and strive hard to reach the goal. This is the long cherished desire of one that lives by the code of Okinawan karatedō."

For Quinn, these words left by Gōjū-ryū master Toguchi Seikichi in his book "Karate no Kokoro" summarize the meaning of "Makoto" and show the most important aspect of karate.

Published on 2019/6/30

01 Ireland

Shōgen-ryū Makoto Dōjō

Daily training as a life support method

2018年05月13日

02 イギリス

「精励刻苦」指導に力

MATS道場

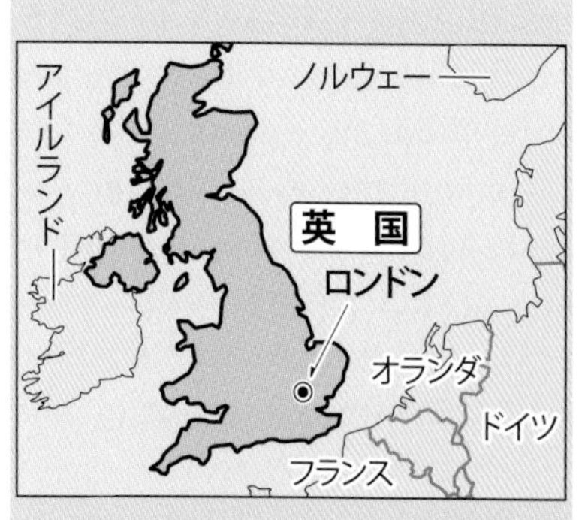

イギリス王室のヘンリー王子が19日、結婚される。王室で名を成す英国。空手の歴史は1950年代後半に遡り、今も「空手王国」の一つとして開花し続けている。

50年生まれのジョージ・アンドリューズ氏は17歳の時空手に入門し5年後2段に昇段した。73年に沖縄剛柔流に触れ、県出身故知念輝夫氏らに師事した。

食肉加工所で仕事をしながらアンドリューズ氏は、74年にロンドン南部のエレファント&キャッスル区で「マーブルファクトリー」道場を開設した。

77年に、県指定無形文化財保持者の東恩納盛男氏(当時39歳)がイギリスを訪れ指導した。以降アンドリューズ氏は、東恩納氏を離れず沖縄剛柔流の道を歩んできた。85年に初めて日本に滞在し、6週間空手を学んだ。その後、毎年のように沖縄を訪れ、尊敬する師の下で技法の再確認を行ってきた。↗

空手の環境で恵まれる一方、アンドリューズ氏はさまざまな困難に立ち向かってきた。その中で最も苦労したのは、「人生で一番辛かった困難」と語る2001年の道場の全焼だった。

すべてが消えても、無形である空手に打ち込

セミナーで指導するアンドリューズ氏(中央)=ローマン・ボードリエフ氏提供
Andrews (center) teaching at a seminar (photo from Roman Boldyrev).

み近隣の学校で指導を続けた。その決意を受けた弟子たちが募金活動を行い、数週間で約125万円が集められ、焼けてしまった道場が現在の「MATS道場」として再生された。

「マーシャル・アーツ・トレーニング・スクールの頭文字であるマッツは、剛柔流開祖の武士宮城長順の幼名の『松(マツー)』にも重なる」と説明する。現在、本部道場に50人、全国12道場に約350人がアンドリューズ氏の下で鍛錬している。

「全く資格の無かった私は、空手道を通して自らの教育を追求してきた。空手に出合えたことは本当に運命でした」と振り返る。人生のすべてを空手に捧げたアンドリューズ氏は、その経験を活かし、20年前から妻と共に児童の養育里親になり、これまで62人の児童を養育してきた。自信、社会スキルとチームワークにつながる空手も勧めるという。

「死、政治、財政、社会などの変化で多くの人々が空手を始めたり離れたりしてきた。しかし、東恩納先生に導かれるように、剛柔流を通して謙虚と誠実な人になり、完璧さを達成するために精励刻苦するべきです」

2012年8段に昇段し、半世紀の武歴を土台とするアンドリューズ氏は今も「言えば忘れる、見せれば覚える」という教えで英国、タイ、ポーランドなどで指導に力を注ぐ。

Prince Harry, Duke of Sussex will be married on May 19th, 2018. In Great Britain, a nation proud of its royal family, the history of karate dates back to the late 1950s and the country continues to bloom as one of the "karate kingdoms".

Born in 1950, George Andrews started karate at the age of seventeen, and 5 years later, he was promoted 2nd dan. He discovered Okinawa Gōjū-ryū in 1973 and studied under the late Okinawan instructor Chinen Teruo.

In 1974, while working in a meat market, Andrews opened The Marble Factory dōjō in the Elephant & Castle area in southern London.

Three years later, Higaonna Morio visited England and taught karate. Since then, Andrews has been following the path of Okinawa Gōjū-ryū staying close to Higaonna. Andrews first stayed in Japan in 1985 where he studied karate for 6 weeks. After this first sojourn, he has visited Okinawa almost every year to have his technique corrected under his respected master.

Published on 2018/5/13

02 United Kingdom 

MATS Dōjō

Diligence with an emphasis on teaching

While blessed with his karate environment, Andrews had to face various challenges, the hardest one being the complete burning of his dōjō in 2001. "The worst difficult time of my life," he recalls.

Even if all had been lost, he continued to teach at a nearby school, devoting himself completely to the intangible art that is karate. Impressed by his determination, his disciples raised funds, collected about 1.25 million yen in a few weeks, and the burnt dōjō was reborn as the current MATS Dōjō.

The acronym for "Martial Arts Training School" MATS also overlaps "Matsu", the childhood name of Miyagi Chōjun, the founder of Gōjū-ryū. Today, 50 people at the honbu dōjō and approximately 350 people in 12 dōjō nationwide train under the guidance of Andrews.

"I had no qualifications and so I pursued my education through karatedō. I look back now and think how lucky I was to be involved with martial arts." Andrews has used his experience to become child fostering parents with his wife. For 20 years, they have raised 62 children so far. He also recommends karate, which builds self-esteem, social skills and teamwork.

"There has been many people come and go due to death, political / financial changes, etc. However, as guided by Higaonna sensei, we should all become humble and sincere and strive for perfection through Gōjū-ryū."

Promoted to 8th dan in 2012 and with a half-century of martial art experience, Andrews still focuses on teaching in the UK, Thailand, Poland, etc. with the motto "If you say it, people forget. If you show it, people remember."

2019年09月22日

03 イギリス

宗家の教え 礎に稽古

上地流空手道協会(GB)

上地流空手道協会が1977年に発刊した『精説沖縄空手道-その歴史と技法』の中で当時、世界で上地流を指導する外国人空手家が紹介されている。グレートブリテン(GB)についてはデイビッド・スコット氏が支部の代表として記載されている。

44年生まれのスコット氏は、20歳のころ、沖縄を訪れ二代目宗家・上地完英氏に師事。帰国後、リバプールで道場を開設し空手の普及に励んだ。しかし82年に禅の道に入ったスコット氏は、後に指導から引退し、禅僧になった。

現在GBでは、桃原慶長氏が会長を務める沖縄空手道協会(沖空会)に所属する支部は数カ所あり、上地流空手道協会はスコット氏の空手を継承する。↗

2008年から10年間、上地流空手道協会の会長を務めたマイク・パッパス氏は、1975年からスコット氏に師事。82年にパッパス氏は、沖縄市民会館で開催された上地流空手道開祖上地完文翁三十三回忌追悼演武大会に参加した。「本部道場生の高いレベルに驚いたが、指導は優しく、細かくそして友好的だった。また、完英先生の自宅でのディナーに誘われ、畏敬の念に打たれた」

仲程力氏(2列目右から4人目)らによるセミナーに参加したデイリー氏(同6人目)=提供
Daly (6th from the right in the 2nd row) participating in a seminar by Nakahodo Tsutomu and other Okikūkai masters.

と当時のエピソードを思い返す。87年にオックスフォードに移り、道場を開設したパッパス氏は、故高宮城繁氏など沖空会の高段者を招き数回セミナーを開催した。

現在、同協会の会長を引き継いでいるのはテリー・デイリー氏。57年ロンドン生まれのデイリー氏は74年に、両親と共に米国に移り住んだ。同年、ボストンで米国の上地流先駆者ジョージ・マットソン氏の道場に入門。2年後に帰国したデイリー氏は、稽古を続け、80年に「ロンドン上地流空手スクール」を開設した。現在も、2カ所で指南し、60人ほどが学ぶ。2016年に7段に昇段した。現在上地流空手道協会では3人の7段保持者の下、加盟8道場で190人のメンバーが同系を学ぶ。

デイリー氏の高弟には、ウエイン・オット氏(53)がいる。「足払いと中段突きの鬼」と称され、世界空手道選手権大会を数回制覇した。その功績が認められ、2001年にエリザベス2世より「大英帝国勲章」を受賞し、最も多くのメダルを獲得した者としてギネス世界記録にも記載された。

上地流5段のオット氏は現在、ノルウェー組手チームのナショナルコーチを務める。師のデイリー氏も王者のオット氏も「伝統と競技」を両輪と位置づけているが、その礎は伝統の上地流に深く根ざしている。

Published on 2019/9/22

03 United Kingdom 

Uechi-ryū Karatedō Association (GB)

Training with the teachings of the founder as basis

In the book "Seisetsu Okinawa Karatedō - History and Techniques" published in 1977 by the Uechi-ryū Karatedō Association are introduced foreigners who led Uechi-ryū outside of Okinawa at that time. For Great Britain (GB), David Scott is listed as the school's representative.

Born in 1944, Scott visited Okinawa at the age of 20 and trained under the second generation Sōke, Uechi Kanei. After returning home, he opened a dōjō in Liverpool and worked hard to popularize karate. However, Scott later on entered the path of Zen in 1982 and retiring from teaching karate, he became a Zen priest.

Currently in GB, there are several organizations belonging to the Okinawa Karatedō Association (Okikūkai) chaired by Tōbaru Keichō and among them, the Uechi-ryū Karatedō Association inherits the karate legacy of David Scott.

Mick Pappas, who was the chairman of the Uechi-ryū Karatedō Association for 10 years from 2008, started training under Scott in 1975. In 1982, Pappas participated in the 33rd memorial service demonstration of Uechi Kanbun, the founder of Uechi-ryū, held at the Okinawa City Civic Center. About his memories of the trip, he recalls, "The level of the honbu dōjō's students was high but they were very helpful, knowledgeable, and friendly in their corrections. And as we were being invited to Master Uechi's home for dinner, we were in awe." In 1987, Pappas moved to Oxford and opened a dōjō. He later invited various Okikūkai's leaders to teach seminars.

Currently, Terry Daly is the chairman of the association. Born in London in 1957, Daly moved to the USA with his parents in 1974. That same year, he entered the Boston dōjō of the pioneer of Uechi-ryū in the USA, George Mattson. Returning to England two years later, Daly continued to practice and opened the London Uechi-ryū Karate School in 1980. Today, about 60 people train in two locations. Daly was promoted to 7th dan in 2016.

Currently, the GB association counts 190 members who are training in eight dōjō under the instruction of three 7th dan holders.

Among Daly's high-ranked student is Wayne Otto (53). Nicknamed the "Sweep and reversed punch demon", Otto won the World Karate Championships several times. His achievements being recognized, he was awarded the Most Excellent Order of the British Empire by Queen Elizabeth II in 2001 and was listed in the Guinness World Records as the athlete with most awarded medals.

Otto, a 5th dan in Uechi-ryū, is currently the national coach of the Norwegian kumite team. Like his teacher, Otto regards "tradition and competition" as the two wheels of a bicycle, but the foundation of it all is deeply rooted in traditional Uechi-ryū karate.

イングランドのリヴァプールと言えば、ビートルズが浮かぶが、実はこの街、空手と深い関わりもある。

1965年、同国での空手普及のため、日本空手協会が数人の指導者を派遣した。その一人の故榎枝慶之輔氏は、リヴァプールにある「レッドトライアングル」道場を拠点に指導し、同市出身のテリー・オニール氏など多くのチャンピオンを育てた。

62年リヴァプール生まれのポール・ベミリーオ氏は、8歳の時、ボクサーの祖父から手ほどきを受け、その後、約20年間柔術を学んだ。商船隊員になった氏は、世界の海を航海しながらも稽古を休まなかった。

92年に、蹴り技を改良しようと故郷にあった「レッドトライアングル」道場に入門した。3年後、オニール氏が発行していた武道雑誌で、琉球古武道の赤嶺栄亮氏のことを知り、96年に赤嶺氏の指導を受けるため沖縄に出向いた。

6年間、豊見城市にある平信賢氏の高弟赤嶺氏の道場で内弟子として琉球古武道と小林流を学びながら、アルバイトなどもした。「多くの沖縄人に助けられ、その人は今私の家族のような存在」と氏はコメントする。

古武道指導のためイスラエルに出向いたベミリーオ氏(右から3人目)
Vermiglio (third from the right) during a kobudō seminar in Israel.

2022年2月27日

04 イギリス

伝統通して極致追求

部見亮(ブミスケ)会国際

沖縄を後にした氏は、イスラエルに滞在し、古武道の普及に励んだ。そして、ヨーロッパ各国を訪れて後、2006年に帰郷した。

現在ベミリーオ氏は、イギリスの特別自然美観地域にあるコッツウォルズに住む。道場「部見亮会国際」は、ウィルトシャーのオークシー村にある。

名の意味を問うと、氏はこのように説明する。「沖縄に住んでいた時、赤嶺会長の奥さまは、私の名字のベミリーオの発音をもとに、道場のある地名の根差部(ねさぶ)の"部"(「べ」とも読める)"見"と栄亮先生の"亮"で"部見亮"という当て字を与えてくれた。道場や赤嶺先生とのつながりが込められた意味で、光栄なことで、私にとって大切な名です」。

道場を開設した際に、氏は「部見亮会国際」を名乗った。当会は、赤嶺浩氏が主宰する琉球古武道信武舘・沖縄小林流無拳会に所属する。両館の7段であるベミリーオ氏は国内2道場、イスラエルと米国でも道場を監督する。

今日、ベミリーオ氏は健康、安全、消防の専門家として陛下の刑務所と保護観察サービスに従事しながら、村内の小学校の児童にも空手を指導している。

氏は沖縄の武術の魅力について「伝統と歴史を通して極致を追求し、空手愛好家や非愛好家に空手と古武道の生き方を共有することは、実に価値のある魅力的な目的」と述べ、献身的な活動に心を込める。

The city of The Beatles, Liverpool has also a deep connection with karate.

In 1965, the Japan Karate Association dispatched several instructors to promote karate in the country. One of them, the late Enoeda Keinosuke, taught at the "Red Triangle" dōjō in Liverpool and raised many champions including Terry O'Neill, born in the same city.

Born in Liverpool in 1962, Paul Vermiglio was taught boxing by his grandfather from the age of eight and then studied jūjitsu for about 20 years. As a member of the Merchant Navy, he sailed the world's oceans but never stopped training.

In 1992, Vermiglio entered the "Red Triangle" dōjō to improve his kicking skills.

Published on 2022/2/27

04 United Kingdom

Bumisukekai Kokusai

The pursuit of perfection through tradition

Three years later, he learned about Akamine Eisuke of Ryūkyū kobudō in a martial arts magazine published by O'Neill and in 1996, he went to Okinawa to learn from Akamine himself.

For six years, he studied Ryūkyū kobudō and Shōrin-ryū as an in-house student at the dōjō of Akamine in Nesabu, Tomigusuku while working part-time. "I had a lot of assistance from brilliant Okinawan people who all became my friends and family" he comments.

After leaving Okinawa, Vermiglio stayed in Israel and did his best to popularize kobudō in the country. After touring various European countries, he finally returned to England in 2006.

Today, Vermiglio lives in the Cotswolds, England's largest Area of Outstanding Natural Beauty. His dōjō, Bumisukekai Kokusai, is located in the Oaksey village in Wiltshire.

Asked about the meaning of his organization, he answers as follow. "When I lived in Okinawa, the wife of Akamine sensei chose three characters based on the pronunciation of my surname Vermiglio: 'bu' of Nesabu ('bu' being also read 'be'), 'mi' as in 'miru' (to watch) and 'ryo' of Eisuke sensei, 'ryo' being another way to read 'suke'. Together the 3 characters gave Bumisuke. Deeply connected to the dōjō and Akamine sensei, it is an honor and an important name for me".

When he opened his dōjō, he called it the Bumisuke International Association. It belongs to the Ryūkyū kobudō Shinbukan and Okinawa Shōrin-ryū Mukenkai led by Akamine Hiroshi. A 7th dan in both systems, Vermiglio also supervises two clubs in the country and chapters in Israel and the USA.

Meanwhile, he is a health, safety & fire professional and currently works for Her Majesty's prison and probation services while teaching karate to the local primary school children.

Regarding the charms of Okinawan martial arts, the fully devoted man he is says, "To pursue perfection through history and sharing the karate and kobudō way of life to students and non-students is simply a worthy charming cause."

多くの国々では、単独の空手道連盟がその国での空手種目を主管する。イタリアの場合、競技空手はイタリアオリンピック委員会に加盟する「イタリア柔道レスリング空手武道連盟(FIJLKAM)」が管轄している。同連盟は1902年に設立され、54年から柔道、94年から空手を主管する立場にある。

なお、ヨーロッパ各地での空手普及は主に松濤館系の日本人指導者によって行われており、イタリアも例外ではない。

60年イタリアに移住した静岡出身の故・杉山庄治氏は、5年後、サッカークラブのユベントスと自動車メーカー、フィアットのホームタウンであるトリノ市に「杉山道場」を開設し、柔道、空手道などを指導した。今日でも同道場は活動している。

57年同市生まれのマウリツィオ・カネパロ氏は、71年に「杉山道場」で武道を習い始めたが、90年代前半、2人の空手家との出会いが氏の武の道の方向性を変えた。

1人目は、イタリアに移住しパレルモを拠点に小林流究道館の空手を指導するオスカー・まさと・比嘉氏。もう1人は、49年ベネズエラ生まれの空手家、リビオ・リベラニ氏。70年代松濤館系の空手を学んだリベラニ氏は、後にイタリアに移住した。

琉棍会の伊波光忠氏(後列左)のセミナー時、カネパロ氏(後列左から2人目)と道場のメンバー=イタリア(提供)　At a seminar in Italy with Ryūkonkai Iha Mitsutada (left in the back row), Caneparo (second from the left in the back row) and some members of the dōjō.

2022年2月13日

05 イタリア

二つの武術 普及継承

ASD小林流空手道 トリノ・琉棍会支部

「リビオ先生は、沖縄を数回訪れ、琉球古武道琉棍会の伊波光太郎先生に師事。彼は、イタリアにおける琉棍会古武道のパイオニアだ」と友人と良きトレーニングパートナーを懐かしむカネパロ氏は解説する。

93年にカネパロ氏とリベラニ氏は共に、トリノ市で小林流と古武道の道場を開設し、今も両武術が継承されている。

道場名にあるASDは、アマチュアスポーツ団体という意味を持ち、両道場主は空手のプロ指導者にはならなかった。2015年、若くして亡くなったリベラニ氏は観光案内の仕事に従事し、カネパロ氏はエネルギー企業の従業員として生計を立てながら指導に励んだ。

現在同道場では30人ほどが稽古に励み、カネパロ氏は道場の高弟のフランコ・マンテッロ氏と共に他の二つの松濤館系の道場で古武道を指南している。他の究道館所属の空手家も、古武道を習いに来るという。

50年余り空手の道を歩むカネパロ氏に沖縄の武術の魅力を問うと「究道無限である空手と古武道は武術であり、型の稽古と呼吸法を通じて健康を保ち精神力も高められる」と答える。

琉棍会のモットー「錬心守道」を心に刻むカネパロ氏は、次回の訪沖を待ちながら琉球生まれの武術の継承と普及に励む。

Published on 2022/2/13

05 Italy

ASD Shōrin-ryū Karatedō Turin–Ryūkonkai Shibu

Transmitting and popularizing two martial arts

In many countries, a single national karate federation is in charge of managing karate. In the case of Italy, sport karate is under the jurisdiction of the "Italian Jūdō Wrestling Karate and Martial Arts Federation (FIJLKAM)", which is a member of the Italian Olympic Committee. This federation was established in 1902 and has been overseeing jūdō since 1954 and karate since 1994.

The spread of karate in various parts of Europe was mainly carried out by Japanese Shōtōkan instructors, and Italy is no exception.

Having moved to Italy in 1960, the late Sugiyama Shōji, who was born in Shizuoka, opened the Sugiyama Dōjō in Turin five years later and started teaching jūdō and karate. The dōjō is still active today.

Born in the same city in 1957, Maurizio Caneparo began learning martial arts at the Sugiyama Dōjō in 1971, but his encounter with two karateka would change the direction of his martial path in the early 90s.

The first encounter was with Oscar Masato Higa, who immigrated to Italy and teaches Shōrin-ryū Kyūdōkan karate in Palermo. The other one was with Livio Liverani, a karateka born in Venezuela in 1949. Liverani, who learned Shōtōkan karate in the 1970s, later moved to Italy.

"Livio sensei visited Okinawa several times and studied Ryūkonkai's Ryūkyū kobudō under its leader, Iha Kōtarō sensei. He is the pioneer of Ryūkonkai in Italy," explains Caneparo.

In 1993, the two good training partners and friends Caneparo and Liverani opened their dōjō and started teaching Shōrin-ryū and kobudō in Turin.

In the dōjō's name, ASD means an amateur sports organization. The two owners did not become professional karate instructors; before passing away in 2015, Liverani was a tourist guide while Caneparo worked in an energy business company.

Currently, about 30 people practice at the dōjō. Caneparo, along with his high-ranked member Franco Mantello, also teaches kobudō at two other Shōtōkan clubs. He says that Kyūdōkan karateka also visit to learn weaponry.

When asked about the charms of Okinawan martial arts, Caneparo, who has walked the path of karate for more than 50 years, answers, "Karate and kobudō are bujutsu of permanent practice in the spirit of 'Kyūdō Mugen', meaning that the study of the way never ends. Furthermore, the unique kata of Okinawa and breathing technique benefit health and beauty."

Keeping in mind the Ryūkonkai's motto "Ren Shin Shū Dō - Forge the heart to protect the way," Caneparo strives to preserve and popularize the Ryūkyū-born martial arts while waiting for his next visit to Okinawa.

2021年08月08日

06 イタリア

沖縄を訪れ原点回帰

黒鳥会

2000年に行われた九州・沖縄サミットの翌年、同首脳会議は、クリストファー・コロンブスの故郷イタリアのジェノヴァで開催された。

リグーリア州の州都のこの港町生まれのロベルト・ゴネッラ氏(64)は、16歳の頃空手を始めた。空手を学ぶ者が少ない時代に氏は多国籍海運会社で働き、沖縄を数回訪れたユーゴスラビア系イタリア人のレズビッチ氏に手ほどきを受けた。

「レズビッチ先生からは、仲里常延先生の型、ナイハンチや那覇手系の型などを習った。中には、上地流に似ている開手の三戦(サンチン)も教わった」と氏は語る。数年後、師匠は南米に移住し師弟関係が終わった。ゴネッラ氏は、多くのメモを基に導かれた少林寺流の研究を続け、1970年代後半に指導にも挑んだ。

30年間余り同じ武の道を歩み続けたゴネッラ氏は、歴史が好きで、自身の組織を「黒鳥会」と名付けた。「鳥は常にリグーリアのエンブレムです。トロイ戦争の数世代前、リグーリアの王キュクノスは、親友の死後、鳥に変身したとされている。イタリアで広く普及している競技空手と区別するために、私たちはしばしば黒い空手着を着ています」と意味を説明する。同じ情熱と熱意によって団結した友人のグループであるこの集団の下、故郷ジェノヴァの4道場で130人が鍛錬をしている。トスカーナ州やロンバルディア州にも支部がある。

審査会を終えたゴネッラ氏(後列中央)と門弟たち=イタリア・ジェノバ(提供)
Gonella (center in the back row) and his students after an examination.

退職するまでに技術者と指導士として情報技術に携わってきた氏は、主観的なだけでなく、客観的にものを観察するように努めたという。流動性とパワーの適切な組み合わせが少林寺流の良さだと実感するようになり、自身の空手の道を逸脱することはなかった。

しかし、あまりにも長い間、沖縄のルーツから離れたため、黒鳥会の代表としてゴネッラ氏は原点回帰を目指した。弟子が故仲里氏の高弟で沖縄空手道少林寺流振興会に所属する親川仁志氏に出会えたことから、2016年にゴネッラ氏も訪沖を果たし、自らの空手の更新作業を始めた。

恵まれた新たな出会いに感謝しながら、レズビッチ氏と出合った半世紀後、師から学んだ技術と教訓は、今も、宝物として大切に守られている。黒鳥会の道場訓の「流水先不競」(流水先を競わず)もその一つで、最初の師の教えが今日も研究の源となる。

バジル香るペースト・ジェノヴェーゼ発祥の地生まれのゴネッラ氏は、イタリア人らしく料理と音楽が趣味だというが、家族と空手が核心とも打ち明ける。謙虚に受け継ぐ沖縄空手の普及を誓う。

Following the 2000 Kyūshū-Okinawa Summit, the G8 summit was held in Genoa, the hometown of Christopher Columbus.

Born in this capital of Liguria, Roberto Gonella (64) started karate at the age of 16, studying the basics with a man by the name of Lesevich, a Yugoslav-Italian who worked for a multinational shipping company and had visited Okinawa several times.

"From Lesevich sensei, I learned the kata Naihanchi of Nakazato Jōen and some Nahate kata, including an open hands Sanchin similar to the Uechi-ryū version." A few years later, Lesevich immigrated to South America and the master-student relationship ended. Guided by many memos he took while training, Gonella continued his research on Shōrinji-ryū and started teaching karate in the late 1970s.

Published on 2021/8/8

06 Italy

Kokuchōkai

Returning to the roots in Okinawa

Gonella loves history and named his organization Kokuchōkai, meaning the Company of Black Swans. He explains the name as follows: "The swan is the emblem of Liguria. A few generations before the Trojan War, Ligurian king Cygnus is said to have transformed into a swan after the death of his best friend. The color black is because we often wear black karategi to distinguish ourselves from the modern karate that is widespread in Italy." In this group of friends united by the same passion and enthusiasm, 130 people are training in four dōjō in Genoa. There are also branches in Tuscany and Lombardy.

Before retirement, Gonella worked in the information technology, both as a technician and an instructor, and thus tries to observe things objectively as well as subjectively. Along the way, he came to realize that the technique of Shōrinji-ryū is close to what he feels is the best way to manage the body, that is, the right combination of fluidity and power. So believing, he didn't deviate from his karate path.

However, because he had been away from his Okinawan roots for so long, Gonella, as the head of the Kokuchōkai, aimed at returning to the origin. Following his student who met Oyakawa Hitoshi, a senior student of late Nakazato, Gonella visited Okinawa in 2016 and started updating his own karate.

While grateful for this new encounter, the techniques and lessons he learned from Lesevich half a century ago are still carefully preserved as treasures today. Among them is a precept of the Kokuchōkai, "Ryūsui saki wo kisowazu" which could be interpreted as "flowing water competes with nothing."

Born in the birthplace of Pesto Genovese, Gonella says that he enjoys cooking and music like a true Italian, but he confesses that his family and karate are the core of his life. As a humble inheritor, he vows to keep spreading Okinawa karate.

2017年07月30日

07 イタリア

古武道普及に使命感

順眞館

イタリアで空手が始めて指導されたのは1955年の頃だという。その後60年代前半に来伊した故村上哲次や白井寛（80）の各氏が本格的に松濤館系の空手を広めた。

剛柔流が同国で紹介されたのは70年代。61年ヴェローナ県生まれのアンドレア・グァレッリ氏は12歳の時、日本人に師事したマリオ・ボスィオ氏の下で剛柔流と古武道を習い始めた。77年、故郷のブッソレンゴで道場を開設。社会人になり鉄鋼会社の経営をしながら、両武術の研究を深めた。

そして、88年に念願の空手の本場沖縄へ旅立った。那覇市安里にある順道館で故宮里栄一氏、同市楚辺にある金硬流唐手又吉古武道総本部光道館の2代目宗家又吉眞豊氏に師事した。

帰国後の89年、剛柔流開祖の宮城長順氏の「順」と又吉家の「眞」の字をもって道場を命名し、93年にイタリア沖縄古武道協会も創立した。94年に武術指導者のプロとなり、翌年、又吉氏をイタリアに招きセミナーを開催した。

その古武道の普及への努力が認められ、97年に又吉氏から古武道錬士6段を授与されたが、同年師は亡くなった。99年に行われた故又吉眞豊追悼演武大会においてグァレッリ氏は、招待演武として三節棍を披露した。

サイ術の指導をするグァレッリ氏（右）＝提供
Andrea Guarelli (right) teaching saijutsu.

2004年には県指定無形文化財保持者故伊波康進氏より空手教士7段、08年には、又吉氏の直弟子の外間哲弘氏より古武道8段を授与された。

使命感に駆られた氏は、執筆を通して古武道の普及も行った。98年に『沖縄の棒』、13年に『サイ術・沖縄の三つ叉』などの書籍を著した。そして、14年に16の武器術などを紹介する書籍『沖縄古武道、歴史と技』をイタリア語で発行し、後に英訳もされた。

軌道に乗り15年にグァレッリ氏は、国際又吉古武道協會を立ち上げた。これまでの動機について氏は「運よく優れた二人の大家に師事した。沖縄の武道の文化、精神、技を伝えると共に、できるだけ多くの人に空手が日本ではなく、沖縄で生まれたことを知らせたい」と言う。

現在、本部道場の順眞館には180人が稽古する。さらに国内16道場700名、海外12カ国58道場で又吉氏の直弟子である氏の指導を受ける者がいるという。

毎年のように沖縄を訪れ、3代目宗家の又吉靖氏の自宅にある師匠の仏前へお参りするグァレッリ氏。空手・古武道は常に、謙虚と尊敬を持って歩むべき道である。

Karate is said to have been taught for the first time in Italy around 1955. Later in the early 1960s, the late Murakami Tetsuji and Shirai Hiroshi (80) spread Shōtōkan karate there. Gōjū-ryū was introduced in the country in the 1970s.

Born in the province of Verona in 1961, Andrea Guarelli began learning Gōjū-ryū and kobudō at the age of 12 under Mario Bosio, who had studied under a Japanese instructor. After opening a dōjō in 1977 in his hometown of Bussolengo, he deepened his research on both martial arts while managing a steel company.

Travelling to Okinawa in 1988, Guarelli studied under the late Miyazato Eiichi at the Jundōkan in Asato, and under Matayoshi Shinpō at the Kōdōkan, the honbu dōjō for Kingai-ryū karate and Matayoshi kobudō located in Sobe, Naha City.

Published on 2017/7/30

07 Italy

Junshinkan

On a mission to popularize kobudō

Upon his return in 1989, he named his dōjō Junshinkan using the letters 'Jun' of Miyagi Chōjun and 'Shin' of the Matayoshi family's given names. In 1993, he also founded the Italian Okinawa Kobudō Association. Becoming a professional martial arts instructor in 1994, he invited Matayoshi Shinpō to Italy to hold a seminar the following year.

In recognition of his efforts to popularize kobudō, he was awarded the Renshi 6th Dan in kobudō by Matayoshi in 1997, the year of his death. 2 years later, Guarelli performed sansetsukon, the three-section staff, at the Matayoshi Shinpō Memorial demonstration.

In 2004, he was promoted to 7th dan in karate by the late Iha Kōshin, a direct student of Miyagi Chōjun and a holder of the Okinawa Prefecture's designated intangible cultural asset "Okinawa karate and kobujutsu," and 8th dan in kobudō in 2008 by Hokama Tetsuhiro, a direct student of Matayoshi.

Driven by a sense of mission, Guarelli also spread kobudō through his writing, authoring books on bōjutsu and saijutsu, respectively the staff and trident systems. In 2014, he published a book "Okinawa Kobudo, History and Techniques" that introduces 16 weapons techniques in Italian, book which was later translated into English.

In 2015, he launched the International Matayoshi Kobudō Association. Regarding his motivation so far, he said, "I was lucky enough to train under two excellent masters. While passing on the culture, spirit and skills of Okinawan martial arts, I want to let people know that karate was born in Okinawa, not in Japan."

Currently, 180 people are practicing in his dōjō. Furthermore, 700 people in 16 dōjō in Italy and 58 dōjō in 12 countries follow his guidance.

Visiting Okinawa almost every year, Guarelli makes sure to pay his respect at the Buddhist altar in the home of Matayoshi Yasushi, the third generation Sōke. Karate and kobudō are paths that should always be walked with humility and respect.

2020年06月14日

08 イタリア

剛柔流の奥義を追究

空手ウーディネ道場

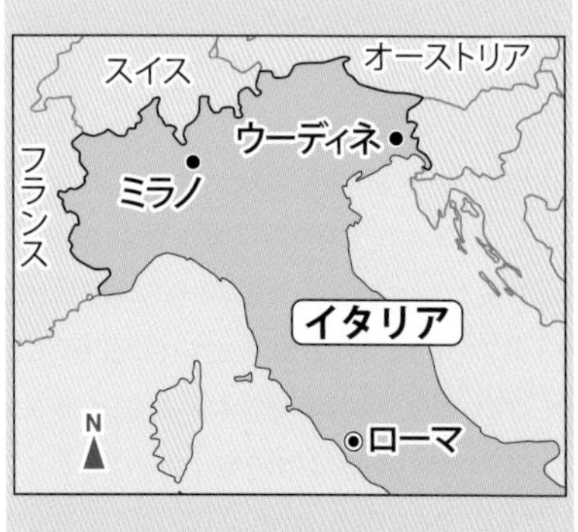

イタリア北東部フリウリ=ベネチア・ジュリア州の都市ウーディネ生まれのアンドレア・ブタゾーニ氏(56)は、13歳の時、空手の道を歩み始めた。

当初、入門したのはカンフー系の空手道場。しかし、軍人でもあった道場主が帰郷することになり、隣の州ベネチア近くのパドヴァで剛柔流を指導するジャンニ・ロッサート氏の道場に行くよう勧められた。

ロッサート氏は、日本本土で剛柔流の普及に貢献した山口剛玄氏を師とする「アメリカン剛柔」の創始者ピーター・アーバン氏の弟子だった。ロッサート氏は後に独立し「剛柔イタリア」を立ち上げている。

ベネチアで徴兵されたブタゾーニ氏は、ロッサート氏の「サムライ道場」に弟子入り。その後、剛柔流のルーツを求めて1989年に中国の少林寺で2カ月間の修行も積んだ。「それでも私が望んでいたものを見つけられなかった」とブタゾーニ氏は振り返る。

翌年、イタリアで柔道の普及に貢献した故矢野秀信氏やローマにある在イタリア日本国大使館の招待状を携えてブタゾーニ氏は、那覇市安里にある宮里栄一氏が創立した順道館の門をくぐった。

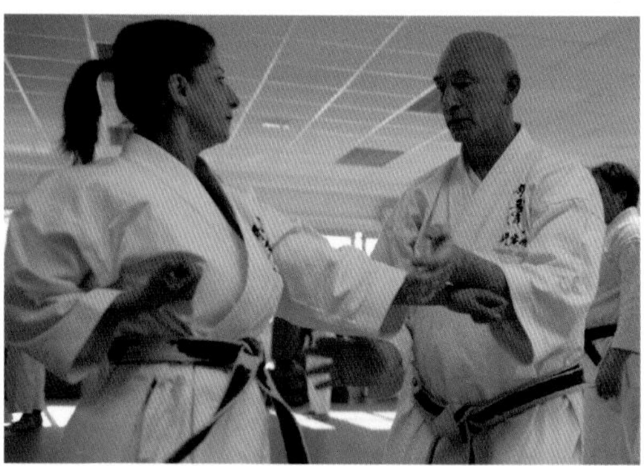
妻ジョビーナ氏(左)と技の研究に励むブタゾーニ氏=提供
Buttazzoni training with his wife Giovina.

「沖縄への最初の旅は人生の最も重要な経験の一つとなった」と当時を懐かしむ。「先生方と先輩方の技術に魅了されたが、道場内外の人々の優しさと人間性にも感動した。その時から沖縄に恋に落ちた。沖縄は私にとって精神性の高い場所です」

訪沖を重ねる中、面倒を見てくれた先輩の中に平良正次氏がいた。「平良先生の技術に感動しすぎて、97年まで先生から学ぶことができずひたすら基本に打ち込んだ」。その後、平良氏と交流を深めながら指導を受け、剛柔流の奥深さを求めるようになったという。

帰国したブタゾーニ氏は稽古に打ち込み、友人と研究を重ねた。訪沖する以外にも、平良氏などの高段者をイタリアに招いてセミナーも開催した。

2012年に道場を開設した。それまで25年間経営していたスポーツジムを閉じ、妻のジョビーナ氏の協力を得て空手のプロになる覚悟を決めた。

道場開設と同じ年に7段に昇段したブタゾーニ氏は翌年、平良氏が会長を務める沖縄剛柔流空手道研究会のイタリア支部長にもなった。現在ウーディネの道場では、子どもや大人200人以上が剛柔流を学ぶ。

「自分の中の愛を見つけること」が空手の本来の目的と考えるブタゾーニ氏。イタリア人であることの誇りを保ちながら、沖縄生まれの剛柔流一筋で人生を歩む。

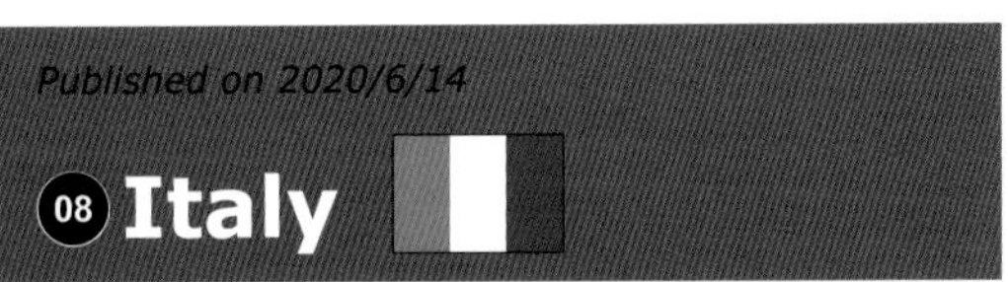

Karate Udine Dōjō

Pursuing the mysteries of Gōjū-ryū

Andrea Buttazzoni (56) was born in Udine, a city in the Friuli Venezia Giulia region, and started karate at the age of 13.

Initially, he started in a kungfu karate club. As the owner, a military man, returned home, he advised Buttazzoni to go to the dōjō of Gianni Rossato who was teaching Gōjū-ryū in Padua, in the neighboring region of Venetia.

Rossato was a student of Peter Urban, the founder of "American Gōjū", whose teacher was Yamaguchi Gōgen. Later on, Rossato became independent and established "Gōjū Italy".

While Buttazzoni served in the army in Venice, he joined the Samurai Dōjō of Rossato. Later, as he was looking for the roots of Gōjū-ryū, he went training for two months at the Shaolin monastery in China in 1989. "But still, I had not found what my heart wanted," Buttazzoni recalls.

The following year, with two letters of introduction which were written by Yano Hidenobu, who contributed to the spread of jūdō in Italy, and the Embassy of Japan in Rome, Buttazzoni entered the Jundōkan founded by Miyazato Eiichi in Asato, Naha City.

"My first trip to Okinawa was one of the most important experiences of my life" he recalls. "I was fascinated by the technical skill of the senpai and sensei of the dōjō, but what made me fall in love with Okinawa was the kindness and humanity of all the people I met. For me, Okinawa is a place of high spirituality."

During his various trips to Okinawa, Taira Masaji was one of the seniors who took care of him. "At the beginning, I was too impressed by the skills of Taira sensei and until 1997, I didn't feel able to learn from him. I just focused on basic training." As time passes, he started receiving instruction from Taira and began seeking the mysteries of Gōjū-ryū.

Returning to Italy, Buttazzoni devoted himself to training and deepened his research with his friends. In addition to visiting Okinawa, he also held seminars in Italy, inviting Jundōkan instructors among which Taira.

Deciding to become a karate professional with the help of his wife Giovina, his dōjō was opened in 2012 after Buttazzoni closed the sport center he had been running for 25 years.

Promoted to 7th dan the same year as the dōjō was opened, he became the head of the Italian branch of the Okinawa Gōjū-ryū Karatedō Kenkyūkai chaired by Taira Masaji the following year. Currently, more than 200 children and adults practice karate at the Udine dōjō.

Buttazzoni believes that the original purpose of karate is to "Find love within oneself." While maintaining his pride as an Italian, he dedicates his entire life to Okinawa-born Gōjū-ryū.

モーツァルトの国、オーストリア。1944年、シュタイアーマルク州生まれのフリードリッヒ・グソーダム氏は、14歳のころ柔道に入門した。66年に大学に入学した際、空手の偉人とされるピーター・ランド氏の下、松濤館空手を始めた。そのころは、同国で空手の歴史の始まりでもあった。

陸軍専門官になろうと71年に入隊し、基地で空手を指導していたもう一人のパイオニア、ジョゼフ・ヘルゾグ氏にも師事。75年ウィーンに移り、国防省に勤めた。そのとき、小川武治氏に出会い、本土系の剛柔流に転向した。

小川氏は70年代、オーストラリアと近隣国に山口剛玄と改名した山口實美氏の全日本空手道剛柔会を広めた人。今も、オーストリアに住み、指導している。

軍のパイロットになったグソーダム氏は、准将まで進むと同時に、78年に基地内で道場を開設した。教授をしていたホッラブルンの専修学校でも道場を開いた。

90年に、剛柔流のルーツと発祥の地への理解を深めようと沖縄に目を向けた。92年に知り合ったキャサリン・ルコプロス氏を通じて県内の米軍基地と故上原恒氏の道場で稽古した。技術のほ

約束組手を指導するグソーダム氏(左)=提供　Gsodam (left) teaching yakusoku kumite.

2019年01月27日

09 オーストリア

伝統と競技両輪に

剛柔流順道館空手

かに、沖縄と本土のアイデンティティーの違いに気付き始めた。96年3度目の訪沖の際に、那覇市安里の順道館に招待され、宮里栄一と安田哲之助両氏に師事し、順道館に入門した。

「本土系も沖縄の剛柔流も素晴らしい。比べるとすると、本土の剛柔流はより厳密に規制されていて、スポーツの側面に重点を置いていると感じます。それに対し、伝統ある沖縄の剛柔流はより自然な動きを強調する。また、分解も柔軟で実用的になっているから、研究は永遠にできる」と解説する。

陰と陽であるかのように、二つの道場の館長であるグソーダム氏は、教育現場の道場でスポーツを、基地内の道場で武術を指導している。「本拠地の基地内道場は、招待者のみが見学できる。稽古法とメンバーと気が合い、入門を希望する者は、きめ細かい審査に合格した上で入門できる」とする。

ノイジードル湖でのセーリングが趣味のグソーダム氏は今、首都ウィーンで退職後の生活を楽しむ日々だ。しかし、空手には終わりがない。

北海道の面積とほぼ同じオーストリアでは現在、130道場で約1万人がさまざまな空手に取り組んでいるという。15回以上沖縄を訪れ、2013年に順道館の宮里善博館長より9段に昇段が認められたグソーダム氏は、7道場、500人にスポーツと伝統空手を伝え、指導している。

Born in Styria in 1944, Friedrich Gsodam began learning jūdō at the age of 14. When he entered university in 1966, he started Shōtōkan karate under karate legend Peter Land. At that time, it was the beginning of karate in the country.

Joining the army in 1971, Gsodam studied under another karate pioneer, Josef Herzog, who was teaching karate on base. Moving to the capital Vienna in 1975, Gsodam served at the Ministry of Defense. It is at that time that he met Ogawa Takeji and switched to mainland Japanese Gōjū-ryū. Ogawa was the person who spread All Japan Karatedō Gōjū-kai of Yamaguchi Gōgen in Austria and neighboring countries in the 1970s. He still lives and teaches in Austria.

Published on 2019/1/27

09 Austria

Gōjū-ryū Jundōkan Karate

Tradition and sport as the two wheels of a bicycle

While advancing to become a Brigadier General, Gsodam opened a dōjō in the base he was stationed at in 1978. He also opened a dōjō at a college in Hollabrunn, where he was a professor.

In 1990, he turned to Okinawa to deepen his understanding of the roots of Gōjū-ryū. Through Catherine Loukopoulos, who he had met in 1992, Gsodam practiced at a US military base in Okinawa and the dōjō of the late Uehara Kō. Besides technique, he began to notice the difference in identity between Okinawa and mainland Japan. When he visited Okinawa for the third time in 1996, he was invited to the Jundōkan in Asato, Naha City and studying under Miyazato Eiichi and Yasuda Tetsunosuke, he joined the Jundōkan.

"Okinawan and Japanese Gōjū-ryū are really great. Comparatively speaking, I feel that Okinawan Gōjū-ryū is more natural in its movement, more traditional and even the applications are more flexible and more practicable; it allows to come in with your own ideas. In contrast, Japanese Gōjū-ryū seems to be more strictly regulated and more focused on sporting aspects."

As in yin and yang, Gsodam is the head of two dōjō teaching both sport karate in his college's dōjō and traditional karate in his on base dōjō. "In the main dōjō located on-base, only licensed people are allowed to enter. And if we have the impression that a guest will fit in with our members and with the philosophy of our club, a detailed examination has to be fulfilled. If the guest succeeds, he could become a full member."

Fond of sailing on Lake Neusiedler, Gsodam now enjoys his retirement life in Vienna. However, karate has no end.

In Austria, which is almost the same area as Hokkaido, about 10,000 karateka train in various systems of karate in some 130 dōjō. Gsodam, who has visited Okinawa more than 15 times and was promoted to 9th dan in 2013 by Miyazato Yoshihiro, the kanchō of Jundōkan, teaches sport and traditional karate to 500 people at 7 dōjō.

琉球とオランダは1859年に両王国が条約を締結した時からつながりがある。

九州とほぼ同じくらいの大きさのオランダといえばチューリップを思い浮かべるが、格闘技も盛ん。同国の格闘技界のパイオニア故ジョン・ブルミン氏に師事し、日本で格闘技を学んだオランダ人は後に、オランダ系キックボクシングを考案し、ピーター・アーツ氏など多くの王者を育てた。その影響で現在、競技空手約8500人の登録者に対し、格闘技家は1万2千人いると言われている。

マセル・ポースト氏は、1969年、ドイツとの国境近くにあるエンスヘデに生まれた。7歳の時、インドネシア系の武術と空手と柔術からなる武道の道場に入門し、後に松濤館空手道に転向。99年には、道場「無我無心」を開設した。

自身の空手のルーツを探し、ポースト氏は小林流に興味を持つようになった。2014年に多くのメンバーと開設した道場を離れ、沖縄空手の研究をする決心をした。ポースト氏の子どもたちが自立し、旅行する余裕ができた16年に沖縄を訪れた。

小林流の故宮平勝哉氏や高弟の真栄城守信氏の動画を見て、宮平氏の志道館本部道場を探したが見つけることはできなかった。滞在中に知

宮平勝哉氏の考案した型「鉄掌（テッショウ）」を指導するポースト氏（後列右端）＝提供　Proost (in the back) teaches the kata Tesshō devised by Miyahira.

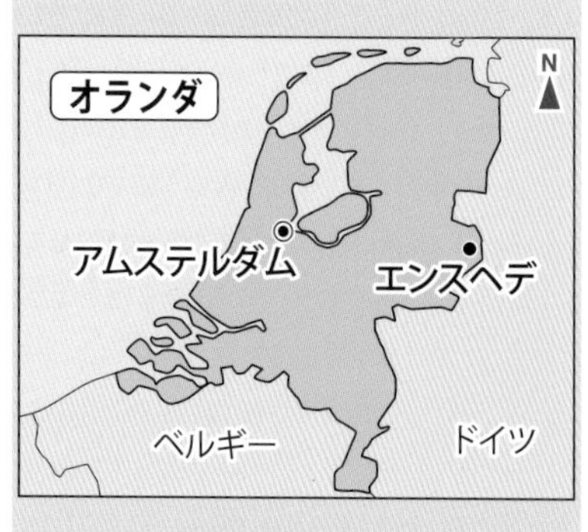

2021年05月09日

⑩ オランダ

小林流に出合い精進

白鷺志道館オランダ

念賢祐氏の小林流セミナーに参加し、少林流の島袋善保氏に紹介され町道場の雰囲気を味わい、首里手への関心がますます高まった。

帰国後、ドイツの志道館「白鷺道場」代表ヨアヘム・ラウプ氏の元へ出向き、その流れで真栄城氏に紹介された。「志道館ファミリーに招かれ、求めていたオリジナルの空手を習える素晴らしい機会が与えられた」とポースト氏は振り返る。

エンスヘデの道場を「白鷺志道館オランダ」に改名し、現在は25人が汗を流す。ポースト氏は19年に沖縄小林流空手道協会の審査会で5段に昇段した。

ポースト氏は、病院と精神科クリニックでソーシャルワーカーとして生計を立てる一方、空手で規律、自制心、集中力を養った。そのため職場で落ち着きを保った対応ができるという。

空手の魅力は、空手のパラドックスと強調する。「一方で有効な護身の技を磨き、一方でますますより良い人になること、人格改善に努める」と解説する。その意味で、真栄城氏に教えてもらった言葉「鬼手仏心」を座右の銘とする。

「志道館で感じる温かいフレンドリーな雰囲気と個人的な友情は、競技空手とはまったく異なる感情を与える」。教えとエネルギーが心から心へと伝わることを実感し、たどり着いた空手の道を大切に、一歩一歩精進していく。

Published on 2021/5/9

⑩ Netherlands

Shirasagi Shidōkan the Netherlands

An encounter with Shōrin-ryū that led to devotion

Ryūkyū and the Netherlands have been connected since the two kingdoms signed a treaty in 1859.

In a country known for tulips, martial arts are also popular. Many Dutch studied under late John Bluming, a pioneer in the Holland's martial arts world. Some of them having trained in Japan, they later devised Dutch kickboxing raising many champions like Peter Aerts. Today it is said there are 12,000 fighters for about 8,500 registered karate athletes.

Marcel Proost was born in 1969 in Enschede, near the German border. At the age of seven, he entered a mixed martial art club and later switched to Shōtōkan. In 1999, he opened the karate school Muga Mushin.

Looking for the roots of his karate, Proost became interested in Shōrin-ryū. In 2014, he left Muga Mushin together with the majority of his black belts and started studying Okinawa karate. After his children came of age and left the parental home, he headed to Okinawa in 2016.

Having watched videos of late Miyahira Katsuya and his disciple Maeshiro Morinobu, Proost aimed for the Shidōkan dōjō of Miyahira but could not find it. Instead, he attended a Shōrin-ryū seminar by Chinen Kenyū and trained with Shimabukuro Zenpō, experiences that confirmed his increasing interest in Shurite.

Back home, he turned to Joachim Laupp of the Shidōkan Shirasagi Dōjō in Germany and along the way, was finally introduced to Maeshiro. "I was invited by the Shidōkan family to have the great opportunity to learn the original karate I was looking for," he recalls.

Today, 25 people train at his dōjō in Enschede that he renamed Shirasagi Shidōkan the Netherlands. Proost himself was promoted to 5th dan by the examination committee of the Okinawa Shōrin-ryū Karatedō Association in 2019.

While earning a living as a social worker in a hospital and psychiatric clinic, Proost uses karate to develop discipline, self-control and concentration. He says that this is valuable to respond calmly to situations encountered at his workplace.

According to him, the charm of karate resides in its paradox. "On the one hand, train yourself in effective self-defense skills and at the same time, strive for character improvement, to become an increasingly better person." In that sense, the saying "Kishu Busshin" (Devil's hands - Buddha's heart) that he learned from Maeshiro has become his favorite motto.

"The warm, friendly atmosphere and the personal friendships I have felt at the Shidōkan give a totally different impulse compared to sport karate." Realizing that teaching and energy are transmitted from heart to heart, he wishes to cherish the path of karate that he has reached and devote himself to its pursuit one step at a time.

2019年02月24日

⑪ギリシャ

伝統空手普及に努力

志道館白鷺道場アテネ

120年前の1899年に、ギリシャは日本と修好通商航海条約を締結した。それから60数年後、オリンピック発祥の地では、初めて空手が米軍基地で紹介され、その後、柔道の道場や大学で広まった。

しかし、それ以前にもギリシャ人ジャーナリストで柔道家のヨルゴス・カラギョルガス氏が1949年の来日時に「近代空手の父」と称される船越義珍氏に面会したとの記録もある。

船員として日本を訪れ、柔道と松濤館空手を習った同国の空手パイオニアの一人ヤニス・ヴェロニス氏は69年の帰国後、アテネで初の道場を開設した。そして「武道館道場」と命名されたこの道場に、13歳の一人の少年が入門した。

76年アテネ生まれのヴァシリス・ラフトポウロス氏は6年間、武道館道場で空手を習った。

19歳の時、スポーツ科学を学ぶためドイツのパーダーボルンに移った。学問と同時に空手を続けたが、そこでは競技に重きが置かれていたため、伝統空手を指導する者を求めた。

2002年に、トリーア市で沖縄小林流を指導するヨアヘム・ラウプ氏の動画を発見したのが人生の転機となった。「型と分解を披露していたラウプ先生のオーラと強力な技に深く感銘を受けた。これまで探していたものを見つけた」とラフトポウロス氏は当時を振り返る。

型を指導するラフトポウロス氏（左）=提供
Raptopoulos (left) teaching kata in his dōjō.

すべてを捨てラフトポウロス氏は、トリーア市に移住した。人生を変えるため心の決断だったという。そこから、故宮平勝哉氏の沖縄小林流志道館に所属し、ラウプ氏の下で沖縄の伝統空手の研さんを積んだ。

2009年、母国に戻ったラフトポウロス氏はラウプ氏に許可を得て、首都の中心部で「志道館白鷺道場アテネ」を開設し指導者となった。自宅を兼ねたこの道場では現在、大人約40人、子供17人が首里手系の空手を学んでいる。

空手の魅力を問うと「稽古で得られる力量と権威を高めると共に謙虚であり続けることは挑戦である。他の活動と違って、特定の目標がない空手の稽古を休まずに規律を持って続けることも大きな魅力」と見解を示す。

09年と18年に沖縄を訪れたラフトポウロス氏は現在5段だが、まだ空手の道を歩み始めたばかりだと言い、その姿勢に変わりはない。沖縄空手と出合って以降、日々稽古を重ね、教わったように指導をする義務があることも肝に銘じている。師のラウプ氏から教わった「正しく習った人は、正しく指導する」という言葉を大切に、アクロポリスの街で沖縄空手の正しい普及に努める。

Sixty years after Greece signed a treaty of commerce and navigation with Japan in 1899, karate was first introduced in the birthplace of the Olympic Games on US military bases, and then spread in jūdō dōjō and universities.

Interestingly, there is a record of a Greek journalist and jūdō practitioner Giorgos Karagiorgas who met with Funakoshi Gichin, the "father of modern karate" when he came to Japan in 1949.

Giannis Veronis, one of the country's karate pioneers who visited Japan as a sailor, learned jūdō and Shōtōkan karate and opened the first dōjō in Athens after returning to Greece in 1969.

Twenty years later, a 13-year-old boy entered the very same dōjō, which was named the Budōkan Dōjō.

Published on 2019/2/24

11 Greece

Shidōkan Shirasagi Dōjō Athens

Striving to popularize traditional karate

Born in Athens in 1976, Vassilis Raptopoulos learned karate at the Budōkan Dōjō for six years. When he was 19, he moved to Paderborn, Germany to study sports science. He continued to practice karate while studying but because of the emphasis on competition, he sought a teacher of traditional karate.

The year 2002 was a turning point in his life as he watched a video of Joachim Laupp who was teaching Okinawa Shōrin-ryū in Trier. "As he demonstrated kata and applications, Laupp sensei impressed me so greatly with his aura and his powerful techniques that I felt right away that this was what I had been looking for," he recalls.

Leaving everything, Raptopoulos moved to Trier. "It was a decision of the heart, a decision that was meant to change my life." From this time on, he belongs to the Okinawa Shōrin-ryū Shidōkan, and under Joachim Laupp, keeps researching Okinawa's traditional karate.

As he returned to Greece in 2009, Raptopoulos opened the Shidōkan Shirasagi Dōjō Athens in the center of the capital with Laupp's permission. At this dōjō, about 40 adults and 17 children are currently learning Shurite karate with him.

When asked about the charms of karate, he says "The charm and also the challenge of karate is to remain humble while you develop your abilities and charisma. I find great charm in the practice of karate with discipline, without pausing while there is no specific goal or target as we often see in other activities."

Raptopoulos, who visited Okinawa in 2009 and 2018, is currently a 5th dan, but he says he has just begun to follow the path of karate, and his attitude has not changed. Since his encounter with Okinawa karate, he has been practicing every day and feels an obligation of teaching the way he was taught. Valuing the teaching of his German master "He who learns correctly, will teach correctly!" Raptopoulos strives to spread authentic Okinawa karate in the city of the Acropolis.

2017年11月12日

⑫スイス

ぶれない魂 交流深化

沖縄シャブレ空手クラブ

ドイツ語、フランス語、イタリア語、ロマンシュ語を公用語とする小さな国際的な国、スイス。

1957年、スイス人のベルナー・シェリクス氏がパリで空手と出合い、同年スイスで初の空手道場を開設した。その後、空手が盛んになり、現在スイス空手連盟には250以上の道場が加盟している。沖縄の三大流派と古武道も根付き、少なくとも12の支部があるという。

67年南スイスに生まれたロアン・モラン氏は10歳の頃、望月拡雄氏が考案した日本総合格闘技「養正館武道」に入門した。後に86年、パリで小林流の知念賢祐、古武道の大城善栄両氏の演武を見て、沖縄へ関心を持った。

20歳前後の頃モラン氏は、大工職人の修業を重ねる一方で空手を指導し、92年にサビエズ市で道場をオープンさせた。

95年、沖縄空手・古武道世界大会プレ大会に参加したモラン氏は、大城氏を通じて首里空手古武道と小林流を継承する守武館上間空手道場の上間康弘氏に紹介され、新たな空手人生を歩み始めた。

現在モラン氏は、サビエズ市の道場で80人、90年に創立された「沖縄空手古武道スイス協会」

型の分解を解説し、指導するモラン氏(左)=提供
Morand (left) teaching the application of a kata section.

加盟の11道場600人に技術指導を展開。その内、七つの道場で直接指導を行う。

今年3月、本部道場開設25周年と沖縄・スイス交流20周年記念事業が行われた。上間康弘氏はこれまで20回スイスへ渡航しているが、息子の建氏も師匠でもある父と同様に20回訪問し、交流を重ねてきた。今回、沖縄から児童と大人20人を連れ、技術交流と親睦を深めた。カナダ、チェコ、スペイン、フランス、ドイツから多くのメンバーも集い、記念演武大会には370人の児童と180人の大人が技を披露し、大会を盛り上げた。

「25年という節目もあるが、康弘先生が初めてスイスを訪れてから20周年の記念も祝うことができた」と振り返るモラン氏。「守武館との交流は技術の面はもちろんだが、家族のような交流が何よりも大切で大事にしたい」と強調する。さらに「空手は、日々新たな真のエネルギーを与えてくれる。毎日、技の発見もあれば、人間そのものについての再発見もある」と語った。

きちょうめんな性格で知られるスイス人。永世中立国のこの国は、本土系の空手やそのほかの武術も盛んだ。モラン氏はスイスの重要な空手連盟に参加しながら、ぶれることなく沖縄の空手・古武道と文化を選んだ。そして一歩一歩、上間家と大城氏と手を繋ぎ、発祥の地沖縄との交流を深めている。

Published on 2017/11/12

⑫ Switzerland 

KC Okinawa Chablais

Deepening exchanges with an unshakable spirit

Switzerland, a small international country whose official languages are German, French, Italian and Romansh.

In 1957, Swiss Bernard Cherix discovered karate in Paris and opened the first dōjō in Switzerland the same year. Quite popular in the confederation today, the Swiss Karate Federation counts more than 250 registered clubs, and there are at least 12 branches of Okinawan organizations.

Born in southern Switzerland in 1967, Roan Morand began karate at the age of 10 in the Japanese mixed martial arts Yōseikan Budō devised by Mochizuki Hiroo. Later, in 1986, he became interested in Okinawa after seeing a demonstration in Paris of Shōrin-ryū karate by Chinen Kenyū and kobudō by Ōshiro Zenei.

Since the age of 20, Morand is a trained carpenter who teaches karate, having opened his dōjō in Savièse in 1992.

In 1995, Morand participated in the Okinawa Karate and Kobudō world pre-tournament. Through Ōshiro, he was introduced to Uema Yasuhiro of the Shūbukan Uema Karate Dōjō which inherits the karate and kobudō of Shuri and Shōrin-ryū. This was the start of a new karate life.

Today, Morand teaches 80 people in his dōjō and guides 600 people who train in the 11 dōjō that form the Association Okinawa Karaté Kobudo Suisse, an organization created in 1990. He physically teaches in 7 of these dōjō.

In March of this year, the 25th anniversary of the opening of the main dōjō and the 20th anniversary of the Okinawa-Switzerland exchanges were held. The son of Uema Yasuhiro, Takeshi, brought 20 children and adults from Okinawa to deepen technical exchanges and friendship. Many members from Canada, Czech Republic, Spain, France and Germany also gathered, and 370 children and 180 adults demonstrated their martial skills at the commemorative demonstration that was quite successful.

"Although 25 years is a milestone, we were also able to celebrate the 20th anniversary of Yasuhiro sensei's first visit to Switzerland," recalls Morand. He emphasizes that, "The interaction with the Shūbukan is of course technical, but the family-like exchange is above all important and worth being preserved". Furthermore, he says that, "karate brings me every day a new energy, as well as great technical and human discoveries."

Swiss are known for their punctuality. This eternally neutral country is thriving with mainland karate and other martial arts. While being active within the Swiss Karate Federation, Morand follows the path of Okinawa karate and kobudō without blurring. Step by step, he deepens exchanges with the birthplace of karate that is Okinawa by joining hands with the Uema family and Ōshiro Zenei.

北欧スウェーデンと言えば、人気ポップグループ「アバ」の世界的ヒット曲「ダンシング・クイーン」を思い浮かべる人も多いだろう。

スカンジナビア半島にあるこの王国には1960年後半、日本の研究者や技術者が訪れ、空手の普及に貢献した。現在の空手人口は1万7千人に上るという。

空手の先駆者の一人、70年代に移住し、通信機器メーカーエリクソン社に勤めていた依田昭次氏は、喜屋武朝徳氏の高弟であった故奥原文英氏の少林流を広めた。79年には全日本少林流空手道スウェーデン支部を開設した。

74年生まれのロバート・イバーション氏は、10歳の時、依田氏の道場に入門した。20歳のころ、スウェーデン軍に入隊。99年から2007年まで、ボスニアで平和安定化部隊、コソボで治安維持部隊の一員として4度配置された。退役後は、警備会社に入社し、今に至っている。

1990年代初期、依田氏が帰国。そこからイバーション氏は、少林流のルーツを研究し始めた。調べるうちに、41年奥原氏と仲里常延氏の組手の写真を発見し、トンネルの奥に光が見えたように感じた。

直ちに訪沖を決めたイバーション氏は、県指定無形文化財保持者の仲里氏に手紙を出し、2000年に南城市知念にある仲里氏の「求道館」の門をくぐった。その後、弟子入りも認められた。「あのころ、外国の門弟はいなかった。先生いわく、私は一番目の外国の弟子」と語る。

子どもたちを指導するイバーション氏(中央)=提供
Iversen (center) teaching young students.

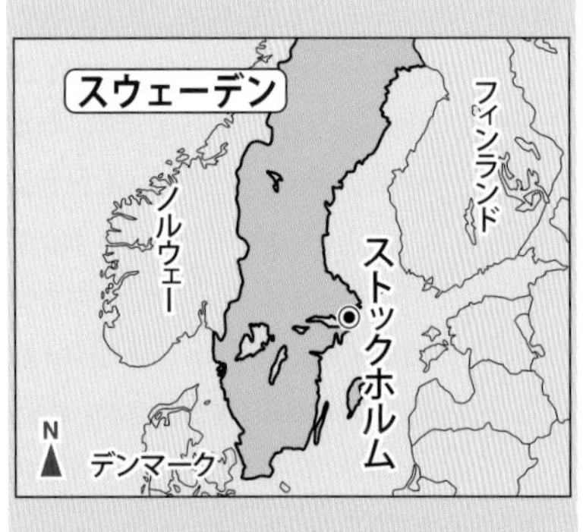

2019年04月28日

⑬スウェーデン

「一挙必勝」胸に鍛錬

ミャルスタ沖縄空手道協会

03年に許可を得て、ストックホルム郊外に道場を開設した。以降、同国で唯一の少林寺流のこの道場で、16人の有段者を含む74人が空手と沖縄古武道の稽古に励んでいる。イバーション氏はこれまで11回沖縄を訪れている。17年に故仲里氏の高弟親川仁志氏により、教士7段の昇段を認められた。

「厳しい指導者でありながら、常延先生は控えめで優しい人でした。教わった一番大切なことは、稽古に対する心構え。『この技が失敗したら次の技があるという考えの稽古では、真の技は体得できない。一拳必勝をもって稽古すべきだ』といつも話していた」と今は亡き師をしのぶ。

今年4月には、第2回北欧空手・古武道セミナーがフィンランドのヘルシンキで開催された。チャンミグヮーと呼ばれた喜屋武朝徳氏の空手を継ぐ少林流聖武館、一心流、少林寺流の35人が技術交流を行い、切磋琢磨(せっさたくま)した。セミナーは「3流派の始祖である喜屋武先生の足跡を歩み、我々の系統の原理を伝えたい」とイバーション氏が発案したという。

仲里氏が好んだ禅の教え「一器の水を一器にうつす」を胸に刻むイバーション氏は、これからも喜屋武氏の空手の神髄を探求し続けていく。

Published on 2019/4/28

⑬ Sweden 

Märsta Okinawa Karatedō Association

Training in the spirit of "succeeding with one fist"

In the late 1960s, Japanese engineers visited Sweden and contributed to the spread of karate. The current karate population in the country is said to be 17,000.

One of the karate pioneers was Yoda Akitsugu who emigrated in the 1970s and worked for the telecommunication company Ericsson. Next to his work, he spread the Shōrin-ryū of the late Okuhara Bunei, a disciple of Kyan Chōtoku and in 1979, the Shōrin-ryū Karatedō Sweden Branch was opened.

Born in 1974, Robert Iversen entered Yoda's dōjō at the age of 10. When he was 20 years old, he joined the Swedish army and from 1999 to 2007, he did 4 international tours in Bosnia and Kosovo. After his retirement, he joined a security company and continues in this field to this day.

As Yoda returned to Japan in the early 1990s, Iversen began to research about the roots of the system he practiced. Along his investigation, he discovered some photos from 1941 of Okuhara Bunei practicing together with Nakazato Jōen. Immediately deciding to visit Okinawa, Iversen wrote a letter to Nakazato and in 2000, he entered the Kyūdōkan dōjō of Nakazato in Chinen, Nanjō City, later to be welcomed as a student. "I was surprised that there were no foreign students in the Kyūdōkan, and Nakazato sensei told me later that I became his first foreign student."

Permission being granted, he opened a dōjō in the suburbs of Stockholm in 2003. Since then, 74 people, including 16 black belt holders, have been practicing karate and Okinawa kobudō at this dōjō, which is the only Shōrinji-ryū dōjō in the country. Having visited Okinawa 11 times, he was promoted to Kyōshi 7th dan in 2017 by Oyakawa Hitoshi, a high-ranked student of the late Nakazato.

Remembering the late master, he says, "Jōen sensei was a very strict teacher but as a person, he was very kind, humble and caring. The best teaching I learnt from him was the attitude towards karate training. He used to say: Do not think that if you don't succeed with one technique, there is a next one. You must train your mind to succeed with the first punch".

This last April in Helsinki, Finland, was held the 2nd Okinawa Karate & Kobudō Nordic Seminar. 35 people from different schools following the lineage of Kyan Chōtoku gathered and trained together. The purpose of the seminar was to "show the similarities between the styles of Kyan sensei and to research the principles of his karate".

Keeping at heart Nakazato favourite saying "Pouring to the last drop the water from one bowl to another," Iversen continues to explore the essence of Kyan's karate.

首里手を母体に沖縄出身の祝嶺正献氏(1925-2001)は本土で玄制流を創始し、1965年に新しい武道として「躰道」を立ち上げた。現在この躰道は11カ国に普及している。

スウェーデン南西にあるウッデバラ生まれのウルフ・カールソン氏(50)は、84年に躰道の道場に入門した。92年に初来日し、躰道を深く理解しようとルーツの調査を始めた。99年から2005年までは東京や京都に住み、武術の鍛錬や大学留学も行った。

日本に住んだ後、母国のマルメに拠点を置いた。以来、躰道の普及に励み、現在同国の躰道連盟の理事長も務めている。

カールソン氏は研究を深めるうち、祝嶺氏の師である岸本祖孝氏(1869-1945)に興味を抱いた。琉球王国時代の士族「武士武村(タチムラ)」の弟子だった岸本氏は名護で指導していたという。戦後受け継いだのは祝嶺氏と武芸館初代の比嘉清徳氏の二人だった。

躰道の関係者が比嘉家と交流を持っていることを聞き、カールソン氏も2009年に那覇市首里にある武芸館を訪れ、2代目比嘉清彦氏に師事した。

ナイハンチの分解を鍛錬するカールソン氏(左)＝デビッド・リンドルム氏提供
Karlsson (left) training an application of Naihanchi (photo from David Lindholm).

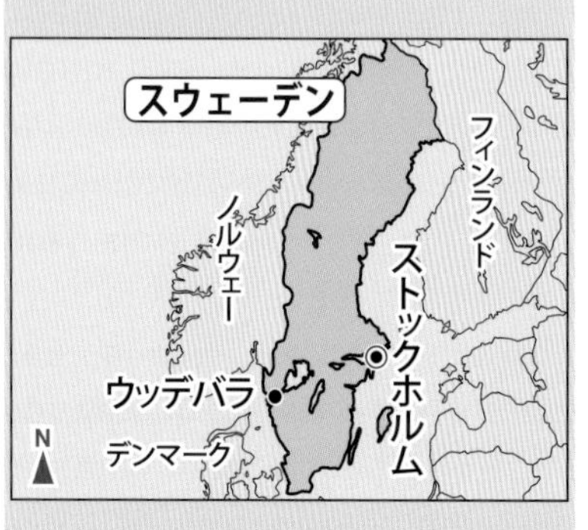

2020年05月10日

⑭スウェーデン

歴史探り 普及へ信念

岸本手研究会

「一度限りの訪問予定でしたが、比嘉家に岸本先生の武術が残っていることに気づいた。2年間の稽古と調査を経て、この武術が絶滅の危機にあると感じ、継承と普及を決めた」。武芸館はこの武術を「武士武村・岸本伝」と称することから、カールソン氏はその後「岸本手研究会」を立ち上げた。

躰道6段のカールソン氏は2015年に比嘉清彦氏より岸本手の師範免許を取得した。現在地元の人材派遣会社の代表を務めつつ、国内外で岸本手を指南している。21年秋には自身の道場開設も検討中だ。

自身の稽古では、五つの型以上に取り組むと真の研究ができないという信念から武士武村の型であるナイハンチ、パッサイ、クーサンクー、二段武の四つの型を中心に汗を流す。

また、この系統の理解を深めるためには、空手と琉球の歴史を知る必要があると感じ、毎年沖縄に滞在し、身体と文献の研究にも励んできた。取り組みには研究者である大阪の本部直樹氏やドイツのアンドレアス・クアスト氏の協力も得ている。

「空手の魅力の一つは、どこでもできる武芸ということ。沖縄は研究に最適な行き先。ぜひ多くの空手愛好者が発祥の地を訪れ、空手を体感してほしい」。カールソン氏は北欧の地と世界を舞台に、沖縄の武術へ理解を深め続けていく。

The Okinawan Shukumine Seiken (1925-2001) founded Gensei-ryū in mainland Japan with Shurite as the basis of his system. In 1965, he launched the new martial art of Taidō which is currently present in 11 countries.

Born in Uddevalla in southwestern Sweden, Ulf Karlsson (50) entered a Taidō dōjō in 1984. He first came to Japan in 1992 and began investigating the roots of his martial art in an attempt to gain a deeper understanding of Taidō. From 1999 to 2005, he lived in Tōkyō and Kyōto, where he trained in martial arts while studying. Returning home, he established himself in Malmö and strived to popularize Taidō.

Published on 2020/5/10

⑭ Sweden

KishimotoDi Kenkyūkai

Devoted to history exploration and promotion

As he deepened his research, Karlsson became interested in Kishimoto Sokō (1869-1945), the teacher of Shukumine. It is said that Kishimoto, who taught martial arts in Nago, was a disciple of Bushi Tachimura, an expert during the Ryūkyū Kingdom era. After the war, the two who inherited Kishimoto's martial material were Shukumine and Higa Seitoku of the Bugeikan.

After hearing that a few Taidō officials had had some interaction with the Higa family, Karlsson also visited the Bugeikan in Shuri, Naha City in 2009 and trained under Higa Kiyohiko, the son of Higa Seitoku.

"After what was intended as a onetime research trip, I realized that the Higa family still had the Kishimoto Sokō material. After a couple of years of training and research, with the authorization of Higa, I decided to teach the material more openly." As the Bugeikan calls this martial art "Bushi Tachimura – Kishimoto Den", Karlsson established the KishimotoDi Kenkyūkai.

In 2015, already a Taidō 6th dan, Karlsson obtained a KishimotoDi master's license from Higa Kiyohiko. He is currently teaching KishimotoDi at home and abroad, while heading a staffing agency. He is considering opening his own dōjō in the fall of 2021.

As he believes that "Three to five kata is training, more is a hobby!" Karlsson concentrates on four kata of the Tachimura lineage, namely Naihanchi, Passai, Kūsankū and Nidanbu.

Furthermore, in order to deepen his understanding of this system, Karlsson felt that it was necessary to better know the history of karate and Ryūkyū. In order to do so, he resides in Okinawa every year and trains while delving in documentation. He is supported in his endeavors by researcher Motobu Naoki in Ōsaka and Andreas Quast in Germany.

"The charm of karate is that it can be practiced anywhere. And Okinawa is a great destination to train. I encourage everyone who does karate to visit Okinawa and experience karate in its birthplace." In Scandinavian land and on the world stage, Karlsson continues to deepen his understanding of Okinawan martial arts.

日本とスペインの関係は1549年にさかのぼるが、この王国での空手の夜明けは1960年以降となった。

空手作家のサルバドール・エライス氏は「危険であるとの言い伝えのため、空手は長年、禁じられた。62年以降に空手が正式に認められ、66年頃から多くの日本の指導者がイベリア半島に定着した」と語る。

フラメンコが盛んなこの国では約8万人が空手を稽古しているという。世界空手連盟の本部も首都のマドリードにある。その競技空手の拠点から直線距離にして約5キロに小さな沖縄空手の道場がある。

「カマニー道場」は、1946年南米アルゼンチン生まれリカドー・カマニー氏が開設した。スポーツが大好きだったカマニー氏は大学時代、上地流の喜屋武昇氏の道場に入門した。69年に、比嘉仁達氏とオスカル・比嘉氏の道場を見つけ、両氏が当時指導していた松林流に「一目ぼれ」して転向を決めた。後に、同国に移民した松林流の赤嶺茂秀氏に師事した。大学を卒業したカマニー氏は、米大手自動車メーカーに入社した。

78年に松林流宗家の長嶺将真氏がアルゼンチンを訪問。感動したカマニー氏は、80年4月5日、

型を鍛錬するカマニー氏（提供） Camani practicing kata.

2018年06月24日

⑮スペイン

「拳禅一如」守り稽古

カマニー道場

那覇市で開催された宗家の県スポーツ功労賞と古希祝賀の記念演武大会に参加した。「大会が地元新聞で掲載され、自分が写真に写ったことが驚きだった」とカマニー氏は語る。

しかし86年に勤め先の販売率が落ち、社員を減らすこととなった。自発的に退職したカマニー氏は、歯科医の妻と息子たちと一緒にオーストラリアへの移住を決めた。そこでカマニー氏はすぐに自分に合った仕事を見つけたが、妻の歯科免許が認められなかった。また息子が学校になじめないことからカマニー夫妻は新たな移住先を考えた。

87年に、妻と息子が先にマドリードに移住。カマニー氏は、家族を支えるためにシドニーで働き、約1年の遠距離生活となった。「息子たちの発音が変わり、長男が大人になっていくことが、離れている父として一番辛い時期でした」と思い返す。

妻が仕事に成功し、88年にカマニー氏は家族と再会した。苦労や悩みを支えたのは、沖縄空手だった。97年の来沖の際に、長嶺氏の許可を得て「カマニー道場」を開設。現在、空手7段のカマニー氏は退職し、スペイン2道場とドイツとオランダ2道場で指南している。

松林流の教えである「拳禅一如」を守り、稽古中では常に警戒する無心を目指す。競技空手が人気の中、強い心を培う沖縄空手を離れず、探求し続ける。

The relationship between Japan and Spain dates back to 1549, but the dawn of karate in this kingdom dates back to 1960. Spanish karate writer Salvador Herráiz tells that, "Karate was banned for many years because of the legend that it was dangerous. It was officially recognized after 1962, and many Japanese leaders have been residing on the Iberian Peninsula since around 1966."

Currently, about 80,000 people practice karate in Spain. In Madrid, about 5 km away from the headquarters of the World Karate Federation, there is a small Okinawa karate dōjō named the Camani Dōjō. It was opened by Ricardo Camani, who was born in Argentina in 1946.

Published on 2018/6/24

15 Spain

Camani Dōjō

Training in accordance to "Kenzen Ichinyo"

Camani entered the Uechi-ryū dōjō of Kyan Noboru when he was in college. In 1969, he found the dōjō of Higa Jintatsu and Oscar Higa, who at that time were teaching Matsubayashi-ryū. It was "love at first sight" and Camani decided to change style. After graduating from college, Camani started working for a major US car maker while continuing karate with Akamine Shigehide, an instructor who had immigrated to the country.

Having met the Sōke Nagamine Shōshin in 1978 in Argentina, Camani participated in the celebrative demonstration for the master's 70th anniversary held in Naha City on April 5th, 1980.

However, in 1986, the sales of the company he worked for dropped and the personnel was reduced. Voluntarily resigning, Camani decided to move to Australia with his wife and sons. Unfortunately, his wife's dentist license was not validated. As their elder son did not adapt to the Australian school system, the family considered Spain as a new destination.

In 1987, his wife and sons moved to Madrid first as Camani stayed working in Sydney to support his family. "The change of accent of my sons, not being able to see my eldest son becoming an adult gave me the saddest of all feelings. It was the worst year of my life."

After his wife succeeded in her work field, Camani reunited with his family in 1988. It was karate that supported him in these times of hardships. In Okinawa in 1997, he received the authorization to open the Camani Dōjō. Currently retired and a karate 7th dan, he instructs in two dōjō in Spain, one in Germany and another one in the Netherlands.

Within his practice, preserving the style's teaching "Kenzen Ichinyo" - The essence of karatedō and Zen as one -, he aims at having the mind and body together towards a 'no-mind' flow of energy, always in alert. While competitive karate is the most popular, he continues to explore Okinawa karate, an art that cultivates a strong heart.

2019年08月25日

⑯スペイン

施設充実 稽古に専心

修武館道場

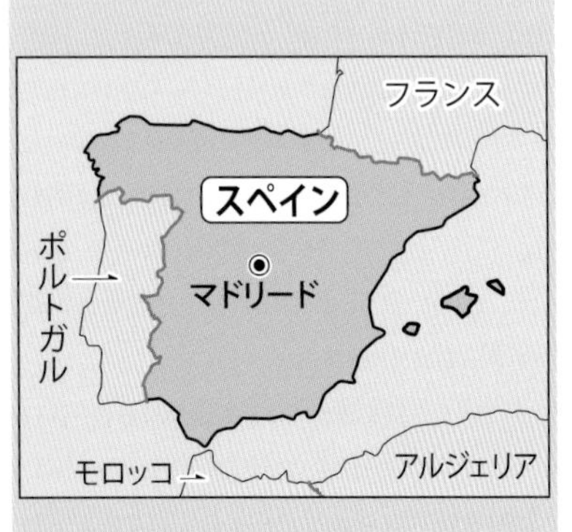

今年で創設200年を誇るスペイン、マドリードのプラド美術館から南西へ18キロほど離れたモストレスに大型の専用道場「修武館道場」はある。

1967年マドリード生まれのホセ・シフエンテス・ガルシア氏は10歳の時、糸東流空手道に入門。83年から指導にも携わった。

96年9月、翌年に開催される沖縄空手・古武道世界大会のPRを目的に、第3次キャラバン隊がスペインを含む4カ国を訪れた。硬軟流の糸数盛昌氏を含む各流派の代表5人が、セミナーや演武を実施した。

「会場には、セミナー受講者が300人位、見学者も2300人位いて熱気にあふれていた」と団員の會澤卓司氏は報告した。当時ガルシア氏も来場し、上地流系の硬軟流の演武を見て魅了された。直ちにその系統を学ぼうと、スペインで上地流を指導する久野泰氏の門をたたいた。↗

上地流2代目上地完英氏の高弟故新木覚氏に師事した久野氏は、83年にイベリア半島に移住し、3年後バルセロナで上地流の指導を始めたという。ガルシア氏は、久野氏の下で上地流の空手を研究し始めた。

長年、警備会社やジムで働いたガルシア氏は、2009年に空手のプロとして羽ばたこうと決意。16年に念願の専用道場「修武館道場」をオープンさせた。

修武館道場で先頭に立ち指導するガルシア氏（提供）
García leading a class at the Shubukan Dōjō.

「私の夢は、古典的な沖縄空手の練習のために特別に設計された道場を開設することでした」。完全木製で500平方メートルのこの道場は200人が一同に集い、稽古に専心できる充実した施設だ。巻き藁42個、手首や下半身の強化のための道具チーシやサーシー100個、多くの武器と鍛錬具、園庭、休憩場などが完備されている。

現在修武館道場では大人100人が上地流、糸東流、又吉古武道を学び、別館で子供60人も稽古に励む。

「夢がかなった気分です。これから私の目標は、この道場を多くの空手愛好家やほかの武道家と共有することです」。開館以降、多数のセミナーを受け入れ、昨年2月、沖縄県主催の海外指導者派遣事業兼第1回沖縄空手国際大会周知キャラバンがガルシア氏の道場を訪れ、新城清秀氏ら4人が指導に当たった。

「私は、空手のすべてが好きです。理由その一、空手には、欠けてはならない礼儀作法がある。その二は空手は求道無限であること。そして一定かつ真剣な練習は良い人間に育てるからです」。太陽と情熱の国で、ガルシア氏は未来を見据え、空手の鍛錬と交流に力を注いでいく。

About 18 km southwest of the 200 years old Prado Museum in Madrid, there is a large martial facility in Móstoles called the Shūbukan Dōjō.

Born in Madrid in 1967, José Cifuentes García began Shitō-ryū karate at the age of 10 and started being involved in teaching from 1983.

In September 1996, in order to promote the Okinawa Karate and Kobudō World Tournament to be held the following year, an Okinawan delegation visited four countries including Spain. Five representatives of Okinawan schools, including Itokazu Seishō of Kōnan-ryū, were dispatched for some seminars and demonstrations.

Published on 2019/8/25

16 Spain

Shūbukan Dōjō

Dedicated to training in a great environment

A member of the delegation, Aizawa Takuji, reported that "There were about 300 seminar participants and about 2,300 visitors, and the venue was filled with enthusiasm." As he participated, García was fascinated by the demonstration of Kōnan-ryū, a branch system of Uechi-ryū. Eager to learn this system of karate, he immediately visited the dōjō of Kuno Yasushi, who teaches Uechi-ryū in Spain.

Kuno studied under late Shinki Satoru, a disciple of Uechi Kanei, 2nd heir of Uechi-ryū, and moved to the Iberian Peninsula in 1983. Three years later, he began teaching Uechi-ryū in Barcelona. García began studying Uechi-ryū karate under Kuno.

Having worked for many years for security companies and gyms, García decided to become a karate professional in 2009 and in 2016, he opened his long-cherished dedicated dōjō, the Shubukan Dōjō.

This dōjō, which is made entirely of wood and has a floor area of 500 square meters, is a fully equipped facility where 200 people can gather and devote themselves to training. It is equipped with 42 makiwara, 100 chīshi and sāshi, many weapons and training tools, a Japanese garden and a rest area.

Currently, 100 adults study Uechi-ryū, Shitō-ryū, and Matayoshi kobudō at the Shūbukan, and 60 children practice at an annex dōjō.

"I feel like my dream has come true. From now on, my goal is to share this dōjō with many karate and other martial arts enthusiasts." Since the opening, many seminars have been organized, and in February last year, an Okinawa karate delegation sponsored by Okinawa Prefecture visited and taught at Garcia's dōjō.

"I like everything about karate. In the first place, the essential etiquette. Second is that karate being endless, one never stops learning. And then the constant and serious practice of karate makes one a better person." In a country of sun and passion, García looks to the future focusing on training experiences and exchanges through karate.

スロバキアは1993年に、チェコスロバキアから分離し独立した。共和国として若い国だが、6千の洞窟と300余りの城・城跡を誇り、兵庫県(人口548万人余)とほぼ同じ人口を有するこの国の歴史は古い。

66年、チェコスロバキアで初めて空手が紹介された。69年に、松濤館系の空手を習っていたヤーン・フラビナ氏は、現首都ブラチスラバで初めての道場を開設した。

54年同市生まれのロドビット・ディビネット氏も、68年に松濤館空手を習い始めた。翌年、近隣国オーストリアからやってきた本土系剛柔会所属の小川武治氏の下で、山口剛玄氏の剛柔流に専念した。

空手の普及を支えようとディビネット氏は、72年に自ら指導を始めた。空手以外でも医学の道に進み、新生児学の専門医となった。忙しい医師としての生活を送りながら、88年には数人の指導者と共に、青少年を中心に指導する道場「TJBUDOブラチスラバ」を開設させた。

スポーツ空手を中心に活動していたディビネット氏は、97年に沖縄県立武道館落成記念行事として開催された沖縄空手・古武道世界大会に参加。その際に、比嘉世幸氏系列のセミナーを通して沖縄の剛柔流を体験した。

弟子と共に型を打つディビネット氏(中央)=提供
Divinec (center) practicing kata with his students.

2019年02月10日

⑰スロバキア 

「平和の武」広め修練

ドゥヴィ館ブラチスラバ

空手の本場において、剛柔流の開祖宮城長順氏の直弟子で大きな組織を立ち上げた人物には、八木明徳氏(明武舘)、宮里栄一氏(順道館)と宮城氏の師・東恩納寛量氏にも師事した比嘉世幸氏がいる。60年に比嘉氏は、尚道館を開設し、剛柔流国際空手古武道連盟も創設した。

伝統ある剛柔流に魅了されたディビネット氏は後に、連盟への加盟が認められ、2006年に、二つ目の道場「ドゥヴィ館ブラチスラバ」を開設し、尚道館の空手を広めた。

密接に運営される両道場では、120人が空手を学ぶ。ディビネット氏はその他5支部、国内空手古武道連盟の技術顧問として34道場でも指導を行っている。2代目比嘉世吉、喜友名朝有、蔵下英喜、又吉清徳ら諸氏の指導を受けるためディビネット氏は、40回余も訪沖を重ねた。

「沖縄の心温かい先生方の下で、古典的な剛柔流の稽古は厳格でありながら気持ちよくできるものです。主に平和というイデオロギーを持つ彼らは、私の心を鼓舞してくれる」とディビネット氏は沖縄とその武術への思いを語る。

精神と肉体の健康を手にした空手8段のディビネット氏。「空手は私の人生の全てですが、家族と仕事も優先する」と最後にコメントした。家族が社会構造の核心であると信じるスロバキア人らしい発言なのだ。

Slovakia separated from Czechoslovakia in 1993 and became independent. Although a young republic, this country has a long and rich history boasting 6,000 caves and 300 castles and castle ruins.

It's in 1966 that karate was introduced for the first time in Czechoslovakia. In 1969, Ján Hrabina, who was learning Shōtōkan karate, opened the first dōjō in the current capital, Bratislava.

Ludovit Divinec, who was born in the same city in 1954, also started learning Shōtōkan karate in 1968. The following year, he switched to the Gōjū-ryū of Yamaguchi Gōgen under the instruction of Ogawa Takeji, who taught mainland Gōjū-ryū in neighboring Austria.

Published on 2019/2/10

17 Slovakia

Duvikan Bratislava

Promoting "the martial art of Peace"

With the aim to support the spread of karate in his country, Divinec began teaching in 1972. Besides karate, he pursued medical studies and became a specialist of neonatology. While living a busy life as a doctor, he and several instructors set up the youth-centered dōjō TJ BUDO Bratislava in 1988.

While active mainly in sport karate, Divinec participated in the Okinawa Karate & Kobudō World Tournament held as a commemorative event for the completion of the Okinawa Prefectural Budōkan in 1997. Joining a seminar during the tournament, he experienced the Okinawa Gōjū-ryū of the Higa Sekō lineage.

In the birthplace of karate, the major figures who started large organizations as direct disciples of Gōjū-ryū founder Miyagi Chōjun were Yagi Meitoku (Meibukan), Miyazato Eiichi (Jundōkan) and Higa Sekō. In 1960, Higa opened the Shōdōkan and also established the Gōjū-ryū International Karate Kobudō Federation.

Fascinated by traditional Gōjū-ryū, Divinec was later admitted to the federation, and in 2006 he opened a second dōjō, the Duvikan Bratislava, in order to spread the karate of the Shōdōkan.

In his two closely operated dōjō, 120 people learn karate. Divinec also oversees 5 branch dōjō and 34 other clubs as the technical director of the Slovak federation of karate and kobudō. In order to receive instruction from 2nd generation Higa Seikichi, Kiyuna Chōyu, Kurashita Eiki and Matayoshi Seitoku among others, he has visited Okinawa more than 40 times.

"Under the supervision of warm-hearted Okinawan masters, classical Gōjū-ryū is rigorous but yet pleasant. Their main ideology which is Peace is inspiring," says Divinec when talking about his thoughts on Okinawa and its martial arts.

A karate 8th dan, Divinec has acquired mental and physical health through training. "Karate is my whole life, but my family and work will always be my priority." Indeed a Slovak-like statement as Slovaks believe that family is the core of the social structure.

イタリアと国境を接する旧ユーゴスラビアの一国であった中央ヨーロッパのスロベニアは、1991年に独立した共和国である。

この国の空手歴は60年代にさかのぼるという。67年にクルシュコ市に初めての空手道場が開設され、急速に国内に9道場がオープンし、約500人が空手を稽古することになった。69年に全国連盟が発足し、初の競技大会が開催された。組手で優勝を果たしたのは、同国の空手パイオニアの一人、レオン・カウザール氏。

59年生まれのボルト・マウラー氏は10歳の時、いとこであったカウザール氏より松濤館を習い始めた。後に加瀬泰治氏の弟子でユーゴスラビアで指導していた徳久隆司氏に師事し、97年まで松濤館の普及にも携わった。

94年に上地流の友人と共に沖縄を訪れたことが転機となった。棒術を習う希望を持っていたマウラー氏は、与那原町に松林流喜舎場塾を構える新里勝彦氏を紹介された。この出会いで、棒術より先に空手とその原理を改めて研究する必要があると感じ、弟子入りした。そこから、新たな空手の世界へ導かれた。

「空手は固定されたものではない。常に手腕を

門下生と共に稽古に励むマウラー氏(中央)=Jane Stravs提供
Mauhler (center) training with his students (photo from Jane Stravs).

2018年02月11日

⑱ スロベニア

名声求めず 鍛錬の道

喜舎場塾

磨き、武術において身体動作の原則への理解を向上させねばならない。固定された着想から解放し、稽古法を再評価するのも必要」と教えられ、研究を続けた。「新里先生の優しさと献身的な姿勢にも驚いた。最後までついていける師を見つけた」と確信したという。

妻のマリナ・グリジニッチ氏は有名な哲学者、芸術家でウィーン美術アカデミー教授。97年、グリジニッチ氏が日本で研究するため、6歳の息子と共に家族で東京に一年間滞在した。マウラー氏はスロベニアに比べ近くなった沖縄を訪れ、稽古を重ねた。

帰国後、忙しい妻を支えながら首都リュブリャナで道場を開設したが、「無償で与えられたものをお金で指導するものではない」と悟ったマウラー氏は、非営利目的の道場「喜舎場塾スロベニア」を誕生させた。現在、15人の弟子と共に、喜舎場塾創設者・故喜舎場朝啓氏の空手の研究に力を入れている。スペインのマドリードやドイツのケルンで空手指南も行っている。沖縄には、これまで16回も足を運んでいる。

人口200万余の小さな国スロベニアでは現在、200道場で6千人が空手を稽古している。マウラー氏は名声を求めず、人生の生きがいである空手の稽古を日々楽しみ、地道に沖縄空手の道を歩んでいる。

A former Yugoslav country bordering Italy, Slovenia became an independent republic in 1991.

It is said that karate was introduced in this country in the 1960s and that the first karate dōjō was opened in Krško in 1967. Later, 6 other dōjō were rapidly opened with about 500 people practicing karate. In 1969, the Karate Union of Slovenia was established, and the first competition was organized. The kumite winner was Leon Kauzar, a karate pioneer in the country.

Born in 1959, Borut Mauhler began learning Shōtōkan at the age of 10 from his cousin Leon Kauzal. Later, he studied under Kase Taiji's student Tokuhisa

Published on 2018/2/11

18 Slovenia

Kishaba Juku

The way of tempering without seeking fame

Takashi who was instructing in Yugoslavia and was even involved in the diffusion of Shōtōkan until 1997.

In 1994 his visit to Okinawa with some friends practicing Uechi-ryū was the turning point. As he wished to study bōjutsu, the technique of the staff, Mauhler was introduced to the head of the Matsubayashi-ryū Kishaba Juku in Yonabaru Town, Shinzato Katsuhiko. After meeting Shinzato, he realized how much more he needed to learn about karate and its principles. Becoming a student, it was an opening to a completely different world of karate.

"Karate is not a fixed box. We have to constantly improve our skills and our understanding of the principles on how our body works in martial arts. We need to be free of fixed ideas, and reevaluate constantly the way we train." Taught in this way, Mauhler deepened his research.

His wife, Marina Gržinić is a famous philosopher and artist who teaches at the Academy of Fine Arts in Vienna. In 1997, they stayed in Tōkyō for a year with their 6 years old son for her studies. Mauhler was also able to visit Okinawa a couple of times to train with Shinzato.

After returning to Slovenia and while supporting his busy wife, he opened a nonprofessional dōjō in the capital Ljubljana as he realized that, "One cannot teach for money something that was given for free". Currently, together with 15 students, he is focusing on researching the karate of late Kishaba Chōkei, the founder of Kishaba Juku. He also teaches at branch dōjō in Barcelona and Cologne. Over the years, he has visited Okinawa 16 times.

Although Slovenia is a small country with a population of around 2 million people, there are some 6,000 people practicing karate in 200 dōjō. Without seeking fame, Mauhler enjoys the practice of karate, which is his ikigai, his purpose in life, and steadily walks along the way of Okinawa karate.

2017年10月08日

⑲ セルビア

訪沖10回 伝統研さん

沖空会セルビア本部

セルビアといえば、テニスのチャンピオン、ノバク・ジョコビッチ選手が浮かぶ。しかし、同国においては空手とマーシャルアーツもとても盛んである。今年4月、同国のチャチャク市で開催された第46回「国際ゴールデンベルト」は、ヨーロッパで最も古い空手大会の一つとされる。

この国で、空手が紹介されたのは、1960年代のころ。セルビア空手連盟は現在、400道場と3万人のメンバーの登録があるという。「だが、この数字は国が支援する競技空手に関するデータで、伝統空手は含まれていない」。そう補足説明するのは、上地流歴44年のヴラディミル・ポポヴィッチ氏、教士七段。58年ベオグラード生まれのポポヴィッチ氏は71年に松濤館空手に入門した。73年、旧ユーゴスラビアで上地流を紹介したマリオ・トポルセク氏の弟子となった。

「72年、ドイツで見つけた小さな本を読んで、空手は沖縄発祥の武術であることを知った。オリジナルの空手を習いたくて、ほかの空手に比べて実践的な上地流を選んだ」と振り返るポポヴィッチ氏。82年の初めての訪沖から、10回も本場で汗を流し研究を重ねてきた。80年代に来沖の際、2代目宗家上地完英氏に師事したことは、忘れられない思い出の一つだという。97年にはベオグラード中心部で現在の道場を開設した。

セミナーで指導するポポヴィッチ氏(右)=提供
Popovic (right) teaching during a seminar.

「空手は、沖縄文化の中で最も高名な部分ですが、空手しかないわけではない。琉球舞踊などもある。空手は日本本土からではなく、沖縄が生んだ文化です。また、スポーツの境界を超える武道である」。そのことをセルビア人に認識させようと、2003年から3回にわたり、沖縄空手と琉球舞踊を中心とした文化事業もベオグラードで開催している。

機械エンジニアで現在沖縄空手道協会(上地流)のセルビア支部長を努めるポポヴィッチ氏は、本部道場で22人に指導し、国内6道場を見守る。また、ギリシャ、ウクライナ、イタリア、ロシアにも交流道場があり、頻繁にセミナーで指南している。

「空手は私の生きがいです。優れた指導者と出会い、世界中多くの友人もできた。自分の素晴らしい財産です。伝統空手でなければできなかったと思う。今日も、日々の稽古を通じて、空手の良さを感じる。技法の研究が無限であるからこそ、空手を基礎にした人生に意義がある」。

長年の鍛錬で築いた強靭(きょうじん)な体のポポヴィッチ氏は、外は固く、中は柔らかい温和な人物。セルビアと発祥の地をつなぐ数少ない“沖縄空手の大使”だ。

When speaking of Serbia, tennis champion Novak Djokovic comes to mind. However, karate and martial arts are also very popular in this country. The International Karate Tournament Golden Belt held in the city of Čačak is considered to be one of the oldest karate competitions in Europe.

Karate was introduced in Serbia in the 1960s. The national federation is said to have currently 400 dōjō and 30,000 members registered. "However, these numbers refer to competitive karate, I don't think they include traditional karate," says Vladimir Popovic, a 7th dan instructor with 44 years of experience in Uechi-ryū.

Born in Belgrade in 1958, Popovic began karate with Shōtōkan in 1971. In 1973, he became a student of Mario Topolsek, the man who introduced Uechi-ryū in the former Yugoslavia.

Published on 2017/10/8

19 Serbia 

Okikūkai Serbia Honbu

Ten visits to Okinawa to study tradition

"In 1972, I read in a small book that karate was originally from Okinawa and looked for the original system. Uechi-ryū seemed to me much more applicable than any other styles which is why I joined".

Since his first visit to Okinawa in 1982, he has travelled 10 times to the birthplace of karate. Being taught by Uechi Kanei - the second Sōke - during his second visit to Okinawa, is one of his most unforgettable memories. In 1997, he opened his current dōjō in the center of Belgrade.

"I think that karate is the most prominent part of Okinawan culture, but not the only one. There are also Ryūkyūan dances, etc. Karate is a culture born in Okinawa, not in mainland Japan, and it is much more complex than a sport." In order to make Serbs aware of this, 3 cultural projects centered on Okinawan karate and dances have been held in Belgrade since 2003.

Popovic, a mechanical engineer, is currently the head of the Serbian branch of the Okinawa Karatedō Association (Uechi-ryū). He teaches 22 people at his dōjō and watches over six dōjō in the country. He also frequently teaches seminars in Greece, Ukraine, Italy and Russia.

"Karate has become the meaning of my life. I had the opportunity to meet wonderful masters, and to make many friends from all over the world. This is a personal treasure that only traditional karate can bring. Even today, I still find the beauty of karate through daily training. Technical research never ends, and that is why a life based on karate is meaningful."

With a strong body built through many years of training, Popovic is yet a gentleman. He is one of the few Okinawa karate ambassadors that connects Serbia and the birthplace of karate.

1966年、コラーシュ兄弟により空手が初めてチェコスロバキアに紹介された。93年に独立したチェコ共和国では現在、約5万人が沖縄生まれの武術を習う。こう話すのは、65年生まれのジャン・ギュウリス氏。

ギュウリス氏は9歳の時に柔道を、13歳の時、同国で一番普及している松濤館の空手を始めた。当初の指導者は、ラディスラブ・デュデック氏。10年間その系統で汗を流した。

88年ギュウリス氏は、プラハで開催されたセミナーで出会ったナカヤ・タカオ氏に技術指導を求めた。ナカヤ氏は首里手の名嘉真朝増氏に師事した空手家で拓殖大学卒。ギュウリス氏は米在住のナカヤ氏の下で、沖縄空手の技法、型と歴史の研究を深めた。同年、ボヘミア北東部に位置するイチーンで道場を開設した。

松濤館から沖縄小林流の転向について「これまで空手に対する疑問を持ち、その答えを求めていた。小林流を選んだ理由は、興味深い真実の空手であることを感じた」と話す。

2000年に、中学校講師の仕事をやめ、プロとして沖縄空手の指導と普及を開始した。

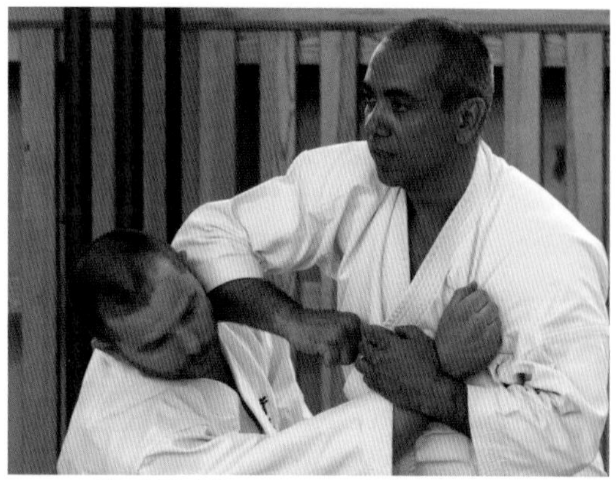

セミナーで型の分解を指導するギュウリス氏(右)=提供
Gyuris (right) teaching a kata application during a seminar.

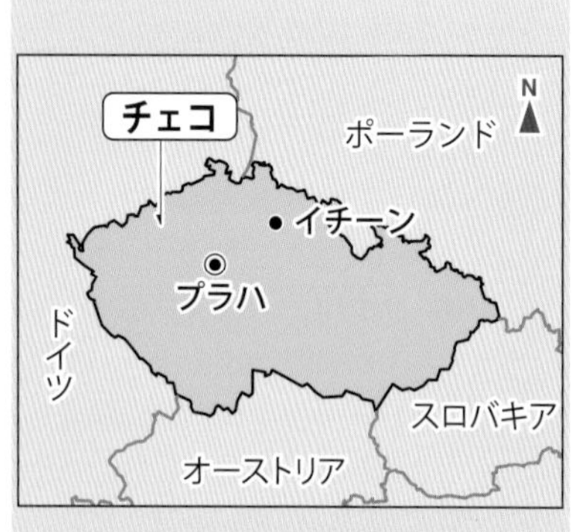

2018年01月14日

⑳チェコ

厳しい稽古 武術の道

守武館上間道場

04年、さらに空手への答えを掘り出すため、初めて沖縄を訪れた。ある人に極真系の道場を案内されたが、そこで小林流を学びたいと話すと、首里鳥堀町にある守武館上間道場に案内された。運良く、道場の館長である上間康弘氏も、名嘉真氏に師事したことがあった。

「鍛えなくてもできるスポーツ空手は簡単。チェコでは、護身術でもある沖縄空手は厳しい練習を意味する。自分との闘いですが、正しい道へと導かれるためには指導者が必要。上間先生の下で疑問を少しずつ解くことができた」とギュウリス氏。

現在、チェコ本部道場で52人、全国で11の道場で約310人の門下生を指導している。国内に定着した他の沖縄空手の流派8団体と交流を深めながら、12年から、守武館上間道場初代館長の故上間上輝氏をしのぶ国際大会を毎年開催している。関係者だけではなく、多くの人々に日本と沖縄の空手と文化を紹介することがこの大会の目的。6歳から70歳の空手家120人が出場している。

17年に15回目の来沖を果たした小林流6段のギュウリス氏は「空手でハッピーライフを得た」と明るい笑顔で語る。そして、沖縄での一番良い思い出を聞くと「ウチナーンチュ、すべての人との出会い」と答えた。

Karate was first introduced to Czechoslovakia by the Kolář brothers in 1966. Nowadays, the Czech Republic counts approximately 50,000 karate practitioners. The one who says so is 1965 born Jan Gyuris.

Gyuris started jūdō at the age of 9 and Shōtōkan at the age of 13, this style of karate being the most popular in the country. Under his first instructor Ladislav Dudek he studied karate for 10 years.

In 1988, Gyuris met Nakaya Takao, a Japanese instructor of Okinawa karate during a seminar in Prague and asked him to become his student. Nakaya was a student of Nakama Chōzō of the Shurite lineage and was residing in the USA after

Published on 2018/1/14

20 Czech Republic

Shūbukan Uema Dōjō

Severe training, the way of martial arts

graduating from Takushoku University. Gyuris started to learn from Nakaya, investigating the techniques of Okinawa karate, its kata and history. Meanwhile, he opened his dōjō in 1988 in Jičín, a small town in eastern Bohemia.

When asked why he changed from Shōtōkan to Shōrin-ryū, he says, “I was seeking the answers for my karate questions. I chose Shōrin-ryū because I considered it as a genuine karate and a very interesting style.”

Having worked as a high school teacher, Gyuris quit his job and started instructing Okinawa karate as a professional in 2000.

Four years later, he visited Okinawa for the first time. As he was led to a Kyokushin dōjō, he explained that he wanted to study Shōrin-ryū and was introduced to the Shūbukan Uema Dōjō in Shuri Torihori-chō. Fortunately for him, the kanchō of the dōjō Uema Yasuhiro had also studied with Nakama Chōzō.

“Not requiring conditioning, sport karate is easy. In my country, Okinawa karate, which is also a system of self-defense, means rigorous practice. It's a fight against yourself, but you need an instructor to be guided on the right path. I was able to solve some of my questions along the way under Uema sensei.”

Currently, Gyuris teaches 52 students at the Czech honbu dōjō and about 310 students in 11 dōjō nationwide. While deepening exchanges with eight other Okinawan karate schools established in the country, he also organizes since 2012 an international tournament every year in honor of the late Uema Jyōki, the first kanchō of the Shūbukan Uema Dōjō. The purpose of this tournament is to introduce the karate and culture of Japan and Okinawa to many people.

In 2017, Gyuris visited Okinawa for the 15th time. A 6th dan in Shōrin-ryū, he says that karate has brought happiness in his life. And when asked his best memory of his visits to Okinawa, he answers, “Meeting Okinawan people, all of them.”

2022年1月23日

㉑ チェコ

空手と研究 努力重ね

拳優会プラハ

中央ヨーロッパにあるこの国での空手は、1960年代から普及していると言われている。後に、70年代前半沖縄で上地流の指導を受けた旧ユーゴスラビア（現クロアチア）出身の故マリオ・トポルセック氏は東ヨーロッパで同系の空手の普及に励み、97年にプラハでヨーロッパ上地流空手協会を立ち上げた。

81年プラハ生まれのトマーシュ・プルスカル氏は、同市で道場を開設するまで沖縄とアメリカで高度な経験を重ねた男である。

17歳の時プラハの松濤館の道場に通ったプルスカル氏は、後にトポルセック氏の門をくぐり上地流を習った。大学で計算機科学を学び、卒業後、沖縄で空手を体験したかった氏は、恩納村にある沖縄科学技術大学院大学（OIST）での仕事に応募し、2005年に採用された。

同年の来沖直後、中部にあるいくつかの上地流の道場を見学し、読谷村にある沖縄上地流空手道拳優会の新城塾に入門した。「新城清秀先生の道場は、先生だけでなく生徒たちの驚くべきエネルギーと勤勉さで際立っていました」と氏は思い返す。

そこから氏は10年間沖縄に滞在。大学院大学内の分子生物学の研究室で働きながら、専門分野であるコンピューターサイエンスを活かし、世界中で人気のソフトウエアを開発した。

トマーシュ・プルスカル氏、道場にて（提供）
Tomáš Pluskal in his Prague dōjō.

同時に生物学そのものにも興味を持つようになり、氏はキャリアチェンジを行い、分子バイオテクノロジーの分野で博士号を取得。高度な研究とともに道場生として空手にも励み、多くの演武にも関われたことも忘れられない思い出だという。

研究を続けようと氏は、15年にマサチューセッツ工科大学（MIT）へ向かい、5年間ボストンで博士研究員として植物にある薬用の分子とそれらを生成する遺伝子を調査した。沖縄で稽古し、上地流拳優会の五段を授かった氏は、米国滞在中、同会所属の道場で汗を流した。

20年故郷に戻り、嘉手納出身の妻と子息2人とプラハ市に住みながら、チェコ科学アカデミーにおいて自身の研究所のリーダーを務める。忙しい研究の傍ら、昨年9月に9世紀に構築されたプラハ城の近くに沖縄空手の道場「上地流空手道拳優会プラハ」を開設し、現在、6人に沖縄空手を指導している。

氏は「毎日の仕事や日常生活に、空手で得られる集中力、スタミナとパワーは欠かせない。護身術だけではなく、複数の利益をもたらす単一の活動である空手は本当に魅力的です」と空手への意気込みを語り、生化学と空手の研究に努力し続ける。

Karate in this Central European country spread in the 1960s. In the early 70s, the late Mario Toposlek from former Yugoslavia (now Croatia), who had trained Uechi-ryū in Okinawa, worked hard to popularize this system in Eastern Europe. In 1997 in Prague, he established the Europe Uechi-ryū Karate Association.

Born in Prague in 1981, Tomáš Pluskal is a man who gained a wide range of experiences in Okinawa and the USA before opening a dōjō in his hometown.

Around the age of 17, he joined a Shōtōkan club in Prague and later enter the dōjō of Toposlek. While studying computer science in university, Pluskal dreamed of experiencing karate in Okinawa. After graduating, he thus applied for a job at the Okinawa Institute of Science and Technology Graduate University (OIST) in Onna Village and was hired in 2005.

Immediately after arriving, he visited several Uechi-ryū dōjō and joined the Shinjō Juku of the Okinawa Uechi-ryū Karatedō Kenyūkai in Yomitan Village. "Shinjō Kiyohide sensei's dōjō stood out with the amazing energy and diligence of the sensei as well as the students."

From there, he eventually stayed in Okinawa for 10 years. While working in a molecular biology lab at OIST, he used his specialty of computer science to develop a software quite popular worldwide.

At the same time, he became interested in biology itself and redirecting his career, he obtained a Ph.D. in molecular biotechnology. While undergoing advanced research, Pluskal persevered in karate as a dōjō student and gained unforgettable memories in various demonstrations.

To continue his research, Pluskal went to the Massachusetts Institute of Technology (MIT) in 2015. Spending 5 years in Boston, he investigated molecules of medicinal interest in plants and the genes that produce them as a postdoctoral researcher. Having been promoted to 5th dan while in Okinawa, he continued training at a Kenyūkai dōjō in the USA.

Returning to his hometown in 2020, he now lives in Prague with his wife from Kadena and their two sons while heading his own research institute at the Czech Academy of Sciences. Aside from his busy research, he opened last September the Uechi-ryū Karatedō Kenyūkai Prague dōjō near Prague Castle, which was built in the 9th century. Currently, he teaches Okinawa karate to six people.

"I use karate every day, in my job as well as in my daily life. The concentration, focus, and strength that I gained from karate are indispensable. Next to teaching self-defense, karate is attractive because it is a single activity that brings multiple benefits." Enthusiastically promoting karate, Pluskal perseveres in his biochemistry and karate research.

Published on 2022/1/23

21 Czech Republic

Kenyūkai Prague

An exertion for karate and research

2018年3月25日

㉒ デンマーク

継承の技 指南に情熱

上心館

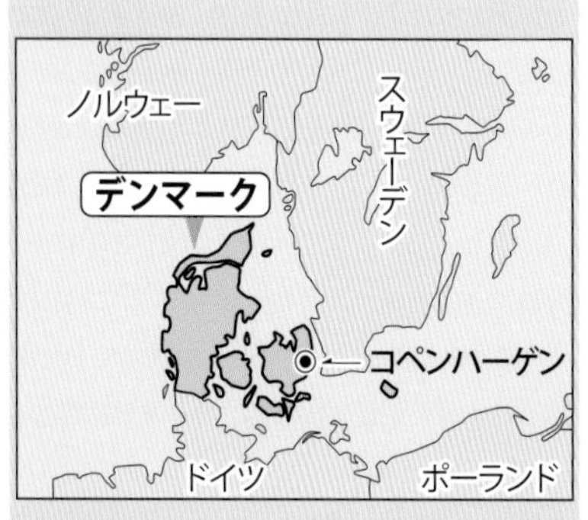

デンマークといえば、ポーク缶詰を輸出し、沖縄で多くが消費されているというイメージが強い。空手との繋がりでは、極真会館・大山倍達氏に師事した格闘家のニコラス・ペタス氏が思い浮かぶ。

空手が同国に紹介されたのは1960年代だという。それ以降、様々な流派が定着したが、現在は極真系と松濤館流が多く普及している。

67年生まれのラース・アンデルセン氏は14歳の時、極真系を始めた。理由は単純に「強い身体で護身術を習いたかったから」。その後88年に米国で一心流空手を学んだジョニー・ジャコブセン氏と出会い沖縄空手に目を向けた。

創始者・島袋龍夫氏により命名された一心流のコンパクトな動き、型の分解と接近戦が魅力的だったとアンデルセン氏は振り返る。

アメリカで研究を深めた後の91年に、デンマークの首都コペンハーゲンに移り、警察に勤めながら署内に稽古場を開き指導を始めた。翌年、首都の空港近くに道場を開設し、96年「上心館」と命名した。

アンデルセン氏は、一心流に興味を持ち始めたとき、同流派の指導者上江洲安儀氏の空手ビデオを購入した。96年沖縄を訪れた際に上江洲氏と上地強氏に師事したことから、両氏の頭文字「上」を引用し道場名を決めた。2001年に支部道場も開き、上心館一心流空手古武道協会を設立した。

型を練習するアンデルセン氏（右）＝提供
Andersen (right) practicing kata.

コソボ紛争後約4年間、アンデルセン氏は、国連国際警察官としてコソボに派遣された。首都のプリシュティナ市で警察指導員コースを指導。現在はコペンハーゲンの国立警察アカデミーで講師を務めている。

多忙な毎日を送るアンデルセン氏は、常に空手普及を考える日々だった。10年に、デンマーク語で情報発信するウェブサイト「空手ニュース」を2人の空手家と共に立ち上げ、今も編集を続けている。

同年沖縄を再度訪れ、琉球古武道徳身流の徳村賢昌氏と出会った。「棒、サイとトンファーの技法が一心流で継承する技と似ていてすぐ興味が湧いた」

現在空手7段、古武道6段のアンデルセン氏は、国内一心流空手3道場、徳身流6道場を監修。ドイツ、ルーマニアとスウェーデンの他流派の空手道場でも古武道を指南し、約1500人に指導している。

「空手は素晴らしい訓練と友人をもたらし、沖縄の文化を学ぶチャンスも与えてくれた」。アンデルセン氏は強い使命感を胸に沖縄空手・古武道の魅力を発信し続けている。

Published on 2018/3/25

22 Denmark

Jōshinkan

A passion for teaching and inheriting the art

When speaking of Denmark, people think of exported canned pork that is highly consumed in Okinawa. As for karate, Danish fighter Nicholas Pettas, who studied under Ōyama Masutatsu, comes to mind.

It is said that karate was introduced in this country in the 1960s. While various systems have spread, today yet, the Kyokushin and Shōtōkan schools are extremely popular.

Born in 1967, Lars Andersen started Kyokushin karate when fourteen. His reason was simple: "I wanted to learn self-defense and get a stronger body."

In 1988 he was introduced to Johnny Jacobsen who had learn Isshin-ryū in the USA and turned his attention to Okinawa karate. Andersen recalls that the short movements, kata's applications and the close combat fighting of this style were attractive.

After training in the USA, he moved to the capital Copenhagen in 1991 and while working as a police officer, he started teaching karate in the police station. The following year, he opened a dōjō near the capital's airport and in 1996, he named it Jōshinkan.

When Andersen began Isshin-ryū, he bought all the videotapes of Isshin-ryū instructor Uezu Angi. When he visited Okinawa in 1996, he studied under Uezu and Uechi Tsuyoshi and thus decided to use the kanji 'Jō', another reading for 'Ue' in both Uezu and Uechi's names. 'Shin' is another reading for 'kokoro', or the heart. In 2001, Andersen established the Jōshinkan Isshin-ryū Karate Kobudō Association.

During the 4 years of the Balkan wars, Andersen was stationed in Kosovo as a United Nations international police officer and taught police instructor courses in the capital Pristina. He now teaches at the national police academy in Copenhagen.

Although busy in his everyday life, Andersen is always thinking about the popularization of karate. In 2010, together with two karate friends, he launched "Karate News", a website that disseminates information in Danish. He still edits the website.

The same year, he visited Okinawa again and met Tokumura Kenshō, head of the Ryūkyū Kobudō Tokushin-ryū. "I was immediately interested as the bō, sai and tonfa techniques were similar to the techniques inherited in Isshin-ryū."

Today a 7th dan in karate and 6th dan in kobudō, Andersen overviews 3 Isshin-ryū dōjō and 6 Tokushin-ryū dōjō in Denmark. He also teaches karate and kobudō in dōjō of different styles in Germany, Romania and Sweden. Altogether he teaches approximately 1,500 people.

With a strong sense of mission, Andersen continues to convey the charm of Okinawa karate and kobudō.

ドイツ西方面に位置するトリーア市は、紀元前4世紀にさかのぼる歴史と伝統を誇る。1957年生まれのヨアヘム・ラウプ氏は、その町の出身だ。

同年にドイツの空手パイオニア、故ジューグン・ジドル氏は同国で初の道場を開設した。松濤館で練習していたジドル氏の有名な弟子は、58年~60年米軍に徴兵されて西ドイツにいた歌手エルビス・プレスリーだという。

その後61年に誕生したドイツ空手連盟は現在、約16万の会員が登録する。沖縄空手、古武道の支部組織は20余も存在している。

ラウプ氏は12歳の頃松濤館の道場に入門したが、直後に、米軍を退役してトリーア市に移住した米国人、沖縄松林流系の有名空手家ウイリアム・マーシュ氏に弟子入りした。「ダイナミックな空手に魅了された」と氏は思い出す。空手のルーツを探るラウプ氏は、76年にはフランスで指導していた小林流の知念賢祐氏に師事し、78年トリーア市で「白鷺道場」を開設した。

転換期は81年、初めて空手の本場・沖縄を訪問。知念氏を通じて氏は、小林流志道館の故宮平勝哉氏に師事した。真の道と師匠と出会ったラ

デュッセルドルフ道場で指導するラウプ氏(右)=提供
Laupp (right) teaching at the Dusseldorf dōjō.

2017年06月25日

㉓ ドイツ

自我抑え 厳しく稽古

白鷺道場

ウプ氏は、ドイツに戻り稽古に励んだ。その鍛錬が認められ91年、ドイツ志道館支部長に任命され、本格的な普及に挑んだ。

非行少年教育者であった氏は、96年から空手を専門職とし、2007年には、230キロ離れているデュッセルドルフで「沖縄小林流志道館ヨーロッパセンター」を設置し、毎週その町に出向いた。

現在、氏が指導するこの2道場のほかに、ドイツに8支部、スイスとギリシャに各2支部、オランダに1支部がある。15年、九段に昇段したラウプ氏の下で800人余が小林流志道館の空手を学ぶ。

03年、あるインタビューでラウプ氏はこのように語った。「海を一回だけ見ても、理解できない。海とその法則を理解するには、短い間だけだと、波しか見えない。長く海を見て、海に没頭するとひと目で見えなかった万の細部の豊富で新たな世界が開かれる。武道も同様です」。きっと、沖縄の美しい海と空手が影響を与えたのだろう。

最初の師であったマーシュ氏からは「敬意を表し厳しい稽古をする」ということを教わったラウプ氏。最上級の稽古が最強の空手家をつくるのだから、自信があっても自我を抑えることが大切。糸満の白銀堂にある「意地ぬ出じらぁ手引き」のような思想だ。

Trier is a city boasting a history and tradition dating back to the 4th century BC. Born in 1957, this is where Joachim Laupp is from.

It is said that that year, German karate pioneer Jürgen Seydel of Shōtōkan opened the country's first dōjō. One of his famous disciple was Elvis Presley who, drafted in the military in 1958-60, was stationed in West-Germany. The German Karate Federation was established in 1961 and now, it has about 160,000 members registered.

Laupp entered a Shōtōkan dōjō at the age of 12, but soon after became a student of William Marsh, a famous Matsubayashi-ryū practitioner who retired from the US military and moved to Trier. "I was fascinated by his dynamic karate," he recalls. In 1976, as he explored the roots of karate, Laupp studied with Shōrin-ryū instructor Chinen Kenyū, and opened the Shirasagi Dōjō in Trier in 1978.

Published on 2017/6/25

㉓ Germany

Shirasagi Dōjō

Controlling the ego and practicing sternly

The turning point occurred in 1981 when he visited Okinawa for the first time. Through Chinen, he trained under Miyahira Katsuya of the Shōrin-ryū Shidōkan. Having found his true way and a master, Laupp deepened his practice and in 1991, as his efforts were recognized, he was appointed as the head of the German Shidōkan branch.

First a juvenile delinquent educator, Laupp has been a karate professional since 1996. In 2007, he also set up the Okinawa Shōrin-ryū Shidōkan Europe Center in Dusseldorf, and since travels there every week to teach.

Currently, in addition to his two dōjō, there are 8 branches in Germany, 2 in Switzerland and Greece, and one in the Netherlands. More than 800 people study karate under Laupp, who was promoted to 9th dan in 2015.

In an interview in 2003, Laupp said, "If you look at the sea only once, you can't understand it. To understand the sea and its laws, if you look only for a short time, you can only see the waves. If you look at the sea for a long time and immerse yourself in it, a new world opens up with a wealth of details you wouldn't have seen at a glance. It is the same for martial arts. I'm sure that the beautiful sea and karate of Okinawa have had a great influence on me."

From William Marsh, Laupp learned to "be respectful and train hard." Even if confident, it is important to control one's ego as a high level of training creates strong karateka. It's the same idea as the one found in Itoman's Hakugindō shrine: "When your temper rises, lower your fists."

2020年10月11日

㉔ドイツ

沖縄武術 真理を追究

大城道場ドレスデン

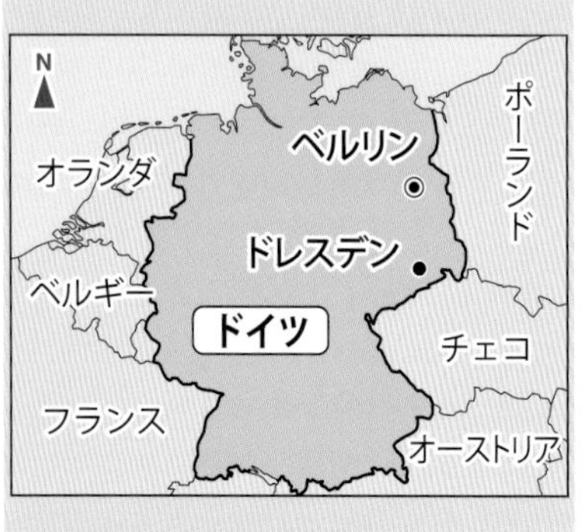

ペルー出身のロベルト・ロメロ氏(52)は、10代のころ松濤館系の道場に入門し、空手の手ほどきを受けた。1988年に東ドイツで進学するための奨学金を得て、ライプチヒに行きドイツ語を学び始めた。空手を続けようと道場を探したが、当時ソビエト連邦占領域では空手が禁じられており、一人で稽古に励んだ。

翌年、ザクセン州のフライベルクに移り、大学に入学、地盤工学を学んだ。そこで、学生が隠れて稽古をすると聞き、稽古会に参加した。「メンバーは本から空手を学んでいた。稽古後、私が経験者と分かった部員から頼まれて空手を教えるようになった」とロメロ氏は振り返る。

90年ドイツ再統一を迎えると、空手が一般に認められた。ロメロ氏は複数の松濤館系の日本人指導者の下で稽古に励み、94年卒業後、空手のプロになることを決断。だが、自らの空手に疑問を感じていたロメロ氏は2001年にインターネットで、島派松林流と山根流棒術を指導する琉球武術研究同友会の代表大城利弘氏の存在を知り、同系主催のセミナーに参加した。

「同年、私は自分の空手のクライシスを経験した。大城先生のセミナーに行く前に、ある松濤館系のセミナーで鉄騎初段という型を練習した。数カ月後、先生のセミナーで同じ型の原型であるナイハンチ初段を教授された。そこでは2時間の修行で松濤館空手の20年間の修行と同じくらい学べた。先生は、明瞭に生体力学の原理でもある沖縄武術の原理を指導している」とロメロ氏は分析する。

道場のメンバーとロメロ氏(前列左から4人目)=大城道場ドレスデン(提供)
Romero (fourth from the left in the front row) with his members at the Dresden dōjō.

ロメロ氏は島派松林流に転じ、後に棒術も習い始めた。「最初、自分の空手にとって古武道の研究は不要と思ったが、空手を理解するには棒術は欠かせないと気づき、山根流も始めた」と研究の意義を説明した。

松林流5段、古武術3段であるロメロ氏は現在、ドレスデンに開設した「大城道場ドレスデン」で指南している。そこでは、子ども約250人と大人70人が沖縄の武術を学ぶ。平日の道場指導のほか、週末はドイツにある同友会加盟15余の道場を訪れ指導に励んでいる。さらにスペイン、オーストリア、ロシアの同友会ヨーロッパメンバーとは、少なくとも年に一度は合同で練習している。

ロメロ氏は、空手を正しく習練すれば、健康法にもつながると考えている。「肩を緩め、上半身と下半身を分けて、重力を尊重し、物事を一方的に見てはいけない」という大城氏の教えを守り、沖縄の武術の研究に専心する。

Roberto Romero (52) from Peru entered a Shōtōkan dōjō when he was a teenager and learned the basics of karate. Earning a scholarship to go study in East Germany, he moved to Leipzig in 1988 and began learning the German language. There, he searched for a club to continue karate but at that time, karate was banned in the German Democratic Republic, and Romero practiced alone.

The following year, he was sent to Freiberg, Saxony, where he entered university and studied geotechnical engineering. Hearing that some students were training karate secretly at the university, he joined a training session. "The students had learned karate from a book.

Published on 2020/10/11

24 Germany

Ōshiro Dōjō Dresden

Pursuing the truth in Okinawan martial arts

After training, as they realized I was more experienced, they asked me to teach them karate," Romero recalls.

With the reunification of Germany in 1990, karate was officially allowed. Romero practiced under several Shōtōkan Japanese instructors and after graduating in 1994, he decided to become a karate professional. In 2001, he accidentally found out about Ōshiro Toshihiro of the Ryūkyū Bujutsu Kenkyū Dōyūkai (RBKD), an instructor of Shima-ha Matsubayashi-ryū and Yamanni-ryū bōjutsu and joined one of his seminar.

"In 2001, I had a karate crisis. Just before I met Ōshiro sensei, I was at a seminar with a Shōtōkan instructor and trained the kata Tekki Shodan. A few months later, I attended a seminar with Ōshiro sensei, where he was teaching the original version of this kata, Naifanchi Shodan. At that seminar, I learned in two hours of training as much as I had learned in 20 years of Shōtōkan training. Ōshiro sensei clearly teaches the principles of Okinawan martial arts, which also represent the principles of biomechanics."

Romero switched to Shima-ha Matsubayashi-ryū and later began to learn bōjutsu, the technique of the staff. "At first, I thought that I would not need kobudō for my personal practice. But then, I quickly understood that one needs to practice bōjutsu in order to understand karate and I started Yamanni-ryū, too."

A 5th dan in Matsubayashi-ryū and a 3rd dan of kobujutsu, Romero currently instructs at his Ōshiro Dōjō Dresden. There, about 250 children and 70 adults learn Okinawan martial arts. In addition to weekdays' instruction, he visits the 17 chapters affiliated with the RBKD in Germany on weekends and at least once a year travels to Spain, Austria and Russia to teach.

Romero sees karate as a good form of health protection, if practiced properly. Valuing Ōshiro's teachings that are "to relax the shoulders, separate your body, respect gravity and question what the eyes see," he concentrates his practice on the study of Okinawan martial arts.

2021年10月10日

㉕ ドイツ

和太鼓も並行し研究

無限道場

ドイツの都市ミュールハイム・アン・デア・ルールには、沖縄空手・古武道と和太鼓を普及する道場がある。「無限道場」の主ライナー・シュメーリング氏（53）は、15歳で柔術や少林寺拳法を習い、1991年に松濤館系の空手を学んだ。

常に物事の根底に到達し、さまざまな見解、文化、視点などを知ることに興味を持つ氏は、数年後、空手のルーツを探り、98年に日本文化の授業も受講した。

訪沖の希望を講師に打ち明けると、89年からドイツを含む世界各地で芸能公演を開催する沖縄文化民間交流協会の玉城正保会長に紹介された。98年10月1日に那覇空港に到着したシュメーリング氏は、玉城氏と面会し比嘉稔氏の小林流究道館へ案内された。初の来沖で3カ月滞在したシュメーリング氏は、那覇市壺屋にある究道館で空手を学び、沖縄の文化を経験した。↗

感慨を受けた氏は、帰国後、究道館をモデルに道場開設の準備を進め、2002年、門弟のハイケ・オプラ氏と共に「無限道場」を開館。オープン以降同館では、沖縄空手と古武道のほか、中国武術の太極拳なども指導している。自然療法医でもあるシュメーリング氏は、健康法でもある沖縄と中国

シュメーリング氏（右端）、オプラ氏（右から2人目）と門弟たち（提供）
Schmäring (far right) and Oprach (second from right) with some of their students.

の武術の類似点に興味を持ち、空手と並行して中国の武術を研究していると解説する。

現在、大人と子ども合わせて約150人が7段のシュメーリング氏と6段のオプラ氏の下で武道を研究する。

世界中、さまざまな国の武術または日本の文化を習う空手家は珍しくない。共同道場主のシュメーリング氏とオプラ氏も例外ではなく、2006年から空手と調和のできる芸能を求め、和太鼓を始めた。

14年の訪沖の際に、和太鼓奏者の金剌凌大氏に出会い、彼のスタイルに惹（ひ）かれ本格的の和の音の旅を始めた。後に、究道館のモットー「究道無限」をコンセプトに太鼓集団「無限太鼓」を立ち上げた。「伝統の太鼓は空手と共通点が多い。例えば、しっかりした立ち方と腹の使い方。両手で太鼓を打つことは、巻き藁（わら）を突く感覚に似ている。空手や太鼓を通して、体のバランスと対称的な能力を養う」と、両芸の研究に勤（いそ）しむシュメーリング氏は分析する。

戦うためではない空手。「人生で何度も直面しなければならない日々の苦労や闘いは、空手の練習を通してより耐えられるようになる」と氏は信じる。他人と道場で得た経験は、人生に応用しなければ価値はないと続ける。人間形成と社会貢献がやはり空手の最も重要な目的だ。

Published on 2021/10/10

25 Germany 

Mugen Dōjō

Studying wadaiko in parallel to karate

In Mülheim an der Ruhr, there is a dōjō that teaches Okinawa karate and various other arts. The head of the Mugen Dōjō, Rainer Schmäring (53), learned jūjutsu and Shōrinji Kenpō from the age of 15 before starting Shōtōkan karate in 1991.

Interested in learning about different views, cultures and perspectives, Schmäring started exploring the origins of karate a few years later and attended a Japanese culture course in 1998.

Revealing his desire to travel to Okinawa to his instructor, he was introduced to Tamaki Masayasu, the chairman of the Okinawa Culture Association, a group which had been holding performances around the world, including Germany, since 1989. Arriving at Naha Airport on October 1, 1998, Schmäring met with Tamaki and was guided to Higa Minoru's Shōrin-ryū Kyūdōkan. Staying for three months, Schmäring experienced both karate at the Tsuboya dōjō and Okinawan culture.

Returning home deeply impressed, he worked on opening a dōjō with the Kyūdōkan as model and in 2002, he opened the Mugen Dōjō with one of his student, Heike Oprach. Since its opening, the dōjō offers Okinawa karate and kobudō classes as well as Chinese martial arts like Tai Chi. Schmäring, who is also a naturopath, explains that he has always been interested in the similarities between Okinawa and Chinese martial arts, and thus studies both in parallel.

Today, about 150 adults and children train under Schmäring and Oprach who are respectively 7th and 6th dan.

It is not uncommon for karateka in the world to learn another martial art or a Japanese cultural art. Schmäring and Oprach are no exception. In 2006, they started playing Japanese drums in search of a performing art that could be performed harmoniously with karate.

When visiting Okinawa in 2014, they met Kanazashi Ryōta, a professional drum player, and charmed by his style, they began a full-fledged journey on the path of Japanese music. Later, they launched the taiko group "Kyūdō Taiko," based on the Kyūdōkan's concept of Kyūdō Mugen. "Traditional taiko has a lot in common with karate. The grounded stances work from the hara and you hit with 2 short sticks. The Taiko responds and gives feedback similar to a makiwara. Through karate and taiko, one can nurture body balance and symmetrical abilities," analyzes Schmäring.

Karate is not for fighting. "I think the everyday struggles that each of us have to face over and over again in life can become more bearable through karate practice" says he. He goes on saying that the experiences that one has in the dōjō together with others are not really worth anything if you do not succeed in transferring them to daily life outside the dōjō. Character building and social contribution are indeed the most important purposes of karate.

人口5百万人のノルウェー王国では、スキーやサッカーが盛んなスポーツ。数十万人の登録者がいるそれらの連盟に比べて、武術愛好者は4万人で、そのうち空手家は1万5千人だ。

そう指摘するのは、同国第2の都市で千年の歴史を誇るベルゲン市生まれのオレビョーン・テュフテダル氏(64)。氏は、同国で数少ない沖縄空手の指導者の一人。

本格的に空手を始めたのは1970年代後半の大学在学中。当時、松濤館系を習った。93年、同大学で道場「BSI空手」を立ち上げた。目的が技の研究と空手のルーツの探求だったため、自然に沖縄空手に目を向けた。

運良く同年に、松林流の開祖長嶺将真氏の洋書『沖縄空手の真髄』を発見し、沖縄空手の基礎の哲学・倫理・技術的な側面を知ることができた。しかし、書籍からは真髄を習えないと感じ、松林流系のセミナーに参加した。

「自然な立ち方、スピードとパワーの出し方、美しくて複雑な型に魅了された。また、生涯を通じて習える空手で、練習生のサイズや強度に関係なく効果的であることも興味深かった」と氏は解説する。99年に松林流2代目で世界中を回り指導していた故長嶺高兆氏を招きセミナーを開き、後に正

空手の技を指導するテュフテダル氏(右)=提供
Tuftedal (right) instructing karate.

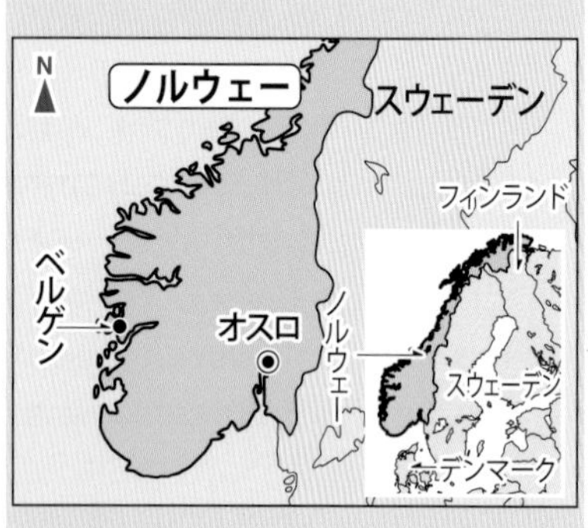

2017年08月27日

26 ノルウェー

自己と戦い 人生探究

BSI空手

式に弟子入りした。

2005年テュフテダル氏は、世界松林流空手道連盟の下でヨーロッパ協会を立ち上げ、会長を任命された。現在ノルウェー2道場のほか、ヨーロッパ5カ国にある11の道場で、松林流の修練が行われている。

プロの道を選ばずベルゲン大学や同市政で情報専門士の仕事に勤め、今年退職をしたテュフテダル氏は、「BSI空手」道場では30人程に指南している。

「西洋の文化はだんだん表面的になり、精神的な深度と濃度が失われている。共に座る人は共に人生を体験せずスマートフォンに集中する。素晴らしい贈り物である人生を実感するには苦労と集中力が必要。空手について長嶺先生は“生死の研究”と言っていた。日々の稽古を通じて身につく知恵と訓練で人間は人生の壊れやすさと大切さを理解できる」とテュフテダル氏。

「最近ヨーロッパでは、伝統空手への興味が増している」とも感じている。9月下旬には、松林流の平良慶孝会長を招いてセミナーを開く。10月には、沖縄を訪れる予定だ。

開祖の長嶺氏が残した心構え「空手は自己との戦いにして　一生のマラソン……これはただ創造の努力あるのみ」のように稽古と研究は無限に続く。

Published on 2017/8/27

26 Norway

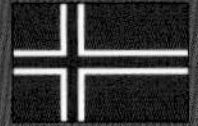

BSI Karate

Fighting with yourself and exploring life

With a population of 5 million, skiing and football are the most popular sports in Norway. In comparison, there are 40,000 martial arts enthusiasts in the country, of whom 15,000 are karateka.

The one who says so is Ole-Bjørn Tuftedal (64). Born in Bergen, he is one of the few instructors of Okinawa karate in the country.

Tuftedal seriously started karate while in college in the late 1970s, learning Shōtōkan karate. In 1993, he established the BSI Karate dōjō in his university. Since his purposes were to study the technique and explore the roots of karate, he naturally turned to Okinawa karate.

Fortunately at the same period, he discovered the book "The Essence of Okinawan Karate-Do" written by the founder of Matsubayashi-ryū, Nagamine Shōshin. This was obviously a very profound explanation of both the philosophical, ethical and technical aspects of the fundamentals of Okinawan karate. However, as one cannot learn a martial art from looking at pictures or reading, Tuftedal looked for a Matsubayashi-ryū instructor and a period of searching and studies followed.

"I was particularly impressed by the effective, natural stances, the way they made it possible to generate speed and force, and by the beautiful and complex kata. It also seemed to be a style anyone could train all life, and be effective, regardless of size and strength." In 1999, Tuftedal organized a seminar inviting the late Nagamine Takayoshi to Bergen and later became his student.

In December 2005 at Nagamine's request, Tuftedal launched the European association under the World Matsubayashi-ryū Karatedō Association and was appointed chairman. In addition to two Norwegian dōjō, 11 dōjō in Germany, Ireland, England, the Netherlands and Spain are practicing Matsubayashi-ryū karate as part of the association.

On what karate brought him, he says, "Western culture becomes more and more shallow, just surface, the mind fluttering from moment to moment without depth and concentration. People sit together but focus on their smartphones, rather than experiencing life in depth. Hard work and the ability to concentrate are important to experience the great gift that life is. 'Karate is the art of death and living,' Nagamine sensei used to say. Through the knowledge and discipline learned by daily practice, one understands how fragile and precious life is."

A retired information and communications technology specialist, Tuftedal trains and instructs about 30 people at the BSI Karate dōjō, following the attitude stressed by Nagamine Shōshin: "Karatedō may be referred to as the conflict within yourself, or a life-long marathon which can be won only through your own creative efforts".

ハンガリーで最も日当たりの良い街として知られるハイドゥーソボスロー市生まれのラズロ・キス氏（51）は、1982年に極真会館館長大山倍達氏のドキュメンタリー映画を見て、故郷で唯一の道場に入門。そこで松濤館空手を始めた。

同国での空手歴は70年代前半にさかのぼるという。72年に極真空手、73年に松濤館空手のセミナーが首都ブダペストで行われ、83年に剛柔流も紹介された。現在の空手人口は4~5万人に及ぶ。

キス氏の最初の指導者が空手から離れ、91年に兵役を終えた後、同門により道場の再編を求められて指導を始めた。後に道場は「天心空手道場」に改名された。

97年頃、東恩納盛男氏が出演した英国BBC制作「The Way of The Warrior」を見て感銘を受けたキス氏は「当時私は有段者で、すでに指導していたが、この番組を見て、日本の空手と沖縄空手の違いにびっくりした」と語る。2000年以降、キス氏は剛柔流の道を歩み始めることになる。

最初は東ヨーロッパで普及していた本土系の剛柔会の数人の高段者に師事した。後にキス氏は沖縄剛柔流に目を向けた。世界で指導する東恩納氏や高弟の中村哲二氏のセミナーを受け、

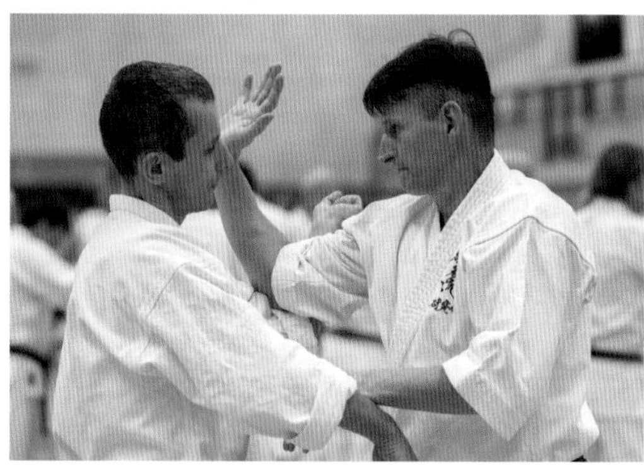
分解の研究に取り組むキス氏（右）＝提供
Kiss (right) working on an application.

2019年11月10日

㉗ハンガリー

剛柔流の奥義を探求

天心空手道場

2013年、宮里栄一氏の順道館で鍛えられた平良正次氏に出会った。

平良氏は、沖縄剛柔流研究会の会長を務め、世界15カ国にある50支部余で定期的に分解セミナーを開いている。

「型にこだわり実戦的な技を指導する平良先生の空手は簡単ではない。心を開き、謙虚でなければ、続けられない。しかし、コードを破り、方法論を変えることによって間違いなく学べるものがある」とキス氏は揺るがぬ信念を抱く。

2015年にキス氏も同研究会ハンガリー支部長に任命され、翌年には剛柔流4段に昇段した。

ハンガリーでは、空手だけで生計を立てる者はほとんどいないという。現在キス氏は地区行政の運転手として働きながら、小さな町道場「天心空手道場」で子どもと大人合わせて30数人に剛柔流を指南している。「この人数だと適切に教えることができる」と説明した。

禅も修行するキス氏は、60年代後半ヨーロッパで禅を広めた弟子丸泰仙氏の教えを心に刻んでいる。

「身体を鍛え、スタミナと持久力を養え。しかし、それらをつかさどる競争と権力の精神は良くありません。その精神は人生のゆがんだビジョンを反映する。武道の根源はそこにはありません」

空手の奥義を求め、18年に夢だった訪沖をかなえたキス氏は、自覚の旅である空手の道をさらに進む。

Published on 2019/11/10

27 Hungary

Ten-Shin Karate Dōjō

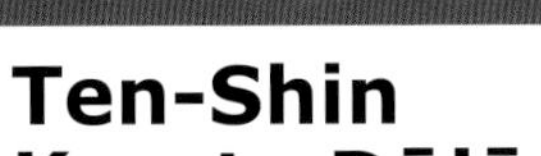

Exploring the inner secrets of Gōjū-ryū

Born in Hajdúszoboszló, László Kiss (51) joined the only karate dōjō in his hometown after watching a documentary about Kyokushin Kaikan in 1982.

Karate in Hungary was introduced in the early 1970s when Kyokushin and Shōtōkan karate seminars were held in Budapest. Gōjū-ryū was brought in the country in 1983. Today, the karate population ranges from 40,000 to 50,000 people.

His first Shōtōkan instructor having quitted karate and Kiss having done his military service in 1991, several people came to him asking him to reorganize his hometown dōjō. That's when he started teaching. Later on, the dōjō was renamed Ten-Shin Karate Dōjō.

Around 1997, Kiss saw the documentary "The Way of the Warrior" on Higaonna Morio which impressed him a lot. "At that time, I was already a black belt and I was teaching, but what I saw in that movie simply amazed me and made me realize that Okinawa karate was very different from Japanese karate." Around the year 2000, Kiss started to investigate Gōjū-ryū.

At first, he studied with several experts of mainland Gōjū-kai which was popular in Eastern Europe. Then, he switched to Okinawa Gōjū-ryū, participating first in seminars with Higaonna and his assistant Nakamura Tetsuji to finally meet in 2013 one of Miyazato Eiichi's top students, Taira Masaji.

Taira, the head of the Okinawa Gōjū-ryū Karatedō Kenkyūkai, regularly holds seminars in some of his 50 branches located in 15 countries around the world.

"Sticking close to the kata and teaching practical skills, Taira sensei's karate is not the easy way. You have to be very open-minded and humble if you want to progress. But it's definitely worth to break the code and change the paradigm," believes Kiss.

In 2015, Kiss was appointed as the head of the Hungarian branch of the Kenkyūkai and was promoted to 4th dan in Gōjū-ryū the following year.

In Hungary, very few people make a living from karate alone. Nowadays, Kiss works as a driver for the district office while he teaches karate to more than 30 children and adults. As he says, "With this headcount, I am able to teach properly."

As he also practices Zen, Kiss has engraved in his heart the teachings of Taisen Deshimaru, who spread Zen in Europe in the late 1960s. "Train the body and develop stamina and endurance. But the spirit of competition and power that presides over them is not good, it reflects a distorted vision of life. The root of the martial arts is not there."

In search of the inner secrets of karate, Kiss, who fulfilled his dream of visiting Okinawa in 2018, keeps walking the path of karate, which he believes is a journey of self-knowledge.

作家トーベ・ヤンソンの「ムーミン」シリーズやサンタクロースの国で知られ、冬は氷点下が続く北欧フィンランド。人口約550万人、人口密度は1平方キロメートルあたりわずか16人の共和国だ。

フィンランド空手連盟の会員数は約6千人と言われる。最も普及している流派は、船越義珍氏に師事した柔術家の大塚博紀氏を開祖とする和道流。1967年に、欧米各国で同系統の普及活動に励んだ鈴木辰夫氏がフィンランドに初めて空手道を紹介した。

カリ・クーシスト氏（60）はタンペレに生まれた。14歳の頃、故郷にある唯一の空手道場に入門。当時タンペレ大学の日本人留学生が本土系の剛柔流を教えていた。留学生が帰国すると、スポーツ系の組手を中心とした稽古が続いたとクーシスト氏は振り返る。↗

10年後、空手のルーツを求めていたクーシスト氏はスウェーデンのストックホルム在住で沖縄剛柔流を指導する鈴木大海氏に出会った。84年から2008年まで鈴木氏の道場を訪れ学び、指導者を招待して国内セミナーも開催した。現在は沖縄剛柔流空手道協会フィンランドの代表として、スペインで指導する同協会ヨーロッパ本部長・翁長良一氏に師事している。

セミナーで指導に当たったクーシスト氏（中央）とフィンランドのメンバー＝提供
Kuusisto (center) and some Finnish members at a seminar.

2021年01月10日

㉘ フィンランド

極寒の北欧 常に挑戦

学生道場

指導者がスウェーデンにいても空手の修行を諦めなかった理由を尋ねると、クーシスト氏は93年の初訪沖の時を思い返す。那覇市にある当時同協会本部の順道館の宮里栄一館長は、フィンランドに指導者が不在、スウェーデンの鈴木氏を訪ねるのも困難と理解し、次の言葉を送ったという。

《昔は沖縄でも同じだった。距離はそれほど遠くはなかったが、現代のような交通手段はなく、弟子は道場に来るまで数週間から数カ月かかることもあった》

この大切な教えを心に刻んだクーシスト氏は30年間以上金融業界で働き、出張なども多かったが、どこでもできる空手の稽古は休まなかった。

26年前に開設された「学生道場」は、タンペレ工科大学の敷地内にある。当初はクーシスト氏の弟子で同大学の学生がクラブを開いていた。後に95年に帰郷したクーシスト氏が首席師範となった。「国内に本格的な道場は少なく、市町村のスポーツ施設等を利用して活動する団体が多い」（クーシスト氏）。現在国内の3道場で約100人が6段のクーシスト氏の下で剛柔流の流祖・宮城長順氏の空手を学ぶ。

「自分自身に挑戦を与え、学ぶこと」をモットーに空手の道を歩むクーシスト氏。空手でより良い人が育つという意義も併せ持ち、指導と普及に励んでいる。

In a country known for Moomins and Santa Claus, the number of members registered with the Finnish Karate Federation is said to be about 6,000.

The most popular system in the country is Wadō-ryū as in 1967, Suzuki Tatsuo, who worked hard to spread Wadō-ryū in Western countries, introduced karate to Finland for the first time.

Kari Kuusisto (60) was born in Tampere city. Around the age of 14, he entered the only karate dōjō in his hometown where a Japanese student at the Tampere University was teaching Japanese Gōjū-ryū. When the student returned to Japan, Kuusisto recalls that the training continued focusing mainly on sport oriented kumite.

Published on 2021/1/10

28 Finland

Gakusei Dōjō

Challenges in the severe Scandinavian weather

Ten years later, as he was looking for the roots of his karate, Kuusisto met Suzuki Hiromi who lives and teaches Okinawa Gōjū-ryū in Stockholm, Sweden. From 1984 to 2008, he visited Suzuki's dōjō to learn and invited instructors for seminars. Kuusisto is currently the head of the Finish chapter of the Okinawa Gōjū-ryū Karatedō Association (OGKK) and studies with Ōnaga Ryōichi, the head of OGKK Europe who lives in Spain.

When asked why he didn't give up although his instructor was in Sweden, Kuusisto recalls his first visit to Okinawa in 1993. At that time, the head of the OGKK and the Jundōkan, Miyazato Eiichi, knew that Kuusisto and his members had no instructor in Finland and that it was difficult to visit Suzuki in Sweden. He then offered them the following words. "In the old days it was the same in Okinawa. Distances were not as long but there were no modern ways of transport. Sometimes it took several weeks or even months until long distance students could be training again at their sensei's dōjō."

Keeping this important teaching in mind, Kuusisto, who worked in the financial industry for more than 30 years and had to make many business trips, never stopped practicing karate.

Established 26 years ago, the Gakusei Dōjō is located on the Tampere Technical University premises and was initially opened by a student of Kuusisto. When Kuusisto returned home in 1995, he became the chief instructor of the club. He explains that "In Finland, we have very few actual dōjō. Karate clubs mainly rent training premises from the city sport centers, schools, etc." At the moment, about 100 people train Gōjū-ryū in 3 clubs under the guidance of 6th dan Kuusisto.

Kuusisto walks the path of karate with the motto "Challenge yourself and learn." As this maxim also has the significance of nurturing better people through karate, he keeps on working hard to teach and disseminate the spirit of Okinawa karate.

新大統領マクロン氏を選んだばかりのフランスは、実は、空手王国でもある。2016年現在、仏空手連盟は25万人余の会員を誇り、そのうち約20万人は空手、残りは養正館武道、中国の武術、クラヴ・マガ（イスラエル式護身術）などの関連武術を学ぶ。

フランスに空手が紹介されたのは、1950年代初期、仏人故アンリ・プレ氏の活動にまでさかのぼる。後に57年から望月拡雄氏など本土の指導者が渡仏し、本土系の空手を広めた。現在それらの空手は、フランスの空手家人口の90％を占めている。

同国には約20の沖縄空手を普及する団体が存在する。沖縄県出身の師範もフランスを拠点にヨーロッパ各地で普及活動に取り組んでいる。小林流・古武道の知念賢祐氏を除く、島袋幸信（上地流）、安谷屋政助（小林流・古武道）、大城善栄（剛柔流・古武道）の各氏は仏空手連盟に加盟し、「日本人エキスパート」として認められており、大城氏は、同連盟の剛柔流責任者でもある。

54年那覇市生まれの大城氏は、16歳から剛柔流を宮里栄一そして比嘉世吉の両氏に師事した。現在尚道館の最高師範、喜友名朝有氏（86）の下で技を磨き研究を続けている。古武道では又吉眞

武道祭で白鶴拳を披露する大城善栄氏＝提供（Denis Boulanger / FFKDA） Ōshiro Zenei demonstrating white crane fist at a martial arts festival (photo from Denis Boulanger/FFKDA)

2017年05月14日

㉙フランス

不撓不屈
心と技探究

尚道館

豊氏に師事。現在、空手・古武道8段である。

大城氏は78年に、フランスとドイツを訪問した後、一時帰郷。しかし沖縄で暮らすと仕事をしながらの稽古となり時間に制約が出てくることから、86年に再びフランスに渡り、移住を果たした。「沖縄剛柔流、古武道を広めるのはもちろんですが、私自身が空手、古武道を納得いくまで稽古したかった」という。

さらに大城氏は、パリ尚道館を拠点に、フランス国内20支部・約1500人、外国8カ国の支部・約800人の弟子を数える組織を築いた。年間25回の尚道館関係セミナーに関わり、連盟責任者として段位審査や講習会も担う。

だが、2013年2月に、脊柱管狭窄症の手術をした結果、大城氏は一時歩けなくなった。それでも、武術で築いた不撓不屈（ふとうふくつ）の精神と剛柔流に欠かせない型「三戦（サンチン）」を通して復活を遂げた。「空手がなかったらできなかった」とコメントする。

20年に大城氏は沖縄に帰国する計画を立てているが、「私の仕事は、定年したから辞めるというわけにはいかないので半年沖縄、半年フランスに行き来する」と考えている。沖縄にいる間は「道場を開いて初心者を育てていくより、本場の先生方と技術や情報交換の場ができれば」という構想を持っている。国境を越えた沖縄空手と古武道の普及活動に終わりはない。

Published on 2017/5/14

㉙ France

Shōdōkan

Indomitably exploring the mind and technique

France is known as a karate kingdom. As of 2016, the French Karate Federation had 250,000 members, of which about 200,000 are karateka.

Karate was introduced in France in the early 1950s, dating back to the activities of the late Henri Plée. From 1957, Japanese instructors came to spread mainland Japanese karate and today, this karate makes up 90% of the French karate practitioners population.

There are about 20 organizations that spread Okinawa karate in France. Except for Chinen Kenyū who is not part of the Federation, Shimabukuro Yukinobu, Adaniya Seisuke, and Ōshiro Zenei are members of the French Karate Federation and recognized as "Japanese experts". Ōshiro is also the person in charge for Gōjū-ryū within the national federation.

Ōshiro was born in Naha City in 1954. From the age of 16, he studied Gōjū-ryū under Miyazato Eiichi and later on with Higa Seikichi. Currently, he continues his research under the supervision of the Shōdōkan's supreme instructor Kiyuna Chōyū (86 years old). For kobudō, he studied under Matayoshi Shinpō. Today, is an 8th dan in karate and kobudō.

After visiting France and Germany in 1978, Ōshiro returned home temporarily. But in Okinawa, he had to practice while working and his training time was limited, so he moved again to France in 1986 and established himself there. "Of course, I wanted to spread Okinawan martial arts, but I also wanted to practice as much as I wanted."

Ōshiro went on building an organization based in Paris, the Shōdōkan, which counts about 1,500 disciples in 20 branches in France and about 800 people in eight foreign countries. He teaches 25 seminars per year, and is also in charge of dan examinations and seminars as the head of the federation.

However, as a result of an operation for spinal canal stenosis in February 2013, Ōshiro was temporarily unable to walk. Even so, he was able to walk again through an indomitable spirit built by martial arts and the kata Sanchin that is indispensable in Gōjū-ryū. "I couldn't have done it without karate," he says.

Ōshiro plans to return to Okinawa in 2020, but he thinks that, "In my profession, I can't quit my job because I have reached retirement age, so I will keep going back and forth between Okinawa and France." In Okinawa, he has the idea that "Rather than opening a dōjō and raising beginners, I wish for a place to exchange skills and information with other local experts." Regardless of borders, there is no end to the promotion of Okinawa karate and kobudō.

2019年07月14日

㉚ フランス

研究に情熱 心技磨く

上地流

230年前の1789年7月14日、バスチーユ監獄襲撃が起こった。フランスの各市町村ではこの日、「パリ祭」と称した建国記念日を祝う。

フランス革命の発端から170年後の1959年に、ディディエ・ロルホ氏はブルターニュ地方の海軍基地があるブレスト市に生まれた。18歳で海軍に入隊し、26歳の時、和道流を継承する道場「山クラブ」に入門した。

82年には海上憲兵隊に移り、2018年まで36年間憲兵として勤めた。1987年に、転勤でパリ地域圏に移った際に、自宅から一番近い道場を探し、上地流の指導をしていた島袋幸信氏に弟子入りした。

「上地流の技の効率性と独特な鍛錬に魅了された。実用的な側面は、私が考える空手とマッチしている」とロルホ氏は同系統への熱い思いを語る。

特殊部隊でも学んだロルホ氏は、勤務の一環でボディーガードも務めた。職務中、空手を活用する機会があったかと問うと「ほとんどなかった。でも、空手の稽古は自信につながった。また、上地流の基礎であるサンチン立ちは、安定性と固定が絶対不可欠の射撃に有用になった」と振り返る。

ロルホ氏が所属するキャリエール=シュル=セーヌのスポーツクラブに空手部ができたのは71年。当初は松濤館の空手が指導されていたが、86年に島袋氏が指南役についた。師の下ロルホ氏は、28年前から部長を務め、空手と護身術を週3回指導している。道場では子ども37人、大人73人の合計110人が上地完文氏を流祖とする空手を学ぶ。フランス全土で約800人が同系統を学んでいるという。ロルホ氏が会長を務める欧州上地流空手道協会のメンバー1100人が、5カ国で島袋氏に師事している。

宜野湾市普天間の上地流宗家修武館で腕を磨くロルホ氏(右)=提供
Lohro (right) honing his skills at the Uechi-ryū Sōke Shūbukan in Futenma, Ginowan City.

ロルホ氏は、毎年下地康夫氏が開催している東京の国際大会で過去5回の優勝を誇る。自身が関わるフランス空手連盟の上地流杯も14年間で大きな大会に育った。

「尊敬としつけのほか、空手は左右分化と身振りの精度を子どもに教える。大人にとっては良好な物理的運動にもなれる」。スポーツが好きで常に競争心を燃やすロルホ氏は、空手の傍ら毎日体を鍛え、高強度のインターバル運動にも取り組んでいる。

ロルホ氏は沖縄にいる時、人々の歓迎ぶりと優しさで癒やされるという。仕事で「天国に一番近い島」仏領ニューカレドニアに2年間駐在したロルホ氏は「大好きなこの両島に類似点を感じる」と語る。

4代目宗家上地完尚氏により6段に昇段したロルホ氏は、空手の研究と親睦を深めるため、8月に7回目の訪沖を計画している。

230 years ago, on July 14, 1789, the storming of the Bastille occurred.

170 years after the beginning of the French Revolution, in 1959, Didier Lohro was born in Brest, a maritime city in Brittany. At the age of 18, he joined the Navy and at the age of 26, he entered the Yama Club, a dōjō that taught Wadō-ryū karate.

In 1982, Lohro moved to the Maritime Gendarmerie and served in the military police for 36 years until 2018. Transferred to Paris in 1987, he became a student of Shimabukuro Yukinobu, who was instructing Uechi-ryū. He recalls, "I was attracted by the effectiveness of the Uechi-ryū's techniques and its unique conditioning practice. This style's pragmatic aspect corresponded to the idea that I have of karate."

Published on 2019/7/14

㉚ France

Uechi-ryū

A passion for research, polishing mind and technique

In his work, Lohro also served as a bodyguard. When asked if he had the opportunity to utilize karate during his duties, he said, "I rarely had the occasion. However, karate's training brought me confidence. Furthermore, the Sanchin stance, the basis of Uechi-ryū, has been very useful for shooting, a skill in which stability and anchoring are absolutely essential."

The karate club to which Lohro belongs was established in Carrières-sur-Seine in 1971. Shōtōkan was initially the style practiced until Shimabukuro took over instruction in 1986. Since, Lohro has been the director of the section for 28 years and teaches karate and self-defense three times a week. At the dōjō, 37 children and 73 adults for a total of 110 people, study the karate of Uechi Kanbun. Approximately 800 people in France and 1,100 people in five European countries train under Shimabukuro, as members of the European Uechi-ryū Karatedō Association, a group Lohro chairs.

In the past, Lohro has won five times the annual international tournament organized in Tōkyō by Shimoji Yasuo and he has been a key figure in making the Uechi-ryū French Cup, sponsored by the French Karate Federation for the last 14 years, a big national event.

"In addition to respect and discipline, karate teaches children left-right lateralization and gesture accuracy. For adults, it can also be a good physical exercise." In love with sport, Lohro trains every day alongside to karate practicing Tabata and HIIT exercises.

When he is in Okinawa, Lohro says that the welcome and kindness of the Okinawan people is like a healing method. As he was stationed for two years in New Caledonia, the "island closest to heaven," he says "I feel similarities between these two islands I love."

Promoted to 6th dan by the 4th Sōke Uechi Sadanao, he plans to visit Okinawa for the 7th time in August in order to deepen his karate research and friendship with other karateka.

フランス南西にあるドルドーニュ県は、先史時代の有名のラスコー洞窟を擁する地方であり、世界三大珍味の一つフォアグラの産地でもある。都会から離れているが、同国で剛柔流が盛んな地域とも言える。

1974年、松濤館の空手を習っていたウイリ・フルシュ氏は、沖縄出身の渡口政吉氏の助手、内藤末吉氏と出会い、剛柔流尚礼館の空手を習い始め、その系統を広めた。

79年、当時17歳のパスカル・イベール氏はフルシュ氏の道場に入門した。85年、東恩納盛男氏の剛柔流を指導する同国支部長故ベーナー・クザン氏の技と迫力に魅了され転向した。

農業・森林生産技術者だったイベール氏は、仕事が忙しくなり、稽古が存分にできなくなったと感じ、早朝業務である清掃業に転業した。「週6日午前4時に起きて、仕事を終えて夜10時まで稽古した。きつかったが、空手はやめられなかった」と振り返る。

指導者になりたかったイベール氏は、再び学問に挑み、フランスでプロに欠かせない「スポーツ教育者国家免許」を取得した。「年数には関係なく、情熱を注げるものを仕事にできるのは、良いことだと思う」と語る。

型セーパイを指導するイベール氏(右端)=提供　Hivert (right) teaching the kata Sēpai.

2018年07月08日

㉛ フランス

困難打破 型反復に汗

アゴラスポー

94年にドルドーニュ県のコミューンブラザックで道場「アゴラスポー」を立ち上げた。現在、5歳から56歳まで約50人が剛柔流を学ぶ。また学校や企業にも指導を行っている。

活動を通じ、狙いは社会に通用する空手の「徳」を伝えること。実は若い時代は乱暴でけんか好きの青年だったという。空手を通してその悪い面を修正した。「静かな空間の中で、ヒーリングの基本技法であるイメージングを行い、再び目標に焦点を合わせることができ、日々の活動を分析することができる」と説く。

空手の素晴らしさについては「ルールに基づいて行われるスポーツと違って空手はゲームではない。相手に自分の体と人生をあずける。しかし、相手と信頼関係を築き、人と人の間の争いを解決できる知恵が生まれる。人としての意識、グループに対する意識、そこから生まれる交流と平和」と答えた。

2015年からイベール氏は、那覇市山下町にある「剛勇館」の新城安勇氏の下で研究を深め、古武道では、琉球古武道保存会の東江三和氏にも技術指導を受けてきた。「反復練習をすることで、出来ないことをやり通す事を体で覚えていく。だから型は、空手の宝物です」。この思いを心に刻んだイベール氏は、これからもフランスの豊かな自然が広がる地域で本場の空手を広め続ける。

Dordogne is home to the famous prehistoric Lascaux cave and to foie gras, said to be one of the world's three delicacies. And although far from the capital, Gōjū-ryū karate is quite popular in this region.

In 1974, Shōtōkan karateka Willy Fruchout met Naito Suekichi, an assistant to Okinawan Toguchi Seikichi, and he started practicing and popularizing the Gōjū-ryū Shōreikan system in the region and in France.

In 1979, then seventeen years old Pascal Hivert entered Fruchout's dōjō. In 1985, fascinated by the skill and power of the late Bernard Cousin, disciple of Higaonna Morio, he decided to change school.

Published on 2018/7/8

31 France

Agora Sport

Breaking through difficulties by repeating kata

Hivert, who was an agricultural and forest production engineer, felt that his work hindered his karate practice, so he changed to an early morning cleaning business. He recalls, "I woke up at 4 am 6 days a week, finished my work and practiced until 9-10 pm. It was hard, but I couldn't give up karate."

As he wanted to become a teacher, Hivert went back to studying and obtained the national licenses for sports educators, which are indispensable for sport professionals in France. He comments, "To associate passion and work seems to me to be a good thing, we do not count the hours and the years."

In 1994, Hivert launched the dōjō Agora Sport in the commune of Boulazac. Currently, about 50 people from 5 to 56 years of age learn Gōjū-ryū there.

Through his activities, his aim is to convey the virtues of karate that can be applied to the society. Young, he says that he was actually a very turbulent boy. He was able to fix his bad habits through karate. "In a quiet space, you can perform visualization, which is the basic technique of healing. Refocusing on your goals, you can analyze your daily activities," he explains.

Asked about the beauty of karate, he answers, "Unlike sports that are based on rules, karate is not a game. You put your body and life in the hands of your partners. However, this can build a relation of mutual trust, which can create a wisdom to solve conflicts. Exchange and peace are born from awareness as a person and consciousness for the group."

Since 2015, Hivert has been deepening his research under Shinjō Anyū, head of the Gōyūkan in Naha City. In kobudō, he studies with Tōe Mitsukazu of the Ryūkyū Kobudō Preservation Society.

"By practicing repeatedly, one will learn physically to do what he/she couldn't do. That is why kata are the treasure of karate." With this in mind, Hivert will continue to spread authentic karate in the rich natural surroundings of France.

2021年02月14日

㉜フランス

平和の武芸 真理探究

上地流・孝武流古武道

多くのフランス人空手家のように、1965年オセール生まれのジャン・スミス氏は、14歳の頃に同国で最も普及する流派、松濤館の空手を始めた。その後パリに移り、日本の古武道を伝授する香取神道流の武術も習った。

研究するうちに、スミス氏は沖縄の武器術にも興味を持ち、89年に6カ月間沖縄に滞在した。空手着メーカーの守礼堂を通して又吉眞豊氏を紹介され、古武道を習った。また高弟の金城孝氏から武器術と上地流系の硬軟流も学んだ。

「金城先生には武道への情熱と献身があった。熱意あふれるコミュニケーションで武道の心と実践を伝えていた」とスミス氏は振り返る。

帰国後パリで道場を開き、10年間古武道を知念賢祐氏、上地流を島袋幸信氏から習った。

娘が生まれ、首都での生活に疲れを感じたスミス氏は地方に移住。最終的に南仏トゥールーズから南30キロにある人口1300人ほどの小さなコミューン、モザックに定住した。そこで指圧と鍼灸(しんきゅう)の治療と指導で生計を立て、同時に沖縄の武道の普及に励んでいる。

30年間にわたる島袋氏の指導の他にスミス氏は64年にフランス王者、72年に第2回世界空手道選手権大会で団体優勝に輝き、長年、空手の効能等を研究するギー・ソヴァン氏にも師事した。

スミス氏(前列中央)と古武道を学ぶ弟子たち=提供　Smith (center in the front row) and his disciples studying kobudō.

古武道を諦めなかったスミス氏は、第1回沖縄空手国際大会(2018年開催)の際、2000年に孝武流を発足していた金城孝氏と再会し、弟子入りした。

「金城先生は自身の武術の変化を説明してくれた。それを受けて、私の研究と完全に一致していたと感じた。そしてソヴァン氏と金城先生の間の類似点に驚いた」

81歳の金城氏と78歳のソヴァン氏の空手の道は一度も交差しなかった。しかし両氏は「力は地面から全身に伝わること・決して後退しないこと・攻防一体など、同じ原理を持つ指導者だ」とスミス氏は見る。

現在スミス氏はモザックの道場で40人、フランス全土で200人に指南する。さらに孝武流古武道のヨーロッパ代表に任命され、6道場で古武道を指導する。

長い武術交流を通じ、文化の違いにもかかわらず、空手は同じ言語を話す方法である、と気づかされたスミス氏。「空手は真に平和の武芸」と考え、世界中の友人と交流を深めながら、自己充足の道である武術の研究に生涯をささげる。

Published on 2021/2/14

32 France 

Uechi-ryū & Kobu-ryū kobudō

A martial art of peace and a quest for truth

Like many French karateka, Jean Smith, who was born in Auxerre in 1965, started karate with Shōtōkan at the age of 14. Moving to Paris, next to karate, he also practiced Katori Shintō-ryū, a style that teaches Japanese ancient martial arts.

Along his research, Smith became interested in Okinawan weapons and stayed in Okinawa for 6 months in 1989. Introduced to Matayoshi Shinpō, he started practicing kobudō. He also studied weapons and the Uechi-ryū related system Kōnan-ryū with Kinjō Takashi, a senior student of Matayoshi.

"Kinjō sensei was passionate and dedicated to the art. He enthusiastically communicated the spirit and practice of martial arts," Smith recalls.

Back in Paris, Smith opened a dōjō and trained kobudō with Chinen Kenyū and Uechi-ryū with Shimabukuro Yukinobu for 10 years.

After his daughter's birth, as he was tired of living in the capital, Smith decided to move in the countryside and settled in Mauzac, a small commune 30 kilometers south of Toulouse. There, he now makes a living by treating and instructing Shiatsu and traditional Chinese medicine while teaching Okinawan martial arts.

In addition to Shimabukuro's guidance for 30 years, Smith also practices with karate researcher Guy Sauvin, who in his younger years won the French championship in 1964 and was part of the French team who won in kumite at the 2nd World Karate Championships in 1972.

In 2018, during the 1st Okinawa Karate International Tournament, Smith reunited with Kinjō Takashi, who had established the Kobu-ryū system in 2000, and became his disciple.

"Kinjō sensei talked about the changes in his martial arts and hearing his explanations, I felt they were in perfect agreement with my research. I was also surprised at the similarities between Guy Sauvin and Kinjō sensei's approaches."

The karate paths of 81-year-old Kinjō and 78-year-old Sauvin have never crossed. However, Smith stresses that both are experts who share the same principles, such as the facts that "power is transmitted from the ground to the whole body, one never retreats, and offense and defense should be simultaneous."

Currently, Smith instructs 40 people at his Mauzac dōjō and 200 people all over France. In addition, he has been appointed as the European representative of Kobu-ryū kobudō and teaches weapons in six clubs.

Through his martial experiences, Smith came to realize that karate is a way to speak the same language with others, regardless of cultural differences. He believes that "karate is a true martial art of peace" and devotes his life to studying martial arts, a way of self-fulfillment, while interacting with friends all over the world.

2019年09月29日

㉝ベラルーシ

伝統武術指導に情熱

ジオン道場

今秋も、ヨーロッパ中央部の共和国ベラルーシで、日本国大使館主催の文化フェスティバル「ベラルーシにおける日本の秋」が開催される。7回目を迎える祭りでは、空手の競技大会やセミナーも行われる。

1958年ウクライナ生まれのセルゲイ・ミルテンコ氏は、1歳の時ベラルーシの首都ミンスクに移った。7歳からフィギュアスケートなどを始め、後に近代五種競技に懸命に取り組み、全国王者となった。

空手は、黒澤明氏の映画を見て魅了され、17歳の時から稽古を始めたという。同国の空手指導者のほか、船越義珍氏の後継者の中山正敏氏、金澤弘和氏らの書籍などから仮想的に学んだとミルテンコ氏は振り返る。

核物理学を専攻する電子エンジニアとして大学を卒業したミルテンコ氏は、88年に、知人と共に「ジオン道場」を立ち上げ、空手の普及に励む決断をした。↗

素手武術の研究のほか、近代五種競技の種目であるフェンシングから「冷兵器（火器以外の武器）」に興味を抱き、90年からヌンチャクなどの武器術を始めた。だが「又吉古武道や山根流の技法を学んだものの、指導者が存在せず、長年独自で

ヌンチャクを指導するミルテンコ氏（先頭右）と息子イゴール氏（同左）=提供
Mirutenko (front line right) and his son Igor (front line left) teaching nunchaku.

断片的な研究だった」と話す。

92年、船越義珍氏の高弟、故西山英峻氏に師事したセルビア人で不動館松濤館の創始者イリヤ・ヨールガ氏がベラルーシを訪れ、指導に当たった。ヨールガ氏の下で、ミルテンコ氏は初段を取得し、ロシアなどで同系の空手の普及に挑んだ。

本格的な古武道の指導を受けたのは2007年。ロシアで琉球古武道哲心館協会ドイツ支部のフランク・ペルニー氏がセミナーを開いた時だった。2年後、哲心館ヨーロッパ合宿がチェコで開催され、初めて同協会の玉寄英美会長に直接師事した。

ミルテンコ氏は15年に初めて来沖した。今年も7月下旬に沖縄を訪れ、第2回沖縄伝統古武道世界大会に出場。ミルテンコ氏は棒で優勝し、息子のイゴール氏はサイで優勝を果たしている。

現在、ミルテンコ氏は国際伝統武術連盟の会長を務める。ミンスク市には8道場あり、400人が学んでいる。また12カ国に渡り、セミナーで指導。その内、6カ国で古武道の支部道場が開設されたという。

空手9段、古武道4段のミルテンコ氏は、自分自身を「情熱の男」と称する。14歳から哲学と天文学が好きで、詩人としての活動にも挑戦している。「空手は、私が最も好む唯一の職業」と語り、40年余りの武歴を生かし文武両道の道を歩み続ける。

Jion Dōjō

A passion for teaching traditional martial arts

This fall, the cultural festival "Autumn of Japan in Belarus" sponsored by the Embassy of Japan will be held. During this 7th edition, there will be a karate competition and a seminar.

Although born in Ukraine in 1958, Sergei Mirutenko moved to Minsk, the capital of Belarus, at the age of one and has been living there since. Practicing figure skating at the age of 7, he later engaged in modern pentathlon and became multiple times national champion.

It is watching the films of Kurosawa Akira that he was charmed by karate and started practicing in 1975. He recalls learning from books by Nakayama Masatoshi and Kanazawa Hirokazu, some of the successors of Funakoshi Gichin, among others.

Although Mirutenko graduated from university as an electronic engineer with a specialty in nuclear physics, he decided to establish the Jion Dōjō with an acquaintance in 1988 and to work on popularizing karate.

Next to researching karate, he became interested in cold weapons as he did some fencing, an event of modern pentathlon, and started training with weapons such as nunchaku in 1990. However, he says, "Although I practiced some Matayoshi and Yamanni-ryū kobudō, it was a fragmentary study for many years that was done without an instructor."

In 1992, Serbian founder of Fudōkan Shōtōkan, Ilya Jorga, who studied under the late Nishiyama Hidetaka, a direct student of Funakoshi, visited Belarus and gave some seminars. Under him, Mirutenko was promoted to 1st dan black belt and strived to spread this system in Russia and surrounding countries.

It was in 2007 that he started receiving some serious kobudō instruction from Frank Pelny, the head of the German branch of the Ryūkyū Kobudō Tesshinkan Association. Two years later, as the association's European seminar was held in the Czech Republic, Mirutenko trained directly with Tamayose Hidemi, the chairman of the association.

Mirutenko visited Okinawa for the first time in 2015. This year in July he also visited Okinawa to participate in the 2nd Okinawa Traditional Kobudō World Championships. He and his son Igor won respectively the bō and sai division.

Today, Mirutenko is the president of an international league that has 8 clubs in Minsk where 400 people train, and branches in 12 countries. Among these, there are kobudō branch dōjō in 6 countries.

A karate 9th dan and kobudō 4th dan, Mirutenko says about himself that he is a "man of passions". He has been fond of philosophy and astronomy since the age of 14, and also likes writing poems. Saying that karate is his only and favorite profession, he continues to pursue Bunbu Ryōdō, the way of the pen and the sword, making the best of his 40-year martial background.

2017年12月31日

㉞ベルギー

極意へ あくなき探究

文武館ブリュッセル

ベルギーで空手が導入されたのは1960年前後。本土系の流派が人気だが、沖縄の小林流、剛柔流、上地流も精力的に活動している。そしてブリュッセルに、琉球生まれの古武術を指導する男がいる。

1957年生まれのアラン・ベルクマンス氏は、16歳の頃、船越義珍氏の空手と柔術を混成し和道流と命名した大塚博紀氏の空手を習い始めた。

後に松濤館も習ったが、80年、友人を通して沖縄出身摩文仁賢和氏が開祖となる糸東流に転向した。糸東流の指導者は、コルシカ島に住む糸東流9段の中橋秀利氏。

組手のナショナルチームで活躍したベルクマンス氏は84年に競技から離れ、首都ブリュッセル圏内のシント=アガタ=ベルシェムにある「武道クラブベルシェム」の空手指導者となった。

90年にベルクマンス氏は初めて日本を訪れ、1カ月間大阪で糸東流2代目宗家故摩文仁賢榮氏に師事した。同年、1660年にさかのぼる日本古流武道「本體楊心流」を始める。

「本来、侍を育てるこの古流武道では柔術の他に刀や棒も習得するが、空手家として、人と自身を守ることを目的とする沖縄空手の理念を受け、空手と連動する武器術を習いたかった」とベルクマンス氏は説く。

棒のセミナー後、弟子と共に。前列中央がベルクマンス氏=提供
Following a bō seminar, Alain Berckmans (front line center) and his students.

この思いを実現するため2002年、南の島沖縄の地を踏み、那覇市首里鳥堀の文武館道場の仲本政博氏に弟子入りした。

それから8回来沖し稽古を重ね、沖縄伝統古武道の5段に昇段。糸東流と本體楊心流の6段にもなった。本體楊心流の奥伝と古武道の師範免許も15年と16年に授与された。

ベルクマンス氏は電気工学士の肩書も持つ。「空手を通して身体能力と抵抗力を養うが、仕事と私生活の中で、稽古をするための調整と努力も精神鍛錬。また、武道における互いの尊重、正義、誠実や意思決定は、毎日の生活の中にも適用できる」と分析する。

10年、県指定無形文化財保持者でもある仲本政博氏の了承を得て、道場を「文武館ブリュッセル」に改名した。文武館館長の仲本守氏の下で首里手の手ほどきも受けている。

3カ国で支部道場を監督するベルクマンス氏は、世界中多くの同門と出会い、国境を越え同作法を重んずる武道の家族の力に気づかされた。2度目の沖縄訪問の際、仲本氏と共に師の家墓を訪れた。先祖を尊敬し、型を披露できたことが大きな感動として胸に刻まれているという。

武の道を歩むベルクマンス氏は、沖縄空手の本来の姿、極意をつかむため、あくなき探求を続けている。

Karate was introduced in Belgium around 1960. While mainland Japanese schools are popular, Shōrin-ryū, Gōjū-ryū, and Uechi-ryū are also present and in Brussels, a man teaches the weapon system born in the Ryūkyū Islands.

Born in 1957, Alain Berckmans started practicing Wadō-ryū when he was sixteen. After training in Shōtōkan, he changed in 1980 to Shitō-ryū and studied under Nakahashi Hidetada, a 9th dan who resided in Corsica.

Once a national kumite team member, Berckmans left competition in 1984 and became a karate instructor at the Budō club Berchem located in the municipality of Berchem Ste Agathe.

Published on 2017/12/31

34 Belgium

Bunbukan Brussels

An insatiable quest toward the innermost secrets

In 1990, Berckmans visited Japan for the first time and trained during one month at the dōjō of Shitō-ryū's Sōke Mabuni Kenei, son of Mabuni Kenwa. Meanwhile, he was introduced to the Japanese school of jūjutsu Hontai Yōshin-ryū, which history traces back to 1660.

"In Japanese martial schools that aimed at training samurai, sword and staff are taught next to jūjutsu. Understanding that the philosophy of Okinawa karate is to protect oneself and people, I wanted to learn weapons' techniques that work along with karate."

In order to do so, he travelled to Okinawa in 2002 and became a student of Nakamoto Masahiro, head of the Bunbukan Dōjō in Shuri Torihori-chō, Naha City.

Having visited Okinawa 8 times since, he was promoted 5th dan in Okinawa traditional kobudō, receiving a teaching license in 2016. He also holds a 6th dan in Shitō-ryū and Hontai Yōshin-ryū.

Out of the dōjō, Berckmans is an electrical engineer specialized in telecommunications. His analyze is that, "Although through karate one develops physical ability and resistance, he/she also trains the mind by adjusting and making efforts to practice on the side of work and personal life. Mutual respect, justice, honesty and decision-making in martial arts can also be applied in everyday life."

In 2010, he received the authorization from Nakamoto Masahiro to rename his dōjō Bunbukan Brussels and since then, has started studying Shurite with the Bunbukan's new kanchō, Nakamoto Mamoru.

As he supervises branches in 3 countries, Berckmans has made friends the world over. It made him aware of the strength of a borderless martial family where the same codes are respected.

When he visited Okinawa for the second time, he visited the grave of the Nakamoto family. Being allowed to perform a few kata on the grave site as an expression of respect towards his master's ancestors left a huge impression on him.

As Berckmans walks the path of martial arts, he continues his quest to grasp the true nature and innermost secrets of Okinawa karate.

オランダ語が公用語のアントウェルペン州生まれ、フーベルト・リーネン氏(60)は、6歳で柔道、11歳になって松濤館空手に入門した。空手6段となり、さまざまな武道に携わってきた中で2002年に初めて沖縄を訪れた。

当時県内では小林流や剛柔流を習ったが、「ある日テレビに映った城間清範先生の演武を見て、この技を習いたいと思った」という。

本部御殿に継承された伝来の流儀は、上原清吉氏に受け継がれ、1961年に本部流と命名された。本部流は、空手の打撃技に取手(関節技・投げ技)や武器術等が混成された総合武術。故上原氏に師事した城間氏は、その流れをくむ。

リーネン氏は、南城市佐敷津波古にある城間氏の湧泉館にたどり着いたが、入門を断られた。

2年後再び湧泉館の門を叩き、初めて舞手本部流合戦取手の手ほどきを受けた。それから城間氏が亡くなる2012年まで毎年来沖し、師の武術を研究した。その後、松濤館、城間派本部流等の技法と原理を統一させようと、リーネン氏は「古流空手術実践流」という護身術を考案した。

「城間先生は、受けてから突くという構想より、型を流ちょうな方法で演武し、分解を先手の時を見てこなす必要があると指摘した。しかし、新流派と舞手は混成するなとも明言した」。リーネン氏は現在、舞手二代目の屋宜勲氏に師事し、両武術を分けて指導している。

セミナーで指導するリーネン氏(中央)=提供
Laenen (center) instructing at a seminar.

2019年07月28日

㉟ベルギー

神髄探究 普及使命に

少林道場

電気技師だったリーネン氏は、22歳の時、武道で生きる覚悟を決め、本部道場「少林道場」をハイスト=オプ=デン=ベルクに開設した。現在、8歳から64歳まで約180人が稽古に励む。毎年数カ国を巡りセミナー指導も行っている。

道場名の意味を問うと、「開設時、私は武術史について無知でした。デビッド・キャラダイン主演のドラマ『燃えよ! カンフー』の品質の高い基準を描写したくて、少林寺を引用して命名した。その後、道場が好評で名が広まったので、道場名を変えなかった」と振り返る。

これまで16回沖縄を訪れているリーネン氏は、武術の神髄を伝えるべく、2017年から毎年「琉球のガーディアンズ」という武芸祭を開催。昨年はヨーロッパ8カ国から200人余りが参加した。「舞手の師範免状を授与された外国人は、私を含めて3人。光栄なことでありながら責任は重い」と胸の内を明かす。

リーネン氏は、城間氏の教え「他人に良いことをする、それがあなたを幸せにする」を心に刻み、沖縄の武術を普及し続けている。

Born in the province of Antwerp, Hubert Laenen (60) began jūdō at the age of 6 and Shōtōkan karate at the age of 11. Having become a 6th dan and experienced various martial arts, he visited Okinawa for the first time in 2002 and studied Shōrin-ryū and Gōjū-ryū.

"One day, I saw a short video of Shiroma Kiyonori sensei in a restaurant and said to myself: that is what I want to learn."

Shiroma was a student of the late Uehara Seikichi who inherited the system passed on within the Motobu family. Named Motobu-ryū in 1961, it is a comprehensive martial art that combines striking techniques with tuite (joint locks and throwing techniques) and weapons techniques.

Published on 2019/7/28

35 Belgium

Shaolin Dōjō

In search of the essence and spreading the art

While Laenen was able to reach Shiroma's dōjō in Sashiki, Nanjō City, he was immediately told to leave. Persisting, he was finally allowed to receive instruction in Mōdi Motobu-ryū Gassen Tuidi two years later. From then and until the passing of Shiroma in 2012, he travelled yearly to Okinawa to study with Shiroma. Later on, in an attempt to unify the techniques and principles of Shōtōkan, Shiroma's Motobu-ryū and other arts he had learned, Laenen devised a self-defense method that he called Koryū Karate Jutsu Jissen Ryū.

"Shiroma Sensei helped me to change my way of thinking about karate in general. He pointed out that we should execute our kata in a fluent way and that bunkai should be focused on the attack opportunities instead of the 'block-punch' approaches. But, he also clearly stated that I could not mix Mōdi and my new system." Today, Laenen keeps studying Mōdi under the second heir Yagi Isao and teaches it separately.

At the age of 22, Laenen decided to live for the martial arts and opened his main dōjō, the Shaolin Dōjō, in Heist-op-den-Berg. Currently, about 180 people from 8 to 64 years old practice with him. He also teaches seminars in several countries every year.

The name of his dōjō was inspired to him by the drama series "Kung Fu" starring David Carradine. "I chose the name Shaolin as I wanted to describe the high quality standards found in the drama."

Having visited Okinawa 16 times so far, Laenen has been holding a martial arts festival called "Guardians of Ryūkyū" every year since 2017 to convey the essence of martial arts. Last year, more than 200 people from eight European countries participated.

"Including me, there are only 3 foreigners that have been handed teaching license for Mōdi. It's an honor, but also a heavy responsibility."

Keeping at heart Shiroma's words "Who does good things to others, will receive good things in return," Laenen continues to popularize Okinawan martial arts.

2018年07月22日

36 ポーランド

原型を追求 日々精進

ピンクゾブクラブ 小林流

日本とポーランドは2019年に国交樹立100周年を迎える。

作曲家ショパンの故郷でもある同国。ここでは70年代前半に松濤館系と極真系の空手が紹介され、広まった。今では東欧で最大の武道施設と言われる「道場Stara Wies」を松濤館系組織が運営する。施設はワルシャワから南方約150キロのスタラビエシ村にある。

1955年生まれのアレキサンデル・スタニシェヴ氏は73年に極真系道場に入門した。氏が手に入れた米国の書籍に「小林流が最も古い流派である」を発見すると、空手の原型を追い求めた。その後、知花朝信氏を開祖とする小林流の流れをくむ米国小林舘と連携を取った。

81年、故郷ピンクゾブ市に道場を開設。10年後、フランスを拠点に活動していた知念賢祐氏に出会い、氏が会長を務める王修会に加盟した。冶金技師だったスタニシェヴ氏は、空手の指導のため国内外のさまざまな大学で学び、体育博士号を取得した。学校や大学で体育を教えながら、趣味である沖縄の武術の稽古と指導を続けてきた。

現在、ピンクゾブの道場で大人約50人が汗を流し、国内42の道場で黒帯210人を含む1750人が小林流を学ぶ。「毎月2回指導者向けのセミナーを開き、各道場に出かけて指導もしている」とスタニシェヴ氏。研さんのため、積極的に知念氏が開催する国際セミナーにも参加。これまで110以上の国際セミナーで腕を磨いてきた。

型の分解を説明するスタニシェヴ氏(中央)=提供
Staniszew (center) explaining an application of a kata.

沖縄空手の優位性を問われると45年の空手歴を持つスタニシェヴ氏は「沖縄空手は原型で非常に論理的」と説く。「絵画と同じ。誰もがダ・ヴィンチ、ゴッホ、ボッティチェッリの原画を持ちたい。空手も同様。美しいフレームに入ったコピーで満足する人はいますが、私は違う」。

知念氏の外国で得た長年の体験と研究に基づく理論を受け継ぐスタニシェヴ氏は「沖縄空手のすべては論理的。型を習ってから分解を学び、その技を道場組手で応用する。近代競技では型と組手を分けるが、無意味です」と強調する。さらに「30歳代半ばまでの人を対象とするスポーツ空手に対し、沖縄の伝統空手は生涯武道として練習できる」と熱く語った。

スタニシェヴ氏は現在、空手8段、古武道7段でワールド王修会の常任理事4人の一人。会の活動を支え、沖縄の空手と古武道の精進に毎日をささげる。

Published on 2018/7/22

36 Poland

Pinczow Club Shōrin-ryū

Pursuing the original form and training daily

In 2019, Japan and Poland will celebrate the 100th anniversary of the establishment of their diplomatic relations.

In the country of Chopin, Shōtōkan and Kyokushin karate were introduced in the early 70's.

Born in 1955, Aleksander Staniszew entered a Kyokushin dōjō in 1973. When he discovered in an American book that "Shōrin-ryū is the oldest style", he started pursuing the original form of karate. Later on, he collaborated with the USA Shōrinkan, a system that inherits Chibana Chōshin's Shōrin-ryū karate.

In 1981, Staniszew opened his dōjō in his hometown of Pinczow. Ten years later, he met Chinen Kenyū who was established in France and decided to join his organization, Oshūkai. A metallurgical engineer, Staniszew studied at various universities in Poland and abroad and obtained a PhD in the field of sports. While teaching physical education in schools and colleges, he continued to practice and teach his passion, Okinawan martial arts.

Currently, about 50 adults are training at the Pinczow dōjō, and 1,750 people, including 210 black belts, are learning Shōrin-ryū in 42 domestic dōjō under Staniszew's guidance. "We hold seminars for instructors twice a month and I go teach in each dōjō too," he says. To deepen his knowledge, he actively participates in international seminars held by Chinen and has so far taken part in more than 110 international events.

When asked about the superiority of Okinawa karate, Staniszew explains that, "Okinawa karate is the original form and is very logical. It is the same with painting. Everyone would prefer to have the original Leonardo da Vinci, Van Gogh or Botticelli paintings. It's the same with karate. There are people who accept a copy because it is in a beautiful golden frame. It is not my case - I prefer the original."

Staniszew inherits Chinen's theory based on many years of experience and research gained overseas. He stresses, "Everything is logical in karate from Okinawa. You learn kata, after that you practice its use in applications and you apply them in dōjō kumite. In modernized sport, kata and kumite are separate things. It does not make sense." He adds, "As opposed to sports karate which is for people up to the age of 35, Okinawan traditional karate can be practiced as a lifelong martial art."

Staniszew is currently one of the four permanent directors of the World Oshūkai and an 8th dan in karate and 7th dan in kobudō. Supporting the activities of the association, he devotes every day of his life to Okinawa karate and kobudō.

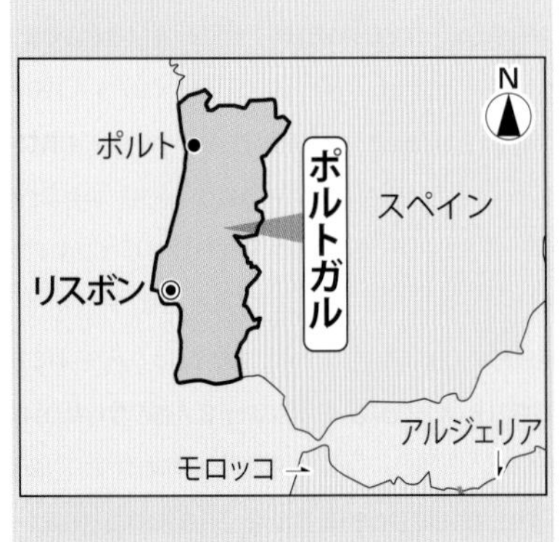

2018年08月12日

㊲ ポルトガル

心と技教え人間形成

IOGKF 本部道場

日本と長い交流の歴史をもつポルトガル。最初は歴史の教科書にもある、1543年、ポルトガル人が種子島に漂着したことにさかのぼる。同じ頃、中国を訪れたポルトガル人のトメ・ピレスが、琉球王国のことを「レキオ」と呼んでいたことを世にあらわした。

沖縄生まれの武術がポルトガルに紹介されたのは1960年代後半。首都のリスボンで初めての空手クラスが同国の「空手の父」とされる故ピレス・マーティンズ氏により設置された。後に、船越義珍氏を始祖と仰ぐ松濤會が大きく普及した。

1961年北部ポルト県のガイア市生まれのジョージ・モンティロ氏は、74年に松濤會の道場に入門した。「当時の多くの子どものように、私は少し反抗的でした。常に友達とけんかしていた。自分を守る方法を学びたくて空手を始めた」と振り返る。

2年後、当時松濤館流を指導していたアンゴラ出身のジャイミ・ペレイラ氏の道場に移った。77年に、剛柔流に転向したペレイラ氏が同系の東恩納盛男氏を招き、ポートワインで有名な町ポルトでセミナーを開催。その際に、モンティロ氏は初めて東恩納氏に出会い、魅了された。若きポルトガル人にとっての空手の道が開いた瞬間だった。

空手に専念したかったモンティロ氏は、80年か

子供に護身術を教えるモンティロ氏（左から2人目）＝提供
Monteiro teaching self-defense to children (second from left).

ら数道場を任せられ、空手のプロとなった。「そのころから、高段者の生徒に道場を開くように勧めた」。88年に主席師範を務める東恩納氏の組織IOGKFのポルトガル支部長になった。現在モンティロ氏の下で、約4千人が140道場で沖縄剛柔流を習う。

恒例のサマー合宿も活動の一環として毎年開催している。今年も補助運動、三戦（サンチン）と子ども向けの護身術を中心と実施されたこの取り組みには1100人が参加し、稽古で汗を流した。

「今日の社会では、多くの若者は規則を分からず、親や学校の担任が教わることを素直に受け入れられないケースが増えている。空手を通して、社会に生きるための良いルールを伝えたい。空手をする子どもは師匠を尊敬する。空手の指導者として、親や学校関係者を支えて良い人間を形成することが我々の義務」とモンティロ氏。

船越氏の「空手道二十ヶ条」には「道場のみの空手と思うな」という格言がある。その言葉を高く見上げるように、空手を通した社会貢献を目指している。

2015年には空手発祥の地・沖縄で8段を付与された。「空手のおかげで、幸せな人生を送ることができ、世界中に多くの仲間がいる」。モンティロ氏は、歴史深き「郷愁の国」で、空手が与えてくれた恵を分かち合いながら、弟子たちを先導している。

Published on 2018/8/12

37 Portugal

IOGKF Honbu Dōjō

Character building by teaching the spirit and skills

Portugal shares a long history with Japan. As written in history books, it dates back to 1543, when Portuguese drifted to Tanegashima. Around the same time, Portuguese Tomé Pires, who travelled to China, mentioned in his diary about "Lequio", the Ryūkyū kingdom.

Karate was introduced in Portugal in the late 1960s. The first class in the capital, Lisbon, was set up by the late Pires Martins, considered as a "father of karate" in the country. Later, Shōtōkai which inherits Funakoshi Gichin's karate spread in Portugal.

Born in 1961 in Gaia in the Porto District, Jorge Monteiro entered a Shōtōkai dōjō in 1974. "At that time, like many kids, I was a bit rebellious and was always fighting with my friends, so I wanted to learn how to defend myself."

Two years later, he moved to the dōjō of Angolan Jaime Pereira who was instructing the Shōtōkan style of karate at that time. In 1977, Pereira, who had switched to Gōjū-ryū, invited Higaonna Morio to hold a seminar in Porto. It was on this occasion that Monteiro met Higaonna for the first time and he was fascinated. For him, it was the beginning of a new karate path.

Monteiro, who wanted to focus on karate, became a karate professional after being entrusted with several dōjō from 1980. "From that time on, I motivated several senior students to teach and to open their dōjō". In 1988, Monteiro was promoted to Portuguese representative for Higaonna's International Okinawa Gōjū-ryū Karatedō Federation (IOGKF). Currently, about 4,000 people are learning Okinawa Gōjū-ryū under him in 140 dōjō.

The annual summer training camp is also held every year as part of the association's activity. This year too, 1,100 people participated in the event, which was centered on the practice of supplementary exercises known as hojo-undō, the kata Sanchin and self-defense for children.

"In today's society, many young people have no rules and have difficulty accepting what teachers and even parents teach them. Through karate, I always try to teach good ways of living in society. All kids who practice karate respect their sensei and so it is our duty, as karate teachers, to help both parents and even schoolteachers to form good human beings," Monteiro explains.

In his "Karatedō Nijū-kajō," Funakoshi wrote: "Do not think that karate is restricted to the dōjō." Valuing these words, Monteiro tries, through karate, to help the students to contribute to a better society.

In 2015, he was awarded the 8th dan in Okinawa, the birthplace of karate. "Karate made me what I am today. I am a happy person and know people from all over the world." In the land of "Saudade", Monteiro keeps leading his disciples sharing the blessings of karate.

1976年、英国生まれのジョエル・リーブズ氏は、10歳の誕生日に親から空手の体験をプレゼントされた。その体験を機に武術の道を歩むことになる。

松濤館空手を学び、94年に1年間、東京で同系統を学んだ。来日中、浪越指圧を知り、帰国後、指圧の指導者を探し求めた。

巡り合えたのはマーク・ビショップ氏だった。英語教師もしていたビショップ氏は72年から90年まで沖縄に在住。リーブズ氏は95年から2008年までビショップ氏の下で武術と指圧を習った。

師のビショップ氏は、武術では故比嘉清徳氏や子息の清彦氏に師事していた。清徳氏は、戦前の大家たちのさまざまな武術を習得し、無党派の道場「武芸館」を開設した武術研究家。また、清彦氏についてビショップ氏は「手（てぃ）と指圧が相互に関連する芸術であるという考えを復活させた先生」とコメントする。↗

多くの空手関係者を取材して回ったビショップ氏は、89年に『沖縄空手:師範、流派、秘密技』を著し、有名になった。沖縄では「ヤッサイビンドー」のフレーズが印象的な電化製品のコマーシャルにも出演している。

セミナーで指導するリーブズ氏（手前右）=提供
Reeves (front right) instructing at a seminar.

2020年03月22日

㊳ポルトガル

空手と健康探究に力

武芸館

ビショップ氏の指導を受けたリーブズ氏は2011年に初めて訪沖した。「比嘉清彦先生は門弟を取らない」と聞いても、那覇市首里にある武芸館を訪ね、指導を受けるようになった。

98年にロンドンで開設した道場で、武芸館の武術の研究と普及に励んだ。現在では4道場で約120人が鍛錬を積んでいる。

空手の系統を問うとリーブズ氏はこう答える。「比嘉清彦先生は、花城長茂先生に師事した仲村渠完蔵先生の指導を受けた。私も武芸館で継承されるこの空手を教えている」。加えて、比嘉氏に習った太極拳と同様の健康上の利点を共有する生道流神気古武道なども指南しているという。

自然に親しみを抱くリーブズ氏は、大都会ロンドンで長く住むのは難しいと感じ、昨夏、英国の道場を高弟に預け、ポルトガルへ移住した。現在はコインブラ県の山中のロウザンに住居を置く。指圧療法士兼ファーマーとして生計を立て、妊娠中の妻と共に古い農場をリフォーム。そこに沖縄空手、指圧、健康法などが研究できる隠れ家的な道場を整備するという。

武芸館5段のリーブズ氏は「真剣に稽古すれば、親切さと理解の感覚をもってどんな敵でも克服することができるはずだ。これが、私が求める武術。そのためにも『健康第一』」と、あくなき探究への思いを示した。

Bugeikan

Deeply investigating karate and health

Born in England in 1976, Joel Reeves was offered a karate lesson by his parents on his 10th birthday. This is how he started to walk the path of martial arts.

Practicing Shōtōkan karate, he stayed in Tōkyō for one year in 1994 in order to further his training. While in Japan, he discovered Namikoshi Shiatsu and after returning from Japan, he sought out an acupressure instructor.

The one person he found was Mark Bishop, an English teacher who lived in Okinawa from 1972 to 1990. From 1995 to 2008, Reeves learned martial arts and hand related bodywork under Bishop.

In Okinawa, Bishop studied martial arts under the late Higa Seitoku and his son Kiyohiko. Higa Seitoku was a martial art researcher who learned various systems from prewar experts and later established a nonpartisan dōjō, the Bugeikan or hall of martial arts. Regarding his son Kiyohiko, Bishop comments, "It was him who revitalized the idea of te – martial art – and shiatsu being a combined and interrelated art."

While in Okinawa, Bishop visited many karate experts and became famous for his 1989 published book "Okinawan karate: Teachers, styles and secret techniques."

After training with Bishop, Reeves travelled to Okinawa for the first time in 2011 and visiting the Bugeikan in Shuri, Naha City, he began his training with Higa Kiyohiko.

Back to England, Reeves strived to popularize the martial arts of the Bugeikan at the dōjō he opened in London in 1998. Today, about 120 people are training in 4 dōjō within the capital.

When asked about the style he practices, Reeves replies: "Higa sensei studied Hanashiro Chōmo sensei's karate from Nakandakari Kanzō. Myself too, I teach this karate that is inherited at the Bugeikan." In addition, he offers classes in Seidō, a type of natural exercise taught by Higa that shares similar health benefits to Tai Chi.

Having a close affinity to nature and struggling to live in London for too long, Reeves left his dōjō to his most senior student and moved to Portugal last summer. He currently lives in Lousã in the mountains of Coimbra District. While working as a professional shiatsu therapist, he is remodeling an old farm with his pregnant wife. He says that he will set up a hideaway dōjō there where he and visitors can research Okinawa karate, acupressure and health methods.

A Bugeikan 5th dan, Reeves analyzes his research. "If we train seriously, then perhaps we can aim to overcome any adversary with a sense of kindness and understanding. This is the high level martial technique I seek." Adding that without health nothing else matters, he reiterates his desire for an endless quest.

2020年09月27日

㊴ モルドバ

不屈の魂 強い体培う

柔道・空手道場「バッサイ」

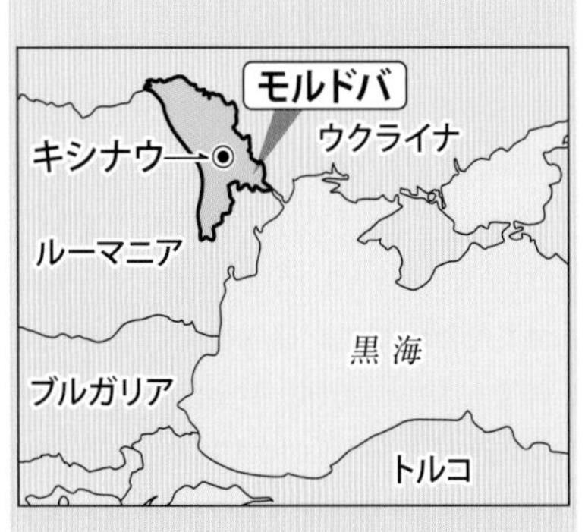

1965年モルドバ生まれのミハエル・ドビチェンコ氏は13歳から柔道専門学校で柔道、5年後軍隊に入営した際に旧ソビエト連邦で開発された格闘技サンボを学び始めた。両スポーツに一身をささげ、モルドバ王者になること数回、さらに旧ソ連の柔道とサンボのチャンピオンにも輝いた。国際柔道大会でも数多くのメダルを獲得している。

柔道と並行して87年から船越義珍氏の弟子で米国の空手パイオニアの一人故西山英峻氏の松濤館空手道を学び、2000年までに三段へ昇段した。「松濤館空手は本当に好きだったが、数年の練習を続けても、進歩がないことに気づいた。柔道での進化と比較したところ、何か物足りないのではと思った」と振り返る。

5年後、疑問を感じたドビチェンコ氏はこの系統から退いた。しかしその後も諦めることなく根源の空手とその指導者を探し続け、剛柔流の友人を通して、上地流空手道拳優会の新城清秀氏の存在を知った。

「身体的にも精神的にも、平易、容易、そして力強さがあふれるもので、新城先生の空手に一目ぼれでした。総合的に考え、この道に決めた。受け入れてくれた新城先生には感謝の気持ちでいっぱい」とドビチェンコ氏は新城氏と拳優会への思いを語る。

ドビチェンコ氏(後列左から4人目)と門下生ら=提供　Vdovicenco (fourth from the left in the back row) and some of his students.

3年かけて入門を願い、09年に初めて訪沖。3週間超、空手の本場・沖縄で上地流を学んだ。11年、2度目の来沖の際に新城氏が空手を指導する沖縄尚学で三戦と試割りを披露し、師の演武補助も務めた。

現在、04年に故郷モルドバの首都キシナウに開設した道場「バッサイ」で柔道と共に上地流を指導している。柔道と空手の指導は分けて行うが、両武術の長所をそれぞれ取り入れている。「理想的に戦闘システムとして互いに補完し合うことから、空手と平行して柔道を教え続けていきたい」。道場生30人は、ほとんどが松濤館から転向した空手家だという。

ドビチェンコ氏は現在5段。本業は国家憲兵隊を預かる内務省内の柔道道場「ディナモクラブ」でコーチであり、さらには銀行業の経済専門家としての顔もあわせ持っている。

13歳から武道に人生を託したドビチェンコ氏にとって、稽古は空気と同じであり、必要不可欠なもの。不屈の精神と強い身体を築きながら、モットーとして「空手に先手なし」を掲げる。身体と精神バランスの完全な調和を求め、鍛錬を続ける。

Born in Moldova in 1965, Mihail Vdovicenco began studying jūdō at a jūdō vocational school at the age of 13 and sambo when he joined the army five years later. Devoting himself to both sports, he became champion of Moldavia several times, as well as former Soviet Union jūdō and sambo champion. He has also won numerous medals at international jūdō competitions.

In parallel with jūdō, Vdovicenco studied the karate of the late Nishiyama Hidetaka, a disciple of Funakoshi Gichin and one of the pioneers of karate in the USA. In 2000, he was promoted 3rd dan. "I really liked Shōtōkan but after several years of practice, I realized that I was not

Published on 2020/9/27

39 Moldova

Jūdō & Karate Dōjō "Bassai"

Cultivating an indomitable spirit and a strong body

making any progress. Comparing with my evolution in jūdō, I thought that I was missing something," he recalls.

Five years later, a skeptical Vdovicenco retired from this line of karate. However, he continued to train and search for the root of karate and a suitable instructor. Coincidentally, he learned from a friend who practiced Gōjū-ryū about Shinjō Kiyohide, head of the Okinawa Uechi-ryū Karatedō Kenyūkai.

"I fell in love with Shinjō sensei's karate from the first move. Simplicity, ease and strength both physical and spiritual, have undoubtedly been the reasons why I chose this way. I thank from the bottom of my heart Shinjō sensei for having accepted me as a student," says Vdovicenco as he tells his feeling toward Shinjō and the Kenyūkai.

After about 3 years of trials, he finally made it to Okinawa in 2009 and trained Uechi-ryū for 3 weeks in the birthplace of karate.

Visiting Okinawa for a second time in 2011, he performed the kata Sanchin at Okinawa Shōgaku, where Shinjō teaches karate, and assisted him for the board breaking demonstration.

Currently, he teaches Uechi-ryū along with jūdō at the dōjō "Bassai" that he opened in 2004 in Chișinău, the capital of Moldova. While he teaches both arts separately, he incorporates the strengths of each art in the other one. "I want to continue teaching jūdō in parallel with karate because they complement each other ideally as a battle system." Most of the 30 dōjō students are karateka who switched from Shōtōkan.

Presently 5th dan, Vdovicenco works as a jūdō coach at the Dinamo Club of the Ministry of Internal Affairs while also being an economist in the banking system.

Having practiced martial arts since the age of 13 without interruption, training for him is as indispensable as air. While cultivating an indomitable spirit and a strong body, his motto is "There is no first attack in karate". Seeking the perfect harmony between physical and mental balance, Vdovicenco keeps on conditioning himself.

モルドバの首都キシナウ生まれのビクトール・パナシウク氏(53)は、11歳のころ、格闘技専門誌で日本の武術空手を初めて知った。その後、友人と共に記事を繰り返し読み、記載されていた三つの技法絵を見習って突きと蹴りを練習したことを覚えている。

当時モルドバは旧ソビエト連邦の構成国であり、情報はほとんどなく、空手について多くのうわさと伝説が流れていた。1979年以降、ソ連で空手の指導が認められたが、指導できる者は少なかった。68万人の市民を数える首都に指導者は4人しかいなかったという。パナシウク氏は、その一人のロマン・リチェヴスキ氏を訪ね、純粋な気持ちで82年まで稽古した。

しかしその年、「事件」が起こった。「ある日、暴力的な男とけんかになった。相手の頭を何度も蹴っても、効果なしでした!結局、レスリングの技で相手を押さえた。これまで習っていた空手の技は、ストリートファイトでは使えない」と振り返る。そこから多くの格闘技を習ったが、それでも空手に惹(ひ)かれていた。船越義珍氏の弟子で日本空手協会の設立者故中山正敏著『ダイナミック空手』を手に入れ一撃技などを独学で研究した。

弟子と共に型を修練するパナシウク氏(中央)=提供
Panasiuk (center) practicing kata with his students.

2019年04月14日

㊵ モルドバ

厳しい鍛錬 精神磨く

IOGKFモルドバ

しかし83年に、ソ連は空手を禁止し、応じない指導者は刑務所に送られたという。「夜になって公園で中山先生の本を参考に稽古を続けた」と当時を思い出すパナシウク氏。隠れても弟子が集まり、掛け試しも少なくなかった。87年に、武術の専業指導者となった。空手はまだ禁じられていたため、道場の正式なカリキュラムは合気道とレスリングだったが、実際には空手の稽古に取り組んでいた。

89年に、空手の禁止は解除された。90年に東恩納盛男氏の国際沖縄剛柔流空手道連盟(IOGKF)の存在を知り、カザフスタンのアルマトイに出かけ、初めて剛柔流のセミナーに参加した。翌年パナシウク氏は、直接東恩納氏から教えを受けた。「先生の強さ、スピード、パワーと同時に優しい笑顔がとても印象的でした!」

94年に正式に同連盟に加盟し、現在国内7道場で300人が沖縄剛柔流を学ぶ。訪沖15回を数える七段のパナシウク氏は、研究熱心で剛柔流と共通点の多い中国の白鶴武術も研究している。

「空手は人間形成を大いに促進し、人々を幸せにする。きれいな手と心を重んずる空手を考案してくれた沖縄人に感謝の意を表したい」とパナシウク氏。師の名言「空手は仕事であり、人生であり、趣味である」を心に刻み、「厳しい鍛錬は幸せな人生」をモットーに剛柔流の道を歩み続ける。

Published on 2019/4/14

40 Moldova

IOGKF Moldova

Severe training to polish the spirit

Born in the capital Chișinău, Victor Panasiuk (53) first learned about karate in a martial arts magazine when he was 11 years old and remembers practicing punching and kicking following the three techniques described in the article.

At that time, Moldova was a member of the former Soviet Union. In 1979, karate training was allowed in the USSR but there were very few instructors. In the capital, there were only four accredited instructors. Panasiuk visited one of them, Richevsky Roman, and practiced with him until 1982.

However this same year, an incident happened. "I had to fight with an aggressive-minded young man in real conditions. Although I hit his head several times with my foot, it did not affect him. I was rescued by wrestling applications I had learned. I was surprised to find that the karate method I thought I had mastered did not work in a street fight!"

Panasiuk went on exploring various martial arts but he was still attracted to karate. Coming across the book "Dynamic Karate" by Nakayama Masatoshi, he studied striking techniques on his own.

In 1983, karate was banned in the Soviet Union. Non-obeying instructors were sentenced and spent several years in jail. "I used to train in a park at night, repeating the techniques described by Nakayama sensei in his book" remembers Panasiuk. Although hiding, students came and so did challenges.

Panasiuk became a professional martial art instructor in 1987. While his students were officially training wrestling with elements of aikido, he was actually teaching karate.

As the ban on karate was lifted in 1989, Panasiuk, having heard about Higaonna Morio of the IOGKF, went to Almaty in Kazakhstan to participate in a Gōjū-ryū seminar for the first time. The following year, he received direct instruction from Higaonna. "Sensei's strength, speed and power and at the same time his soft and pleasant smile made a huge impression on me!"

Officially joining the IOGKF in 1994, there are now 300 people who study Okinawa Gōjū-ryū in seven Moldovan dōjō. Having visited Okinawa 15 times and holder of a 7th dan, Panasiuk is an enthusiast researcher who also studies Chinese White Crane, which has much in common with Gōjū-ryū.

"Karate helps thousands of people around the world to change and develop their character and thus to become happier! I want to express my gratitude to all the people of Okinawa for creating the art of Clean Hands and Clean Heart."

Inspired by his master's words "My job is karate. My life is karate. My hobby is karate," Panasiuk keeps walking the path of Gōjū-ryū following his own motto: "Hard training is a happy life!"

2020年02月23日

㊶ラトビア

師の教え胸に魂培う

神人武館リガ道場

北ヨーロッパの国ラトビアは1990年に独立した共和国。現在、この国の副首相で防衛大臣のアルテイス・パブリクス氏は沖縄空手4段の実力を持つ。

旧ソ連支配時代の66年生まれのパブリクス氏は、小学生のころから武道に興味を示した。「武道は強くなれる、学校でのいじめから身を守る魔法のようなものに見えた」と若き日の意気込みを振り返る。

しかし当時、空手の稽古は禁じられていて、KGB（ソ連国家保安委員会）等のみが学べたという。87年ごろ、カンフーを学び始めたパブリクス氏は、デンマークへの留学時に中国武術を続けた。

ラトビア大学で歴史と哲学を学んだパブリクス氏は、フルブライト奨学金を受け、96年にニューヨークのコロンビア大学に留学。神人武館の空手を指導するジミー・モラ氏に出会い、沖縄空手の手ほどきを受けた。神人武館は、小林流究道館の比嘉佑直氏に師事した翁長良光氏が1988年に那覇市で開設している。

茶帯を取得し帰国したパブリクス氏はヴィドゼメ大学で政治学准教授になった。同時に空手道場を探し、喜屋武朝徳氏などに師事した千歳強直氏（旧姓・知念）の空手の流れをくむ養秀会（故山元勝王宗家）のラトビア支部に入門した。

翁長良光氏（右から4人目）とパブリクス氏（同5人目）、門下生ら=提供
Onaga (fourth from the right), Pabriks (fifth from the right) and some students.

国のために尽くしたいとパブリクス氏は2004年に政界に入り、外務大臣を拝命した。同年の秋に、翁長氏に初めて会い、神人武館の初段を獲得。翌年以降沖縄を数回訪れ、翁長氏から直接学び、ラトビアにも師を招き合宿も行った。

07年には、沖縄とラトビアの橋渡しができるよう在那覇ラトビア共和国名誉領事館が設置され、翁長氏は名誉領事に就任している。

さまざまな政治職を担い、欧州議会の議員にもなったパブリクス氏は、19年1月から副首相と防衛大臣を兼務している。時間を見つけてはリガの道場などで指導に励む多忙な日々を送る。「名誉、強さ、誠実さ、一意専心という翁長先生の教えは毎日の支えになる」と空手と仕事に情熱を注ぐ原動力を語った。

「空手は対立の回避術であり、哲学につながる芸術。空手をすることで、生き生きとした精神を維持し、体調を整えることもできる。若さの源泉」というパブリクス氏。仕事と空手、家族との生活以外に、チェスに情熱を注ぐ一面もある。子どものころから楽しむチェスは戦略ゲームで知性を育み、日常生活、仕事にも役立つという。

人間力の向上を人生の目標とするパブリクス氏は常に前を見据え、心技体の鍛錬・継承とともに、国への貢献に努めていく。

Published on 2020/2/23

41 Latvia

Shinjinbukan Riga Dōjō

Keeping to heart the teacher's teachings and cultivating the soul

Latvia, a republic in Northeastern Europe, became independent in 1990. Currently, the country's Vice Prime Minister Artis Pabriks is a 4th dan in Okinawa karate.

Born in 1966 at a time when the country was under Soviet occupation, Pabriks showed an interest in martial arts already since elementary school. "They seemed a magic way on how to learn to be strong and to defend oneself against bullying in school" he recalls.

However, at that time, karate practice was forbidden by Soviet authorities and only organizations like KGB were allowed to learn martial arts. Having started Kungfu around 1987, he continued Chinese martial arts when he went to study in Denmark.

After studying history and philosophy at the University of Latvia, Pabriks received a Fulbright scholarship to the Columbia University in New York in 1996. There, he met Jimmy Mora, who teaches Shinjinbukan karate and started training with him. The Shinjinbukan was established in 1988 by Onaga Yoshimitsu, a disciple of Higa Yūchoku of the Shōrin-ryū Kyūdōkan.

Returning home after earning a brown belt, Pabriks became an associate professor of political science at Vidzeme University. Meanwhile, he joined the Latvian branch of the Yōshūkai founded by the late Yamamoto Katsuō, a student of Chitose Tsuyoshi (former name Chinen).

As he wanted to serve his country, Pabriks entered politics in 2004 and was appointed Minister for Foreign Affairs of Latvia. In the fall of the same year, he met Onaga for the first time and was promoted 1st dan in Shinjinbukan. From the following year, he visited Okinawa several times to train directly with Onaga, and invited him for seminars.

Having held various political positions as well as having been elected as a member of the European Parliament, Pabriks now serves as Vice Prime Minister and Minister of Defense since January 2019. When he finds time in his busy schedule, he trains at the Riga dōjō. Talking about the driving force behind his passion for karate and work, he says, "Honor, strength, integrity and wholeness, the teachings of Onaga sensei, help me daily."

"Karate is an art of avoiding conflict and closely relates to philosophy. By practicing karate, one can maintain a lively spirit and improve his/her physical condition. It is a source of youth," says he. Besides work, karate and family life, Pabriks also has a passion for chess, a strategy game he practices since childhood and which also helps him in his daily life and work.

Pabriks, whose life's goal is to improve human skills, looks ahead and strives to contribute to the country while training and passing on spiritual, technical and physical skills.

2020年08月23日

㊷リトアニア

強い身体と精神培う

こころ道場

バルト海に面するリトアニア。長年旧ソビエト連邦の一つだったが、90年に独立回復を果たした。

同国で空手の起源は72年頃といわれている。当時フルコンタクト系や松濤館の空手が導入され、現在も両系統の人気が高いという。

80年代にソ連は「社会主義的な生き方と両立しない残酷なスポーツ」として空手を禁じた歴史もある。

アイバラス・エンゲライティス氏は73年、同国第3の都市のクライペダに生まれた。14歳から兄と共に格闘技を学び、柔道も試したが、体力がなくやめた。「森の中で違法に空手の練習をしている秘密集団はあったが、指導料が高く入門できなかった。代わりに太極拳を始めた」と振り返る。

禁止令が解除されると、エンゲライティス氏は空手を習い始めたが、スポーツ空手に失望し、より伝統ある系統の空手を求めた。↗

93年、英国で沖縄剛柔流を指導するボブ・ホニボル氏と出会い、弟子入り。帰国後道場を開き、研究に励んだ。英国での修行も毎年続けた。

10代から仏教に興味を持っていたエンゲライティス氏は、英国在住で当時「霊友会」の教えを

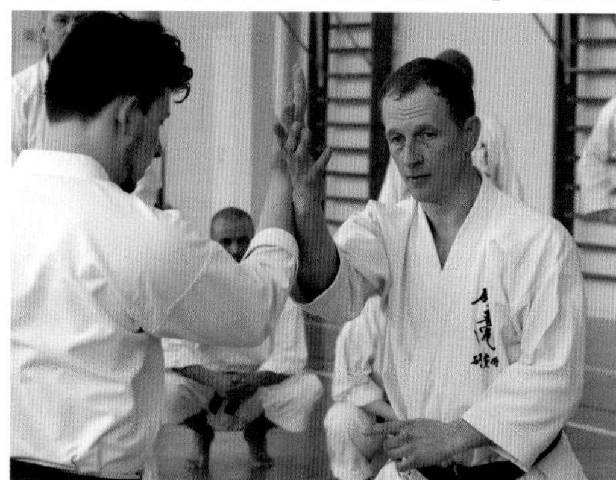

分解を指導するエンゲライティス氏(右)=提供
Engelaitis (right) instructing an application.

普及していた長谷川和己氏に出会った。訪英するたびに長谷川氏の下で法華経の研究を続け、98年にはさらに実践、取り組みを深めるため初めて日本を訪れた。

この年故郷クライペダで同会支部を開設。現在は霊友会から独立した「在家仏教こころの会」のリトアニア代表を務める。「こころの会は常に自己啓発を強調する。空手と太極拳の練習はそのための良い手段だと感じた」と説明する。

2006年に来日した際、初めて那覇市安里の順道館で稽古を体験した。現在、同館出身の平良正次氏の沖縄剛柔流研究会に所属。ヨーロッパ各地で普及活動に励み、毎年日本と沖縄を訪れている。

01年に「こころ道場」と改名した道場では現在、大人20人、子ども40人が剛柔流を学ぶ。空手指導のほかエンゲライティス氏は、週5日午前8時から夜10時まで太極拳、古武道、在家仏教の教えの普及にも努めている。89年から日本語を学び、日本語会話のクラスも開設している。

コロナ感染の影響でアウトドア稽古が続いたが、6月以降は制限やマスク着用もなく、コロナ禍前と同様の活動が再開した。「空手の魅力は体力、精神的に弱い人でも健やかになり、強くなること」。エンゲライティス氏は空手の力に信念を持ち、指南に励んでいる。

Published on 2020/8/23

42 Lithuania

Kokoro Dōjō

Cultivating a strong body and spirit

Facing the Baltic Sea, Lithuania was part of the former Soviet Union for many years, but in 1990 it regained its independence. It is said that karate started spreading in the country around 1972 when full contact and Shōtōkan karate were introduced.

Then karate was prohibited in the 1980s in all USSR as it was considered "a cruel sport, not compatible with a socialist way of living".

Aivaras Engelaitis was born in 1973 in Klaipeda. He studied martial arts with his brother from the age of 14 and tried jūdō, but quit because he was too weak physically he says. "There were some secret groups which practiced karate illegally in the woods, but it costed too much. Instead, I started learning Chinese Wushu," he recalls.

When the ban was lifted, Engelaitis began practicing karate but was disappointed with sport karate and sought a more traditional system. He then met Okinawa Gōjū-ryū instructor Bob Honiball from the UK in 1993 and became his student, visiting him every year to train.

Engelaitis, who had been interested in Buddhism since his teens, met Hasegawa Kazumi, who lived in the UK at that time and was spreading the Buddhist teachings of the "Reiyūkai". Every time he visited the UK, Engelaitis continued to study the Lotus Sutra under Hasegawa and in 1998, he visited Japan for the first time to further his practice.

This year in Klaipeda, he opened a branch that represents Kokoro No Kai, an international Lay Buddhist Association, independent from Reiyūkai. He explains, "As Kokoro No Kai's philosophy stresses constant self-development, I see karate and Taijiquan practices as good means for it."

When he came to Japan in 2006, Engelaitis trained at the Jundōkan in Asato, Naha City, for the first time. He now belongs to the Okinawa Gōjū-ryū Karatedō Kenkyūkai chaired by Taira Masaji who is originally from the Jundōkan. While working hard to spread the system all over Europe, Engelaitis visits Japan and Okinawa every year.

At the dōjō, which was renamed "Kokoro – heart – Dōjō" in 2001, 20 adults and 40 children are currently studying karate. In addition, Engelaitis teaches Tai Chi, kobudō and Buddhism from 8 am to 10 pm five days a week, as well as Japanese that he has been learning since 1989.

Due to the Covid-19 pandemic, training continued outdoor but after June, with the lifting of restrictions, activities will resume as before. "The charm of karate is that it can make a physically and mentally weak person to become healthy, strong inside and outside." Believing in the power of karate, Engelaitis strives to guide people around him on the way of the empty hand.

2019年03月10日

㊸ルーマニア

禁断の時代超え修練

アレキス武術クラブ

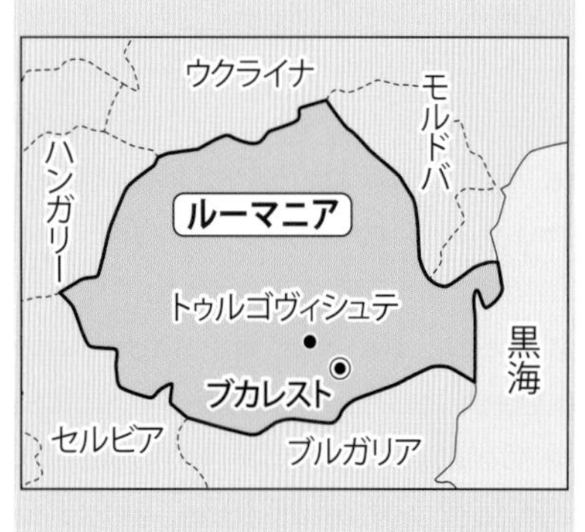

ルーマニアの南にあるトゥルゴヴィシュテ市は、アイルランド人の作家ブラム・ストーカーの恐怖小説『吸血鬼ドラキュラ』のモデルとなった、15世紀に生きたヴラド3世の町として知られている。

1957年北ルーマニア生まれのドミトゥル・アレキサンドル氏は、現在この町で沖縄空手を指導している。

空手との出合いは70年代後半。当時、日本の企業がルーマニアでステンレス工場を建設するためエンジニアが派遣された。20歳のときに陸軍に入ったアレキサンドル氏は、空手をたしなんでいた技師のタワダ・アサオ氏に剛柔流を1年間教わった。

「冷戦時代、空手について情報が少なく、フーリガンがやるスポーツ、反社会的勢力の人がやるものだと思われていた。82年に法律によって空手が禁じられた。そのため、柔道を稽古していると当局に報告していた」とアレキサンドル氏は振り返る。

門下生と共に笑顔を見せるアレキサンドル氏（前列右から2人目）=提供
Alexandru (second from the right in the front row) with his students.

同門がイギリスへ出張した際に、長嶺将真著『沖縄空手道の神髄』の英書を手に入れた。同書をもとにアレキサンドル氏は沖縄空手を独自で学び、隠れて稽古を続けた。87年にアレキサンドル氏は、駐留していたトゥルゴヴィシュテ市の基地内で道場「アレキス武術クラブ」を開設した。

90年、共産党政権の崩壊を機に空手の各流会派が集う初の武術連盟が発足。アレキサンドル氏は創設者の一人となった。

沖縄との交流がなかった時代、長嶺氏の空手を求めるアレキサンドル氏は、93年からアメリカに目を向けた。松林流2代目・長嶺高兆氏の高弟ジム・ドリッグス氏との交流が始まり、書籍やDVDが送られ、松林流の道を本格的に追求した。

2000年には、沖縄で長嶺将真氏に直接指導を受け、後に宇江城安盛氏にも師事したジェムス・ワックス氏の弟子パーカー・シェルトン氏に技術指導を受けることとなった。長嶺高兆氏と交流があった松村正統少林流のフィリップ・コープル氏にも分解組手を教わったという。

09年、中佐として退職したアレキサンドル氏は、教育現場と自らの道場で空手指導に人生をささげている。現在、本部道場で65人、国内7の加盟道場に松林流と山根流の古武術を指導する。

日本とルーマニアは今年で、外交関係再開60周年を迎える。沖縄と縁が少ないなか、7段のアレキサンドル氏は、約40年間沖縄空手の道を歩み、2017年に初めて空手の発祥の地を訪れ、松源流の玉城剛氏に師事した。沖縄の人々の愛情と文化に魅了され、沖縄の武術のみならず、沖縄の文化への理解も深めていく決意を胸に刻んでいる。

The city of Targoviste, south of Romania, is known as the town of Vlad III, who lived in the 15th century and was the model for the Irish writer Bram Stoker's novel "Dracula". Born in Northern Romania in 1957, Dumitru Alexandru is currently teaching Okinawa karate in this town.

Alexandru started karate in the late 70's at a time he already had joined the Army. He first studied Gōjū-ryū karate for a year under Tawada Asao, an engineer who was dispatched to build a stainless steel factory in Romania.

"During the Cold War, there was little information about karate. It was considered to be a sport for hooligans and something that anti-social people would do. In 1982, karate was banned by law. Therefore, we used to fool the authorities by making them believe that we were practicing jūdō," recalls Alexandru.

Published on 2019/3/10

43 Romania

Alex Martial Arts Club

Overcoming the ban and keeping training

Through a karate friend who travelled to the UK, Alexandru was able to get a copy of the book by Nagamine Shōshin "The Essence of Okinawan Karate-Do". Based on the book, Alexandru learned Okinawa karate on his own and continued to practice secretly. In 1987, he opened the dōjō Alex Martial Arts Club at the base he was stationed at in the city of Targoviste.

In 1990, the collapse of the Communist regime led to the establishment of the first martial arts federation in which all karate styles found their place. Alexandru was one of the founders.

Having no connection with Okinawa, but still seeking Nagamine's karate, Alexandru turned to the USA in 1993. He started exchanging with Jim Driggs, a student of Nagamine Takayoshi, and receiving books and DVDs, he started pursuing earnestly the path of Matsubayashi-ryū.

In 2000, he received technical guidance from Parker Shelton, a disciple of Jim Wax who had trained with Nagamine and Ueshiro Ansei and learned bunkai kumite with Phillip Koeppel of Matsumura Seitō Shōrin-ryū.

Having retired as a lieutenant colonel in 2009, Alexandru now devotes his life to teaching karate in educational institutions and at his dōjō, where 65 people study Matsubayashi-ryū and Yamanni-ryū kobujutsu. There are also 7 branch dōjō in the country.

This year, Japan and Romania celebrate the 60th anniversary of the reopening of diplomatic relations. With few ties to Okinawa but having walked the path of Okinawa karate for about 40 years, Alexandru visited the birthplace of karate for the first time in 2017 and studied under Tamaki Tsuyoshi of Shōgen-ryū. Charmed by the warm-hearted Okinawan people and their culture, he is determined to deepen not only his knowledge of Okinawan martial arts but also his understanding of Okinawan culture.

2018年05月27日

㊹ロシア

ルーツ学び 型を鍛錬

アルファ武道クラブ

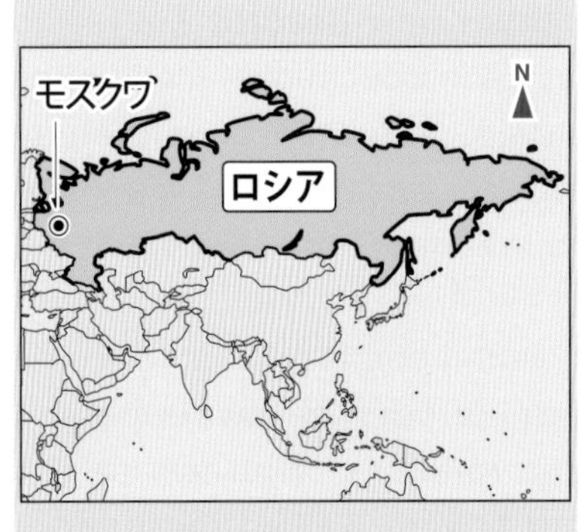

総合格闘王者エメリヤーエンコ・ヒョードル氏を生んだ大国で、空手の歴史は1960年代にさかのぼる。北朝鮮の武道家から空手に似た武術「クワオンフー」を習ったアレックシ・シトルミン氏は、師匠の帰国後「セネ(朝鮮語で“生涯”)」という空手の流派を創設し普及に努めた。

「セネの受け技と手の攻撃技は空手に似ている。猫足立ちも使う。しかし他の立ち方は、松濤館と同様で低く大きい。蹴りは高く、ジャンプも多い」とロマン・ストョーピン氏は説く。

1958年モスクワ生まれのストョーピン氏は、75年からシトルミン氏の空手を習い始めた。81年、ロシアで最も有名な道場「空手中央スクール」で黒帯を取得した。

空手中央スクールで指導するストョーピン氏(中央)=提供
Stepin (center) teaching at the Central School of Karate.

92年に、自らの道場「武道」を開設して指導。セネのほか、ロシア独特の護身術も研究している。後に、ストョーピン氏の弟子が反テロリスト組織アルファで仕事し始め、同部隊員が道場に通うことから、道場は「アルファ武道クラブ」に改称した。青少年のスポーツ育成と同部隊ベテランの支援が道場のミッションに加わった。

「空手の組織で数千人の弟子が一人の師匠を尊敬することに恐れを感じた政府は、長年国内で空手を禁じた。80年代、社会の変化に伴い、空手の稽古が許され、今日国内にはほぼすべての流派が存在する。空手人口は100万に及ぶのではないか」とストョーピン氏。

格闘技好きのロシア人は、サンボを国技として誇っている。組手を重視するフルコンタクト系の空手は人気だが、型を中心とする沖縄空手の流会派はまだ多くはない。

2008年、友人を通じて、訪露中の小林流守武館の仲里秀雄氏を紹介された。空手のルーツを求めていたストョーピン氏は、仲里氏の指導を受け、小林流を追求することを決めたという。仲里氏の下で、古武道の世界も知った。

現在、ストョーピン氏は、プロ指導者として数カ所で子ども100人余、大人50人程にセネと小林流を指南している。「小林流の型は、容易だが爆発的なスピードを用いるから魅力的だ。沖縄空手の型と歴史を学ぶことで、先達の伝統を重んじるようになる」

本場で継承される小林流の指導を受けるためこれまで6度、沖縄を訪れた。8月に開催される第1回沖縄空手国際大会では首里・泊手系の部に出場する。

Published on 2018/5/27

44 Russia

Alfa-Budō Club

Learning at the roots and training kata

In the country that has given birth to MMA champion Fedor Emelianenko, the history of karate dates back to the 1960s. Alexey Shturmin, who learned the karate-like martial art “Kwong-thu” from a North Korean martial artist, founded and popularized the karate school “Sen-E” (which means “a lifetime” in Korean) after his teacher returned to his country.

As Roman Stepin explains, “In Sen-E, blocking techniques and hand strikes are similar to karate. We also use the cat stance nekoashi-dachi. However, other stances are low and large as in Shōtōkan and kicks are done high and there are many jumps too.”

Born in Moscow in 1958, Stepin began learning Shturmin’s karate in 1975. In 1981, he received his black belt at the most famous dōjō in Russia, the Central School of Karate.

In 1992, he opened his own dōjō called “Budō” and started teaching. In addition to Sen-E, Stepin also studied Russian-specific self-defense. Later, his disciples began to work for the counter-terrorist organization Alpha Group, and the dōjō was renamed Alfa-Budō Club as Alpha members came to train at the dōjō. Youth sports training and support to veterans of the Alpha Group were tasks added to the dōjō’s mission.

“For many years, karate was forbidden because the government didn’t like groups of thousands of people respecting and obeying one individual. In the 1980s, with the changes in society, karate practice was allowed, and today almost all styles are represented in Russia. The number of karate practitioners may reach 1 million,” says Stepin.

Russians who like combative sport are proud of Sambo, the national sport. Full-contact karate, which puts an emphasis on kumite, is popular, but there are not many Okinawan karate schools available.

In 2008, a friend introduced Stepin to Nakazato Hideo of the Shōrin-ryū Shūbukan who was visiting Russia. As he was looking for the roots of karate, Stepin trained with Nakazato and decided to pursue Shōrin-ryū under him. Later on, he also learned about the world of kōbudo with the Okinawan master.

Currently, as a professional instructor, Stepin teaches Sen-E and Shōrin-ryū to more than 100 children and 50 adults in several places. “The kata of Shōrin-ryū are attractive because they are easy to perform but make use of explosive speed. By learning the kata and history of Okinawa karate, we come to respect the traditions of our predecessors.”

Stepin has visited Okinawa six times so far to receive guidance in Shōrin-ryū the way it is inherited in the birthplace of karate. At the 1st Okinawa Karate International Tournament to be held in August, he will participate in the Shurite & Tomarite division.

Glossary-Index

Akamine Eisuke	(1925~1999) Born in Tomigusuku Village (present Tomigusuku City). Studied kobudō with Taira Shinken among others. Became the second chairman of the Ryūkyū Kobudō Preservation and Promotion Society after the passing of Taira. Opened the Shinbukan in Tomigusuku in 1971.
Bunbu Ryōdō	A Japanese expression meaning that one should follow the way (dō) of excellence in both academic or cultural matters (bun) and martial art (bu).
Chibana Chōshin	(1885~1969) Born in Shuri. Studied Shurite under Itosu Ankō. Named his system Shōrin-ryū in 1933 and established the Okinawa Shōrin-ryu Karatedō Association in 1948.
Dan	A word meaning a step or a rank. Achieving the black belt level means reaching Shodan, the 1st dan or first rank. Depending on organizations, the highest rank is 5th dan (Godan) or 10th dan (Jūdan).
Dōjō	The place (jō) to study the way (dō).
Funakoshi Gichin	(1868~1957) Born in Shuri Yamagawa. Studied under Asato Ankō and Itosu Ankō among others. Went to Mainland Japan to introduce and spread karate in 1922, teaching karate in many universities in Tōkyō. Known as the father of modern karate. Originally a Shurite expert, his system was reformatted with time and renamed Shōtōkan, the name of the dōjō his students built for him in the capital in 1939.
Gōjū-kai	A branch of Gōjū-ryū. In Mainland Japan, it usually relates to Yamaguchi Gōgen's karate while in Okinawa, it is synonym to Yagi Meitoku's karate.
Gōjū-ryū	Meaning hard (gō) and soft (jū), this name was chosen by Miyagi Chōjun in 1930 to describe his style of karate which is rooted in Nahate and Higaonna Kanryō's teachings. One of the 3 main styles of Okinawa karate as well as one of the 4 styles of mainland Japanese karate together with Shōtōkan, Wadō-ryū and Shitō-ryū.
Hanshi	The highest title in martial arts following Renshi and Kyōshi titles.
Higa Minoru	(1941~) Born in Naha City. The Nephew of Higa Yūchoku and current head of the Shōrin-ryu Karatedō Kyūdōkan.
Higa Seikichi	(1927~1999) Born in Naha City. Son of Higa Sekō and second chairman of the Gōjū-ryū International Karate and Kobudō Federation and the Shōdōkan dōjō.
Higa Sekō	(1898~1966) Born in Naha. Trained karate under Higaonna Kanryō and Miyagi Chōjun. Founder of the Gōjū-ryū International Karate and Kobudō Federation and the Shōdōkan dōjō in 1960.
Higa Yūchoku	(1910~1994) Born in Naha. Trained karate under Shinzato Jinan, and Chibana Chōshin among others. Started teaching at his home in 1941, dōjō known today as the Kyūdōkan. A policeman and later a Naha City Council member, he was involved with the reviving of the Naha Great Tug of War in 1971. After WWII, one of the four giants of the karate world along with Nagamine Sōshin, Uechi Kanei and Yagi Meitoku.
Higaonna Kanryō	(1853~1915) Born in Naha. Known as the forefather of Nahate. Studied martial arts in China. Among his top students are Kyoda Juhatsu and Miyagi Chōjun.
Higaonna Morio	(1938~) Born in Naha City. Studied Gōjū-ryū with Miyagi Anichi among others. Recognized in 2013 as a holder of the Okinawa Prefecture's designated intangible cultural asset "Okinawa karate and kobujutsu".
Honbu dōjō	The headquarters of an organization.
Iha Kōtarō	(1940~) Born in Gushikawa Village (present Uruma City). Studied karate under Chibana Chōshin and Higa Yūchoku and kobudō under Izumikawa Kantoku and Ishikawa Hōei among others. Opened a dōjō in 1974, and later established the Ryūkonkai. Recognized in 2020 as a holder of the Okinawa Prefecture's designated intangible cultural asset "Okinawa karate and kobujutsu".
Iha Seikichi	(1932~) Born in Nishihara Village (present Nishihara Town). Studied karate under Gusukuma Shinpan and Miyahira Katsuya. Taught in the Philippines before moving to the USA in 1967. Still teaches in Lansing, Michigan. Recognized in 2020 as a holder of the Okinawa Prefecture's designated intangible cultural asset "Okinawa karate and kobujutsu".

用語集（敬称略・アルファベット順）

赤嶺栄亮	（1925～1999）豊見城村（現豊見城市）生まれ。平信賢等らに古武術を習う。師の死去後、琉球古武道保存振興会の2代目会長になる。1971年に豊見城村に信武館を開設。
文武両道	空手や武道の世界では、主に、学芸と武芸の両道に努めること。
知花朝信	（1885～1969）首里生まれ。首里手の糸洲安恒に師事。1933年に、自身の空手を小林流と名付け、1948年に沖縄小林流空手道協会を結成。
段	空手に於いてのレベルを表す「段」は、黒帯の初段から始まる。組織によって、最高段位は5段又は10段となっている。
道場	武道や芸を学ぶ場のこと。ちなみに、海外では、道場以外にクラブという呼称がよくつかわれている。
船越義珍	（1868～1957）首里山川生まれ。安里安恒、糸洲安恒等に師事。1922年に日本本土で空手を紹介し普及活動に励む。都内の多くの大学で指導し、「現代空手の父」と称する。首里手を嗜んだ船越の空手は、時間と共に再編され、後に、弟子が1939年に建設した道場名にちなみ「松濤館」として知られるようになった。
剛柔会	剛柔流に属する。日本本土では主に山口剛玄の空手、沖縄では八木明徳の空手に関係を持つ団体を示す。
剛柔流	那覇手と東恩納寛量の武術にルーツがある空手で、1930年に宮城長順が名乗った流派名である。沖縄空手三大流の一つであり、松濤館、和道流、糸東流と共に、日本本土空手4大流派の一つである。
範士	錬士と教士の上、武道において最高位の称号。
比嘉稔	（1941～）那覇市生まれ。比嘉佑直の甥であり、現在、小林流究道館の代表である。
比嘉世吉	（1927～1999）那覇市生まれ。比嘉世幸の子息。尚道館及び剛柔流国際空手古武道連盟の2代目会長。
比嘉世幸	（1898～1966） 那覇生まれ。東恩納寛量や宮城長順に師事。1960年に尚道館を開設し、剛柔流国際空手古武道連盟を結成。
比嘉佑直	（1910～1994）那覇生まれ。新里仁安、知花朝信等に師事。1941年に指導を始めた自宅が現在の小林流究道館道場である。警察官と那覇市議会議員を務め、1971年に那覇大綱挽の復活に大きく貢献した。戦後、上地完英、長嶺将真、八木明徳と共に、空手界の4大巨星の一人と称される。
東恩納寛量	（1853～1915）那覇生まれ。那覇手の中興の祖として知られる。中国で武術を学ぶ。高弟には、許田重発と宮城長順がいる。
東恩納盛男	（1938～）那覇市生まれ。宮城安一等に師事。2013年に沖縄県指定無形文化財「沖縄の空手・古武術」保持者に認定。
本部道場	ある組織の本部となる道場
伊波光太郎	（1940～）具志川村（現うるま市）生まれ。空手は、知花朝信や比嘉佑直に師事。古武道は、泉川寛得、石川逢英等に師事。1974年に道場を開設し、その後「琉棍会」を発足。2020年に沖縄県指定無形文化財「沖縄の空手・古武術」保持者に認定。
伊波清吉	（1932～）西原村（現西原町）生まれ。空手は、城間眞繁と宮平勝哉に師事。フィリピンで指導し、1967年にアメリカに移住。今も、ミシガン州のランシングで指導する。2020年に沖縄県指定無形文化財「沖縄の空手・古武術」保持者に認定。

Isshin-ryū	Style founded in 1956 by Shimabukuro Tatsuo. The curriculum includes Shurite and Nahate related kata as well as weapons forms. The founder taught karate to many military servicemen stationed in Okinawa thus the style is well spread in the USA.
Jōshinmon	A mainland Japanese karate style that follows the tradition of Kyan Chōtoku and that was founded by Ikeda Hōshū in 1969.
Jundōkan	Following the passing of Miyagi Chōjun, this dōjō was built by Miyazato Eiichi in 1956, and then rebuilt as it stands today in 1970. Nowadays, it is known as the Okinawa Gōjū-ryū Karatedō Sōhonbu Jundōkan under Miyazato Yoshihiro, son of Miyazato Eiichi.
Kanchō	Meaning the head (chō) of a hall (kan) or a dōjō.
Karateka	Meaning a karate practitioner, to be differentiated with "karate aikōka", a karate enthusiast who doesn't always practice karate.
Kobudō	A general term used for the systems of weapons found in Okinawa. The major systems are Ryūkyū kobudō, Matayoshi kobudō, Yamanni-ryū, etc. A similar word used is kobujutsu.
Kōnan-ryū	A style related to Uechi-ryū founded in 1978 by Itokazu Seiki (1915-2006), who was recognized in 1997 as a holder of the Okinawa Prefecture's designated intangible cultural asset "Okinawa karate and kobujutsu".
Kote-kitae	Forearms conditioning. Sometimes complemented by Kashi-kitae (leg conditioning) and Tai-kitae (body conditioning).
Kyan Chōtoku	(1870~1945) Born in Shuri. An expert of Shurite and Tomarite who trained under Matsumura Sōkon, Matsumora Kōsaku, Chatan Yara and Oyadomari Kōkan among others. Son of Kyan Chōfu, a karate expert and magistrate who served under the last King of Ryūkyū, Shō Tai. Among his disciples are Nagamine Shōshin, Shimabuku Tatsuo, Shimabukuro Zenryō and Nakazato Jōen.
Kyokushin	A full-contact karate system established in 1964 by Ōyama Masutatsu (1923~1994).
Kyōshi	The second title in martial arts preceded by Renshi and followed by Hanshi titles.
Kyū	Before testing for black belt, a karate practitioner usually starts at a 10 kyū level (white belt) and progresses until 1 kyū (brown belt) level.
Kyūdōkan	The name of two different dōjo in Okinawa. One is the Kyūdōkan (究道館) founded by Higa Yūchoku in Naha City while the other one is the Kyūdōkan (求道館) established by Nakazato Jōen in Chinen Village. The styles of the two masters are different.
Mabuni Kenwa	(1889~1952) Born in Shuri. Studied karate with Itosu Ankō and Higaonna Kanryō. Moved to mainland Japan and founded Shitō-ryū in 1934, one of the 4 styles of mainland Japanese karate.
Matayoshi Shinpō	(1921~1997) Born in Yomitan. Studied martial arts with his father Shinkō, Kyan Chōtoku and Go Kenki. Founded the Okinawa Kobudō Federation in 1972 and established his dōjō, the Kōdōkan in 1976. His system is known as Kingai-ryū Karate & Matayoshi kobudō.
Matsubayashi-ryū	A karate style founded by Nagamine Shōshin in 1947. "Matsu" stands for Matsumura Sōkon and Matsumora Kōsaku, two masters from which Nagamine's instructors studied karate with.
Matsumura Sōkon	(Approximately 1809~1899) Born in Shuri and known as Bushi Matsumura. Considered the forefather of Shurite. Said to have studied martial arts in China and sword fighting in the former Satsuma domain in Kagoshima. Two of his most famous disciples are said to be Asato Ankō and Itosu Ankō.
Meibukan	The dōjō founded by Yagi Meitoku in 1952.
Miyagi Chōjun	(1888~1953) Born in Naha. Studied karate with Higaonna Kanryō. Chose the name Gōjū-ryū in 1930 to describe his system of karate. Travelled to mainland Japan and Hawaii to spread karate.
Miyahira Katsuya	(1918-2010) Born in Nishihara Village (present Nishihara Town). Studied karate with Chibana Chōshin, Tokuda Anbun and Motobu Chōki. Established the Shidōkan in 1948. Succeeded to Chibana as the chairman of the Okinawa Shōrin-ryu Karatedō Association. Recognized in 2000 as a holder of the Okinawa Prefecture's designated intangible cultural asset "Okinawa karate and kobujutsu".

一心流	1956年に、島袋龍夫が命名した流派。首里手や那覇手の型と古武術で構成する。流祖が、沖縄に駐留する多くの米兵に指導したことから、一心流は米国に於いてかなり普及している。
常心門	喜屋武朝徳の流れを汲む空手で、1969年に池田奉秀により創立された日本本土の流派。
順道館	宮城長順の没後、1956年に宮里栄一によって建設された道場。1970年に今の道場として再構築された。現在、宮里栄一の息子・宮里善博が館長を努める沖縄剛柔流空手道総本部順道館として知られている。
館長	ある空手の館又は道場の代表のこと。
空手家	空手を修練する人の事。意味が異なる愛好家は、必ずしも修練するとは言えない。
古武道	沖縄生まれの武器術を総称する言葉。主な系統は、琉球古武道、又吉古武道、山根流などがある。古武術ともいう。
硬軟流	1978年に、糸数盛喜(1915～2006)によって命名された上地流系の流派。糸数は、1997年に沖縄県指定無形文化財「沖縄の空手・古武術」保持者に認定。
小手鍛え	小手を鍛える鍛錬法。下肢鍛えと体鍛えもある。
喜屋武朝徳	(1870～1945)首里生まれ。松村宗棍、松茂良興作、北谷屋良、親泊興寛等に師事した首里・泊手の大家。武術家で最後の琉球国王・尚泰の讃議官を務めた喜屋武朝扶の子息。弟子には、長嶺将真、島袋龍夫、島袋善良と仲里常延がいる。
極真	1964年に、大山倍達(1923～1994)によって設立されたフルコンタクト空手。
教士	武道において錬士の上、範士の下の称号。
級	有段者になるまで、空手家は十級(白帯)から一級(茶帯)のレベルに進める。
究道館・求道館	究道館は、比嘉佑直が那覇市で、求道館は、仲里常延が旧知念村で開設した道場のこと。両氏の流派は異なる。
摩文仁賢和	(1889～1952)首里生まれ。糸洲安恒、東恩納寛量に師事。日本本土に渡り、1934年に日本本土空手4大流派の一つ糸東流を命名した。
又吉眞豊	(1921～1997)読谷生まれ。父・眞光、喜屋武朝徳、呉賢貴に師事。1972年に社団法人沖縄古武道連盟を設立し、1976年に道場「光道館」を設立。流派は、金硬流唐手又吉古武道として知られている。
松林流	1947年に長嶺将真が命名した空手の流派。「松」は、長嶺将真の師が空手を習った松村宗棍と松茂良興作の頭文字を意味する。
松村宗棍	(およそ1809～1899)首里生まれ。「武士松村」として知られ、首里手の中興の祖とされる。中国で武術を学び、鹿児島の旧薩摩藩で剣術を学んだとされている。最も有名な高弟は、安里安恒と糸洲安恒と言われている。
明武館	1952年に、八木明徳が開設した道場のこと。
宮城長順	(1888～1953)那覇生まれ。東恩納寛量に師事。1930年に自身の空手を「剛柔流」と命名。空手を広めるために日本本土やハワイを訪れる。
宮平勝哉	(1918～2010)西原村(現西原町)生まれ。知花朝信、徳田安文、本部朝基に師事。1948年に「志道館」を開設。知花から引き継ぎ、沖縄小林流空手道協会会長に就任。2000年に沖縄県指定無形文化財「沖縄の空手・古武術」保持者に認定。

Miyazato Eiichi	(1922~1999) Born in Naha City. Studied karate under Miyagi Chōjun. Established the Jundōkan in 1956 and the Okinawa Gōjū-ryū Karatedō Association in 1969. Served as a police officer and also excelled in judō.
Nagamine Shōshin	(1907~1997) Born in Naha. Trained under Kyan Chōtoku and Motobu Chōki among others. Named his karate system Matsubayashi-ryū in 1947. Established the Kōdōkan dōjō in 1953, using the first kanji of Matsumora Kōsaku's given name. Recognized in 1997 as a holder of the Okinawa Prefecture's designated intangible cultural asset "Okinawa karate and kobujutsu". A prolific author who served as a police officer and Naha City municipal assemblyman. After WWII, one of the four giants of the karate world along with Higa Yūchoku, Uechi Kanei and Yagi Meitoku.
Nagamine Takayoshi	(1945~2012) Son of Nagamine Shōshin. Second heir of Matsubayashi-ryū. Traveled the world over and spend many years in the USA to popularize Okinawa karate.
Nahate	Before styles were born, karate is said to have been separated into Shurite, Nahate and Tomarite, although this terminology was used for the first time in 1927 for a karate demonstration for Kanō Jigorō of judō. These terms were used as a matter of convenience to classify the various karate systems demonstrated. Nahate represents the system(s) taught in the Naha area.
Nakahodo Tsutomu	(1933~) Born in Yuntanza Village (present Yomitan Village). Studied Uechi-ryū under Shinjō Seiyū and Uechi Kanei. Recognized in 2020 as a holder of the Okinawa Prefecture's designated intangible cultural asset "Okinawa karate and kobujutsu".
Nakamoto Masahiro	(1938~) Born in Naha City. Studied mainly karate under Chibana Chōshin and kobudō under Taira Shinken. Established his dōjō in 1971 and the Okinawa Traditional Kobudō Preservation Society (Bunbukan) in 1983. Recognized in 2013 as a holder of the Okinawa Prefecture's designated intangible cultural asset "Okinawa karate and kobujutsu". Prolific author and painter.
Nakazato Shūgorō	(1920~2016) Born in Naha City. Studied karate under Chibana Chōshin. Established his dōjō "Shōrin-ryū Shōrinkan" in 1953. Travelled in Japan and overseas to popularize Okinawa karate and kobudō. Recognized in 2000 as a holder of the Okinawa Prefecture's designated intangible cultural asset "Okinawa karate and kobujutsu".
Renshi	The first title in martial arts that precedes Kyōshi and Hanshi titles. In many organization, is bestowed at a 5th dan level.
Ryūkyū	A name that relates to the chain of island known today as the Okinawa Prefecture, and the name of the kingdom that ruled over these islands until 1879.
Sanchin	Although the content is different, this kata exists in Gōjū-ryū and Uechi-ryū. It is said to be the most important kata in both systems and is practiced to develop and maintain a correct posture, forms and breathing among others.
Seibukan	The Shorin-ryū karate dōjō founded by Shimabukuro Zenryō and his son Zenpō in 1962 in Jagaru, Chatan. There is taught the karate received from Kyan Chōtoku by Shimabukuro Zenryō.
Shidōkan	The name of the Shōrin-ryū karate dōjō founded by Miyahira Katsuya in 1948. Seniors students of the late master still train regularly there.
Shimabukuro Tatsuo	(1908~1975) Born in Gushikawa Village (present Uruma City). Studied under Kyan Chōtoku and Miyagi Chōjun. Founder of Isshin-ryū in 1956. (Also pronounced Shimabuku)
Shimabukuro Eizō	(1924~2017) Born in Gushikawa Village (present Uruma City). Studied under Kyan Chōtoku and Miyagi Chōjun. Younger brother of Shimabukuro Tatsuo, the founder of Isshin-ryū.
Shimabukuro Zenryō	(1909~1969) Born in Shuri Kubagawa. Studied karate under Kyan Chōtoku. Established the Shōrin-ryū Seibukan in Chatan Town with his son Zenpō in 1962.
Shitō-ryū	A style founded by Okinawan Mabuni Kenwa in 1934 and considered one of the 4 styles of mainland Japanese karate together with Shōtōkan, Gōjū-ryū and Wadō-ryū.
Shurite	Represents the system(s) taught in the Shuri area. For more, see Nahate.
Shōdōkan	The name of the dōjō founded by Higa Sekō in 1960.
Shōgen-ryū	A Matsubayashi-ryū related style of karate founded in 2002 by Taba Kensei (1933~2012), a senior student of Nagamine Shōshin.

宮里栄一	(1922～1999)那覇市生まれ。宮城長順に師事。1956年に「順道館」を開設し、1969年に沖縄剛柔流空手協会を設立。警察官を務め、柔道にも優れていた。
長嶺将真	(1907～1997)那覇生まれ。喜屋武朝徳、本部朝基などに師事。1947年に松林流を名乗る。松茂良興作の「興」を選び、1953年に空手道場「興道館」を開設する。1997年に沖縄県指定無形文化財「沖縄の空手・古武術」保持者に認定。空手史研究者として著作も多く、警察官と那覇市議会議員を務めた。戦後、上地完英、比嘉佑直、八木明徳と共に、空手界の4大巨星の一人。
長嶺高兆	(1945～2012)長嶺将真の息子。松林流2代目宗家。沖縄空手の普及のため、世界中を巡回し、アメリカにも長年滞在した。
那覇手	空手の流派が名乗られる前に、空手には、首里手、那覇手、泊手の三つの区分があったと言われている。しかしこの区分は、1927年に、柔道の嘉納治五郎のために行われた空手演武で初めて便宜上使用されたという。那覇手は、那覇地域を中心に発達した武術のことと考えられている。
仲程力	(1933~)読谷山村(現読谷村)生まれ。新城清優や上地完英に上地流を師事。2020年に沖縄県指定無形文化財「沖縄の空手・古武術」保持者に認定。
仲本政博	(1938~) 那覇市生まれ。主に空手を知花朝信、古武道を平信賢に師事。1971年に道場を開設し、1983年に沖縄伝統古武道保存会(文武館)を設立。2013年に沖縄県指定無形文化財「沖縄の空手・古武術」保持者に認定。著作や画家としての作品多数。
仲里周五郎	(1920～2016) 那覇市生まれ。知花朝信に師事。1953年に道場「小林流小林舘」を開設。国内外を訪れ沖縄空手古武道の普及に努める。2000年に沖縄県指定無形文化財「沖縄の空手・古武術」保持者に認定。
錬士	教士と範士の称号に先行する武道の最初の称号。多くの組織では、五段に達した者に与えられる。
琉球	琉球列島や琉球王国に関する名称。
三戦	内容は異なるが、剛柔流と上地流の鍛錬型。両流派で最も重要な型と言われている。正しい姿勢、技と呼吸法等を発達・維持のために鍛錬される。
聖武館	1962年に北谷町謝苅で、島袋善良と息子の善保によって設立された少林流の空手道場。島袋善良が受け継いだ喜屋武朝徳の空手が継承されている。
志道館	宮平勝哉が1948年に開設した小林流の空手道場。宮平の高弟は今も定期的にこの道場で稽古している。
島袋龍夫	(1908～1975)具志川村(現うるま市)生まれ。喜屋武朝徳や宮城長順に師事。1956年に一心流を名乗る。
島袋永三	(1924～2017)具志川村(現うるま市)生まれ。喜屋武朝徳や宮城長順に師事。一心流流祖島袋龍夫の弟。
島袋善良	(1909～1969)首里久場川生まれ。喜屋武朝徳に師事。1962年に北谷町において、子息の島袋善保と共に少林流聖武館を設立。
糸東流	1934年に沖縄県出身の摩文仁賢和が名乗った流派。松濤館、和道流、剛柔流と共に、日本本土空手4大流派の一つである。
首里手	首里地域を中心に発達した武術のことと考えられている。補足は「那覇手」を参照。
尚道館	比嘉世幸が1960年に開設した道場のこと。
松源流	2002年に、長嶺将真の高弟・田場兼靖(1933～2012)が名乗った松林流系の流派のこと。

Shōrin-ryū	An appellation for various Shurite & Tomarite related systems. It includes Shōrin-ryū (readable as kobayashi-ryū) established by Chibana Chōshin, Shōrin-ryū (written in kanji as Sukunai-hayashi-ryū) which relates to Kyan Chōtoku, Matsubayashi-ryū founded by Nagamine Shōshin, Shōrinji-ryū founded by Nakazato Jōen as well as Shimabuku Tatsuo's Isshin-ryū among others.
Shōrinkan	The dōjō founded by Nakazato Shūgorō in 1953.
Shōtōkan	Also known as Shōtōkan-ryū. A style that relates to Funakoshi Gichin. One of the 4 styles of mainland Japanese karate together with Gōjū-ryū, Shitō-ryū and Wadō-ryū. Originally, the name of the dōjō his students built for Funakoshi in the capital in 1939.
Soken Hōhan	(1891~1982) Born in Nishihara Village (present Nishihara Town). Said to have studied the martial art of Matsumura Sōkon. Founder of Shōrin-ryū Matsumura Seitō.
Sōke	The head of a family or a school.
Takara Shintoku	(1930~) Born in Motobu Village (present Motobu Town). Student of Uechi Kanei. Recognized in 2020 as a holder of the Okinawa Prefecture's designated intangible cultural asset "Okinawa karate and kobujutsu".
Toguchi Seikichi	(1917~1998) Born in Naha. Studied karate under Higa Sekō and Miyagi Chōjun. Founded the Shōreikan dōjō in 1954. Later moved to Tōkyō to spread Gōjū-ryū.
Tomarite	Represents the system(s) taught in the Tomari area. For more, see Nahate.
Uchinā	Meaning Okinawa in Okinawan language. Some related terms is this book are Uchinānchu (Okinawans) and uchināmuku (son of law of Okinawans).
Uechi Kanbun	(1877~1948) Born in Motobu Village (present Motobu Town). Went to China and studied martial arts. Returned to Okinawa after more than 10 year bringing with him with 3 kata. Moved to Wakayama in Mainland Japan and taught his system first called Pangainūn-ryū but renamed Uechi-ryū in 1940.
Uechi Kanei	(1911~1991) Born in Motobu Village (present Motobu Town). Son of Uechi Kanbun and second heir of Uechi-ryū. Opened a dōjō in Ginowan Futenma after WWII, dōjō which was moved in 1957 to the present location where stands the headquarters of the style. Worked hard to develop the system handed down by his father. After WWII, one of the four giants of the karate world along with Higa Yūchoku, Nagamine Shōshin and Yagi Meitoku.
Uechi-ryū	The karate system of the Uechi family and one of the 3 major styles of Okinawa karate.
Uehara Kō	(1929~2018) Studied Gōjū-ryū with Miyazato Eiichi and operated the Okinawa Shōrei Bujutsu Association Jikishinkan founded in 1974 in Naha City.
Wadō-ryū	A style founded by Ōtsuka Hironori(1892~1982) who studied Japanese jūjutsu and karate with Funakoshi Gichin among others. One of the 4 styles of mainland Japanese karate together with Shōtōkan, Gōjū-ryū and Shitō-ryū.
Yagi Meitoku	(1912~2003) Born in Naha. Studied karate with Miyagi Chōjun. Opened the Gōjū-ryū Meibukan in 1952. Recognized in 1997 as a holder of the Okinawa Prefecture's designated intangible cultural asset "Okinawa karate and kobujutsu". After WWII, one of the four giants of the karate world along with Higa Yūchoku, Nagamine Shōshin and Uechi Kanei.
Yamaguchi Gōgen	(1909~1989) Born in Kagoshima Prefecture. His original name is Yamaguchi Jitsumi. Studied karate and later received some instruction from the founder of Gōjū-ryū, Miyagi Chōjun while attending Ritsumei University. Opened a dōjō in 1949, and established the All Japan Karatedō Gōjūkai in 1950.

※ Reference materials: Okinawa Karate Kobudō Encyclopedia (edited and authored by Takamiyagi Shigeru, Shinzato Katsuhiko and Nakamoto Masahiro), Okinawa Karate People's Directory (1993 edition, Okinawa Ken Karatedō Rengōkai), etc.

しょうりん流	首里手・泊手系の空手の総称的な名称。知花朝信の小林流、喜屋武朝徳の流れを汲む少林流、長嶺将真の松林流、仲里常延の少林寺流、島袋龍夫の一心流等が含まれている。
小林舘	仲里周五郎が1953年に開設した道場のこと。
松濤館	松濤館流ともいう。船越義珍を開祖とする流派。剛柔流、糸東流、和道流と共に、日本本土空手4大流派の一つである。本来「松濤館」は、1939年に船越の門弟が建設した道場の名称である。
祖堅方範	(1891～1982)西原村(現西原町)生まれ。松村宗棍の武術を学んだとされる。少林流松村正統の創始者。
宗家	ある一族或いは道場の当主のこと。
髙良信徳	(1930～)本部村(現本部町)生まれ。上地完英に師事。2020年に沖縄県指定無形文化財「沖縄の空手・古武術」保持者に認定。
渡口政吉	(1917～1998)那覇生まれ。空手は、比嘉世幸、宮城長順に師事。1954年に「尚礼館」を設立。後に、剛柔流を広めるために東京に移住。
泊手	泊地域を中心に発達した武術のことと考えられている。補足は「那覇手」を参照。
ウチナー	沖縄語で「沖縄」のこと。
上地完文	(1877～1948)本部村(現本部町)生まれ。中国に渡り10数年武術を学ぶ。三つの型を持ち帰り帰郷。後に和歌山に移り、「パンガヰヌーン流」と呼ばれた空手を指導し、1940年に「上地流」と改名した。
上地完英	(1911～1991)本部村(現本部町)生まれ。上地完文の子息で、上地流の2代目継承者。戦後、宜野湾普天間に道場を開き、1957年に道場を移し現在の宗家本部道場を築いた。父の空手を発展させるように努力した。戦後、比嘉佑直、長嶺将真、八木明徳と共に、空手界の4大巨星の一人。
上地流	上地家の空手流派であり、沖縄空手3大流派の一つである。
上原恒	(1929～2018)剛柔流を宮里栄一に師事。1974年に沖縄昭霊武術協会・剛柔流直心館上原空手道場を設立。
和道流	日本の柔術などの武術と船越義珍等の空手を学んだ大塚博紀(1892～1982)が創始した流派のこと。松濤館、剛柔流、糸東流と共に、日本本土空手4大流派の一つである。
八木明徳	(1912～2003) 那覇生まれ。宮城長順氏に師事。1952年剛柔流明武館道場を開設。2013年に沖縄県指定無形文化財「沖縄の空手・古武術」保持者に認定。戦後、比嘉佑直、長嶺将真、上地完英と共に、空手界の4大巨星の一人。
山口剛玄	(1909～1989)鹿児島県生まれ。本名山口実美。空手を学び、立命館大学で剛柔流開祖の宮城長順の指導を受ける。1949年に道場を開設し、1950年に全日本空手道剛柔会を発足。

※参考資料　沖縄空手古武道事典(高宮城繁・新里勝彦・仲本政博編著)、平成5年度版　沖縄空手人名録(沖縄県空手道連合会)等

出版に寄せて

万国津梁 世界に響く拳音
挑戦と勇気 絆結ぶ

首里城正殿の鐘に刻まれた銘文「万国津梁」は「世界の架け橋」を指すとされる。碧い空と海に抱かれた沖縄。その重きキーワードは、遥か琉球王国時代から海を越え、世界との交易を通じて文化、友好の架け橋を目指した先人達の熱き志とも言える。そして今もウチナーンチュの心にDNAとして受け継がれ、誇れるアイデンティティーとなって人々を迎え入れている。

フランスの西地域、ブルターニュの小さな町。沖縄空手の達人ミヤギとひ弱な少年の闘いの成長を描いた映画「ベストキッド」に感動し、「いつか空手の聖地・OKINAWAへ行きたい」と夢見た青年は、片道切符で故郷を飛び出し、東恩納盛男氏の道場の門を叩いた。清掃業、通訳業、空手誌発行など様々な職種、人生の紆余曲折を経て沖縄空手の研究家へ。沖縄在住30年余。今や沖縄空手界に欠かせないキーパーソンとなるまで、不屈の魂を持って一つの頂(いただき)にその身を到達させた。

2017年春。沖縄タイムス「週刊沖縄空手」の企画を持ちかけた際、自信に満ちた表情で「90カ国までなら書けるよ」と言い放った言葉に偽りはなかった。第1回「ミゲールの世界の沖縄空手事情」、アルゼンチンの宮里昌栄氏の初出の原稿は歴史・人物像まで記され、読み応えある内容に、編集者として「これは行ける」と安堵し、確信を持った。連載開始から100回を超えるまで担当したが、世界に広がる沖縄空手への知見と交流の幅、卓越した日本語能力で編集作業の修正点も少なくて済み、助けられた。あれから5年余。自身初の空手書刊行にあらためて深い感慨と感動を抱く。

この書はかつてなかった、世界に広がる沖縄空手を実証すると共に、海外道場の修練の日々を深く刻んだ沖縄空手の「モニュメント」でもある。沖縄空手と沖縄文化のすべてを愛してやまない、陽気な笑顔の男の挑戦と勇気、そして努力と絶え間ない探究心に感服するのは、はたして元編集者だけだろうか。どうか、一空手家でもある男の軌跡、いや奇跡の「物語」と同時に、このモニュメントの確かな手触りを感じてほしいと願う。それはさらに沖縄空手の現在のワールドワイドな評価、空手家たちの敬意を夢にさえ見ず、情熱だけでひたすら伝統と技を紡いできた沖縄空手の先人達へのレクイエムともなろう。

著者がたびたび口にする「空手とは受けである」という言葉は、言うまでもなく己の心身を強くし、暴心を諌(いさ)める「平和の武」を示している。日英併記の珠玉の各ページをめくれば、なぜ沖縄空手が「平和の武」と言われるのか、各回に刻まれている空手家たちのコメントを拾えば、そこに集約されていることがより理解できるはずだ。今、こうして拙文を記す間にも、世界各地の道場では空手家たちの拳の空気を切り裂く音、魂から発せられる気合がこだましあっている。それは「万国津梁」の鐘の音とも重なると言えようか。

ただ、51歳のフランス人-いや前世はウチナーンチュのはずだ-の沖縄空手という宇宙の旅路はまだ志半ばのはずである。真の沖縄空手を世界に広め、交わり深めるという使命の炎を消すことなく、引き続きあくなき探究と奮闘に期待したい。なぜなら、ミゲール・ダルーズ氏の活躍が沖縄空手という無形文化の至宝を世界に証明し、絆を結び、継承へと導く確固たる熱源となるのだから。

(中島一人　沖縄タイムス「週刊沖縄空手」　2017年4月~21年3月編集担当)

Postface

Bankoku Shinryō
- The sound of fists echoing in the world -
Challenge and courage that connect people

The inscription "Bankoku Shinryō" engraved on the Shuri Castle's bell means "Bridge to All of Nations". Okinawa, embraced by the blue sky and sea. The important keyword is the passionate desire of our Ryūkyūan predecessors who, crossing the oceans since the time of the Ryūkyū kingdom, aimed to build bridges of friendship and culture through trade with the world. And even today, as this DNA has been passed down in the hearts of Uchinānchu as an identity they can be proud of, Okinawans welcome all visitors.

A small town in Brittany, France. Touched by the movie "The Karate Kid" which depicts Okinawa karate master Miyagi and the growth of a weak boy, a young man dreamed of "someday going to Okinawa, the birthplace of karate" and, buying a one way ticket to Okinawa, knocked at the door of the dōjō of Mr. Higaonna Morio. After working in various fields like cleaning business, interpreting and karate magazine publishing, and through the twists and turns of life, he has become a researcher of Okinawa karate who has been living in Okinawa for almost 30 years. With an indomitable spirit, he has reached the top of the mountain becoming an indispensable key person in the Okinawa karate world.

Spring of 2017. When he was approached by the Okinawa Times about the "Weekly Okinawa Karate", he confidently said, "I can write about up to 90 countries." In the 1st article of Miguel's "Overview of Okinawa Karate in the World" introducing Miyazato Shōei in Argentina, the manuscript included history and background information about the featured personality, and was a worthwhile read. As the editor, I was relieved and confident that "this could work". I was in charge of over 100 articles from the beginning of the serialization, but thanks to his knowledge of Okinawa karate, which is spreading around the world, and his excellent Japanese language skills, corrections were minimal, which was all together a great help when it came to editing. It's been over five years since then. The publication of this karate book brings strong feelings and is deeply moving.

This book proves that Okinawan karate has spread to the world like never before. It is an Okinawa karate monument, deeply carved by the days of training in overseas dōjō. Am I the only one, as the former editor, to admire the challenge, courage, effort and ceaseless spirit of inquiry of a man with a cheerful smile who loves Okinawa karate and all aspects of Okinawan culture? Realizing the trajectory of a man who is also a karateka and his miracle "story", I hope that you will somehow feel the solid touch of this monumental book. Furthermore, it is a requiem for the Okinawa karate predecessors who have never dreamed of the current worldwide reputation of Okinawa karate and the respect of karate practitioners, who devote themselves passionately to the tradition and techniques of karate.

The expression "Karate is about uke - the act of receiving" that the author often uses, refers, needless to say, to a "martial art of peace" which strengthens one's mind and body and discourages violence. If you turn each page of this bilingual book and read the comments of karate practitioners that are engraved in each episode, you will find out why Okinawa karate is called a "martial art of peace". Even as I write these words, the sounds of karate practitioners' fists tearing through the air and their spirit are echoing in dōjō around the world. Doesn't it overlap with the sound of the bell of the "Bridge to All of Nations"?

Yet, the 51-year-old Frenchman - no, he must have been an Uchinānchu in a previous life - is still only halfway through this space journey that is Okinawa karate. I hope that he will continue to explore and struggle without extinguishing the flame of his mission to spread true Okinawa karate to the world and deepen fellowship among enthusiasts. This is because the activities of Miguel Da Luz will prove to the world the beauty of the intangible culture that is Okinawa karate, and will become a solid source of energy that will lead to the creation of bonds between people and the inheritance of the art.

(Nakajima Kazuto, editor of Okinawa Times "Weekly Okinawa Karate" April 2017 to March 2021)

あとがき

私自身の空手に関連する活動として、沖縄空手が実際にいくつの国に存在するかを調査したことがある。世界空手連盟によると空手は193ヵ国や地域で鍛錬されているが、これらの多くの空手家は、沖縄空手の組織に所属せず空手を習っている。私が個人的に調べた結果によると、沖縄空手の組織が有する支部道場は少なくとも90カ国に広がっていることが分かった。

沖縄タイムス「週刊 沖縄空手」における私の連載は2017年4月9日に始まった。それ以来、71の国と地域に指導する沖縄空手家を取材することができた。

2017年に沖縄タイムス社に私を紹介してくれた現沖縄県副知事の照屋義実氏、沖縄タイムス社と記事の編集をいつもサポートしてくれた中島一人氏、私の記事を読んで訂正してくれた妻の寛子に感謝の意を表します。また、この本に掲載されている記事英訳の校正をしてくれたバンサン・ハイニガー氏にも感謝致します。

結びに、インタビューに応じてくれたという理由だけではなく、沖縄の空手と古武術を世界に普及する、この本で紹介したすべての人々に感謝の意を表したい。彼らは、この本に紹介していない多くの人々とともに、沖縄空手の大使である。この本は、彼らに捧げる・・・そしていつかこの本を読んでくれる息子の航と健汰にも捧げる。

ミゲール・ダルーズ

Afterword

Along my karate related activities, I once researched in how many countries and regions Okinawa karate was actually present. While for karate in general, the official World Karate Federation number is 193, people in many of these countries simply practice karate with no connection with an Okinawan dōjō or organization. My personal research's result was that Okinawa karate organizations are represented in at least 90 countries.

Since the beginning on April 9th, 2017 of my serialization in the Okinawa Times "Weekly Okinawa Karate," I was able to interview Okinawa karate personalities from 71 countries and regions.

I want to thank the vice-governor of Okinawa Prefecture Teruya Yoshimi for suggesting my name to the Okinawa Times in 2017, the Okinawa Times newspaper and especially Nakajima Kazuto for always supporting me in the editing of my articles and my wife Hiroko who read and corrected my Japanese written articles. Also, my gratitude goes to Vincent Heiniger for editing my English translations of the articles published in this book.

Finally, I would like to express my gratitude to all the people who are introduced in this book. Not simply for agreeing to my request of an interview but more important, for spreading worldwide the art of Okinawa karate and kobujutsu. They are, next to the many others not in this book, the ambassadors of Okinawa karate. This book is dedicated to them... and my two sons, Wataru and Kenta, who maybe one day will read this book...

Miguel Da Luz

ミゲール・ダルーズ

1971年フランスブルターニュ地方生まれ。14歳のころ空手に興味を持ち、故郷で沖縄剛柔流を学ぶ。93年9月11日に来沖。2005年以降、様々な空手事業等に携わり、月刊誌「沖縄空手通信」の編集を始める。2011年以降、沖縄空手の情報発信と国内外の空手家の受け入れに携わる。仲本政博著『沖縄の伝統古武道』(文武館、2008年)、外間哲弘著『沖縄空手7人の侍』(琉球新報社、2015年)等の書籍の英訳を担う。舞台「沖縄空手御庭」をプロデュース。沖縄ニューカレドニア友好協会の副会長。那覇市在住。

Miguel Da Luz

Born in Bretagne, France, in 1971. Became interested in karate when 14 years old and trained Okinawa Gōjū-ryū in his hometown. Landed in Okinawa on September 11th, 1993. Since 2005, engaged in various karate projects among which the editing of the monthly publication “Okinawa Karate News”. Since 2011, involved in the promotion of Okinawa karate and supporting national and foreign karate visitors. Translated various books in English among which “Okinawa Kobudō” (Bunbukan, 2008) by Nakamoto Masahiro and “The Seven Samurai of Okinawa Karate” (Ryūkyū Shinpō Sha) by Hokama Tetsuhiro. Producer of the spectacle “Okinawa Karate Garden”. Vice president of the Okinawa New Caledonia Association. Resides in Naha City, Okinawa.

ミゲールの世界の沖縄空手事情／
Overview of Okinawa Karate in the World

2022年10月9日 初版第1刷発行/
First edition October 9th, 2022

著　者　ミゲール・ダルーズ／
Author:Miguel Da Luz

発 行 者　武富和彦／
Publisher:Taketomi Kazuhiko

発 行 所　(株)沖縄タイムス社／
Publishing company:OKINAWATIMESSHA Co.,Ltd
〒900-8678 沖縄県那覇市久茂地2−2−2
2-2-2 Kumoji Naha-city Okinawa 900-8678, Japan
TEL 098-860-3000 FAX 098-860-3830
URL https://www.okinawatimes.co.jp

デザイン　イエスデザイン／
Designed by YESDESIGN

印　刷　(株)東洋企画印刷／
Printed by TOYO Planning & Printing, Inc.

ISBN 978-4-87127-294-0